3/10

Kentucky

Kentucky

Deborah Kohl Kremer

The Countryman Press ✷ Woodstock, Vermont

FIRST EDITION

We welcome your comments and suggestions. Please contact Explorer's Guide Editor, The Countryman Press, P.O. Box 748, Woodstock, Vermont 05091; or e-mail countrymanpress@wwnorton.com.

Copyright © 2010 by Deborah Kohl Kremer

First Edition

Kentucky: An Explorer's Guide
ISBN 978-0-88150-746-1

Interior photographs by the author unless otherwise specified
Maps by Erin Greb Cartography, © The Countryman Press
Book design by Bodenweber Design
Text composition by PerfecType, Nashville, TN

Published by The Countryman Press, P.O. Box 748, Woodstock, VT 05091
Distributed by W. W. Norton & Company, Inc., 500 Fifth Avenue, New York, NY 10110
Printed in the United States of America

10 9 8 7 6 5 4 3 2 1

To my parents, Paul and Peg Kohl: Thanks for being such great parents and proud Kentuckians. Those early road trips through the state really inspired me, but now I stay home when they predict sporadic showers. Love you both.

EXPLORE WITH US!

Welcome to the first edition of *Kentucky: An Explorer's Guide.* All attractions, activities, lodgings, and restaurants have been selected based on recommendations and personal experiences, never through paid advertising. This book is laid out in a user-friendly manner, but go ahead and familiarize yourself with the following information to make the most of it.

WHAT'S WHERE

This section is an alphabetical list of the state's highlights as well as important information you might need as you travel.

ALCOHOL

Kentucky's 120 counties all have different laws regarding the sale of alcohol. A *wet* county is one in which alcohol sales are permitted everywhere. A *dry* county allows no alcohol sales within the county borders. And, just to confuse the situation, some counties are *moist*. This means that selected restaurants in selected cities of a dry county are permitted to sell alcohol by the drink. So my advice is to always call ahead if you want a drink with dinner.

LODGING

The hours and price ranges listed after each entry are correct as of press time. This is subject to change at the owner's discretion. Please call ahead or check the web site if you're ever in doubt.

Lodging prices
Less than $100 = $
$101–150 = $$
$151–200 = $$$
$201 and up = $$$$

DINING

Restaurants listed under the Dining Out heading are typically a little higher end. Those listed under the Eating Out heading are generally less expensive and casual.

Restaurant entrée prices
Less than $10 = $
$11–20 = $$
$21–30 = $$$
Above $30 = $$$$

KEY TO SYMBOLS

- ∞ **Weddings.** The wedding-ring symbol indicates establishments that frequently serve as venues for weddings and civil unions.
- ❧ **Special value.** The special-value symbol appears next to lodgings and restaurants that combine high quality and moderate prices.

- ❦ **Pets.** The dog-paw symbol shows those lodgings that accept pets (usually with a reservation and a deposit) as of press time.
- ✎ **Child-friendly.** The kids-alert symbol indicates those lodging places, restaurants, activities, and shops of special appeal to youngsters.
- ♿ **Handicapped access.** The wheelchair symbol appears before lodgings, restaurants, and attractions that are partially or fully handicapped accessible.
- ⁽ᵗ⁾ **Wireless Internet.** This symbol shows establishments that offer WiFi or computer access.
- 🍸 **Beer/Alcohol/Wine.** This symbol appears beside establishments that serve alcohol.

I welcome your comments or corrections about places you discover or know well in Kentucky. Please email me at deb@deborahkohlkremer.com or address correspondence to Explorer's Guide Editor, The Countryman Press, P.O. Box 748, Woodstock, VT 05091; countrymanpress@wwnorton.com.

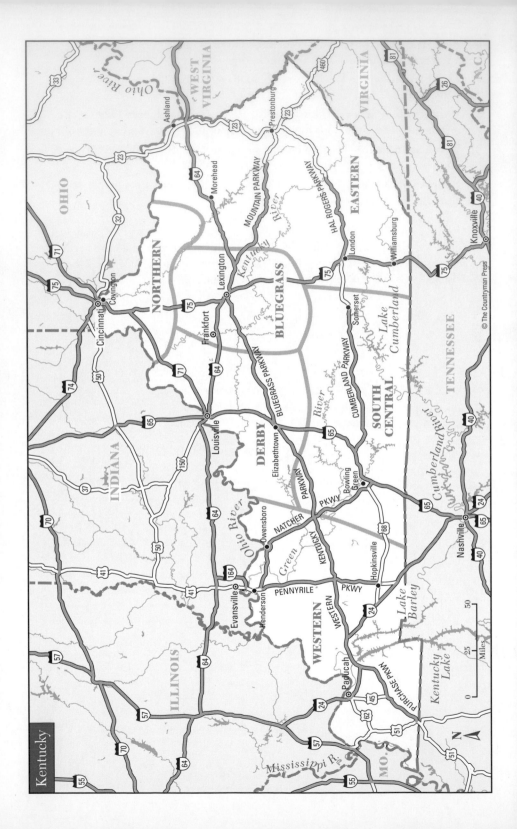

CONTENTS

ACKNOWLEDGMENTS

Writing a book about a place as large and diverse as Kentucky is a job not to be tackled alone. Well armed with that knowledge, I went about alerting everyone that I knew, and some I didn't, that I was writing a book. Funny thing is, when people know that you're interested in their part of town, they can't wait to tell you about it. If you mention that you're on your way to Bardstown, chances are the next words out of your listener's mouth will be, "Bardstown? Did you ever try that little restaurant . . ." And if you are planning an outing at the track, you're likely to hear, "After the races, you need to stop and get a piece of pie at this little place . . ."

People are forever recommending places to eat, and luckily for me, that's one of my favorite activities.

In addition to my friends, relatives, neighbors, and business associates, who all recommended great places to go, I need to thank the total strangers, too. So to the guy in Paintsville who was fixing his front porch on a Sunday morning when I showed up lost and asked the direction to Prestonsburg . . . thanks for putting down your tools, coming across your yard, standing outside my car, and giving me fantastic guidelines. All he had to do was point, but the guy wanted to make sure we got there. And thanks to the woman in a parking lot in Russellville. When I asked if she knew of a particular bakery, she replied, "Well bless your heart, you are lost, honey. Just follow me and I'll take you there myself." And she did.

So as much as I attempt to list all the people who helped make this book possible, even after several tries I'll never be able to thank them all.

Specifically though, I do have to thank my parents, Paul and Peg Kohl, who are the best parents a girl could ever have. They raised me right and began teaching me about Kentucky at an early age. The combination of Mom's enthusiasm and Dad's sarcasm gave me just the right mix to be excited, but sometimes cynical in my writing endeavors.

To my sister Nancy Hoffman, who gallivanted around the state with me, as well as Emily Hoffman, Ben, Deneen, Trey, and Bray Zimmerman, Michael Embry, Jodi Karem, Gina Johnson, Sue Gladding Carpenter, Heather Jordon, Chris Hoffman, Nancy Stephen, David Dominé, Kathy Witt, Mike and Ann Wright, and all my friends at *Kentucky Monthly Magazine*, who helped in ways too numerous to mention. Special thanks go to my acquisitions editor Kim Grant, who stood by me and helped to get this book off the ground.

But the group that certainly deserves the most accolades would be my husband, Nick, and my children, Ellie and Paul. Nick believed in me and encouraged me

ACKNOWLEDGMENTS

when things got tough. His love and support have been priceless. Ellie has helped me spread the word about the book, as well as told me her honest opinion of some of the restaurants and attractions we found along the way. Paul saw little details that I might have missed and reminded me to include them in my descriptions. So really, this book belongs to all four of us, not just me. As we spent weekends traveling around the state, stopping in antiques shops, visiting historical sites, touring horse farms, and generally eating our way across Kentucky, they were troopers. Although we all love the Bluegrass State, I'm sure there might have been a time or two when they wished they could've just stayed home. Thanks for not staying home. Thanks for all your help in writing this book. Thanks for being you.

INTRODUCTION

Writing a book about a place as vast and exciting as Kentucky is a dream come true for me. I've lived here all my life, and I've been writing about it for the last 20 or so years. It only makes sense that I finally put it into book form to share with you.

This book is divided up regionally, hopefully to aid you in your travels. You won't find any chain restaurants or chain lodging choices in this book, but all the biggies are well represented throughout the state if that is what you are looking for. The reasoning behind this is you can stay at a chain, anywhere. But you are in Kentucky, and the best way to explore the state is by patronizing the antiques-filled, historic B&B mansion, the locals' favorite greasy spoon, and the secluded barbecue joint just on the outskirts of town.

Traveling through Kentucky will lead you high atop mountains, through gentle rolling plains of bluegrass, to major metropolitan cities, and to small towns that are so cute, you wish you could pinch their cheeks. I hope you will use this guide to take you to these amazing places.

After you visit the awe-inspiring mountains, canyons, lakes, or forests, and when you've made your way through the skyscrapers, tourist attractions, and shopping malls, then you'll be on your way to knowing Kentucky.

Because, you see, for the best part, you need to get out of your car and possibly your comfort zone. You have to talk to the people. Kentucky people are the abundant natural resource that gives the state its beauty. They give it character, life, and personality.

So whether you're in a bustling downtown or a local coffee shop, pull up a chair and ask the natives about their hometown. You'll see the sparkle in their eyes, the genuine kindness in their hearts, a sprinkle of southern hospitality in their voices—and then you'll know what Kentucky is all about.

Welcome to Kentucky. I hope you love it here as much as I do.

WHAT'S WHERE IN KENTUCKY

AIRPORTS AND AIRLINES Kentucky is served by three primary airports, which include all the major airlines. Even though it sounds like it's in Ohio, the **Greater Cincinnati/Northern Kentucky Airport** (859-767-3151; www.cvgairport.com) is in Hebron. Serving the rest of the state are the **Louisville International Airport** (502-368-6524; www.fly louisville.com) and **Lexington's Bluegrass Airport** (859-425-3114; www.bluegrassairport.com). There are a scattering of small regional airstrips for private airplanes throughout the state.

AMUSEMENT PARKS The state's biggest amusement park, **Six Flags Kentucky Kingdom** (www.sixflags.com/kentuckyKingdom), is located in Louisville. With attractions like heart-stopping roller coasters, kiddy rides, and a great water park, it's a great place for family fun. On a smaller scale, but just as fun, is the **Beach Bend Amusement Park** (www.beachbend.com) in Bowling Green. They have great rides, a splash park, and a drag strip.

AQUARIUMS Sure, Kentucky is about 1,000 miles from the nearest ocean, but you can learn all about our friends from the sea at the state's only aquarium, **Newport Aquarium** (859-

photo courtesy of www.kentuckytourism.com

261-7444; www.newportaquarium.com). Surrounded by one million gallons of water, the aquarium offers huge exhibits that allow visitors to actually walk through the natural habitat of man-eating sharks, piranhas, and alligators. Listen to classical music and enjoy the ballet of the jellyfish or sit and watch the antics of the penguins.

AREA CODE The area codes for Kentucky are 270, 502, 606, and 859. The central part of the state uses the newest area code, 859. If turned to text, 859 reads *UKY*, which the University of Kentucky is quite happy about.

ART MUSEUMS The state's oldest museum is the **Speed Art Museum** (502-634-2700; www.speedmuseum

.org) in Louisville. With more than 12,000 pieces in its permanent collection, it is the state's largest, too. The second oldest is the **Owensboro Museum of Fine Art** (270-685-3181; www.omfa.museum). The **University of Kentucky Art Museum** (859-257-5716; www.uky.edu/ArtMuseum) also has a fascinating collection. Be sure to stop in while browsing around campus.

BED & BREAKFASTS Kentucky has a huge assortment of B&Bs to meet the needs of any traveler. Whether you're traveling with your children or your horses, Kentucky has inns that accept both. Choices include Victorian-era mansions in the historic district of a downtown, and secluded mountain hideaways where you can snuggle up with a quilt and a book next to a fieldstone fireplace and unwind. A great place to look first is the **Kentucky Bed and Breakfast Association** (www.kentuckybb.com).

BICYCLING With so much of Kentucky's countryside devoted to outdoor recreation, you can be sure there are lots of opportunities to bike. Several state parks offer biking trails (see www.parks.ky.gov) as well as the mountain bike trails in the **Daniel Boone National Forest** (www.fs.fed.us/r8). An organization called **Bike Kentucky** (www.bikekentucky.com) lists great trails on their web site.

BIRDING Bird-watching is a popular attraction in Kentucky; after all, John James Audubon himself called Henderson home. Audubon, who painted and classified native birds throughout the early 1800s, supplied us with information that is still used today. Opportunities for birding are great at the **John James Audubon State Park** (270-826-2247; parks.ky.gov) in Henderson. The **Land Between the**

Lakes Recreational Area (800-455-5897; www.lbl.org) offers 170,000 acres of unspoiled forest. Just outside Bardstown, in the tiny town of Clermont, you'll find the **Bernheim Arboretum and Research Forest** (502-955-8512; www.bernheim.org), offering more than 14,000 acres of bird lovers' paradise.

BOAT EXCURSIONS In Louisville, take a ride aboard a historic paddlewheeler, the *Spirit of Jefferson* or the *Belle of Louisville* (502-574-2355; www.belleoflouisville.org). These grande dames of the Ohio River offer excursions and dinner cruises daily. In Northern Kentucky, **BB Riverboats** (859-261-8500, 800-261-8586; www.bbriverboats.com) offers sightseeing tours and meal packages year-round. The **Dixie Belle Riverboat at Shaker Village** (859-734-5411, 800-734-5611; www.shakervillageky.org) offers tours of the Kentucky River and the scenic palisades and cliffs that surround it.

photo courtesy of www.kentuckytourism.com

BOAT RENTALS Known for its natural and human-made lakes, Kentucky offers boat rentals all over. In addition to **Lake Cumberland** (www.cumber landlake.com), **Kentucky Lake** (www .kentuckylake.com), and **Lake Barkley** (www.lakebarkley.org), there are also marinas and docks at some of the smaller bodies like **Green River Lake** (www.greenrivermarina.com).

BOOKS In the urban areas of the state, you find the big-box book sellers, but in the small communities you'll find the treasured old-time bookstores. Try **Bardstown Booksellers** (502-348-1256) or Maysville's **Market Street Bookstore** (866-571-5036), tucked into their respective historic downtown storefronts.

CAMPING Nearly all of Kentucky state parks (see parks.ky.gov) offer camping options that range from primitive tent sites to deluxe accommodations for the biggest rig. Another great place to rough it is the **Daniel Boone National Forest** (www.fs.fed.us/r8/ boone), which is sprawled across 700,000 acres in 21 Kentucky counties.

CANOE AND RAFTING So many streams and lakes, so little time. You'll find canoe rentals at all the major marinas and docks. Head for **Sheltowee Trace Outfitters** (800-541-7238; www.ky-rafting.com) to hook you up with canoe and rafting trips on all the major waterways near Corbin.

CAVES As home to the world's largest cave, known as **Mammoth Cave** (270-758-2180; www.nps.gov/maca), Kentucky is the place to come for underground natural wonders. There are many caves in Western Kentucky but also a few lesser-known caves in the northeast region. Try **Carter Caves State Park** (606-286-4411;parks.ky.gov) to learn more about the caves there.

photo courtesy of www.kentuckytourism.com

CHILDREN, ESPECIALLY FOR Kentucky is bursting at the borders with family-style fun, historical learning opportunities and recreation. One location that focuses directly on the kids is the **Explorium** (859-258-3253; www.explorium.com). Formerly known as the Lexington Children's Museum, this great place changed their name because the emphasis is more on exploring than observing. Fun for adults, too.

CIVIL WAR Although Kentucky was officially neutral in the War Between the States, the Bluegrass State saw her share of action. Today there are many historic sites, driving tours, and museums that focus on how the war affected that area of the state. The largest battle, the **Battle of Perryville** (www .perryville.net) pitted 18,000 Confederates against 20,000 Union troops. Today Perryville is a historic site with a preserved battlefield. In Northern Kentucky, you can see the site high atop a mountain where Union forces gathered to defend Cincinnati—but the Confederates, hearing they were outnumbered, turned back and headed home. Tour the **James A. Ramage Civil War Museum** (859-344-1145), which is on the grounds of this historic outlook. In Lexington, you can visit **Hunt Morgan House and Civil War Museum** (859-233-3290; www.blue

grasstrust.org), which has an impressive collection of Civil War artifacts as well as memorabilia that belonged to the infamous Confederate raider John Hunt Morgan.

CLIMBING One of the best places for rock climbing in Kentucky is the **Red River Gorge** (www.redriver gorge.com). Located in the east-central part of the state, this intricate canyon system features sheer limestone cliffs and more than 80 natural bridges.

COVERED BRIDGES The Bluegrass State, once dotted with more than 400 covered bridges, now has 13 remaining. Most are located in the northeastern section of the state. Flemingsburg, in Fleming County, is home to three and is known as the **Official Covered Bridge Capital of Kentucky**.

CRAFTS Kentucky's rich Appalachian heritage has resulted in generations of craftspeople who produce art in all forms and now sell their wares throughout the state. Berea, which is known as the Folk Arts and Crafts Capital of Kentucky, is home to the **Kentucky Artisan Center** (www .kentuckyartisancenter.ky.gov), a 25,000-square-foot facility offering a huge variety of crafts all under one

roof. In Louisville, the **Mellwood Arts and Entertainment Center** (502-895-3650; www.mellwoodartcenter .com) is home to 180 art studios, galleries, and specialty shops where you can purchase crafts as well as watch the artists working in their studios.

DRIVE-IN MOVIES If drive-in movies were wild animals, they would be on the endangered list—not quite extinct, mind you, but not as many around as there used to be. Although their predator, the multiplex, has been gobbling them up for years, there are currently 13 standing strong in Kentucky. Tucked into places where you would least expect them, like the **Twin Hills Drive-In Theatre** in Harrodsburg (859-734-3474) and the **Mountain View Drive-In** in Stanton (606-663-9988), they're all great places to go for family-style entertainment. There's a great web site that can help you locate all of them: www.drive -ins.com.

EMERGENCIES Dial 911 anywhere in the state for emergency help.

FACTORY OUTLETS Bargain shoppers have two great options when looking for outlet malls in Kentucky: the **West Kentucky Outlet Center** (305-893-5018; www.wkyfactoryoutlet.com) in Eddyville, and **Factory Stores of America** (502-868-0682; www.factory stores.com) in Georgetown. Shop for factory direct bargains all in one place.

FACTORY TOURS There are many things made in Kentucky, and luckily for us, some of the manufacturers offer tours. You might be surprised to learn that **General Motors** builds Corvettes in Bowling Green (www.bowlinggreen assemblyplant.com) or that **Toyota** churns out Camrys in Georgetown (www.toyotageorgetown.com/tour.asp),

photo courtesy of www.kentuckytourism.com

but the Bluegrass state is home other products, too. Winchester's **Ale 8 One** (859-744-3484; www.ale-8-one.com) offers tours of their soft-drink manufacturing plant. The **Louisville Slugger** (www.sluggermuseum.org) factory lets visitors see how a big hunk of wood can be transformed into a sleek baseball bat, headed for the major leagues.

FARMER'S MARKETS Rich farmland and a good climate have produced bountiful crops for Kentuckians for generations. This is evident in summer and fall as local farmers bring their wares to the farmer's markets held in most counties and roadside stands that pop up in the farmers' own front yards and at busy intersections. Farmer's markets by county are listed on the **Kentucky Department of Agriculture** web site: www.kyagr.com.

FISHING Fishing is available all over the state, but you're going to need a Kentucky State Fishing License to be legal. To get yours, just contact Kentucky Department of Fish and Wildlife Resources at 800-858-1549.

FORTS Get a taste of the frontier life at **Fort Boonesborough State Park** and **Fort Harrod State Park** (parks.ky.gov). When our forefathers made it through their arduous journey over the mountains and through the Cumberland Gap, the first settlements took root in the Bluegrass Region. Unfortunately the Native Americans in the area weren't standing here with a bottle of Champagne and basket of cookies to welcome them. The threat from the Indians was very real and very dangerous, so the settlers erected huge forts for protection. Today these state parks have re-created the forts to give visitors a feel for how these brave pioneers lived.

FREE FAMILY FUN You can see and do quite a bit in Kentucky without ever spending a dime. There are endless opportunities to swim, fish, and hike at the Kentucky state parks (parks.ky.gov).

GARDENS The Kentucky climate is great for growing stunning flowers as well as tobacco. Outside Owensboro you'll find a breathtaking daylily and hosta farm called **Pinecliffe Gardens** (270-281-9791) where you can enjoy peak bloom season in mid-June. In Lexington, visit the **University of Kentucky Arboretum** (859-257-6955), where you can see 1,500 varieties of roses in bloom. Bet it smells heavenly.

GOLF With more than 300 courses to choose from, the Bluegrass State's beautiful courses are always nearby. The web site www.golflink.com can help you find one near you, listed by city.

HIKING Kentucky has wonderful trails, whether you want the rugged terrain of the **Daniel Boone National Forest** or the flat, wooded trails of the **Land Between the Lakes** region. It's beautiful whichever end of the state you choose. Most parks offer trail maps that let you know how long the trail is and how difficult it might be.

HISTORIC HOUSES Touring a historic home is like a brush with greatness. There are lots of Lincoln-related cabins in the state, including Abraham's birthplace (www.nps.gov/abli) in Hodgenville. In Bardstown, you'll find the Rowan estate, also known as **My Old Kentucky Home** (parks.ky.gov). You can also tour **White Hall**, the 1800s-era home of Cassius Clay, which is near Richmond.

photo courtesy of www.kentuckytourism.com

livestock. There are hundreds of categories and thousands of entrants; it really is unbelievable. People also come for the Thrillway rides, the Championship Horse Show, and the Pride of the Counties exhibit, where each of Kentucky's 120 counties gets its chance to brag.

LAKES In addition to the big three, **Lake Cumberland**, **Kentucky Lake**, and **Lake Barkley**, you'll find nice-sized lakes all over the state. Whether

HORSE RACING What's a trip to Kentucky without a little horse racing to really get a feel for the place? **Turfway Park** (www.turfway.com) in Florence, **Keeneland** (www.keeneland .com) in Lexington, **Churchill Downs** (www.churchilldowns.com) in Louisville, and **Ellis Park** (ellisparkracing .com) in Henderson all offer live thoroughbred racing. If you're into harness racing, the **Red Mile** (www.theredmile .com) in Lexington is a great place to go. The schedules vary, so call ahead for post times.

KENTUCKY STATE FAIR For more than 100 years, the **Kentucky State Fair** has been drawing crowds to Louisville vying for the coveted blue ribbon in competitions ranging from home-grown produce to handmade quilts, bunnies, roosters, pigeons, and

photo by Paul Kremer

you're into houseboating, fishing, or waterskiing, Kentucky's lakes have you covered.

MAGAZINE *Kentucky Monthly* magazine is for sale at newsstands throughout the state. This magazine gives a glimpse into the life of Kentuckians, and usually shines a spotlight on a few restaurants or B&Bs in each issue. There is also a monthly calendar to tell you what's going on around the state.

MAIN STREET Main Streets, the ever-present commercial centers of downtown cities across the country, are alive and well throughout Kentucky. Although some cities have replaced their city center to the outskirts of

photo courtesy of www.kentuckytourism.com

town—where you'll find the chain stores and big-box retailers—there's still something special about walking down Main Street and browsing through the shops. In Danville, the historic downtown includes well-kept storefronts, charming shops, and pristine churches. In Covington, the area once populated by German immigrants is host to Mainstrasse. This neighborhood, sprinkled with galleries, antiques shops and cool restaurants, has hints of the motherland apparent in the amazing architecture.

MUSEUMS Kentucky offers a variety of museums; you just have to look for them. Get a feel for the "Greatest Two Minutes in Sports," at the **Kentucky Derby Museum** (www.derbymuseum .org) in Louisville. You'll enjoy the interactive exhibits and huge multi-screen movie, where you can learn all about a Kentucky tradition that has been around since 1875. For a not-so-common museum experience, Lexington's **Headley-Whitney Museum** (www.headley-whitney.org) is known for their stunning collection of bibelots—small intricately jeweled baubles. The museum also houses unique art pieces, jewelry, and pieces from the Smithsonian.

photo courtesy Kentucky Monthly Magazine

NATIVE AMERICANS The **Trail of Tears Commemorative Park** (www .trailoftears.org) in Hopkinsville is dedicated to the remembrance of the Cherokee people who traveled the trail in the mandatory migration westward of the 1830s. Hopkinsville was a stop on the trail; the park pays respect to all who passed through, and those who did not make it.

POPULATION Kentucky is home to more than four million people. The largest concentration lives in the triangle that includes Louisville, Lexington, and Northern Kentucky.

QUILTS For quilters, there is no other destination than the **National Quilt Museum** (www.quiltmuseum .org) in Paducah. The museum showcases quilts both old and new, and the exhibits tell the stories behind them. For those not so well versed in the art of quilting, this is a great place to learn about this intricate craft.

RAILROAD AND RAILROAD MUSEUMS The railroad is credited with bringing people, news, supplies, and life to Kentucky, so it is only fitting that there are several museums around the state that pay it homage. On the far eastern tip of the state is the **Elkhorn City Railroad Museum** (606-754-8300; elkhorncityrrm .tripod.com). Centrally located in Versailles is the **Bluegrass Scenic Railroad and Museum** (859-873-2476, 800-755-2476; www.bgrm.org); tucked into the Big South Fork Recreation Area in Stearns, you'll find the **Scenic Railway** (606-376-5330; www .bsfsry.com), where you can take a 16-mile ride on the 100-year-old Kentucky & Tennessee Railroad.

SCENIC BYWAYS Hopping onto a well-marked scenic byway is a great way to see the natural beauty of Kentucky, all from the comfort of your car. There are three **National Scenic Byways** in the state: the **Country Music Highway**, the **Red River Gorge Scenic Highway**, and the **Wilderness Road Heritage Highway**. The state has also designated several **Kentucky Scenic Byways**, too. A great drive through horse country is along US 68 in the Lexington area. The route encompasses 106 miles of sprawling horse farms, complete with hand-laid fieldstone fences, chandeliered horse barns, and horses grazing in the rolling pastures. To find route information, go to www.kentucky tourism.com.

WELCOME CENTERS Kentucky is a welcoming state, and all that down-home hospitality has to start somewhere. So you'll find eight interstate highway welcome centers located near the state borders. Stop in to be welcomed by the friendly staff, and feel free to grab some brochures, use the clean restrooms, and buy a can of cola and a pack of M&M's before getting back on the road. The centers are:

Bullitt County Welcome Center, I-65 South (502-543-5900)

Christian County Welcome Center, I-24 West (270-439-7505)

Florence Welcome Center, I-75 / I-71 South (859-384-3130)

Franklin Welcome Center, I-65 North (270-586-6292)

Grayson Welcome Center, I-64 West (606-474-4333)

Shelby County Welcome Center, I-64 East (502-722-9383)

Whitehaven Welcome Center (Paducah), I-24 East (270-554-2077)

Williamsburg Welcome Center, I-75 North (606-786-4474)

WINERIES Napa Valley has nothing on Kentucky. The fertile soil, good climate, and determined winemakers are turning out wonderful "vino" from the Bluegrass State. **Ruby Moon Vineyard & Winery** (270-830-7660; www.rubymoonwinery.com), Henderson, produces award-winning wine at their wonderful vineyard. They also have a tasting room, a gift shop, and events like art shows on the grounds. The folks at **Elk Creek Vineyards** (www.elkcreek vineyards.com) in Owenton produce a huge selection of wines as well as offering tours, cooking classes, and some really great concerts on their scenic rolling pastures. In all Kentucky has more than 40 wineries; check out the Kentucky Grape and Wine Council (www.kentuckywine.com) to find them all.

ZOO Kentucky has one zoo: the **Louisville Zoo** (502-459-2181; www.louisvillezoo.org). It's a beautiful zoo, with wonderful adaptations that allow the animals to live in their native environments.

photo courtesy of www.kentuckytourism.com

Eastern Appalachian Region

1

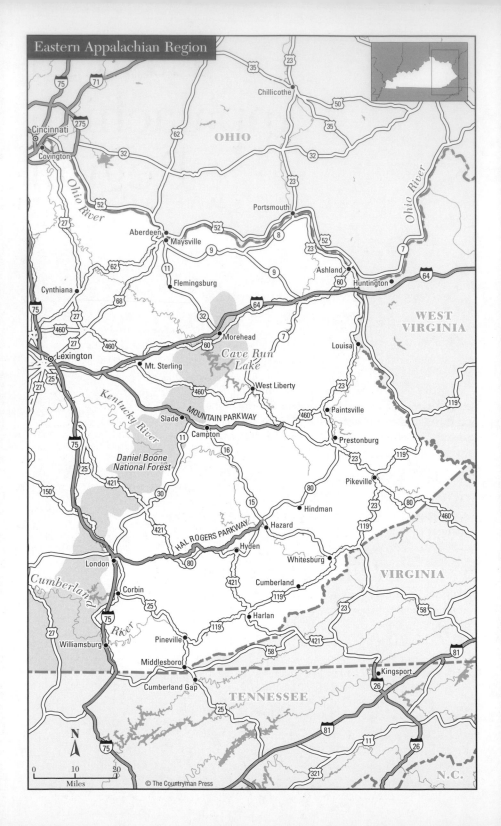

OHIO

WEST VIRGINIA

VIRGINIA

TENNESSEE

N.C.

Cincinnati
Covington
Aberdeen
Maysville
Flemingsburg
Cynthiana
Lexington
Mt. Sterling
Morehead
Cave Run Lake
West Liberty
Louisa
Ashland
Huntington
Portsmouth
Chillicothe
Slade
Campton
Daniel Boone National Forest
Paintsville
Prestonburg
Pikeville
Hindman
Hazard
Hyden
Whitesburg
Cumberland
London
Corbin
Harlan
Williamsburg
Pineville
Middlesboro
Cumberland Gap
Kingsport

Ohio River

Kentucky River

Cumberland River

MOUNTAIN PARKWAY

HAL ROGERS PARKWAY

N

0   10   20
Miles

© The Countryman Press

INTRODUCTION:
EASTERN KENTUCKY APPALACHIANS

The rugged, natural beauty of the eastern side of Kentucky is reflected vividly in the people and culture. The high mountains and the low scenic valleys, which are known as hollows to locals, include coal mines, state parks, and even the massive Daniel Boone National Forest. Although some of the terrain is jagged and rough, you'll find small storybook towns and people with enough charm to make it all feel smooth.

The Appalachian Mountains—pronounced *appa-LATCH-an* or *appa-LAY-sion*, depending on your location and who you're talking to—run in a north–south direction through Eastern Kentucky. The Appalachian lifestyle is tied to the mountains and the hardworking people who reside there. This culture is readily apparent in the crafts and folk art produced in the region. Another boon to the area is its ability to turn out nationally known country music artists. Tour the Country Music Highway, also known as US 23, to learn about these famous locals. As this scenic byway stretches through eight counties, it takes you through hometowns and birthplaces of superstars like Loretta Lynn, Billy Ray Cyrus, the Judds, and Dwight Yoakam.

With so much natural scenic beauty, it seems like there is a state park around every bend. The state of Kentucky created these parks to capture the mountains, lakes, and rolling plains before development took hold, resulting in one beautiful park after the next. Although most boast camping, boating, and fishing, some offer a unique magnet, like elk viewing, outdoor Broadway-style shows, and even black bear sightings, that you won't want to miss.

Sprinkle in a little history with your commune with nature by learning about legendary frontiersman Daniel Boone. One of Kentucky's first explorers, Boone led literally thousands of pioneers into Kentucky through the Cumberland Gap, in the southeast corner of the state. Today visitors will find that progress has been hidden, and the area near the gap looks as it must have when those brave pioneers found this convenient cut-through in the mountains. Hike or horseback ride along the historic Wilderness Road, which was cut down by Boone himself, and you can really see what our forefathers' first glimpses of Kentucky were like.

You will find nods of appreciation to Boone, who never actually wore a 'coonskin cap, all over the region. One of the largest tributes is the enormous **Daniel Boone National Forest**. This wooded wonderland covers 694,985 acres and most of Eastern Kentucky, touching 21 counties. It includes the stunning Red River Gorge Geological Area and Natural Bridge State Park, a mecca for hikers, rock climbers, and campers.

Eastern Kentucky, not known as the most affluent part of the state, is steeped in riches that money can't buy. It is bursting with natural beauty, recreational opportunities, a rich artistic culture, and mountainfuls of friendly people who can't wait to meet you.

ASHLAND AREA

Ashland is the welcome mat into Kentucky if you're arriving from the east, and what a warm welcome you'll receive. Ashland is a charmer, built around the lush, 47-acre Central Park, breathtaking 100-year-old homes, and a vibrant central business district made up of both new and old buildings that are well maintained.

When the Poage family arrived from Staunton, Virginia, in October 1799, they promptly named the area Poage's Landing. In 1854, the city name was changed to Ashland after statesman Henry Clay's Lexington estate.

The area became prosperous due to its prominent natural resources and proximity to the Ohio River, where these resources could be easily distributed. The Kentucky Iron, Coal and Manufacturing Company was incorporated on March 8, 1854, and they are credited with laying out the town of Ashland. The company purchased thousands of acres of coal, timber, and ore throughout the area; as the firm flourished, so did Ashland. Known today as AK Steel, the industry remains a major employer in northeastern Kentucky.

While downtown Ashland offers restaurants, art galleries, and shops, do venture into the surrounding communities like Russell and Flatwoods for even more mom-and-pop shops, one-of-a-kind eateries, and some real friendly folks.

About 30 miles west of Ashland, in Carter County, you'll find Grayson, known as the Heart of the Parks. It's located in the center of a triangle formed by three of the commonwealth's most beautiful state parks: Carter Caves, Greenbo Lake, and Grayson Lake. These parks offer outdoor recreation as well as a taste of the region's natural beauty.

GUIDANCE **Ashland Area Convention & Visitors Bureau** (606-329-1007, 800-377-6249; www.visitashlandky.com), 1509 Winchester Ave., Ashland. Open weekdays 9–5. You can't miss this visitors center, which is located on Winchester Avenue, the main route through town. The staff are eager to help with info, maps, and tips.

GETTING THERE Northeastern Kentucky is served by several state routes as well as Interstate 64, which runs east–west across the state, and the AA Highway, which runs from Alexandria to, you guessed it, Ashland. The nearest commercial airport is the **Tri-State Airport** (304-453-6165; www.tristateairport.com), located about 30 minutes from Ashland in Huntington, West Virginia. **Greyhound Bus Lines** serves the northeastern Kentucky area (800-231-2222; www.greyhound

.com). The depot operates out of the Ashland Transportation Center, 99 15th St., in Ashland.

GETTING AROUND It is easy to get around the area by car. Streets are well marked, and parking in the downtown areas is free. Public transportation is available through the **Ashland Bus System** (606-327-2025; www.ashlandky.org/abs .htm), 99 15th St. Buses blanket the area weekdays 7–6 and Sat. 9–6.

MEDICAL EMERGENCY King's Daughters Medical Center (606-408-4000; www.kdmc.com), 2201 Lexington Ave., Ashland. Established in 1899, King's Daughters Medical Center (KDMC) is a 385-bed center that covers a 150-mile radius including southern Ohio, Eastern Kentucky, and western West Virginia.

ALCOHOL Both Carter and Boyd are dry counties, which means they prohibit alcohol sales. Alcohol sales by the drink are permitted in Ashland restaurants that seat more than 100 people, making it a wet city. If you want a drink with dinner, call ahead to make sure you are in the city limits.

✳ To See

✆ ✿ ♿ **Highlands Museum & Discovery Center** (606-329-8888; www.highlands museum.com), 1620 Winchester Ave., Ashland. Open Tue.–Sat. 10–5. Housed in the former Parsons Department Store, this interactive museum features exhibits where you can learn about the history of Ashland and Eastern Kentucky. Learn about caves, coal mining, and life on the river; lots of hands-on activities for kids. $6 adults, $5 seniors, $5 children ages 2 and over; under 2 free.

Jesse Stuart Foundation (606-326-1667; www.jsfbooks.com), 1645 Winchester Ave., Ashland. Call for hours. Visit this former post office, which was built in 1917, and learn about the career of world-renowned writer and area native Jesse Stuart. This former poet laureate published more than 460 short stories and used Northeastern Kentucky as the setting of many of his works. This foundation is dedicated to preserving his literary works, and visitors can enjoy viewing some of his personal belongings and signed manuscripts. The foundation sells works by Stuart as well as books other Appalachian authors.

♿ ✿ **Catlettsburg Floodwall Murals** (606-329-1007), Center St. in downtown Catlettsburg. Many of Kentucky's river cities boast intricately painted floodwall murals, and Catlettsburg is no different. Stop and get a closer look at these magnificent murals that tell the story of the history of Catlettsburg.

✿ **Northeastern Kentucky Museum** (606-286-6012; www.kymuseum.org), 1385 Carter Caves Rd., Olive Hill. Open seven days 9–5. Open until dark in summer. This area of Kentucky features caves, rugged terrain, and fossils, and this is the place to learn all about

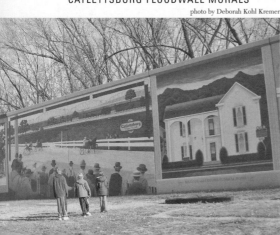

CATLETTSBURG FLOODWALL MURALS
photo by Deborah Kohl Kremer

it. They have collections covering Indian artifacts, fossils, and war memorabilia. Tours of privately owned caves can be arranged here, too. Free.

✳ To Do

GOLF Sandy Creek Golf Course (606-928-6321; www.sandycreekgc.com), 9701 Meade Springer Rd., Meads. This public, 18-hole course measures 5,538 yards. Short and hilly, it has a few elevated greens, a chipping area, and a practice bunker.

Sundowner Golf Course (606-329-9093), 4135 KY 5, Ashland. This 9-hole, par-33 bent grass course has lots of obstacles and traps. It measures 2,009 yards and is somewhat hilly.

Hidden Cove Golf Course at Grayson Lake (606-474-9727; parks.ky.gov), 314 Grayson Lake Park Rd., Olive Hill. This public 18-hole, par-72 course hugs the shores of Grayson Lake.

✳ Green Space

Central Park (606-327-2007), bounded by Lexington and Central Ave., and 17th and 22nd Sts., Ashland. The crown jewel of the Ashland city parks sits right in the downtown area. This 47-acre gem is a perfect place to eat a picnic lunch surrounded by the 1,100 trees, with each identified and located on maps of the park. If you're looking for recreation, there are three separate children's playgrounds, several baseball diamonds, and tennis and volleyball courts. In summer the city offers outdoor concerts; in winter you can ice skate. It really is a year-round park.

Tygarts State Forest (606-286-4411; www.forestry.ky.gov), KY 182, Olive Hill. Adjacent to Carter Caves State Park is this lush 874-acre forest. They offer hiking and picnicking, but camping is not allowed.

STATE PARKS Grayson Lake State Park (606-474-9727; parks.ky.gov), 314 Grayson Lake Park Rd., Olive Hill. Enjoy this former camping area of Shawnee and Cherokee Indians, full of beautiful sandstone canyons and scenic terrain. There are 74 miles of shoreline on this 1,500-acre lake where you can rent fishing and pontoon boats, and enjoy the sand between your toes at the sand beach. The park offers a spacious 71-site campground (606-474-6856, 606-474-5815). They have utility hookups, a dump station, a bathhouse, and laundry facilities. The check-in station has a small store with some necessities like ice and firewood. Closed mid-Nov.–mid-Mar.

& ❝✝❞ **Carter Caves State Resort Park** (606-286-4411, 800-325-0059; parks .ky.gov), 344 Caveland Dr., Olive Hill. This is the perfect park for nature lovers and spelunkers alike. Hidden under the park are 20 natural caves, with 4 open for touring. Tours are available for every level of caver. Bat Cave, the largest, is home to more than 40,000 Indiana bats that come to hibernate each winter. Each cave has its own natural wonders—but don't miss Cascade Cave, where you can enjoy the Cathedral Room and a 30-foot underground waterfall. Not all the natural beauty is underground, though. Carter Caves State Park has several natural bridges, one with a paved road on top. The park offers more than 20 scenic miles of trails for hiking, horseback riding, and mountain biking. The 45-acre **Smokey Lake** offers fishing, boating, and water sports. And if you have any time left, they also have an outdoor pool, a 9-hole golf course, tennis courts, and miniature golf. Stay on site at the **Lewis Caveland Lodge**, where you'll find 28 rooms, all with outdoor balconies where you can take in the scenery. The resort also offers 10 rustic cottages, 8 with wood-burning fireplaces, all equipped with modern conveniences such as dishwashers and microwave ovens. If outdoors is more your style, **Carter Caves Campground** has 89 campsites with utilities, a dump station, and a bathhouse. They also have 30 tent sites that do not have water or electric. Closed mid-Nov.–mid-March. **Tierney's Cavern Restaurant** is open seven days a week. Breakfast 7–10, lunch 11:30–2, dinner 5–9. Sun. brunch is served 11–3. Enjoy fine dining while surrounded with caving artifacts, photos, and memorabilia. The menu offers steaks and seafood as well as appetizers and sandwiches. People come from miles away to enjoy the Sunday brunch, which is loaded with entrées like fried catfish, turkey and dressing, fried chicken, and Kentucky hot brown. $–$$

    🚫 ⁹¹ **Greenbo Lake State Resort Park** (606-473-7324, 800-325-0083; parks .ky.gov), 965 Lodge Rd., Greenup. At the confluence of Clay Lick Creek and its tributaries, Buffalo Fork and Pruitt Fork, sits the 300-acre Greenbo Lake. Its name reflects the two counties, Greenup and Boyd, and recognizes the efforts of the citizens who worked so hard in the late 1940s to establish a recreational park in this area. Greenbo is a fisherman's dream, stocked full of largemouth bass, bluegill, crappie, catfish, and trout. In addition to boating and fishing, this 3,330-acre park offers more than 25 miles of trails for all levels of hikers. Along the trails you can enjoy the seasons as well as sightings of grouse, deer, squirrels, and many different birds. Stay in one of the 36 rooms of the **Jesse Stuart Lodge** overlooking beautiful Greenbo Lake. This lodge was named in honor of Jesse Stuart—a native of Greenup County and Kentucky's poet laureate. The lodge has a welcoming reading room where you can enjoy some of Stuart's works and personal artifacts. If you would rather camp, they offer 63 sites with utility hookups; or you can rough it on one of the 35 primitive sites. At the **Angler's Cove Restaurant**, open seven days a week 7 AM–9 PM, you can enjoy your meal with a relaxing view of the lake. The menu features tasty catfish and seafood entrées, legendary corn chowder, and fresh salads. $–$$

✳ Lodging

∞ 🚫 **Ashland Plaza Hotel** (606-329 0055; www.ashlandplaza.net), 15th and Winchester Ave., Ashland. Known as the jewel in the crown of Ashland, this independently owned 126-room hotel feels like an upscale chain, but the personal service indicates otherwise. Spacious rooms, workout facilities, and a complimentary continental breakfast make the Plaza a good choice. $$

∞ ⁹¹ **The Presidents' House Bed & Breakfast** (606-739-8118, 877-500-3452; www.bbonline.com), 2206 Walnut St., Catlettsburg. Just south of Ashland is this stately B&B in the former home of Levi Hampton, one of

the first settlers in the Big Sandy Valley. Built in 1847, this five-guest-room-home has all the authentic historic touches, mixed with modern amenities to ensure a comfy stay. Innkeepers Mark and Aleceia Anderson have one of the largest private collections of authentic presidential memorabilia and autographs, and it is all displayed meticulously. At the President's House, they say your family is always the first family, and they really mean that. $–$$

CAMPING Yatesville Lake State Park Campground (606-673-1492, parks.ky.gov), Louisa. This 47-site campground offers 27 full-hookup campsites and 20 primitive campsites. Sixteen of the sites are "boat-in" sites that can only be reached via the 2,300-acre lake, and four are "hike-in" sites offering complete seclusion. The campground also has a playground facility, nature trails, laundry room, restrooms, showers, and a dump station. Closed mid-Nov.–mid-March.

✳ Where to Eat

Ⴠ **Chimney Corner Café** (606-324-7500), 1624 Carter Ave., Ashland. Open Mon.–Fri. 11–10, Sat. 4–10. This restaurant has been a staple in Ashland for years, and locals turn to it when they want an upscale meal with reasonable prices. Thorough assortment of steaks, seafood, and chicken available. $$

Giovanni's Pizza (606-324-5157), 724 Greenup Ave., Ashland. With six locations in the area, you're probably already close to one. This pizza is a local favorite as well as a first stop for those revisiting the area. The pizza is delicious, but they also have good sandwiches, salads, and pasta dinners. At lunch, there's a pizza buffet where you can try all different kinds of pizza and pasta. You might want to wear loose clothing, because you'll be full when you leave. $

Ⴠ **C. J. Maggie's American Grill** (606-324-7895; www.cj-maggies.com), 1442 Winchester Ave., Ashland. Open Mon.–Thu. 11–10, Fri.–Sat. 11–11, and Sun. 11–4. Look for the historic building in the center of town to find this warm and welcoming restaurant. Inside, the decor includes a little bit of Americana: license plates on the walls, farm equipment scattered about; you can even write on the walls. They have a huge selection, like handmade brick-oven pizzas, giant fresh salads that come with french fries mixed in, and

really big burgers. Their chicken tenders are worth the trip alone, but while you're there, try the Alfredo pieces—an appetizer made up of deep-fried Alfredo sauce. Rich but good. $–$$

"Ⴠ" & Cafe Zeal (606-324-8565; www.theframeupgallery.com), 1436 Winchester Ave., Ashland. Open Mon.–Sat. 11–8. Located inside the Frame Up Gallery in downtown Ashland, Café Zeal offers a relaxing place for lunch right in the heart of downtown. Surrounded by soothing music and work of local artists, you'll enjoy the salads, sandwiches, desserts, and specialty coffee drinks while you unwind. The Italian cream cake consists of three layers of unbelievable happiness. $

SNACKS Randy's Roadside Market and Deli (606-474-6455), 431 E. Main St., Grayson. Open 7 AM–9 PM every day. Disguised as a market, this is a favorite of locals for burgers and loaded hot dogs smothered in homemade chili sauce, coleslaw, and shredded cheese. They've been around for more than 20 years serving up hearty breakfasts, hand-dipped ice cream, and old fashioned homemade shakes, too. $

CHIMNEY CORNER CAFÉ

photo by Deborah Kohl Kremer

✳ Entertainment

Paramount Arts Center Theatre
(606-324-3175; www.paramountarts
center.com), 1300 Winchester Ave.,
Ashland. Visit this historic art-deco-
inspired theater from the 1930s. You
can take in a tour, or take in a show;
either way you'll see how an old-time
theater is supposed to look. It was constructed by Paramount Pictures, whose
plan was to have one of these theaters
in each of the 48 states. Unfortunately,
only three were completed, and Ashland's version is the only survivor.
Shows vary throughout the year, so
check the web site to see what's coming. Paramount's claim to fame is that
it was the location site of native Billy
Ray Cyrus's "Achy Breaky Heart" video
shoot.

**GALLERIES Pendleton Arts Cen-
ter** (606-920-9863; www.pendletonart
center.com), 1537 Winchester Ave.,
Ashland. Artists and craftspeople come
to Pendleton to work on their art and
offer their wares. Enjoy watching the
painters, woodworkers, and potters as
they hone their craft. Hours vary by
artist, so check the web site for times.

The Frame Up Gallery (606-324-
8565; www.theframeupgallery.com),
1436 Winchester Ave., Ashland. Open
Mon.–Sat. 11–8. This funky but relaxing shop offers a mix of art, framing,
and gifts.

✳ Selective Shopping

🖉 Rail City Hardware Company
(606-836-3121), 520 Belfonte St., Russell. Even if you don't need any home
repair items as you travel, this 100-
year-old hardware store is worth a
stop. People have been coming here
for years to enjoy the fantastic service
and the darling model train that runs
around the circumference of the store,
up near the ceiling. When you walk in

photo by Deborah Kohl Kremer

RAIL CITY HARDWARE

the front door, just look up, wait a
minute, and that train will be making
her way around in no time.

**ANTIQUES Chicken Coop Art &
Craft Mall** (606-474-9690), 10813 KY
9, Grayson. Open Mon.–Sat. 10–5,
Sun. 1–5. Sited in a former chicken
house, this 7,000-square-foot shop
offers the works of more than 150 local
crafters. The shop is rustic, and the
merchandise is fabulous. You'll find
antiques, crafts, handmade furniture,
and more. It's different every time you
go.

Catlettsburg Antique Mall (606-
739-9786), 2606 Louisa St., Catlettsburg. Open Wed.–Sat. 10–5, Sun.
1:30–5. A roomy store with about 10
vendors, each offering a variety of
antiques, collectibles, and estate items.

Old Friends Antiques and Uniques
(606-928-2181), 6118 W. US 60, Ashland. Open Mon.–Fri. 9–5. Call if you
want to come on Saturday. This place
is big. It's spread out over two floors of
a retail store, the first floor of a house,
and an entire mobile home, so be care-
ful not to miss anything. More stuff
than you can imagine, from tiny knickknacks to huge pieces of furniture and
everything in between.

✴ Special Events

✤ *July:* **Summer Motion** (www
.summermotion.com). For more than
20 years, this festival, held in the Central Park in Ashland, has been entertaining huge crowds who come for
well-known musical acts like Wynonna,
Billy Ray Cyrus, Merle Haggard, Herman's Hermits, Grand Funk Railroad,
Trace Adkins, and John Michael Montgomery. They also have a craft show, a
petting zoo, games and carnival rides, a
10K race, and a soapbox derby.

✤ *September:* **Ashland Poage Landing Days** (poagelandingdays.com).
Named for the first immigrants in the
area, the Poage family, who settled the
area in 1786, this annual festival celebrates the town's roots right in downtown Ashland. The celebration features
big-name live entertainment, a 5K run,
a skateboarding competition, a car and
bike show, and regionally inspired arts
and crafts.

✤ *December:* **Christmas festivities**.
The city of Ashland knows how to celebrate Christmas. If you are in the area
on the Tuesday evening before
Thanksgiving, head for the Christmas
Parade along Winchester Avenue. This
is a huge parade, with more than 200
entrants that come from three states in
a 50-mile radius. Fans line the route—
which is at least a mile long—to cheer
for the marching bands, fire trucks,
and Shiners in their little cars. This
parade, which ought to be called the
Macy's Parade of the South, is a perfect way to get the hometown feel of
Ashland. While you're in town, drive
through the town's Central Park for
the **Winter Wonderland of Lights
Festival**, a phenomenal display of
800,000 Christmas lights open for five
weeks every year. Another fun event in
Ashland is the **Festival of Trees and
Trains**, held annually at the Historic
Paramount Arts Center. Wander
through the historic theater and enjoy
the hundreds of Christmas trees, each
with its own theme and decorated by
community groups, schools, and area
businesses. They also have a huge train
display and a gingerbread house competition. Ashland at Christmastime is a
treat for your senses.

MOREHEAD AND DANIEL BOONE NATIONAL FOREST

M orehead, which is the county seat and largest city in Rowan County, is located in the mountainous region of Northeastern Kentucky. It's about halfway between Lexington and Huntington, West Virginia.

Established in the mid-1800s, Morehead and Rowan County were known for coal production and timber, but by the mid-1900s the area was committed primarily to tobacco farming. Today the county has a population of about 22,000, and its biggest employer is Morehead State University. Established as a teachers' college in 1887, MSU now offers more than 80 academic majors. The scenic campus makes the most of its mountain and forest location.

Even though they had a college, the people of Morehead faced challenges of poverty and illiteracy in the early 1900s. Cora Wilson Stewart, from the nearby community of Farmers, was elected superintendent of Rowan County Schools. She knew the key to ending poverty was education, so she established the Moonlight Schools Movement in 1911. Her plan was to open school buildings to students of

RED RIVER GORGE

photo by Nick Kremer

all ages in the evenings so adults could learn to read and write when they finished work for the day. This movement is credited with teaching more than 1,200 people from the area to read and write. One of these school buildings still stands on East 1st Street in downtown Morehead.

The Daniel Boone National Forest spans Kentucky, from the Tennessee border on the south on about 150 miles or so to just north of Morehead, so most outdoor recreation in this area is linked to this precious behemoth. The forest is so massive and full of opportunities to camp, mountain bike, fish, hunt, and rock climb, you could easily stay for weeks at a time, and some people do.

GUIDANCE **Morehead Tourism Commission** (606-780-4342, 800-654-1944; www.moreheadtourism.com), 111 E. 1st St., Morehead. Open weekdays 8:30–4:30. Located in the Morehead Conference Center, it's easy to find, right downtown. They have maps, brochures and lots of helpful tips.

For information about the **Daniel Boone National Forest**, go to www.fs.fed.us/ r8/boone/recreation or stop by the **Cumberland Ranger District**, 2375 KY 801 S., Morehead. They have maps and information about the entire forest as well as local information about Cave Run Lake and Red River Gorge.

GETTING THERE Morehead sits just south of Kentucky's east–west expressway, I-65, so it's easy to access. For air travel, the closest airport is **Lexington's Bluegrass Airport** (859-425-3114; www.bluegrassairport.com). It is located about 70 miles from Morehead, and car rentals are available.

GETTING AROUND **Federated Transportation of the Bluegrass** (888-848-0989) operates bus routes through Morehead. They run Mon.–Sat., 6 AM–8 PM. the cost to ride the bus is $1 each way. They do not have a web site, so please call for routes and information.

MEDICAL EMERGENCY **St. Claire Regional Medical Center** (606-783-6500; www.st-claire.org), 222 Medical Circle, Morehead. This 119-bed hospital was practically a gift to the area from the Sisters of Notre Dame in Covington, Kentucky. Prior to its 1947 opening, residents of the region had to go to Lexington or Northern Kentucky, both more than an hour's drive, for medical care. Local doctor Claire Louise Caudill set up a practice in Morehead but spent most of her time driving to homes delivering babies. A priest from Northern Kentucky was spending some time in the area, following the plight of this country doctor. When he returned home, he asked the good sisters if they could help, and they did by sponsoring the hospital.

ALCOHOL Rowan County is a moist county, which means that alcohol is prohibited except in the city of Morehead, which allows packaged alcohol sales. Kentucky law prohibits consumption of alcohol in public places and prohibits open containers of alcohol, so don't bring it to the Daniel Boone National Forest.

✳ To See

Morehead State University (800-585-6781; www.moreheadstate.edu), 150 University Blvd., Morehead. Founded in 1887 as Morehead Normal School, they currently have an enrollment of about 9,000 students, in about 80 degree programs.

Take a tour of this scenic campus, which lies on the fringes of the Daniel Boone National Forest.

✔ **Tater Knob Fire Tower** (606-784-6428), Morehead Ranger District, 2375 KY 801S, Morehead. Visit the last remaining fire tower in the Daniel Boone National Forest. Climb up into this 10-by-10 foot building that sits high above the forest and take advantage of the view. The 35-foot tower, which was once used for spotting fires, was closed in the mid-1970s. It has now been restored and is open to the public. It's open dawn to dusk, but you might want to call the ranger district for directions on how to get there.

Kentucky Folk Art Center (606-783-2204; www.kyfolkart.org), 150 University Blvd., Morehead. Open Mon.–Sat. 9–5, Sun. 1–5. KFAC is closed on Sunday Jan.–March. Located in the historic Union Grocery building in Morehead, and with a growing permanent collection of over 1,300 works by regional folk artists, the Folk Art Center is a unique cultural experience. You will enjoy the amazing talent that creates this traditional mountain art. $3 adults, $2 seniors; under 12 free.

✔ 🐟 **Minor E. Clark Fish Hatchery** (606-784-6872), 120 Fish Hatchery Rd., Morehead. Open weekdays 7–3. This is one of the largest state-owned warm-water fish hatcheries in the nation, with largemouth bass, striped bass, walleye, and crappie. The fish are raised to stock area lakes and streams. Beautiful grounds are also a prime spot for bird-watching. Free.

✳ To Do

G O L F Eagle Trace Golf Course (606-783-9973; www.moreheadstate.edu/eagletrace), 1275 Eagle Dr., Morehead. This semi-private 18 hole golf course covers a maximum distance of 6,902 yards and is a par-72 course. The grounds are lush and challenging with a variety of water, sand, and topographical hazards.

Sheltowee Trail Golf Course (606-784-2582), 1200 Clearfork N., Morehead. This public 9-hole course is surrounded by beautiful Daniel Boone National Forest. It is a par-36 course and covers 3,381 yards. They offer a 15-tee driving range and a snack bar.

B I N G O Cave Run Bingo (606-356-4025), 6950 US 60W, Morehead. Have fun and make some money, too. This bingo hall has 8,000 square feet with two large areas for smokers and nonsmokers. Play in the Tropicana Room or the Vegas Room; monitors are everywhere so you'll always know what's going on. Open Fri. and Sat. at 5 PM.

O U T D O O R A D V E N T U R E Cave Run Lake Area (606-783-7001, 606-784-9709). This giant 8,270-acre lake was created in 1969 to prevent flooding of the Licking River. It lies on the western edge of Rowan County near a small community called Farmers just outside Morehead. The pristine lake is almost entirely within the Daniel Boone National Forest. To preserve its beauty, there has been no private development along the banks, other than campgrounds. Known as the Muskie Capital of the South, the lake is stocked full of these little buggers, but fishermen looking for small- and largemouth bass, bluegill, crappie, White bass, Kentucky bass, channel catfish, flathead catfish, and trout won't go home empty-handed, either. The area also offers boating, swimming, and hiking.

Scott Creek Marina (606-784-9666), 801 S. Morehead. This well-stocked marina offers houseboat, pontoon, fishing. and paddle-boat rentals. While you are there, grab a hearty meal at **Captain Jack's Boat House Grill** (606-784-9666). They are right on the water and offer mouthwatering desserts and glorious sunsets. Open Fri. noon–9, Sat. 7–9, and Sun. 7–6.

Cave Run Bicycle and Outdoor Adventures (606-784-1818; www.caverun bikeshop.com), 995 KY 801S, Morehead. Open Tue.–Sat. 10–6. With hundreds of miles of world-class mountain bike roads and hiking trails in the area, you need to be equipped to start your adventure. They rent canoes, kayaks, and mountain bikes and sell camping equipment, maps, and other gear.

✳ Lodging

🖉 BED & BREAKFASTS Brownwood Bed & Breakfast & Cabins

(606-784-8799; www.brownwood bandb.com), 46 Carcy Cemetery Rd., Morehead. Sleep in the large two-bed suite or in the all-natural one-bedroom wood cabins. Either way you will feel warm, cozy, and right at home in the mountains. Don't miss the southern-style breakfast with jams and jellies made by local Mennonite and Amish communities. Sit on the big front porch and let nature soak in. $

🖉 CABINS Cave Run Lodging

(606-783-1234, 888-276-8759; www .caverunlodging.net), 1190 KY 801 S., Morehead. Offering cabins and A-frame homes minutes to Cave Run Lake or the Daniel Boon National Forest. Each cabin and A-frame is fully furnished with a stove, refrigerator, microwave, and cooking essentials. They all have a deck with a grill, a coffeemaker, and toaster. You'll be comfortable year-round, as all models have central heat and air. $–$$

🖉 Red River Gorge Cabin Rentals

(www.redrivergorgecabinrentals.com). One-stop shopping for your cabin needs in the gorge. They have about 10 secluded cabins, which can provide a romantic respite for two; a couple of families can be housed in their four-bedroom cottage. All have homey amenities, and some even have hot tubs or fireplaces, perfect for relaxing after a day of hiking.

CAMPING Twin Knobs Campground

(606-784-8816, gate, 877-444-6777; www.reserveusa.com), 5195 KY 801 S., Morehead. Right in the middle of Daniel Boone National Forest, this is a big but secluded campground. Reserve a lakeside site or a wooded area to camp. Some sites have electric hookup. They also have a sand beach and a boat ramp. Open Mar.–Oct.

Zilpo Campground (606-768-2722, 877-444-6777; www.reserveusa.com), US 60 E., Salt Lick. Lots to do here, like boating and hiking. They have a paved boat ramp and a sand beach. The mostly shaded campground sits right alongside the lake. The campground store has all the things you need for your stay. Open Mar.–Oct.

✳ Where to Eat

EATING OUT All Seasons Flowers & Gifts & Café

(606-784-4933), 134 E. Main St., Morehead. Open Mon.–Fri. 9–5, Sat. 9–3. This cute florist shop started selling sandwiches, and now it's a huge part of their business. Although the café isn't even listed on their sign, word of mouth has told the locals where to go for chicken salad on giant homemade croissants, deli sandwiches, and pasta salads. They also have delicious desserts, too. $

GREEN SPACE

About an hour east of Lexington, via the Mountain Parkway at the Slade exit, you will find the Red River Gorge and Natural Bridge State Park, two gems that can't be missed.

🔦 🎣 ⛺ **Natural Bridge State Resort Park** (606-663-2214, 800-325-1710; parks.ky.gov/findparks/resortparks/nb), 2135 Natural Bridge Rd., Slade. One the four original Kentucky state parks, this park was established in 1926, but was about 65 million years in the making. Named for the sandstone arch—78 feet long,

NATURAL BRIDGE

photo by Deborah Kohl Kremer

65 feet high, 12 feet thick, and 20 feet wide—it's actually the most famous of the more than 70 natural arches in the area. Situated adjacent to the **Red River Gorge Geological Area** (www.redrivergorge.org), which covers about 26,000 acres of the Daniel Boone National Forest, this region was created by wind and water, resulting in stunning cliff formations, scenic vistas, and natural rock shelters. With miles and miles of hiking trails, it offers routes for all levels of exertion. But be sure to use extreme caution, as there are many steep cliffs and hair-raising drop-offs along the paths that take lives every year.

The state park encompasses approximately 2,500 acres, with more than 18 miles of hiking trails all leading to the awe-inspiring Natural Bridge. The park also includes a 4-acre pond with an island in the middle of it. Known as Hoedown Island, it is used for square dances in the summer. There is also 54-acre Mill Creek Lake where you can rent pedal boats and hydrobikes; it's an excellent place for fishing for bass, bream, catfish, crappie, and rainbow trout. For those not interested in hiking, take the 22-minute SkyLift up to the breathtaking Natural Bridge. Stay in one of the 35 rooms at the **Hemlock Lodge**; all have private balconies to enjoy the views of the forested mountain area. They also have secluded one- and two-bedroom cottages tucked into the woods. If you would rather camp, Natural Bridge State Resort Park hast two campgrounds,

Whittleton Campground and **Middlefork Campground**. These wooded grounds provide 82 sites with utilities, as well as primitive sites for those who really want to rough it. **The Sandstone Arches Restaurant** is a good place to go relax after a day of hiking. The restaurant overlooks the lake and Hoedown Island, the clogging capital of Kentucky (and you didn't even know there was a clogging capital of Kentucky). Diners can enjoy watching squirrels steal nuts from the squirrel feeders outside. The menu offers choices like fried catfish, fried green tomatoes, and Kentucky hot brown. Although it could be hard to choose among these specialties, the restaurant offers a daily buffet at all three meals, so you won't have to. Open every day. Breakfast 7–10, lunch 11:30–2, dinner 5–9. Sunday brunch is served 11–3. $–$$; children under 5 eat free.

Those new to the climbing world might want to head for **Torrent Falls Climbing Adventure** (606-660-6613; www.torrentfalls.com), 1617 North KY 11, Campton. Open Mar. 1–Dec. 1, 9 AM–dark. This French climbing system, the only one in the United States, is a mixture of rungs and cables connected right to the rock face to aid in climbing or rappelling. Climbers need to be older than 10 and weigh less than 9,500 pounds, which is the amount of weight the rungs can hold.

While you are in the area, don't miss **Miguel's Pizza** (606-663-1975), 1891 Natural Bridge Rd., Slade. This legendary hangout for rock climbers and campers serves excellent home-style pizza. They also offer climbing supplies and overnight camping for climbers. So, if you are not a climber, stop by for some tasty pizza, but if you're there for climbing, stop by for pizza and climbing camaraderie.

TORRENT FALLS CLIMBING ADVENTURE

photo by Tim Durstock

Ÿ **The Front Porch Restaurant** (606-783-1821, 606-780-2548), 303 Old Flemingsburg Rd., Morehead. Open Mon.–Sat. 11–10, sometimes later in summer. Closed Sun. This restaurant, run by a close-knit family, makes you feel like kin when you come in the door. They offer true country cooking with lunch specials like chicken and dumplin's or homemade soup beans, which is a mountain way of describing pinto beans with corn bread. The meals are delicious, but guests have been coming in for more than 10 years just for a slice of coconut cream or butterscotch pie. $

SNACKS Root-a-Bakers Bakery and Cafe (606-780-4282), 313 Flemingsburg Rd., Morehead. Open Tue.–Fri. 7 AM–6 PM, Sat. 8–2. Just follow your nose to this wonderful bakery, where you'll find pastries, breads, cinnamon rolls, and sticky buns. They also have lunch items like soups, salads, and sandwiches. Don't leave without trying one of the world-famous sugar cookies. $

Ole Thyme Sweetshop and Gifts (606-784-6656), 7075 US 60 W., Farmers. Open Thu.–Sat. 10–5. Calm your sweet tooth with some homemade fudge and candy. They also have a small gift shop where you'll find all kinds of quilts and Boyd Bears. $

✳ Selective Shopping

Old School House Antique Mall (606-783-1800), US 60 W., Farmers. Open Mon.–Sat. 10–5. Specializing in Amish furniture and quilts, they also carry a wide range of antiques and collectibles.

Frieda's Antique Shoppe (606-784-5993), 1750 US 60 W., Morehead. Open Mon.–Sat. 10–5. Specializing in antique lamps, lamp parts, shades, and accessories, they also carry lots of small antiques and willow furniture.

Pine Grove Framing and Gallery of Fine Arts (606-784-6238; www.pinegroveart.com), 314 Bridge St., Morehead. Open Mon.–Fri. 11–6, Sat. 11–2. The home showplace for the work of many regional artists. They have dozens of original paintings and hundreds of prints, too. Stop in to see what's new.

Claypool-Young Art Gallery (606-783-5048; www.moreheadstate.edu). Open Mon.–Fri. 8–4. This is the largest exhibiting space in Kentucky east of Lexington, and it's loaded with contemporary art of American as well as international artists. This gallery is located in the Claypool-Young Art Building on the Morehead State University campus.

Calico Patch (606-784-7235; www.calicopatch.net), 155 Bluebank, Morehead. Call for hours. This is quilter's paradise. This shop carries all kinds of designer quilting fabrics, notions, and gifts. They have classes, kits, and a friendly staff who never tire of talking about quilting.

✳ Special Events

June: **Clack Mountain Fest** (606-780-4342; www.clackmountainfest.com). Formerly known as the Bluegrass n' More festival, this weekend of bluegrass, traditional, acoustic, and other music coincides with the "Day in the Country" folk art show and the Appalachian Arts and Crafts Fair. All events are held at or near the historic First Street Arts District.

September: **Poppy Mountain Bluegrass Festival** (606-784-2277; poppymountainbluegrass.com). Featuring five full days of bluegrass music and camping nestled in the 1,000 beautiful acres of Poppy Mountain. This event draws thousands of bluegrass music fans each year.

PAINTSVILLE, PRESTONSBURG, AND PIKEVILLE

These three cities, in the heart of the Appalachian Mountains, are worth the drive to this far eastern corner of the state. Although connected by US 23, the Country Music Highway, they each have their individual personalities that you will definitely want to sample.

Named for the colorful Indian markings on the white birch trees and rocks that lined the banks of Paint Creek, the city of **Paintsville**, which was first known as Paint Lick Station or Paint Landing, established a post office in 1824. The city sits at the confluence of the Big Sandy River and Paint Creek, in the heart of the Appalachian Mountains in Eastern Kentucky.

This remote location kept the city, which is the county seat of Johnson County, from expanding much in those early years. In the early part of the 20th century, John C. C. Mayo, a local teacher, realized the mountains were full of coal and proceeded to become a millionaire from the bounty inside the hills. He lobbied heavily for a railroad, which finally reached Paintsville on September 1, 1904. By 1910, thousands of tons of coal were pouring out of Eastern Kentucky. This influx of money helped Mayo to establish banks, churches, streets, and public utilities of Paintsville.

Today Paintsville is home to about 4,200 people. Visitors can tour Mayo's magnificent home, the Country Music Museum, or even the birthplace of country music legends Loretta Lynn and Crystal Gayle. For outdoor recreation, Paintsville Lake State Park will meet all of your fishing, boating, and water sport needs.

Prestonsburg, the first town in the Big Sandy Valley, was also the first county seat in all of Eastern Kentucky. It lies in a valley along the banks of the Levisa Fork of the Big Sandy River. Prestonsburg was founded in 1797 by Colonel John Preston, who also named it, coincidentally, after himself. Today it is home to about 4,000 people who live surrounded by some of Kentucky's highest mountains.

Known as Star City of Eastern Kentucky, Prestonsburg achieved this name for all the entertainment and star power that comes from the region. Country music stars including Dwight Yoakam—born just a few miles from Prestonsburg in Floyd County—Loretta Lynn, Wynonna Judd, Naomi Judd, Billy Ray Cyrus, Tom T. Hall, and other big names are all from the Big Sandy Valley.

Prestonsburg is a must-see for those looking for a real taste of Eastern Kentucky.

photo courtesy of www.kentuckytourism.com

COUNTRY MUSIC HIGHWAY

Pike County, Kentucky's largest in terms of land area, covers 787 square miles. **Pikeville**, the county seat, was founded in 1823 and named, like the county, for General Zebulon Pike, a US Army officer and explorer who discovered Pikes Peak. The area may not be as steep as Pikes Peak, but it certainly is mountainous. It is located right in the heart of the Appalachian Mountains. Although coal was discovered in the area before the Civil War, Pikeville didn't really start mining until about 1910, when the railroad finally made it to town. Today mining is still the largest employer of Pike County's 68,000 people.

These strong people know they can move mountains. And actually they did. You can see their results at the Pikeville Cut-Through. It was a huge engineering project that actually rerouted the river, the train tracks, and a highway.

Come to Pike County and see what it's all about.

GUIDANCE Call or stop by the **Paintsville/Johnson County Tourism Commission** (606-297-1469, 800-542-5790; www.paintsville.org), 120 Staves Branch, Paintsville. Open 7–4 weekdays only. They are located right beside the Country Music Museum, so you can get directions and brochures and visit the museum at the same time.

Prestonsburg Convention & Visitors Bureau (606-886-1341, 800-844-4704; www.prestonsburgky.org), 113 S. Central Ave., Prestonsburg. Open Mon.–Fri. 8–4. Stop by this historic US Post Office building to get maps and directions. You might want to stay awhile, because they also exhibit and sell locally created arts and crafts.

You can't miss the old train car as you enter Pikeville. It is home to **Pikeville–Pike County Tourism** (606-432-5063, 800 844-7453; www.tourpikecounty.com), 781 Hambley Blvd., Pikeville. They have brochures, maps, directions, and even Pikeville souvenirs.

GETTING THERE These cities are not close to any commercial airport, so driving there is the way to go. If you fly, you can choose either **Bluegrass Airport** in Lexington or **Tri-State Airport** in Huntington, West Virginia. Either is about two hours away. Prestonsburg, known as Star City, is centrally located at the confluence of five major highways. Those highways, which seem to make up a five-point star, are US 23 N., US 23 S., KY 80, KY 3, and KY 114, also known as Mountain Parkway.

GETTING AROUND The mountainside roads offer scenic views, but you'll have to drive yourself, because there is no public transportation. The downtown areas offer free parking everywhere. If you find yourself lost, don't be afraid to ask directions—the people are super-friendly.

MEDICAL EMERGENCY **Paul B. Hall Regional Medical Center** (606-789-3511; www.pbhrmc.com), 625 James S. Trimble Blvd., Paintsville. This 72-bed hospital serves a population base of more than 45,000 people from five counties. Formerly known as Paintsville Hospital, they have been serving Eastern Kentucky since 1920. **Highlands Regional Medical Center** (606-886-8511; www.hrmc .org), 5000 KY 321, Prestonsburg. Serving the areas of Floyd, Johnson, Martin, and Magoffin Counties with a combined population of over 90,000 residents, this hospital was started 33 years ago by a group of concerned citizens from each of these counties. **Pikeville Medical Center** (606-218-3500; www.pikevillehospital.org), 911 Bypass Rd., Pikeville. Founded in 1924 as Pikeville Methodist Hospital, this 261-bed facility serves the counties of Eastern Kentucky.

ALCOHOL Paintsville is situated in a dry county, which prohibits alcohol everywhere. In Prestonsburg, the entire county is wet, which means alcohol sales are allowed throughout the area. If you want a drink while in Pike County, you need to get it in Pikeville, because the rest of the county is dry. Actually Pike County is considered moist, which means, in relation to alcohol sales, that the county is dry but the city of Pikeville is wet.

✳ To See

In the Paintsville area

Loretta Lynn's Birth Place—Butcher Hollow (606-789-3397), Webb's General Store, Millers Creek Rd., Butcher Hollow, Van Lear. Tour the humble four-room cabin that was the girlhood home of the Queen of Country Music, Loretta Lynn. Just stop by **Webb's General Store** and ask Loretta's brother, Herman, for a tour. The authentic, rustic country store is a treat, too.

Coal Miners' Museum (606-789-8540), 78 Miller's Creek Rd., Van Lear. Located in the former headquarters of the Miller's Creek Division of the Consolidation Coal Company, they have a unique collection of tools and artifacts associated with the mining community. It is run by volunteers, so call ahead to schedule an appointment.

Mayo Mansion (606-297-1469), 3rd St., Paintsville. Visit the 43-room mansion of Eastern Kentucky's first coal baron, John Caldwell Calhoun Mayo. The beautiful three-story mansion was

WEBB'S GENERAL STORE

built between 1905 and 1912 in Classical Revival styling. Today it is a parochial school, and tours are by appointment only. It's a beautiful site, even if you just drive by.

Mayo Church (606-789-3296), 3rd St., Paintsville. After completing his spectacular home, John Caldwell Calhoun Mayo realized he needed a church, too. So just across the street from his home, Mayo built a stunning Late Gothic Revival stone church. It is well known for its awe-inspiring stained-glass windows and organ that was donated by Mayo's friend Andrew Carnegie. Tours by appointment.

§ US 23 Country Music Highway Museum (606-297-1469, 800-542-5790), 120 Staves Branch, Paintsville. Open 7–4 weekdays only. Located next to the Paintsville Information Center off the Paintsville exit of US 23, the museum honors many of the country music entertainers who consider US 23 their home.

✎ Mountain HomePlace (606-297-1850), on the grounds of Paintsville Lake State Park, Staffordsville. Open Apr.–Oct.; call for hours. A working 1850s-era farm made up of original structures from the area. Come and see how things used to be. Visit cabins, a schoolhouse, a church, and a blacksmith shop while encountering interpreters, in authentic period costumes, who are performing their chores. The visitors center features a movie depicting the history of the early Appalachian settlers. There is also a small museum full of 1850s-era tools, clothes, and household items.

In the Prestonsburg area

Battle of Ivy Mountain Battlefield (606-886-1341), US Route 23, 10 miles south of Prestonsburg at Ivel. Call the Prestonsburg Visitors Center for directions. This 14-foot-high granite obelisk marks the spot of the Civil War Battle of Ivy Mountain. The conflict, which took place November 8, 1861, was a Union victory as the Confederates were outnumbered more than 12 to 1.

MOUNTAIN HOMEPLACE
photo courtesy of www.kentuckytourism.com

✎ East Kentucky Science Center & Planetarium (606-889-0303; www.wedoscience.org), 7 Bert Combs Dr., Prestonsburg. Open Tue.–Fri. 1–4:30. Not only a science museum, it also features exhibits about math and technology. The 40-foot domed planetarium offers shows with close-up views of the night skies. Check the web site for showtimes.

Middle Creek National Battlefield (606-886-1312; www.middlecreek.org), Route 114, Prestonsburg. Open dawn–dusk. This battle, which took place on January 10, 1862, ended Confederate supremacy in the region. Coincidentally, it also launched the career of James A. Garfield, the 20th president of the United States. Make a visit and see the battlefield where it took place.

Ranier Racing Museum (606-886-1341), 113 S. Central Ave., Prestonsburg. Call for hours. See memorabilia such as trophies, pictures, and uniforms of the former Floyd County coal operator Harry Ranier, who became famous in Winston Cup stock-car racing in the 1980s. Ranier Racing fielded cars that won 24 NASCAR races, including three Daytona 500s. Small fee.

Samuel May House (606-886-9608, 606-432-3528; www.mayhouse.org), 1035 N. Lake Dr., Prestonsburg. Tours of the May House can be made by appointment. Built in 1817, it is the oldest brick house in the Big Sandy Valley. Tour this childhood home of Colonel Jack May, a leading Confederate officer in the Civil War. The 5th Kentucky Infantry was organized at the May Farm, and the house was used as a Confederate recruiting post during the Civil War period. This fine home, and the grounds surrounding it, has been restored to its original grandeur.

In the Pikeville area

& **Big Sandy Heritage Museum** (606-218-6050; www.bigsandyheritage.org), 773 Hambley Blvd., Pikeville. Open weekdays. Located in a historic railroad station in downtown Pikeville, this museum portrays the rich history and culture of Eastern Kentucky. For a snapshot of the region, study the exhibits about coal mining, devastating floods, and the infamous Hatfield–McCoy feud.

/ **Elkhorn City Railroad Museum** (606-754-8300; elkhorncityrrm.tripod.com), 100 Pine St., Elkhorn City. Open Tue.–Sat. 10–4, Sun. noon–4. Closed Jan.–Mar. Even though it's about 35 miles outside of Pikeville, this is worth the drive if you're a train enthusiast. It was founded in 1990 by retired railroad employees whose fascination with trains and their pride in museum's collection is obvious. They have two cabooses, motor cars, antique uniforms, and equipment. They even have a velocipede, a one-man propelled vehicle used by track inspectors. More than 1,000 pieces of rare railroad memorabilia are well displayed.

Historic Dils Cemetery (606-423-5063), intersection of Chloe Rd. and the Bypass, downtown Pikeville. The first integrated cemetery in Eastern Kentucky, Dils is the final resting place for local notables such as Randolph McCoy, who was credited with leading the famed Hatfield–McCoy feud. Graves of soldiers from the Revolutionary War are also on the grounds.

Pikeville Cut-Through (606-423-5063). Residents of Pikeville were plagued with devastating floods from the Levisa Fork of the Big Sandy River for decades. The Cut-Through Project, which was the most extensive land-moving project in the Western Hemisphere after the Panama Canal, moved 18 million cubic yards of earth. By moving the mountain, and diverting the highway, the railroad, and the river itself, the area is safe from flooding. See the whole picture for yourself at the overlook at the top of the mountain. Get directions at the visitors center.

✳ To Do

BASKETBALL The East Kentucky Miners (www.ekminers.com). Pikeville's minor-league basketball franchise is part of the Continental Basketball Association. The team plays home games at the East Kentucky Exposition center, Nov.–Mar. Check the web site for tip-off times.

BOATING/FISHING Paintsville Lake State Park (606-297-8486) in Staffordsville, is 3 miles west of Paintsville. Bordered by steep cliffs and wooded coves, this

1,140-acre lake is just the right size for boating, skiing, and fishing. It's stocked with walleye, bass, trout, and crappie. They also have a full-service marina with docking and boat-launching ramps. Rent a houseboat, pontoon, or fishing boat, or just fish off the dock. Open year-round.

DRIVING TOUR The Hatfield–McCoy Feud Driving Tour (606-432-5063, 800-844-7453). Pick up an audio guide at the tourism center. Listen to the antics of the famous feud between the McCoys of Kentucky and the Hatfields of West Virginia as you drive past authentic sites from their mid-1800s interfamily battle.

GOLF Paintsville Golf Course and Country Club (606-789-4234), 2960 KY 1107, Paintsville. This 18-hole, par-70 course is very well known in the area for its beautiful surroundings. It has a cool swinging bridge that connects the back 9 to the front 9. They also have a well-stocked pro shop.

StoneCrest Championship Golf Course (606-886-1006; www.stonecrestky .com), 911 Clubhouse Dr., Prestonsburg. Come for the golf, stay for the view. Built on a reclaimed strip mine high atop a mountain, this championship-caliber, links-style course offers 18 holes with phenomenal views. Golfers can see about 50 miles in any direction from nearly every spot on the course. They also have a putting green, driving range, and clubhouse.

Mountain Pub-Links (606-437-0339), 8709 Lower John's Creek Rd., Pikeville. Settled right into the mountains, this 18-hole public golf course offers a serene setting. This course offers club rentals, snack bar, and practice green.

HORSE RACING Thunder Ridge Racing & Entertainment Complex (606-886-7223; www.thunderridgeraceway.com), 701 KY 3, Prestonsburg. This track offers harness racing in fall and intertrack wagering year-round. During the off-season, the track is also used for MotoX, rodeos, horse shows, and dog shows. Check the web site to see what's racing.

RACEWAY Mega Raceway (606-874-2484), 194 Cow Creek, Prestonsburg. Mega Raceway features go-cart racing on an asphalt track; rent by the hour or the day. They also have a game room with pool tables and video games. Hours change seasonally, so please call first.

WALKS The Kiwanis Walking Trail (606-297-1850). Located across from the visitors center at the Mountain Home Place. Enjoy a leisurely 1.6-mile walking trail around Paintsville Lake. Take a break on one of the many benches and maybe you'll see one of the many wild turkeys or deer that are abundant in the area. Open from daylight to dark.

Historic Downtown Pikeville Walking Tour. Pick up a map at the tourism center. See 53 historic buildings and homes, some of which are on the National Register of Historic Places, while enjoying a walk through the downtown area.

STATE PARKS Jenny Wiley State Resort Park (606-886-2711, 800-325-0142; parks.ky.gov). Located in the heart of the Appalachian Mountains, this park is named in honor of a brave frontierswoman. Jenny Wiley, who was captured by Native Americans in 1789, witnessed the murder of her children, and endured

photo courtesy of www.kentuckytourism.com

DEWEY LAKE AT JENNY WILEY STATE PARK

months of torture herself. Jenny Wiley escaped and went on to raise more children and live a productive life in nearby Johnson County. The state park is widely known for Broadway-style shows at the Jenny Wiley Theatre. This is Kentucky's only professional theatre east of I-75, and the productions really are first-rate. The park also boasts many outdoor activities on the 1,100-acre Dewey Lake, which covers 18.5 miles and offers 52 miles of shoreline. Fish for largemouth bass, catfish, and crappie. Pontoon boats are available for rent at the marina. They tend to get rented out quickly on weekends in summer, so call ahead and reserve one early. The park offers miles of scenic hiking trails, a disk golf course, and swimming in the lodge pool. Stay in one of the 48 comfy rooms or 18 rustic cottages of the **May Lodge**, which is surrounded by peaceful woods and scenic mountains and over looks Dewey Lake. They also have 117-site campground with utility hookups, a dump station, and a grocery store. Dining is available at the **Music Highway Grill**, open every day: breakfast 7–10, lunch 11:30–2, dinner 5–9. Sunday brunch is served 11–3. Offering bar-style appetizers like a deep-fried onion, mozzarella sticks, and potato skins, as well as entrées ranging from mahimahi to baby back ribs. The menu covers a wide range of favorites and includes locally grown meats and produce whenever possible. The restaurant, which overlooks Dewey Lake, offers a lunch buffet every day and a dinner buffet on weekends. $–$$

"¶" & ✍ **Breaks Interstate Park** (276-865-4413, 800-982-5122; www.breakspark .com), KY/VA 80 E., Breaks, VA. Visit this interstate park—known as the Grand Canyon of the South—and you'll see how it earned its nickname. Located right on the Kentucky–Virginia border, the massive 1,000-foot gorge is the centerpiece of a park made up of 4,500 acres of mountains, forests, and cliffs. The park, which is best known for the rugged and scenic hiking trails, offers a lodge, restaurant, and campground. The 82-room **Rhododendron Lodge**, which is open seasonally Mar. 21–Dec. 21, sits right along the edge of the canyon, so all the balcony rooms have phenomenal views. They also have rustic two-bedroom cottages, which are available year-round. The cottages are tucked into the woods and they are fully equipped. They also have an outside pool and laundry facilities, and they allow pets. **Breaks Interstate Park Campground** is open Mar.–Oct. 31. This wooded

photo courtesy of www.kentuckytourism.com

BREAKS INTERSTATE PARK

campground features 122 sites with full hookup, electricity, water, and sewer. They do not take reservations, however, so it is first come, first camped. The **Rhododendron Restaurant** is open daily 7–9, serving all three meals. This is where you will find fine dining right in the heart of the Grand Canyon of the South. They offer daily lunch specials as well as delicious homemade soups and deserts. $–$$

Fishtrap Lake State Park (606-437-7496; parks.ky.gov), 2204 Fishtrap Rd., Pikeville. Somewhat of an engineering marvel, Fishtrap Lake was created when the Army Corp of Engineers constructed the highest dam in Eastern Kentucky. This giant lake covers about 1,100 acres. Come for boating, fishing, and hiking and enjoy the scenery.

✳ Green Space

Bob Amos Park (606-437-5116). This park, which is adjacent to the famous Cut-Through Project, offers a rubberized oval walking track, horseshoe area, tennis courts, basketball courts, soccer, Little League, and baseball fields. They also have a miniature golf course, a driving range, a picnic shelter with an enclosed grill, and playground equipment. Surrounded by open woodland, a nature trail takes you to "The Overlook," which is the place to get a bird's-eye scenic view of the Cut-Through Project.

Rucker Park (606-789-8540), 78 Miller's Creek Rd., Van Lear. The park is open to the public during daylight hours. Just east of the Coal Miners' Museum, you'll find this cute park. It is owned and operated by the Van Lear Historical Society. The park features an old C&O Railroad caboose, perfect for climbing and exploring. Basketball and volleyball courts, playground equipment, and a picnic shelter, too.

Levisa Fork River Park (606-886-2335) Front St., Prestonsburg. Located right in downtown Prestonsburg, this park includes a boat ramp, picnic shelter, and outdoor stage.

✳ Lodging

& **The Landmark Inn** (606-432-2545, 800-831-146,; www.the-landmark-inn.com), 190 S. Mayo Trail, US 23, 460, and 11, Pikeville. Around since 1962, this 103-room inn offers huge rooms and excellent service. The decor is somewhat dated but the staff of this independently owned hotel are so happy to have you, you won't even notice.

CAMPING **Paintsville Lake State Park Campground** (606-297-8488; parks.ky.gov), 1551 Hwy. 2275, Staffordsville. This campground features 32 developed sites with utility and sewer hookups and 10 primitive sites with terraced pads for tents. All campsites have a picnic table, a campfire ring, and a lantern post. Restrooms, showers, and laundry facilities are close to all sites. Relax and enjoy the playgrounds, a sand volleyball court, basketball court, and horseshoe pits. Open year-round. Leashed pets allowed.

✳ Where to Eat

DINING OUT

In Paintsville

& **Carriage House Restaurant** (606-789-4242), 624 James Trimble Blvd., Paintsville. Open 7–9 daily. Located inside the Ramada Inn Conference Center, this is fine dining in Paintsville. This white-tablecloth, excellent-service kind of place has flame-broiled steak, charbroiled chicken breast, and jumbo fried shrimp. They also offer a jam-packed lunch buffet. $$–$$$

Mandarin House (606-789-5313), 507 S. Mayo Trail, Paintsville. If you are looking for delightful choices from the Orient, this is your place. Asian dishes like spicy-hot General Tso's chicken or hot-and-sour soup are rec-ommended by locals. Fri. and Sat. nights they offer specials on seafood, frog legs, and prime rib. $$–$$$

In Pikeville

& **The Top of the Inn at The Landmark Inn** (606-432-2545, 800-831-1469; www.the-landmark-inn.com), 190 S. Mayo Trail, US 23, 460, and 11, Pikeville. Serving three meals daily. Offers fine dining on the top floor of the hotel. Menu choices range from prime rib to fried oysters to a delicious chicken potpie. $$–$$$

Chirico's Ristorante (606-432-7070), 136 Pike St., Pikeville. Open Mon.–Fri. 10–9, Sat. 3–10. Closed Sun. Located in the historic Pinson Hotel building. The Chirico family, who have roots in southern Italy, have a wide variety of authentic Italian dishes. All menu items are made from scratch, using recipes that have been handed down for generations. Make sure you save room for the homemade bread. $$–$$$

Mona's Creative Catering (606-437-6662), 180 Town Mountain Rd., Pikeville. Open 10–9; closed Sun. Try this little spot for sandwiches and salads. Mona tries to make almost everything low cal or at least healthy. Try the alfa turkado sandwich, which is a tasty combination of turkey, alfalfa sprouts, and avocado. She also makes a heavenly angel food cake from scratch daily. $

EATING OUT

In Paintsville

Wilma's Restaurant (606-789-5911), 212 Court St., Paintsville. Open daily 7–7. Wilma's is a staple in Paintsville. Everyone knows one another, and if you ask for a menu, well, they know you're from out of town. Get a menu anyway so you don't miss anything. Breakfast is available all day with local-recommended choices like biscuits and gravy or home fries. For lunch or dinner, try the open-faced roast beef, mashed potatoes, pinto beans, and corn bread. Wilma also has a mean apple pie. $

Big Sandy Drug Store (606-789-5371), 316 Main St., Paintsville. Open weekdays 9–2. With a pharmacy in the back and a diner in the front, this cute place feels like the 1950s. Sit at the bar or at a table and order up a burger, sandwich, or bowl of soup. In summer they have thick milk shakes and picture-perfect parfaits. $

In Prestonsburg

Billy Ray's Restaurant (606-886-1744), 101 N. Front Ave., Prestonsburg. Open for lunch and dinner. Closed Sun. This family-style restaurant was formerly known as Playhouse Pool Hall, a somewhat seedy bar and pool room. Owner Billy Ray—not *that* Billy Ray, but Billy Ray Collins—has transformed the eatery but managed to keep the pool room burger on the menu, which was a favorite in bygone times, as well as now. They also have juicy prime rib and homemade red velvet cake. The walls are loaded with old

DAIRY CHEER

photo by Deborah Kohl Kremer

photos of Prestonsburg and local sports teams. $

 Dairy Cheer (606-886-8666), 1384 N. Lake Dr., Prestonsburg. Despite the name, this fast-food restaurant specialized in big sloppy cheeseburgers, like their signature Smashburger and crispy onion rings. They also have a tempting array of ice cream, sundaes, and shakes. $

In Pikeville

Rusty Fork Café (606-754-4494), 105 S. Patty Loveless Dr., Elkhorn City. Open daily 9–9. This is a fantastic place to go for a home-cooked meal. They serve hearty breakfasts featuring homemade buttermilk biscuits, which they claim are bigger than a cat's head. They also have daily lunch specials like country-fried steak or chicken 'n' dumplings. Named for the Russell Fork River—which runs through Elkhorn City and right by the café—this cute restaurant is full of antiques, crafts, and locals. Stop by and get a fried apple pie. $

SNACKS Country at Heart & Old Town Fudge Co. (606-886-8957), 128 South Front Ave., Prestonsburg. Closed Sun. Owner Ken Wells makes creamy mountain fudge daily. While you're there have a cup of gourmet coffee or tea or wake yourself up with an espresso. The shop also carries locally made Kentucky crafts.

✳ Entertainment

Historical Sipp Theatre (606-789-9014; www.wkyh.com/sipp.htm), 3302nd St., Paintsville. Originally built as a vaudeville house, the Sipp has hosted the stars in the entertainment world from the 1930s to the present. Today it's both the downtown movie theater and the host of a "Bluegrass at the Sipp" music series. Call to see what's showing.

In The Pines Amphitheater (606-297-1850). In The Pines Amphitheater is located on the grounds of the Mountain Homeplace at Paintsville Lake. It resembles a Greek amphitheater and has the capacity to seat 700. Enjoy outdoor concerts under the stars. The schedule changes throughout the year, so call ahead.

Billie Jean Osborne's Kentucky Opry (606-886-2623, 888-622-2787; www.macarts.com), Mountain Arts Center, 50 Hal Rogers Dr., Prestonsburg. This is the answer to Saturday-night family entertainment. Kentucky Opry troupe, formed in 1990, comprises a cast of very talented individuals, all of whom call Eastern Kentucky home. They present variety-style shows covering everything from musical acts to comedy. Performances are held in the Mountain Arts Center's 1,050-seat theater. Check the web site for show-times and dates.

Artists Collaborative Theatre, Inc. (ACT) (606-754-5137; www.us23 .com/kycycle), 5664 Elkhorn Creek Rd., Elkhorn City. An Appalachian-based theater company whose year-round programming includes dramas, comedies, musicals, and the ACT1 theater for young people. Check the web site to see upcoming shows.

✳ Selective Shopping

Something Old and Something New (606-789-4210), 1057 Broadway St., Paintsville. Open Tue.–Sat. 10–6, Sun. 1–5. Closed Mon. Located in old Hobbs department store building downtown, they do offer both old and new items. This is the place to find used and vintage furniture, antiques, and dishes. They also have new quilts, candles, and crafts for your home. The shop is set up so you can see what the merchandise will look like in your home. Friendly staff, too.

Country Cottage Gifts (606-297-6520), intersection of US 460 and KY 40, Paintsville. Open Mon.–Sat. 10–5; closed Sun. You can't miss this stately historic mansion just off the highway. The home features 15-inch walls, nine fireplaces, and 1800s-era woodwork. While you are there, browse inviting home interior pieces like quilts, trunks, candles, and baskets.

⅁ **David Appalachian Crafts** (606-886-2377; www.davidappalachian crafts.com), KY 404, about 9 miles from Prestonsburg. David Appalachian Crafts is a nonprofit organization aimed at preserving traditional mountain crafts. The people of this region are an extremely talented bunch, and after touring this gallery, you will be convinced, too. You will find beautiful quilts, handmade baskets, woodworking, and other crafting techniques that have been handed down for generations. All items are for sale, so get something for yourself and you will be helping to supplement the income of these local craftsmen.

Pike County Artisan Center (606-433-0193; www.pikeartisancenter.org), Main St., Pikeville. You will enjoy their wide selection of arts and crafts by local artisans. Their slogan, "Where Community Meets Creativity," really is

DAVID APPALACHIAN CRAFTS
photo courtesy of www.kentuckytourism.com

true. You'll find goods such as paintings, pottery, and jewelry, all locally made.

Remember Me (606-437-0444), 645 Hambley Blvd., Pikeville. Located right downtown, this cozy gift shop has home decor items, jewelry, crystal, and Vera Bradley items.

GALLERIES Mountain Arts Center Gallery (606-886-2623; www.macarts .com), 50 Hal Rogers Dr., Prestonsburg. Closed Sun. Enjoy the work of many local artists at this gallery. The exhibits change monthly, so you never know what you'll get to see.

Prestonsburg Community College Art Gallery (606-886-3863; www .prestonsburgcc.com), at Prestonsburg Community College, 1 Bert Combs Dr., Prestonsburg. Open weekdays 10–3. With a mission to enrich the lives of the students and community through exposure to the visual arts, the gallery exhibits a wide range of art. This gallery is located in the Magoffin Learning Resource Building.

ANTIQUES Southern Hospitality Antiques (606-886-9995), 5459 KY 321, Prestonsburg. This is a first-class collection of antiques, furniture, and glassware. They also have new gift items like silk floral arrangements, dishes, linens, and candles. Stop by this renovated service station and have a look around.

✷ Special Events

✧ 🐾 ♿ *April:* **Hillbilly Days** (www .hillbillydays.com). This huge festival, celebrating all things hillbilly, has been a Pikeville tradition since 1977 and draws more than 100,000 people each year. Visitors enjoy live down-home music, rides and carnival games, and a grand parade where you never know

what you'll see—from bands playing in the back of a pickup truck to gaudy jalopies to locals in crazy hillbilly costumes. It's all in fun and it benefits the Shriners Children's Hospital in Lexington, Kentucky.

✧ 🐾 ♿ *June:* **Hatfield–McCoy Heritage Weekend**. This event, founded in 1999 by Ron and Bo McCoy, promotes the cultural heritage of the world's most famous family feud. Although in 2003 the Hatfield and McCoy families signed a truce officially putting an end to the feuding, the festival has a celebration commemorating the signing of the truce. It includes a marathon run, an apple pie and old-fashioned stack-cake bake-off, arts and crafts, and bus tours to feud sites.

✧ ♿ 🐾 *October:* **Kentucky Apple Festival** (606-789-4355; www .kyapplefest.org). For more than 40 years, people have gathered in Paintsville each fall to celebrate all things apple. Purchase homemade apple cakes, pies, and muffins, and breathe in and enjoy the aroma coming from the giant iron kettle of apple butter being cooked over an open fire. This event draws more than 75,000 attendees who come for the free music, arts and crafts, a flea market, rides, car shows, and a parade.

✧ ♿ 🐾 **Jenny Wiley Pioneer Festival** (www.jennywileypioneerfestival .org/events.html). This weekend captures the spirit of Jenny Wiley, a local pioneer woman who survived a brutal Indian attack that took the lives of several of her children. This weeklong festival includes arts and crafts, food, and free entertainment. It takes place at various locations around the area. Check the web site for events and sites.

LONDON AND CORBIN

Geographically, both London and Corbin are situated right along the foothills of the Appalachian Mountains. This location makes you feel like you're verging on an adventure . . . and very likely you are. Both cities are adjacent to the massive Daniel Boone National Forest and feature access to huge lakes and three rivers: the Rockcastle, the Laurel, and the Cumberland. So if you are looking for an outdoorsy getaway, this might be your place.

Recreation is not your only option, though. History buffs can traipse along the Wilderness Road, the route created by Daniel Boone as he brought pioneers into Kentucky. This was also the site of Camp Wildcat, a Civil War battlefield.

If you are in the area in September, don't miss the Annual World Chicken Festival, an homage to native sons Colonel Harland Sanders of KFC, Lee Cummings of Lee's Famous Recipe, and all things chicken.

GUIDANCE **London–Laurel County Tourist Information Center** (606-878-6900, 800-348-0095; www.laurelkytourism.com) is located at I-75, Exit 41. The office is open Mon.–Sat. 9–5, Sun. 10–2. You can't miss this center, right off the interstate. They even have a cute little gazebo out front where you could relax. Inside you'll find maps, brochures and a very friendly staff. **Corbin Tourism Commission** (606-528-8860; www.corbinkytourism.com), 805 S. Main St., Corbin. Open weekdays 8–4. The Tourism Reception Center, right inside Corbin City Hall, has brochures you need no matter which direction you're headed.

GETTING THERE There is a **Greyhound bus station** in London (606-864-2040; www.greyhound.com), 1938 London Shopping Center, London. The nearest commercial airport is 70 miles away, **Lexington's Bluegrass Airport** (859-425-3114; www.bluegrassairport.com). If you can find a better flight into Knoxville, Tennessee's, **McGhee Tyson Airport** (865-342-3000 www.tys.org), you might want to fly there. It is 85 miles from Corbin and an easy commute right up I-75.

GETTING AROUND London is located at the intersection of I-75, the Hal Rogers and Cumberland Parkways, and US 25, so it's easy to find and easy to get around by car once you arrive. There is no public transportation, but you can call **Venture Cabs** (606-526-1211) if you need a taxi.

Corbin straddles I-75 and US 25, which splits into 25E and 25W just north of Corbin. Most everything runs off these two arteries, so make sure you have a good map, and you shouldn't have any trouble getting around. There is no public transportation, but you can call **Park Taxi** (606-549-1977) based out of nearby Williamsburg if you need a ride.

MEDICAL EMERGENCY St. Joseph London (606-878-6520), 310 E. 9th St., London. Changing its name in 2008 from Marymount Medical Center, this hospital covers a population of 50,000 in Laurel, Jackson, Clay, and Whitley Counties. It was founded in 1926, and at the time, it was the most modern hospital in Southeastern Kentucky. In fact, it was the only facility between Lexington and Knoxville located in a building specifically to house a hospital. Today the 89-bed facility provides a full range of medical, surgical, and obstetric services. **Baptist Regional Medical Center** (606-528-1212; www.baptistregional.com), 1 Trillium Way, Corbin. Located in Whitley County off I-75, situated in Southeastern Kentucky's "Valley of Parks," this 200-bed facility has three specialty units: adult and pediatric, burn intensive care, and coronary care.

ALCOHOL Laurel County is a dry county, meaning that alcohol sales are prohibited, but by-the-drink sales are permitted at some London restaurants. Corbin city limits are actually in two counties, Whitley and Knox. Both counties are dry but allow by-the-drink sales in restaurants that serve more than 100 people. Call ahead and ask if a restaurant sells alcohol if you really want a beer or glass of wine with dinner.

✳ To See

Camp Wildcat Civil War Battlefield (www.campwildcatpreservationfoundation .org). This site is slightly complicated to get to, so it is recommended that you grab a map at the London–Laurel County Tourist Information Center. Due to its location on a major north–south artery, the Wilderness Trail, both the North and South wanted control of Camp Wildcat. On October 21, 1861, a battle took place in which the 5,400 Union soldiers defeated 7,500 Confederates. Today you can hike the walking trail to the top of Hoosier Knob, where you can look into the trenches where fighting took place. Stop by in mid-October to see enactments of the battle.

KENTUCKY MUSIC HALL OF FAME
photo by Deborah Kohl Kremer

♿ **Kentucky Music Hall of Fame and Museum** (877-356-3263; www .kymusichalloffame.com), 2590 Richmond Rd., Renfro Valley. Honoring Kentucky performers, songwriters, broadcasters, and other music professionals who have contributed to the music industry in Kentucky and around the world. The museum includes exhibits for instruments, artifacts, costumes, and memorabilia. Some members of the Hall of Fame include famous Kentucky names like Crystal Gayle, Patty Loveless, John Michael Montgomery, Ricky Skaggs, Dwight

Yoakam, and Naomi and Wynonna Judd. Closed Mon. and Tue.

Colonel Harland Sanders Cafe and Museum (606-528-2163; www.kfc.com), I-75 Exit 29, US25W. Visit the colonel's original restaurant, which turned out to be the "Birthplace of Kentucky Fried Chicken." First opened in 1940, this is the home of the still-secret 11-herbs-and-spices recipe still used at KFC restaurants around the world today. See where it all happened and take a look at some of the historic photos and memorabilia of KFC's humble beginnings. Museum-like displays, and a working KFC, too, so stay for lunch.

photo by Deborah Kohl Kremer

THE ORIGINAL KFC

Dr. Thomas Walker State Historic Site (606-546-4400; parks.ky.gov/findparks/histparks/tw), 4929 KY 459, Barbourville. A physician and surveyor, Dr. Thomas Walker led the first expedition through Cumberland Gap in 1750, beating Daniel Boone by 17 years. Dr. Walker built the first cabin in Kentucky, a replica of which stands on the site today. Free.

✷ To Do

GOLF **Crooked Creek Golf Club** (606-877-1993), 781 Crooked Creek Dr., London. Golf at this semi-private club and enjoy the beautiful 18-hole, par-72 championship course. They have a driving range and a pro on site to help you with your swing.

Sweet Hollow Golf Course (606-523-1094; www.sweethollowresort.com), 424 Sweet Hollow Rd., Corbin. This 9-hole public course has 12 water hazards spread out over 125 acres. They also have a lit driving range.

Cedar Rapids Country Club (606-256-4112), 3021 New Brodhead Rd., Mount Vernon. This 9-hole, par-36 public course features 3,228 yards of golf from the longest tees.

OFF-ROAD PARKS **Daniel Boone Motorcross Park** (606-877-1364; www.danielboonemx.net), 775 Falls City Rd., London. Enjoy extreme sports racing featuring motorcycles, ATVs, bicycle Motocross, and cross-country mountain bikes. Weekly racing runs Mar.–Nov. Check the web site for schedule.

London Drag Way (606-878-8883; www.londondragway.com), 3835 White Oak Rd., London. Come watch the excitement on the regulation-sized drag strip every Sat., Apr.–Nov. Family-style entertainment. Call for a complete schedule.

D&K Off-Road Park (606-598-2776; www.dandkoff-roadpark.com). Situated about 30 minutes off I-75's Exit 41, you'll find 3,150 acres of off-road trails, muddy, rocky, and hilly. Drag races every Sat. night, Apr.–Nov.

CANOEING AND RAFTING **Sheltowee Trace Outfitters** (800-541-RAFT; www.ky-rafting.com), KY 90, Whitley City. Just outside Cumberland Falls State

photo by Deborah Kohl Kremer

SHELTOWEE TRACE OUTFITTERS

Park, you'll find this one-stop shop for water sports. In addition to all the supplies you need for a day of outdoor fun, Sheltowee arranges rafting and canoeing expeditions on the Cumberland, Laurel, and Russell Fork Rivers. Call early because these trips fill up fast in the summer months.

FISHING **Lake Cumberland** is the granddaddy of them all. With a shoreline covering over 1,200 miles, it extends from the Cumberland Falls area into seven counties and downstream for more than 100 miles west to Wolf Creek Dam south of Russell Springs and Jamestown. Fish varieties include five species of bass, walleye, crappie, and trout. Bring your rod and reel and toss in a line.

Wood Creek Lake. Located about 6 miles northwest of London, this 900-acre lake offers terrific fishing. In fact, it's the home of the state largemouth bass record of 13 pounds, 10 ounces. Although it's too narrow for pleasure boating, there are lots of docks and ramps available to launch your fishing boat. The lake is stocked with rainbow trout, largemouth bass, smallmouth bass, spotted bass, white crappie, channel catfish, bluegill, red ear sunfish, rock bass, long ear sunfish, and yellow bullhead. While there, stay at the **Wood Creek Lodge** (606-878-0972; www .woodcreeklodge.com), 1961 Moiah Rd., London. Six fully equipped mini cabins are located just 1,000 yards from public boat docks and only 150 feet from the water's edge.

Laurel Lake (606-864-6412), 1433 Laurel Lake Rd., London. With over 200 miles of shoreline and 5,800 acres of water, this lake is protected by the Daniel Boone National Forest. Known for rainbow trout fishing it also offers excellent largemouth and smallmouth bass, walleye, catfish, and crappie. Laurel Lake holds the state record smallmouth, 8 pounds 12 ounces, caught in 1998.

Laurel Lake marinas
Grove Marina (606-523-2323; www.grovemarina.com). Rent fishing, pontoon, and houseboats and stock up on camping and fishing supplies and detailed maps of the lake. The marina is open year-round. They also have a public boat ramp. Other facilities include camping sites, hiking trails, and picnic areas.

Holly Bay Marina (606-864-6542; www.hollybaymarina.com). Get all you need for a boating weekend at this marina, open year-round. You can rent all kinds of boats, stock up on supplies, and purchase your fishing license, too. They have hiking trails and campsites.

Pier 1 Rental (606-864-5196), KY 192, London. Rent boats and Jet Skis as well as tubes, skis, and knee and wake boards. Call for hours.

HIKING Travel the **Sheltowee Trace National Recreation Trail** (www .sheltoweetrace.com), a 269-mile multiple-use recreation trail that traverses the length of the **Daniel Boone National Forest**. The trail is named in honor of Daniel Boone. Sheltowee (meaning "big turtle") was the name given Boone when he was adopted into the Shawnee tribe as the son of the infamous war chief Blackfish. Go to the web site for maps and more information.

✎ ♿ "🍴" **STATE PARKS Cumberland Falls State Resort Park** (606-528-4121, 800-325-0063; parks.ky.gov), 7351 KY 90, Corbin. You've got to see "Niagara of the South." This beautiful 125-foot-wide waterfall drops 68 feet into the Cumberland River. If you can arrange your visit during a full moon, you can witness a moonbow, a rainbow made by the light of the moon. Catch it here because it's the only moonbow in the Western Hemisphere. This park also has 17 miles of scenic hiking trails, fishing, rafting, horseback riding, and playgrounds. Stay at the **DuPont Lodge** with its massive stone fireplaces, solid hemlock beams, and knotty-pine paneling. Enjoy views of the Cumberland River and scenic wooded valley from all rooms and cabins. They have 52 hotel-style rooms in the lodge along with Woodland Rooms, which are adjacent to the lodge but slightly larger than a lodge room. These have kitchenettes and a small porch with a grill. There are also one- and two-bedroom cottages available. They are a little more secluded and private but offer a full kitchen, cozy fireplaces, and private patio or deck. Campers will enjoy

CUMBERLAND FALLS

photo by Deborah Kohl Kremer

THE DUPONT LODGE

photo by Deborah Kohl Kremer

one of the 50 campsites, all with electric and water hookups, showers, grocery, and a dump station. Close to the hiking trails. The campground is closed mid-Nov–mid-March. Dine at the **Riverview Restaurant**, open 7–9 daily, while you enjoy the breathtaking view of the Cumberland River. The menu is full of dishes prepared with locally grown meats and produce. They have a buffet at each meal, or you can order sandwiches, wraps, and salads as well as their famous catfish, hushpuppies, or frog legs off the menu. Make sure to ask for a window seat. $–$$

✎ ♿ **Levi Jackson Wilderness Road State Park** (606-878-8000), 998 Levi Jackson Mill Rd., London. Named for one of the area's first permanent settlers, the park is a tribute to the more than 200,000 pioneers who came through the area between 1774 and 1796. Most of these pioneers followed either the Wilderness Road or Boone's Trace, both of which go through this park's 800 acres. Visit the Mountain Life Museum, a re-created pioneer settlement full of tools and home furnishings from that period. Another section of the park is right on the banks of the Little Laurel River. Here you will find McHargue's Mill, a replica of a mill, surrounded by the largest display of millstones in the country. This state park also has a 146-site campground situated in the middle of a wooded area. The campground has a large swimming pool, mini golf, and planned recreation programs.

MCHARGUE'S MILL AT LEVI JACKSON
WILDERNESS ROAD STATE PARK

photo by Deborah Kohl Kremer

✳ Lodging

♿ **Cumberland Inn** (800-315-0286; www.cumberlandinn.com), 649 S. 10th St., Williamsburg. Owned by the University of the Cumberlands, this inn employs students to help fund their education. This beautiful property features standard rooms as well as suites with kitchens. They also have a heated indoor pool for year-round swimming. If you are traveling with a large group, try their Hearth and Home, a six-bedroom log home with more than 3,000 square feet. It is fully furnished and perfect for relaxing in the cozy family rooms or grilling outside on the deck.

Country Cabin Retreat (606-864-7685, 606-682-0490), 410 W. Pinehill Rd., London. Nestled into the woods on the banks of a 3-acre lake is this cute cabin retreat. Built by the owners from trees on the property, this cabin is authentic, but still has modern amenities like appliances and indoor plumbing.

✳ Where to Eat

In London

GiGee's (606-862-1052) W. 4th Street London. Open Mon-Fri.11–2. Located in an old white house with black shutters, right behind the courthouse, you'll find GiGee's. Nancy, the owner, named the restaurant after the nick name her grand kids bestowed on her. And those are some lucky grandkids, if they get to eat GiGee's cooking all the time. Everything on the menu is homemade, so it's hard to know where to start. But go ahead with salad, loaded baked potato soup or a stuffed sandwich, but save room for dessert. GiGee whips up desserts like homemade pies and cakes every day but her most-ordered item is her strawberry pretzel salad, which locals eat as a salad or a dessert, or possibly both. $ $$

Shiloh Roadhouse (606-877-9363), 218 Russell Dyche Memorial Hwy. Open for lunch and dinner every day. Crack your peanuts and throw the shells on the floor. It's even better than home, because you don't have to sweep them up. This steak house is similar to the chain-style steak houses but with a hometown feel. They have lots of choices of steaks and ribs, but people just rave about the baked sweet potatoes and the homemade rolls that you can cover with their honey butter. $$

&. ✿ **Weaver's Hot Dogs** (606-864-9937), 131 N. Main St. Open Mon.–Wed. 8–3 and then Thu.–Sat. 8–7. This is the town's oldest restaurant, and you will feel the walls can

talk when you eat there. The interior is covered, really covered, with old photos of people and events from the area. Get a history lesson along with one of their famous dogs. Locals come for the sausage and egg breakfast platter, but the chili dogs and wiener buns are worth getting off the interstate for. $

Burger Boy Restaurant (606-864-2675), 1625 S. Main St. Open 7 days 5 AM–10:30 PM. This restaurant looks a lot like it used to be a former chain eatery, the one that has a statue of a large boy out front holding a very big burger. You know the one. Burger Boy's logo is a boy with a large head wearing plaid pants and, well, holding a burger. Copyright infringement aside, this little hole in the wall serves up good burgers. They also have a daily breakfast bar with staples like eggs, sausage, French toast, and biscuits. It's a stick-to-your-ribs kind of place. $

In Corbin

&. **Athenaeum Restaurant** (800-315-0286; www.cumberlandinn.com), I-75 Exit 11, 649 S. 10th St., Williamsburg. Open Mon.–Sat. 7 AM–9 PM and Sun. 7–2. You will find both southern and contemporary menu choices in this white-tablecloth restaurant. Whether you want fried green tomatoes and a

INSIDE WEAVER'S HOT DOGS

photo by Deborah Kohl Kremer

Kentucky hot brown or spicy fajitas, they have what you are in the mood for. $$–$$$

☿ **The Depot on Main** (606-523-1117; www.thedepotonmain.com), 101 N. Main St. Open daily for lunch and dinner. Closed Sun. You'll have lots of fun at this locals' favorite right in the heart of Corbin. They serve certified Angus beef as well as a selection of pastas, seafood, and sandwiches. Try their homemade potato chips for an interesting side dish. Stop in on a weekend to hear some local live music. $–$$

Dino's Italian Restaurant and Lounge (606-877-2525 London; 606-523-0600 Corbin), 384 London Shopping Ctr, London. 1895 Cumberland Falls Hwy., Corbin. Open for lunch and dinner every day. With a location in London and Corbin, if you are in the area, you are close to a Dino's. Although they are known for their pizzas and huge array of Italian pasta specialties, the huge menu will temp you with Greek dishes, steaks and the very popular fried catfish. Dino is a local resident who everyone seems to know, so stop in and say hi. $$

✸ Selective Shopping

& ♦ **Dog Patch Trading Post** (606-864-4531; www.dogpatchtradingpost

THE DEPOT

.com), KY 80 and I-75, London. This family-owned business has been a part of Laurel County since the 1950s. They claim to be the largest and oldest souvenir store in Southeastern Kentucky. Stop by to get Kentucky-related treasures, joke gifts, and discounts on cigarettes.

Paula's Quilting Pantry (606-231-3543), 833 W. Hwy. 3094, East Bernstadt. What could be more charming than a quilting bee? That's what you'll find on Sit and Sew Days. Shop here to pick up all things related to quilting—fabrics, sewing notions, and ideas, too.

Flea Land Flea Market (606-864-3532), KY 229 at 192 Bypass, London. With over 80,000 square feet of shopping and 500 vendors, if they don't have it, you probably don't need it very much anyway.

ANTIQUES Antiques and Accents (606-526-0646; www.antiques-accents.com), US 25E, Cumberland Gap Pkwy., Corbin. This shop is loaded with antiques of all kinds including furniture, quilts, and jewelry. They also have a huge selection of concrete and cast-iron benches and fountains for your yard.

Ona Whim Antiques and Collectibles (606-526-7232), 194 S. Stewart Rd., Corbin. Closed Wed. All kinds of antiques in this brightly colored fun Victorian house, but owner Nancy Chandler specializes in architectural salvage. She grabs the good stuff out of houses due for demolition, like staircases, doorknobs, and mantels. You really never know what you'll find.

✸ Special Events

& ♦ ❧ *September:* **Annual World Chicken Festival** (606-878-6900; www.chickenfestival.com). Celebrating

DOG PATCH TRADING POST

the works of Colonel Harland Sanders, founder of Kentucky Fried Chicken, and Lee Cummings (Sander's nephew), co-founder of Lee's Famous Recipe Chicken. Both got into the chicken restaurant business right here in Laurel County, so what better reason to have a festival? Have a fried chicken dinner, cooked in the World's Largest Skillet, which is more than 10 feet in diameter. Enter the chicken-inspired competitions, like the hot-wing-eating contest, the egg toss, or the Colonel Sanders Look-Alike contest. There is live music all weekend, as well as thrill rides and kids' activities.

 August: **NIBROC Festival**. This festival, which takes its name from *Corbin* spelled backward, began in 1952. People come from all over to enjoy the four nights of free open-air concerts by world-famous performers. In addition to the music, they also have a run/walk, carnival rides and games, food, crafts, and a Closing the Streets Party starts it all off.

HAZARD AND HINDMAN

Hazard is a coal town. This mountain community would not even be on a map had it not been for the discovery of the black gold hidden deep inside. Hazard is the seat of Perry County, which was founded in 1790. Both city and county are named for Commodore Oliver Hazard Perry, an American naval hero in the War of 1812, who had no apparent ties to the area.

This small town, which is not easy to reach, is known as the "Queen City of the Mountains." It is truly in the heart of the Appalachians. In the early years, the isolation of the mountains stunted its growth. It sometimes took more than two weeks to travel about 45 miles out of the valley and reach civilization. That changed in 1912 when the railroad finally made it to town. The area, now accessible, became more prosperous—yet even today, as home to about 6,000 people, it has its share of poverty.

The natural backdrop in the mountains makes a perfect setting for nature lovers. With the creation of Buckhorn Lake State Park and the recent increase in the elk population, tourism is on the rise.

Hazard did receive some notoriety in the early 1980s with the CBS television show *The Dukes of Hazzard*. Even though this show was based on a fictional county in Georgia, tourists began to make Hazard a destination; some of the show's stars have come for Hazard's annual Black Gold Festival.

Hindman, the seat of Knott County, is situated in a narrow valley at the fork of Troublesome Creek along KY 80. It dates back to about 1884, when the tiny berg was named for then Lieutenant Governor James P. Hindman. The town's economy has been largely dependent on coal, but tourism is quickly helping the area become notable.

The area is rich with Appalachian culture and history as home to the Hindman Settlement School and the Kentucky Appalachian Artisan Center, two stops you must make here. Knott County, as well as its surrounding counties, is home to more than 5,000 free-ranging elk, the largest elk herd east of the Mississippi River. These massive elk were transplanted to this area in the late 1990s and now call it home. There are many opportunities to go elk-watching and see them in their natural setting.

Stop by and enjoy the slow pace of Hindman. The rugged terrain prevented the extension of rail service to the town, and its isolated mountain location kept it from growing at the quick pace of more centrally located burgs. The result is a relaxed group of residents who are happy to see visitors. Stop by the courthouse to see a statue of Hindman's best-known native son, Carl D. Perkins, who served Eastern Kentucky as a US representative from 1949 until 1984. He is credited for his work to better the lives of people in the area by bringing in educational opportunities and aiding the underprivileged.

GUIDANCE **Perry County Department of Tourism** (606-487-1580, 888-857-5263; www.hazardperrytourism.com), 481 Main St., Hazard. They are open during the week to help you find your way around Hazard and Perry County. Lots of friendly help to plan your stay. **Knott County Tourism** (606-785-5881), 40 Center St., Hindman. Located right behind the courthouse is the tourism office. They are open weekdays 8–4 and they have maps, directions, and information about your stay in Knott County.

GETTING THERE **Lexington's Bluegrass Airport** (859-425-3114; www.blue grassairport.com) is the nearest commercial airport, about 120 miles away. If you're traveling from the west, the Hal Rogers Parkway—which covers the mountainous region—turns into I-80 in Hazard. Just stay on I-80 and it will bring you right to Hindman.

GETTING AROUND The small mountain town of Hazard has some winding roads that can be difficult to navigate, especially in bad weather. But the downtown streets are marked, and there is plenty of free parking. There is no public transportation but if you need a taxi, call **Miller Cab Company** (606-439-5161). Hindman is a small mountain town which is somewhat remote, but not terribly hard to navigate once you get there. There is no public transportation there either, so get a good map and directions from the tourism office before you head out.

MEDICAL EMERGENCY **Hazard ARH Regional Medical Center** (606-439-6600; www.arh.org/Hazard), 100 Medical Center Dr., Hazard. Dedicated to rural health care, this 308-bed hospital is well respected in the area. Formerly part of the Miners Memorial Hospital Association, they operate hospitals in Harlan, Hazard, McDowell, Middlesboro, Morgan County, South Williamson, and Whitesburg, Kentucky.

ALCOHOL You cannot order a drink in Hindman or surrounding Knott County, which is dry. But in Hazard and Perry County, alcohol is available. If you want a frosty beer with dinner and are not sure which county you're in, call the restaurant ahead of time.

✳ To See

& **Bobby Davis Memorial Park & Museum** (606-439-4325), 234 Walnut St., Hazard. Huge assortment of local memorabilia includes an outstanding photography collection that traces the progress of Hazard from dirt streets at turn of the century through the turmoil of World War II. The museum houses a library and archives containing photographs, historical documents, oral history tapes, and artifact collections. Closed weekends.

Eversole Cabin (606-439-1816), Chavies. This dirt-floor log cabin was originally built around 1789 by Jacob and Mary Eversole. They added on around 1800, making it a dog trot cabin—really two separate cabins connected by a roof. The space between them was an open porch. It still stands today and is privately owned. It is one of the oldest landmarks in Kentucky. Call for directions and a private tour.

✄ **The Mother Goose House**, KY 476, Hazard. You have to see this house to believe it. It is a stone structure made to resemble a goose, complete with a goose head on the top. Built in 1940 by local resident George Stacy, he actually killed a goose to use its skeleton as a model. The oval-shaped base, which resembles a nest, is made of sandstone from nearby creeks. The roof is ribbed just like a goose, and the head is 15 feet high. Drive by, you won't be disappointed.

&. **Kentucky Appalachian Artisan Center** (606-785-9855; www.artisancenter .net), 16 W. Main St., Hindman. Open weekdays 10–6, Sat. 10–4. This is a must-see while in the area. They have an overwhelming display of art exhibits and craft demonstrations of artisans from 49 counties of Eastern Kentucky. The center, which aims to help crafters and artisans make and sustain a living from their art, features works juried by the Kentucky Craft Marketing Program and the Kentucky Guild of Artists and Craftsmen. When you see the talent and dedication these artisans put into their work, you'll want to fill your home with their pieces. The building they call home is a work of art in itself. It was crafted from the sandstone of a nearby mountain around 1913.

Alice Lloyd College (606-785-5475; www.alc.edu), 100 Purpose Rd., Pippa Passes. This private liberal arts college was founded in 1923 by Alice Spencer Geddes Lloyd, a journalist from Boston who wanted to create educational opportunities for residents of Appalachia. Students are required to participate in the work-study program in janitorial, office, or food service jobs. This small college tucked in the mountains has a beautiful campus that you will want to explore.

Hindman Settlement School (606-785-5475; www.hindmansettlement.org), 71 Center St., Hindman. Open weekdays 10–4, Sat. 10–2. Closed weekends Jan.–Mar. Established in 1902, the Hindman Settlement School became the first and most successful rural social settlement school in America. Today you can tour the grounds, which include historic buildings, a museum, and a shop consignment craft shop of juried arts and crafts from the region. Free.

✳ To Do

Saddle Up Elk Tours (606-642-3656; www.trailsrus.com/saddleuptours), 250 Hole Cemetery, Mollie. Ride horseback through the rolling hills of elk country. See magnificent elk as well as other native wildlife while enjoying the scenery on one of their gentle horses. Tours last about three hours. Closed Jan. and Feb.

Knott County Sportsplex (606-785-5932; www.knottcountyky.com), 450 Kenny Champion Loop, Soft Shell. Recreation is the name of the game. They have softball and soccer fields, indoor volleyball and basketball courts, an arcade, a bowling alley, a batting cage, and an indoor walking track. Fun for all ages.

Fugates Entertainment Center (606-439-4613), 197 Entertainment Dr., Hazard. Fun for everyone with bowling, skating, and, in summer, a water park with a wave pool.

Addington Wildlife Management Area (606-785-5881, 606-378-3474), KY 80, Knott County. From December 1997 through March 2002, free ranging Rocky Mountain Elk were released into southeast Kentucky, and this area is the perfect place to get a glimpse of them. The area is also full of wild Canada wild geese and wild turkeys. Open year-round dusk to dawn.

Perry County Park (606-436-5095), 354 Perry Park Rd., Hazard. Swimming pool, tennis and basketball courts, 18-hole miniature golf course, walking track, picnic shelters, and playground equipment.

Battle of Leatherwood Memorial Park, KY 699S, Cornettsville. Named for the Civil War battle that took place nearby, today this is a nice park to shoot some hoops or play a few sets of tennis. There is also a walking track and a picnic shelter.

✦ ♿ "🍴" **STATE PARK Buckhorn Lake State Resort Park** (800-325-0058; parks.ky.gov), 4441 KY 1833, Buckhorn. Located at the northern edge of the Daniel Boone National Forest, Buckhorn Lake State Park has 856 acres of lush Kentucky mountain land for recreational enjoyment. They offer fishing and boating in the 1,230-acre Buckhorn Lake, as well as swimming in the lodge pool and disk golf. Stay at the **Buckhorn Lodge**, a warm and inviting inn featuring 36 rooms with private balconies so you can take in all the mountains have to offer. They also have executive cottages with kitchens and separate bedrooms for even more privacy. The lodge restaurant, **Bowlingtown Country Kitchen**, is open seven days a week 7 AM–9 PM; Sunday brunch 11–3. It is named for a city that was located where Buckhorn Lake is today. This restaurant has a wonderful view. Local favorites are on the menu, but try the Bluegrass Special—country-style beans with home fries, coleslaw, and fried corn bread—if you want to get the feel for the place. $–$$

✦ ♿ "🍴" **Kingdom Come State Park** (606-589-2479, parks.ky.gov), 502 Park Rd., Cumberland. Straddling the Kentucky–Virginia border high atop Pine Mountain, you'll find Kentucky's home for the black bear. Sightings, which are not uncommon, are a huge draw to the park. Park rangers advise that most sightings occur in the summer months, and they can tell you where to go in the park if you really want to see one. But don't come just for the bears. With 1,300 acres of wilderness, forest, caves, and rock formations—including one that lurches 290 feet into the air at a 45-degree angle—there is a lot to see. There are rugged hiking trails, including the most popular, Pine Mountain Trail, as well as a lake for fishing and

BLACK BEARS AT KINGDOM COME STATE PARK

photo courtesy of www.kentuckytourism.com

paddle-boating, a 225-acre nature preserve on the north face of Pine Mountain, and a gift shop. Most Kentucky state parks are named for their geographic location, but this one honors *The Little Shepherd of Kingdom Come*, a popular 1903 novel that was set in Civil War Kentucky and written by Appalachian author John Fox Jr.

Carr Creek Lake State Park (606-642-4050; parks.ky.gov), KY 15, Sassafras. Mostly known for excellent fishing, Carr Creek Lake also boasts the longest sand beach in Kentucky's state park system. So relax and swim or fish for largemouth bass, crappie, and walleye. Located 15 miles southeast of Hazard, Kentucky, this lake covers 750 acres. It was created in 1976 by a 720-foot dam above the mouth of the Carr Fork River. The state park offers a marina where you can rent fishing and pontoon boats and stock up on supplies, as well as a 39-site campground and picnic areas. Keep your eyes open for wildlife. The unusual marsh environment in the area is inviting for ruffed grouse, great blue and green herons, wild turkeys, wood ducks, bobwhites, raccoons, skunks, and even red-winged blackbirds.

✳ Where to Eat

EATING OUT Frances's Diner (606-436-0090), 1315 Combs Rd., Hazard. Stop by and see Frances and she will set you up with a tasty meal. Stop in anytime, because they are open 24 hours per day. Home-cooked meals, like the meat loaf and mashed potatoes, are big sellers. Breakfast is available all day, served with biscuits that are heavenly. Look around at the photos scattered about. They are old pictures of local mines that have since shut down. If you look long enough, someone will probably come over and start telling you about them. $

Circle T Drive In (606-436-6984), 1519 Combs Rd., Hazard. Open daily. This family-style diner is packed on Tuesdays and weekends when the locals know they can get a chicken-and-dumplin' dinner with all the trimmings for under $5. Everything they make is from scratch, so if you're there another day, finding something good won't be a problem. Try the Kentucky silk pie for dessert. $

Kristen's Café (606-398-7250), 18543 KY 28, Buckhorn. Open daily, but hours change seasonally. Stop in for some fried chicken, and while you're there, pick up some bait and maybe some camping supplies. Daily plate lunch specials. $

Holly Hills Mall Restaurant (606-785-0909), 92 Holly Hills Villa Rd., Hindman. Open Mon.–Sat. 11–8. This cute restaurant inside the Holly Hills Shopping Center serves up home-cooked meals and has a locals-favorite lunch special. They have everything from burgers to salads but are best known for steaks and individual home-made pies. Try the butterscotch or coconut cream—or try them both, they're small. $

Five and Dine Café at the Kentucky Appalachian Artisan Center (606-785-9855; www.artisancenter.net), 16 W. Main St., Hindman. Open Mon.–Fri. 10–6, Sat. 10–4. Offering light lunches and unique menu items, the café aims to have as much variety as the Artisan Center itself. They offer sandwiches, soups, and salads and try to use locally grown products whenever possible.

✳ Entertainment

Greater Hazard Area Performing Arts Series (606-436-5721; www .hazardpas.com), 1 Community College Dr., Hazard. Presenting arts and entertainment events in music, drama, and dance, this organization features artists known locally and internationally. Check the web site for the upcoming performance schedule.

✳ Selective Shopping

Buckhorn Lake Gift Shop at Buckhorn Lake State Resort Park (800-325-0058; parks.ky.gov), 4441 KY 1833, Buckhorn. Full of outstanding Kentucky Crafted products—juried craft items made by Kentuckian. You'll find beautiful pottery, handmade baskets, and scented candles. They also carry books by Kentucky authors and Kentucky Proud food items, like jellies, sauces, and candies. Grab a Buckhorn Lake T-shirt while you are there, too.

✳ Special Events

✐ ♿ ❀ *September:* **Black Gold Festival** (606-439-6614; www.blackgold festival.com). Held in downtown Hazard, this tribute to Kentucky coal offers fun for everyone. In addition to the parade, food, arts and crafts, and live entertainment, they also have the Road Hazards Extreme Team Stunt Show, Black Diamond Street Rod Show, and Black Gold Bike Show.

✐ ♿ ❀ **Knott County Gingerbread Festival**. Started in 1981, this festival features the world's largest gingerbread man, made from real gingerbread. He sets a new record each year. Also carnival games, a parade, free bluegrass music, a huge selection of food, and lots of arts and crafts.

October: **Fall Horse Ride** (606-785-5881). More than 6,000 people and their horses from all over the country come together each year for a weekend of horseback riding and camping. There are trails, some up to 37 miles long, over the 60,000 acres of a reclaimed mine site. Although they also have a ride in spring, the fall event seems to be more popular. Bring your own horse—but make sure you have an equine heath certificate with you or you won't be allowed to participate.

PINEVILLE AND MIDDLESBORO

This area is rich in history, nature, and mineral resources. Historically, it encompassed Cumberland Gap, a natural phenomenon in the mountain range that made it possible for thousands of settlers to enter Kentucky between 1750 and the early 1800s. During the Civil War, both the North and the South recognized the value of the Cumberland Gap; it was eventually occupied by both sides during the course of the war.

According to scientists, the small city of **Middlesboro** sits in a valley that was created by an asteroid strike. Although that is an interesting fact, it is not something you would just notice when in the city limits. The small city sits right along the Wilderness Road, traveled first by pioneers but then by explorers who realized the value of land. Middlesboro is the result of the planned mining and manufacturing city, financed by Europeans. Although it never became the manufacturing giant they had envisioned (the backers were bankrupt by 1893), the area did survive on coal- and ironworks.

The city of **Pineville**, which is about 14 miles north of Middlesboro, is located where the Cumberland River cuts through Pine Mountain. It's one of the oldest settlements in Kentucky; it dates back to 1781, when it was called Cumberland Ford.

Today, with a county population of about 30,000, the area still survives on coal and tourism. Pine Mountain State Resort Park and Cumberland Gap National Historical Park are in the 361 square miles of Bell County. Hunting, hiking, and fishing are the huge attractions, and the options are limitless. Come all the way over to Bell County and see where Kentucky really started.

GUIDANCE Come for guidance and tour a local museum at the same time. The **Bell County Tourism Commission and Visitor Center** is housed inside the **Arthur Museum** (800-988-1075; www.mountaingateway.com), 2215 Cumberland Ave., Middlesboro. This museum includes the artifacts and memorabilia of Alexander A. Arthur, founder of Middlesboro. This wonderful 1890s home is on the National Historic Register. Tour the grounds and then get information and maps for the rest of your trip. Closed weekends.

GETTING THERE To get to this mountainous community by private plane, you can fly into **Middlesboro Bell County Airport** (606-242-3134), but if you need to fly commercial, your best bet is **Knoxville McGhee Tyson Airport** (865-342-3000; www.tys.org), which is just 56 miles away.

GETTING AROUND The communities of Middlesboro and Pineville are about 14 miles apart. Middlesboro is about eight times the size of Pineville, the county seat. Both have well-marked streets but neither has public transportation, so you'll have to get around by car.

MEDICAL EMERGENCY Pineville Community Hospital (606-337-3051; www.pinevillehospital.com), 850 Riverview Ave., Pineville. When it opened in 1938 with 40 beds, PCH was a leader in patient care. Today with 150 beds, this tradition continues.

ALCOHOL The county is dry, meaning alcohol sales are prohibited, but Pineville restaurants that serve more than 100 people can sell alcohol by the drink.

✳ To See

✒ **Cumberland Gap Tunnel** (606-248-2817), US 25E, Middlesboro. Experience one of the region's most ambitious construction projects by traveling through the 4,600-foot tunnel that passes under the Cumberland Gap. Seventeen years in the making, at a cost of $280 million, this tunnel was created to replace narrow and dangerous roads through the gap and restore the area to resemble the path used by the pioneers of the late 1700s. It opened in 1996.

Bell County Coal House and Coal Museum (606-248-1075), N. 20th St., Middlesboro. Built in 1926 out of 42 tons of bituminous coal, the Coal House building now houses the Middlesboro Chamber of Commerce. Get glimpses of the coal-mining life at this outdoor museum featuring a mine locomotive, a coal-cutting machine, and other mining equipment from the 1960s.

✳ To Do

FISHING Chenoa Lake (606-337-3011), KY 190, Pineville. This 37-acre lake is well stocked with largemouth bass, green sunfish, white crappie, channel catfish, bluegill, red ear sunfish, and brown bullhead. It is 15 miles west of Pineville.

Cannon Creek Lake, US 25E, Pineville. Six miles south of Pineville, you can fish for rainbow trout, largemouth bass, smallmouth bass, spotted bass, warmouth, channel catfish bluegill, and crappie on this 243-acre lake.

GOLF Wasioto Winds Golf Course at Pine Mountain State Resort Park (606-337-3066; parks.ky.gov), 1050 State Park Rd., Pineville. This course is situated in a valley between two mountains, hence the name (pronounced *wah-see-OH-tuh*), which means "valley of the deer." This championship 18-hole course has a practice range, putting greens, and an indoor-use training center.

✳ Green Space

Shillalah Creek Public Wildlife Area (606-248-2482), 2215 Cumberland Ave., Middlesboro. Running along Brush Mountain just north of Cumberland Gap is this 2,640-acre, old-growth forest. Turkey, deer, raccoons, squirrels, and grouse can all be found here, but you're going to need a four-wheel-drive vehicle to navigate the rugged terrain and steep, undeveloped roads. You can hunt here, too, but you'll need a permit.

⚓ ⚐ "𝗜" **STATE PARKS** **Cumberland Gap National Historical Park** (606-248-2817; www.nps.gov), Middlesboro. This huge national park, which covers 20,000 acres in Kentucky, Virginia, and Tennessee, is the largest historical park in the nation. Known as the Doorway to the West, Cumberland Gap forms a major break in the Appalachian Mountain chain, which covers about 1,500 miles from Canada to Alabama. The gap was first used by migrating buffalo, and then by Native Americans. As pioneers headed west, they, too, used the gap instead of traveling over the 3,000-foot mountains. From 1775 to 1810, around 300,000 people passed through. Today visitors can tour one of the 24 caves and the historic Hensley Settlement, a mountain village that was used in the early 1900s. With 20,500 acres of park (with 14,000 acres of wilderness), the hiking is spectacular. You'll feel like the settlers did as they walked these same trails. Hike to Pinnacle Overlook so you can see the breathtaking view that encompasses four states. There are unbelievable views in each direction, breathtaking waterfalls, and lots of trees, flowers, and wildlife. Keep your eye out for black bears.

⚐ ⚓ "𝗜" **Pine Mountain State Resort Park** (606-337-3066; parks.ky.gov), 1050 State Park Rd., Pineville. Visit Kentucky's first state park, which sits high atop the Kentucky Ridge State Forest. This is Kentucky's second largest state forest, with 11,363 acres of unspoiled wilderness. The hiking alone is fantastic, but you'll also find mini golf, an outdoor pool, and playgrounds. In summer, they have daily recreational activities at the on-site nature center. Stay at the **Herndon J. Evans Lodge** for some for a real getaway. This lodge offers 30 rooms, each with a private patio or balcony to enjoy the mountain views. They also have rustic one- and two-bedroom cottages or one- and two-bedroom log cabins with stone fireplace and

CUMBERLAND GAP

private deck. While you are there, try some local cuisine at the **Mountain View Restaurant**. Open 7 AM–9 PM daily. Enjoy the unforgettable mountain scenery from every seat in the dining room. The menu features a wide variety of choices, using locally raised meats and produce when available.

✳ Lodging

The Cumberland Manor Bed and Breakfast (606-248-4299; www
.cumberlandmanorbedandbreak-
fast.com), 208 Arthur Heights, Mid-
dlesboro. Surrounded by mountains in all directions, guests really feel like they've left their cares behind. Built in 1890, this huge Victorian beauty boasts a gorgeous hand-carved staircase, stained-glass windows, and intricate woodwork and flooring. They have four inviting guest rooms, but you'll want to spend some time on the great big front porch, which offers views of three states. $

✳ Where to Eat

The Flocoe (606-337-2034), 122 W. Kentucky Ave., Pineville. Open for lunch only. Closed weekends. Created as a sweets shop in the 1920s, this for-
mer drugstore is located right on the courthouse square. It is where to get some home cooking. Locals rave about their chicken and dumplings, so try some to see what they are talking about. $

Avenue Cafe & Antiques (606-248-
3958), 1915 W. Cumberland Ave., Middlesboro. Open for lunch only. Closed weekends. Situated right on the main drag of Middlesboro, in a historic building, this is the place to go for a yummy chicken salad sandwich and daily hot lunch specials. Thursday is spaghetti day, really popular with local lunch crowd. $

✳ Selective Shopping

Cumberland Crafts (606-242-3699), US 25E, Middlesboro. Located in the Cumberland Gap National Historical Park Visitors Center, this unique gift shop offers handmade crafts created by members of the Southern Highland Craft Guild. They have beautiful selections of pottery, woodworking, photog-
raphy, paintings, and jewelry.

✳ Special Events

🖉 ♿ ⚘ *May:* **The Kentucky Moun-
tain Laurel Festival** (www.kmlf.org). Started in 1931, this festival celebrates the blooming of the native mountain laurel. It also honors Dr. Thomas Walker, the first European to settle in the region. Walker's settlement was some-
where around 1750, which was 40 years before Kentucky became a state. The festival features entertainment, carnival games, a grand ball, and a street dance. The highlight is the crowning of the Mountain Laurel Queen. The festival is held on the grounds of Pine Mountain State Resort Park.

South-Central Kentucky

2

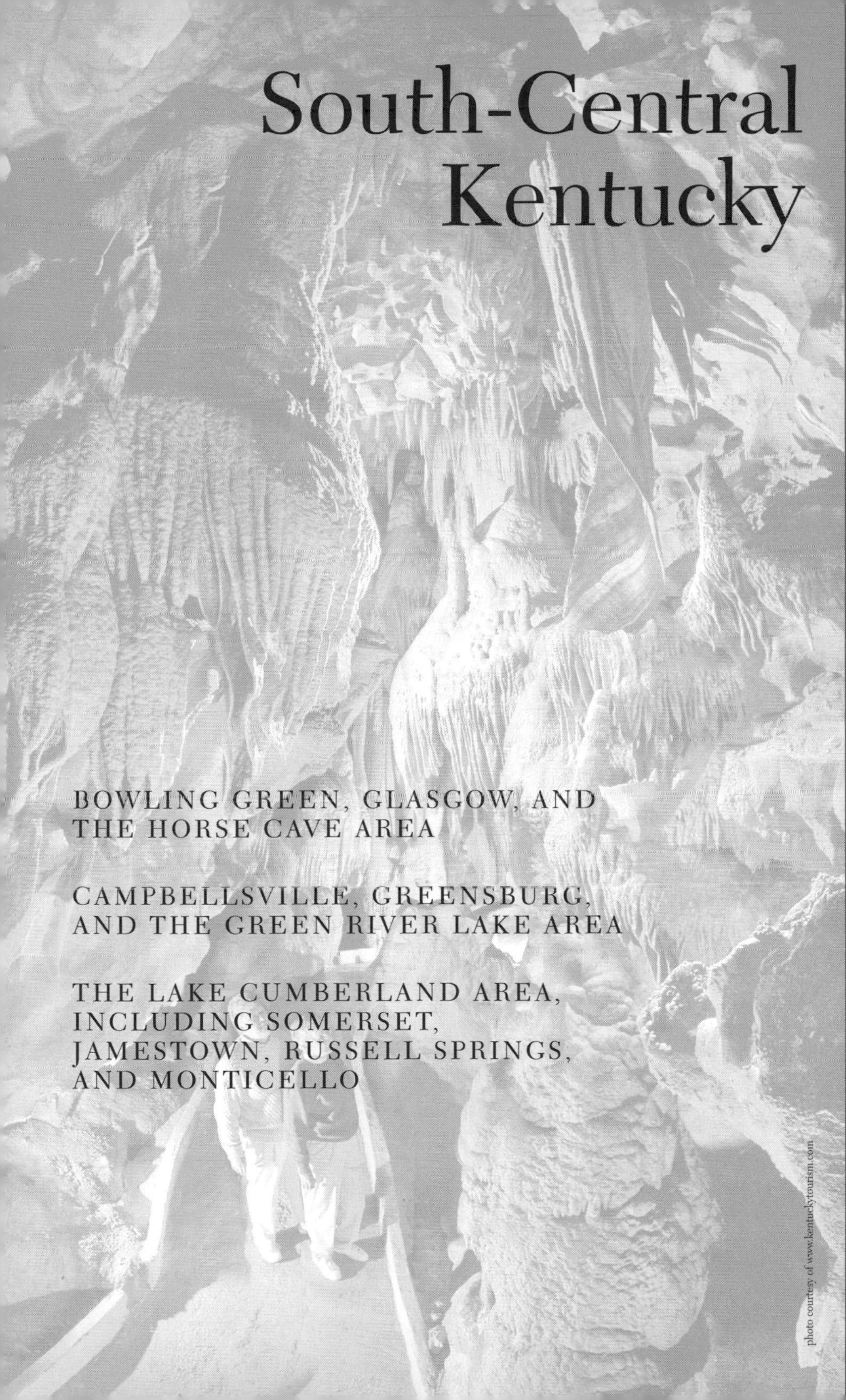

BOWLING GREEN, GLASGOW, AND THE HORSE CAVE AREA

CAMPBELLSVILLE, GREENSBURG, AND THE GREEN RIVER LAKE AREA

THE LAKE CUMBERLAND AREA, INCLUDING SOMERSET, JAMESTOWN, RUSSELL SPRINGS, AND MONTICELLO

photo courtesy of www.kentuckytourism.com

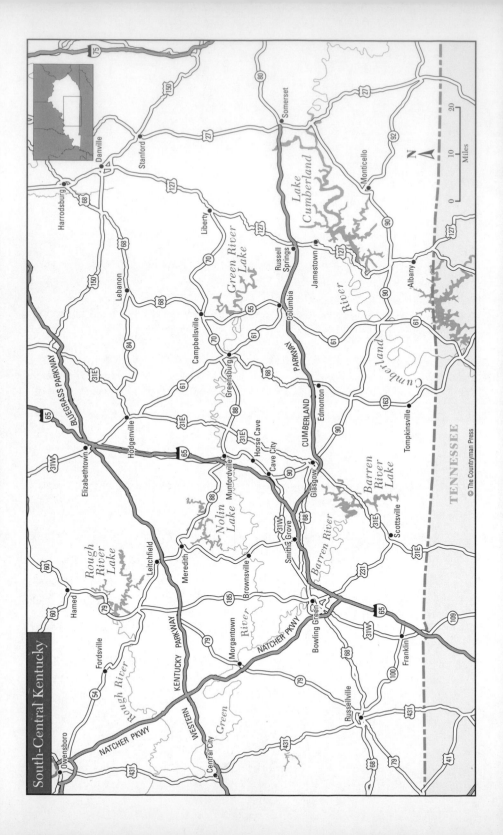

South-Central Kentucky

INTRODUCTION:
SOUTH-CENTRAL KENTUCKY

This southern section of Kentucky is filled with deep lakes and sometimes-raging rivers, which ultimately created caves and caverns, all of which make this Kentucky's recreation mecca.

On the western edge is cave country. Anchored by Mammoth Cave, the largest cave in the world, and surrounded by smaller and privately owned caves, it is a spelunker's paradise. No matter which cave you choose, you'll be sure to see stalactites, which form on the ceiling by slowly dripping water, and stalagmites, which grow upward. If a stalactite and a stalagmite meet, it results in a column. Although these cave decorations are a common occurrence underground, they are a marvel each time you see one.

If hiking is your passion, the heavily wooded terrain and slightly rolling hills of Southern Kentucky could be just what you're looking for. At Mammoth Cave National Park, they have 52,000 acres of wooded trails for hikers and horseback riders. About half of the park's visitors come for the hiking and never even go into the cave. The hiking, hunting, and nature-watching opportunities spread eastward into the area of Green River Lake and Lake Cumberland, which is adjacent to the Daniel Boone National Forest. Just on the border of Tennessee is the Big South Fork National Recreation Area, which offers 125,000 acres of gorges, sandstone bluffs, and miles of trails that lead to waterfalls, natural arches, and other wonders of nature.

But if it's the water that's calling you, your possibilities are vast. With rivers like the Nolin River, Green River, and Cumberland River all flowing through the region, as well as the human-made Nolin River Lake, Green River Lake, and Lake Cumberland, you'll be hard-pressed not to catch some kind of fish while you're there. These lakes are stocked, so do a little research to find the spot that has your choice of catch.

Although the fish are abundant, some people just like to boat. Come to the lakes and rivers of Kentucky to enjoy kayaking, canoeing, and houseboating. If you don't have a boat, all the lakes have various sizes of boat rentals, as well as the supplies you need for your lake outing.

Tucked in among the lakes, caves, and rivers, you'll find the small towns and bergs that make Kentucky special. Tiny towns like Jamestown and Greenville will welcome you with open arms. They offer hometown-style diners, cute specialty shops, and antiques-laden downtown districts. They also have various attractions like parks, old-time drive-in movies, and a few sprinklings of history, just to keep it interesting.

BOWLING GREEN, GLASGOW, AND THE HORSE CAVE AREA

I n the heart of downtown **Bowling Green** is the 2-acre Fountain Square Park, which is the city center and focal point for this charming town. The fountain, statues, landscape, and ages-old trees draw you in, much as the town itself does. The 19th-century buildings, nearby Western Kentucky University campus, and outlying rolling farmland make you want to get to know this area, which has so much more to offer than just the caves and Corvettes that get all the publicity.

As the fourth most populous town in Kentucky, Bowling Green has roots dating back to its incorporation in 1798. Although Kentucky was considered neutral in the Civil War, the Confederate loyalists declared the city to be the state capital in 1861. This honor didn't last long, as it was taken over by the Union army in 1862.

You can tour various aspects of Bowling Green's role in the War Between the States on the Civil War Discovery Trail. This itinerary includes visits to caves where soldiers purportedly hid out, historical markers and homes, and Riverview at Hobson Grove Historic House Museum, a home whose foundation was used as a fort.

FOUNTAIN SQUARE PARK

As home to the largest cave known in the world today, Mammoth Cave has to be seen to be believed. Plan to visit Mammoth Cave National Park and enjoy the forested park and a magnificent cave tour. With more than 70 miles of trails and 52,000 acres of secluded natural preservation available, lots of visitors never even head underground. The park has a plethora of tours and caving adventures, one to meet any and all of your needs. With several smaller, lesser-hyped cave tours in the area, novice cavers could enjoy a privately owned cave just as well. Wherever you go, you'll find stalactites, stalagmites, and formations that were created millions of years before we were born.

If boating and fishing are your calling, you are heading in the right direction. Nolin River, Green River, Barren River, and Barren River Lake State Resort Park offer an assortment of marinas and fishing spots perfect for your catch of choice.

A stop in the area wouldn't be complete, however, without a nod to General Motors and their roadster, the Corvette. Tour the assembly plant and the museum that pays homage to the car. Or stick around for the annual Corvette Homecoming Festival in July, when thousands of loyal 'Vette owners bring their cars and their enthusiasm to Bowling Green for a weekend of fun.

GUIDANCE Pick up advice, maps, and brochures at the **Bowling Green Area Convention and Visitors Bureau** (800-326-7465; www.visitbgky.com), 352 Three Springs Rd., Bowling Green. The Cave City Convention Center and Tourism Bureau, located at the visitors center at I-65 Exit 53, is also jam-packed with maps, coupons, and brochures.

GETTING THERE Bowling Green is about two hours south of Louisville and one hour north of Nashville, Tennessee. For airline travel, check both for deals. The **Louisville International Airport** (502-368-6524; www.flylouisville.com) is located at the intersection of I-65 and I-264. **Nashville International Airport** (615-275-1675; www.flynashville.com) is an easy trip right down I-65. Car rentals are available at both airports. From Nashville, you can take the **Airport Shuttle of Bowling Green** (270-996-1227, 866-234-8705; www.anytimetransport.com). **Greyhound Bus** also serves Bowling Green (270-842-5131; www.greyhound.com). The station is located at 55 Parker Ave., Bowling Green.

GETTING AROUND Bowling Green, with its small-town feel, has well-marked streets and is easy to navigate by car. But if you are looking for public transportation, bus service is available. **Bowling Green Public Transit** (270-782-3162; www.casoky.org/transportation) offers fixed-route bus service Mon.–Fri. beginning at 7 AM and ending at 6 PM. Check the web site for schedules and routes.

MEDICAL EMERGENCY **Greenview Regional Hospital** (277-793-1000; www.greenviewhospital.com), 1801 Ashley Circle, Bowling Green. This hospital has 211 beds and serves Bowling Green and Warren County.

ALCOHOL Although it is the seat of Warren County—a dry county where alcohol sales are prohibited—Bowling Green, does permit alcohol sales within the city limits. Barren County, home of **Glasgow** and Cave City, is also dry, but allows alcohol sales by the drink at restaurants in these two cities.

✳ To See

CORVETTE MUSEUM

✐ ♿ 🐾 **National Corvette Museum and Plant Tour** (270-781-7973, 800-53-VETTE; www.corvettemuseum.com), 350 Corvette Dr., Bowling Green. Museum open 8–5, seven days a week year-round except Easter, Thanksgiving, Christmas Eve, Christmas Day, and New Year's Day. Plant tours are $5 per person, weekdays at 8:35, 11:30, 12:45, and 2; reservations are required, and all participants must have closed-toe shoes and be older than 7. Welcome to the world of the 'Vette. This huge 68,000-square-foot showroom is an ode to the true American sports car, the Corvette. With 75 on display, you can learn about each one and see rare collections and memorabilia. While you are there, sign up to tour the assembly plant. Every Corvette driven is made at this plant, so when you see one on the road, it will remind you of Kentucky.

✐ ♿ **Barren River Imaginative Museum of Science** (270-843-9779; www.brimsbg.org), 1229 Center St., Bowling Green. Open Thu.–Sat. 10–3, Sun. 1–4. Enjoy more than 50 fun science exhibits like the van de Graff Electrostatic Generator, which will make your hair stand on end, and the BRIMS Blaster where you can experience the force of a mini tornado. They have a huge model train exhibit, too. $5 adults, $4 children.

Riverview at Hobson Grove (270-843-5565; www.bgky.org/riverview), 1100 W. Main Ave., Bowling Green. Tue.–Sat. 10–4, Sun. 1–4. This late-1800s Victorian home was used for storage of Confederate munitions when the Rebel forces held Bowling Green. Tour the home and grounds now that it has been restored to its original splendor. On the National Register of Historic Places, this home lets visitors see how families and their servants lived during that time period. $5 adults, $3 students; under 6 free.

♿ **Shaker Museum at South Union** (800-811-8379; www.shakermuseum.com), 850 Shaker Museum Rd., Auburn. Open Mar. 1–Nov. 30, Mon.–Sat. 9–5 and Sun. 1–5. During winter hours (Dec. 1–Feb.), the museum is open for tours Tue.–Sat. 10–4. This site was home to the Shakers, a communal religious sect that lived in the area from 1807 until 1922. The museum is filled with original furniture, crafts, textiles, and manuscripts of this group, named for their extremely active style of worship. $6 adults, $2 ages 6–12; 5 and under free.

Western Kentucky University (270-745-2497; www.wku.edu), 1906 College Heights Blvd., Bowling Green. What started out in 1906 as a teachers' college has grown to 18,000 students and 88 college majors. The campus, built high on a hill overlooking the Barren River Valley, is home to the Hilltoppers. While on campus, plan a visit to the Kentucky Library and Museum, where they collect pieces of Kentucky. View their rich collection of maps, letters, furniture, toys, diaries, and even an 1800s log cabin.

✐ **Historic L&N Depot, Railpark, and Train Museum** (270-745-0090; www .historicrailpark.com), 401 Kentucky St., Bowling Green. Tue.–Sat. 9–5, Sun. 1–4. Housed inside the 1925 Classic Revival–style L&N depot, the museum has interactive exhibits and artifacts from the heyday of train travel. Take a private tour of the real, retired train cars on site like the 1953 Luxury Pullman Sleeper Car and the Chessie Class Caboose. $10 adults, $5 under 12.

✐ ♿ ♞ **Kennys Farmhouse Cheese** (888-571-4029; www.kennysfarmhouse cheese.com), 2033 Thomerson Park Rd., Austin. Mon.–Fri. 9–3, Sat. 9–1, closed Sun. Kenny Mattingly has been making cheese on his 200-acre family dairy farm for about 10 years, and he invites visitors in to see the whole process. Don't leave without some Gouda, Colby, cheddar, or the variety of your choice. Kenny sells 70,000 pounds a year, so he must know what he is doing.

✳ To Do

✐ **Beech Bend Park & Splash Lagoon** (270-781-7634; www.beechbend.com), 798 Beech Bend Rd., Bowling Green. In the business of entertaining Western Kentuckians since 1898, this amusement park has everything you need for a day or two of fun. With more than 40 rides, a miniature golf course, an oval track and drag strip for racing, and a giant water park, this park has it all. Open Memorial Day–Labor Day.

Kentucky Downs (270-586-7778; www.kentuckydowns.com), 5629 Nashville Rd., Franklin. Sitting almost on the Tennessee border is North America's only European-style horse-racing course. The all-turf course makes for exciting racing at their live September meets. Although their live racing meet is short, the track offers year-round simulcasting.

BEECH BEND PARK

photo courtesy of www.kentuckytourism.com

Ballance MotoX (270-792-RACE; www.ballancemotox.com), 13101 Louisville Rd., Oakland. The first state-of-the-art motocross facility in the Southeast features a 1.3-mile lighted track. Check the web site for upcoming events. Open Mar.–Nov.

Race World (270-781-RACE; www.raceworld-bg.com), 255 Cumberland Trace, Bowling Green. Featuring two racetracks for stock-car racing and a state-of-the-art arcade, there is fun here for the whole family. Call or check the web site for hours.

Paul Walker Golf Course (270-393-3821; www.bgky.org/golf/paulwalker.php), 1044 Covington Ave., Bowling Green. This 9-hole, par-36 golf course, right in the center of Bowling Green, is the place to go for a nice break from touring. The course welcomes walk-ins, and tee times are not necessary. Really convenient for those last-minute golfers.

∂ **Guntown Mountain** (270-773-3530; www.mammothcave.com/guntown), I-65 Exit 53, Cave City. Open daily 9:30–8 Memorial Day–Labor Day; weekends only, 9:30–8, the rest of the year. Visit this re-creation of a Wild West town, high atop a mountain. Getting there is half the fun: You ride a chairlift that takes you up 1,360 feet from the parking lot. Watch an old-time Saloon Show, a mock gunfight, or a country-western music show all in one visit. There is also an old-time country store where you can get local products like country hams and preserves. $15 adults, $9 children.

∂ **Kentucky Down Under** (270-786-2634, 800-762-2869; www.kdu.com), 3700 L&N Turnpike Rd., Horse Cave. Open mid-Mar.–Nov. 1; hours change seasonally. Cavern tours offered year-round. Get up close and personal with animals typically found in Australia, like kangaroos, wallabies, and an emu. They also have reptiles, farm animals, an aviary full of lorikeets, and a laughing kookaburra. And you don't have to settle for just looking at the animals in a cage; Kentucky Down Under lets you get in the cage, too. The ticket price also includes admission to Kentucky Caverns (see the sidebar). $22 adults, $13 ages 5–14; 4 and under free.

∂ & *"Ï"* **STATE PARK Barren River Lake State Resort Park** (270-646-2151, 800-325-0057; www.parks.ky.gov), 1149 State Park Rd., Lucas. Indians repeatedly burned this huge area of forest to make it easier to hunt, creating open plains. When settlers discovered this "barren" land, they assumed it was not fertile, but quickly found it was some of the lustiest farmland in the state. With the damming of the Barren River, which created Barren River Lake, the state park soon followed. Created in 1965 this 2,187-acre park boasts a 10,000-acre lake with 140 miles of shoreline. The park offers boating and fishing opportunities as well as an 18-hole golf course, horseback riding, and a public sand beach. Stay at the Louis B. Nunn Lodge, in one of their 51 rooms or one of the two-bedroom cottages that offer lake or wooded views. They also have a

KENTUCKY DOWN UNDER

photo courtesy of www.kentuckytourism.com

99-site campground with utility hookups for the outdoorsy set. **The Driftwood Restaurant** specializes in fresh seafood, like salmon, striped bass, trout, and crab clusters, but they also have salads and burgers. Open seven days a week. Breakfast is 7–10, lunch is 11:30–2, dinner is 5–9. $–$$.

✳ Lodging

∞ **BED & BREAKFASTS Victorian House Bed & Breakfast** (270-563-9403), 110 N. Main St., Smiths Grove. Sit on the huge wraparound porch and enjoy the period antiques that fill this 1875-era home, which is on the National Register of Historic Places. Innkeepers Sharon and Dave Dahle pamper each guest and are full of tips about the 10 antiques stores that are within walking distance. $$

∞ **Federal Grove Bed & Breakfast** (270-542-6106), 475 E. Main St., Auburn. This historic home sits on land that is also historic: It was once owned by Jonathan Clark, the brother of William Clark of Lewis and Clark fame. This Federal-style home is loaded with antiques, most of which are for sale, so if you love that settee in your room, you might be able to buy it. Make sure you don't miss breakfast; the homemade pastries are certainly worth getting up for. $$

& **Shaker Tavern Bed and Breakfast** (270-542-6801, 800-929-8701; www.shakermuseum.com), US 73, South Union. Stay in one of the six guest rooms that are part of the Shaker Tavern, a business venture for the South Union Shakers built in 1869. They hoped to attract "the people of the world" so they used intricate brickwork, an ornate staircase, and a towering columned facade that was very different from the simple style of the Shakers. The rooms are furnished with Victorian-style furniture and equipped with modern-day necessities. $

∞ ✎ "🍴" **Hall Place Bed and Breakfast** (270-651-3176), 313 S. Green St., Glasgow. The pampering and well-appointed antiques-filled rooms almost cause you to miss the architectural and historical wonders of this fine home. Built in 1852 by slaves, who actually created the bricks on site, the Hall family's home once hosted a young Abraham Lincoln. This mix of history (it was even a stop on the Underground Railroad) together with the 12-foot ceilings, original woodwork, and amazing library encourage you to enjoy all four of the splendid guest rooms. $

1869 Homestead Bed and Breakfast (270-842-0510; www.1869home stead.com), 212 Mizpah Rd., Bowling Green. Situated on 55 acres of peaceful farmland, but just minutes from Bowling Green, you'll find this historic home. Offering two guest rooms and one suite, the home also has an amazing spiral staircase and original fireplaces and flooring. Innkeepers Jan and Wendell Strode treat you like family. Corvette lovers need to make note of the fact that Wendell is executive director of the nearby National Corvette Museum, so if you want to talk to someone who knows a thing or two about 'Vettes, well you might want to book a room. $

✎ **CAMPGROUND Bowling Green KOA** (270-843-1919; www.bgkoa.com), 1960 Three Springs Rd., Bowling Green. This 26-acre property has full water and electric hookups, a tent area, and KOA Kamping Kabins. For fun there is an 18-hole mini golf course, hayrides, fishing derbies, paddle-boat races, and live music. Open year-round.

photo courtesy of www.kentuckytourism.com

DIAMOND CAVE

CAVES

The terrain of Kentucky makes it seem an unlikely place to find caves, but caves you will find. Miles and miles of them. Actually, it is probably all one giant cave system, and they are all probably connected, but there are many different caving opportunities available, so choose the one that fits your needs.

In the same class as the Grand Canyon and the giant sequoias, Mammoth Cave is a natural wonder that has been revered since prehistoric times. This is the longest recorded cave system in the world, at least three times longer than any cave known. With more than 348 miles of underground world explored and mapped, the park offers tours for all ages, ability levels, and interests.

Authorized as a national park in 1926 and established in 1941, Mammoth Cave National Park is Kentucky's number one tourist destination and the second oldest tourist attraction in the United States. The cave tours are unbelievable, but with 52,830 acres of park aboveground, there is plenty to do in the lush forested area as well, including hiking, horseback riding, cycling, fishing, and other back-to-nature activities.

Mammoth Cave National Park (270-758-2180; www.nps.gov/maca). The park is open every day of the year (except Christmas Day) 8–5. The visitors center is where you can get maps and cave tour tickets, attend seminars, and watch the informative films *Water and Stone* and *Voices of the Cave* before heading underground. The cost of cave tours varies, but admission to the park and visitors center is free. **Mammoth Cave Hotel** (270-758-2225) offers an assortment of lodging accommodations, from hotel rooms to cottages, rustic cabins, and several campgrounds. There are three restaurants on site; hours vary, so call to make sure they are open. At the **Travertine Restaurant**, you'll find a casual sit-down eatery specializing in southern cuisine. The **Crystal Lake Coffee Shop** is perfect for a light lunch, coffee, or a homemade dessert. You'll also find **Troglo-BITES**, which is Mammoth Cave's answer to a fast-food restaurant, serving burgers, fries, and other typical fare.

The following caves are in the area, but are not part of Mammoth Cave National Park:

Crystal Onyx Cave (270-773-2359), I-65 Exit 53, Cave City. Closed in January. Used by Native Americans as a burial site more than 2,700 years ago, this cave is an important archaeological site as well as a formation-rich cave. The tour allows views of vertical shafts, onyx flowstones and draperies, and limestone dams. Admission charged.

Cub Run Cave (270-524-1444), I-65 Exit 65, Munfordville. Tours available Mar. 24–Oct. 31. Winter tours for groups by appointment. First discovered in 1950, the cave was then closed to the public for more than 50 years. Reopened in 2006, this cave offers a 90-minute tour that is highlighted by wooden walkways, modern electric lighting, and renovated pathways for easy maneuvering and touring. Admission charged.

Diamond Caverns (270-749-2233; www.diamondcaverns.com), 1900 Mammoth Cave Parkway, Park City. Open year-round except for Thanksgiving, Christmas, and New Year's Day. On one of the 0.5-mile-long guided tours, you'll feel like you are in a cathedral while enjoying the intricate drapery deposits of naturally colorful calcite that cover the walls. Thanks to state-of-the-art modern lighting, you won't miss any of it. Tours are available every 30 minutes. The pathways have added handrails but the tour includes 350 stair steps, so it is not handicapped accessible. $15 adults, $8 ages 4–12.

Hidden River Cave (270-786-1466; www.cavern.org), 119 E. Main St., Horse Cave. Open daily 9–5 year-round, 9–7 Memorial Day–Labor Day. Guided cave tours leave hourly, no reservations needed. This cave, as well as the adjacent American Cave Museum, is dedicated to the exploration and preservation of groundwater as well as a reminder of the delicate balance between caves and the sunlit world above. Learn about caves and their connection to groundwater, and then tour the cave where you can see it all firsthand. Descending into the cave includes 230 stairs, but one tour is handicapped accessible and includes an elevator ride into a sinkhole. $15 adults, $10 ages 12–15, $7 ages 3–11. Museum tour (all ages) $6.

Kentucky Caverns (270-786-2634, 800-762-2869; www.kdu.com), 3700 L&N Turnpike Rd., Horse Cave. Tours available year-round. Call for times. Short cave tour included with admission to Kentucky Down Under. Guided tours offer a close-up view of the colorful onyx formations that line the cave from beginning to end. The 45-minute tour is not handicapped accessible and involves stairs and winding passages. $22 adults, $13 ages 5–14; 4 and under free.

Onyx Cave (270-773-3530; www.mammothcave.com/guntown), I-65 Exit 53, Cave City. Open Mar.–Nov. Offering 30-minute guided tours on demand, this is the cave to explore when you don't have time to wait for a schedule. Tour this cave and see walls coated with calcite crystal flowstone, which results in a shimmering, colorful show. The cave tour is not strenuous but does include steps so it is not handicapped accessible. Adjacent to Guntown Mountain. Small fee.

Lost River Cave and Valley (270-393-0077, 866-274-2283; www.lostrivercave.com), 2818 Nashville Rd., Bowling Green. Open 9–5 seven days a week, except for Thanksgiving, Christmas Day, and New Year's Day. Call for tour times. The valley itself is breathtaking, but Kentucky's only Underground Boat Tour is a trip you'll never forget. Travel the lost river in a huge cave where it is always a comfortable 57 degrees. While you are there, you can walk the wooded trails, do a little bird-watching, and enjoy the butterfly garden. Cave and boat are not handicapped accessible. $15 adults, $11 ages 4–11, $4 ages 1–3.

Yogi Bear's Jellystone Park Camp Resort (270-773-3840, 800-523-1854; www.jellystonemammothcave.com), 1002 Mammoth Cave Rd., Cave City. Spend some time with Yogi, Boo Boo, and all the gang at this fun resort. Accommodations include log cabins, Amish cottages, four-bedroom bungalows, and even a bunkhouse that sleeps up to 22 people. They also have campsites ranging from those suitable for the largest RV to the most primitive tent site. The resort itself features a pool and 300-foot waterslide, mini golf, arcade, fishing pond, and planned activities like outdoor movies and a bonfire where you can roast marshmallows. Open year-round.

❋ Where to Eat

♈ **DINING OUT 440 Main Restaurant & Bar** (270-9793-0450; www.440main.com/Home.asp), 440 E. Main Ave., Bowling Green. Serving dinner Mon.–Sat. beginning at 5. Overlooking Fountain Square Park in the downtown area, this restaurant, housed in a historic building, is both warm and elegant. For finer dining they offer a dining room with an upscale feel, featuring steaks, veal, chicken or duck. In the mood for something more casual? Then head for the bar area for delicious appetizers and sandwiches. $–$$

♿ **Mariah's 1818** (270-842-6878; www.mariahs.com), 801 State St., Bowling Green. Open 11–9 daily. Holding the title of the oldest brick home in Bowling Green, this casual eatery is on the National Register of Historic Homes. Menu choices include steaks, salmon, and salads, but they also have the not-so-common barbecue pizza made in their wood-fired brick oven. Have the New Orleans bread pudding for dessert. $–$$

Brickyard Café (270-843-6431), 1026 Chestnut St., Bowling Green. Open for lunch and dinner every day. This is truly a culturally diverse eatery: It's owned by a Bosnian and a Croatian immigrant who specialize in delicious Mediterranean food. The old building, part of an 1857 brickyard, has thick brick walls and intricate masonry from long ago. From pasta to pizza, the typical Italian menu includes four-cheese lasagna and veal Marsala, but the flavors have a slight European twist. Wide variety of pizzas, too. Make sure to try some bread, which is made from scratch daily. $–$$

& EATING OUT **Cambridge Market & Café** (270-782-9366; www .cambridgemarketandcafe.com), 830 Fairview Ave., Bowling Green. Open weekdays 9–8, Sat. 10–3. This soup-and-sandwich deli offers daily gourmet specials like roast pork loin on Mondays and BBQ on corncakes on Thursdays. They have awesome cheesecakes and homemade pies, too. $

Judy's Castle (270-842-8736), 1302 US 31W Bypass, Bowling Green. Open 6 AM–7:30 PM Mon.–Sat. While not exactly a castle, the personal service you'll get at Judy's will make you feel

like royalty. They are truly happy to have you, and you'll be happy to be there when you try their down-home breakfasts, succulent barbecue, and homemade pies. $–$$

Aunt Bee's Family Restaurant (270-786-2020), I-65 (Exit 58) and KY 218, Horse Cave. Open Sun.–Thu. 6 AM–10 PM, Fri.–Sat. 6 AM–midnight. If you are looking for a stick-to-your-ribs home-cooked meal, this is the place. Whether you want breakfast, lunch, or supper Aunt Bee's has something on the menu for you. Stop by on Friday nights for all-you-can-eat catfish. Monday is all-you-can-eat ribs night. $–$$

Teresa's Restaurant (270-782-6540; www.teresas-bg.com), 509 Gordon Ave., Bowling Green. Closed Sun. Teresa's is the kind of place where you can get a hearty southern breakfast all day, but then you might miss out on one of the daily lunch specials like country-fried steak or meat loaf served with three vegetables. Teresa's is also known for country smoked hams. Try some there or order one to go. $–$$

Big Moose's BBQ Smokehouse (270-651-1913), 525 W. Main St., Glasgow. Mon.–Wed. 10:30–2:30, Thu.–Sat. 10:30–8. This is a barbecue joint that is near and dear to the locals of Glasgow. They cook everything out back, so you can smell what's grilling when you are down the street. Everyone loves the barbecue, but a plate of side dishes isn't out of the question. With choices of mayonnaise slaw, vinegar slaw, hush puppies, and sweet potato crunch, there's hardly room left for the pork chops, chicken, or country ribs entrées. $

& SNACKS **Chaney's Dairy Barn** (270-843-5567; www.chaneysdairybarn .com), 9191 Nashville Rd., Bowling Green. Open Mon.–Sat. 11–8, Sun. noon–5. This dairy farm, in the Chaney

DINING ROOM AT MARIAH'S
photo courtesy of www.kentuckytourism.com

family for generations, is a country-style place to go for some homemade ice cream, sandwiches, and desserts. Or make it your destination and take a farm tour and try your luck at the giant corn maze in fall. $

George J's, on the Square (270-651-2161), 144 E. Public Sq., Glasgow. Open Mon.–Sat. 7–2, this former pharmacy with a soda fountain has been transformed into a diner, with its famous fountain still intact. You'll find one of their original milk shake machines still up on the counter, serving up creamy concoctions as it has for generations. The most popular menu item is the Mexican Hamburger, a favorite at the lunch counter of Newberry's, a former rival and now defunct drugstore down the street. The other lunch-of-choice is called The Manhattan—not the cocktail, but an open-faced roast beef sandwich swimming in mashed potatoes and homemade gravy. This place is a big hangout for local politicians, but don't let that keep you away; they are part of the fun.

Riley's Bakery (270-842-7636), 819 US 31W Bypass, Bowling Green. Open Mon.–Fri. 6:45–5, Sat. 6:45–2. Serving up made-from-scratch products for more than 60 years, all the pastries are scrumptious, but the Hungarian coffee cake and the cream horns stand out to the locals. Order a sandwich on their famous Butter Bread and get yours filled with pimiento cheese or egg salad. $

Countryside Bake Shop (270-542-8679), 525 Quarry Rd., Auburn. With everything made one batch at a time, you can taste the difference at this family-run bakery. The Schwartz family gets up about 3 AM each day to bake their signature white, wheat, and honey oatmeal breads. Buy a few loaves and pick up a Hummingbird cake, too; full of bananas, pineapples, pecans, and cinnamon, it is delightful.

✳ Entertainment

Capitol Arts Center Galleries (270-782-2787; www.capitolarts.com), 416 E. Main St., Bowling Green. Gallery open Mon.–Fri. Originally built as a vaudeville house in the late 1890s, this theater is truly an icon in the downtown area. The historic auditorium welcomes touring acts from around the globe. Check the web site to see who is appearing. There are also two galleries, the Houchens and Mezzanine, which feature revolving exhibits throughout the year.

Public Theatre of Kentucky/ Phoenix Theatre (270-781-6233; www.ptkbg.org), 545 Morris Ave., Bowling Green. A talented community theater in the historic downtown area. The lineup features plays and musicals Sept.–May each year. Check the web site for shows and times.

✳ Selective Shopping

Steamboat Salvage and Company (270-796-3606), 1750 Campbell Lane, Bowling Green. This store features an unbelievable collection of one-of-a-kind nautical items, but they are also direct importers of furniture, giftware, and oil paintings. Wander around and see what you find.

Dollar Brothers Shoes (270-842-8141), 419 Park Row, Bowling Green. Open the door and smell the leather—this shop smells like a shoe store should. Located right in the town center and specializing in men's and women's shoes, it has been part of Bowling Green's downtown since 1937. Customers are treated to old-fashioned service, like using a shoe horn to glide your foot into the shoe. For people of a certain age, it will bring back memories.

ART GALLERIES **Memphis Marsha's Art Gallery** (270-843-1726, 877-640-7973; www.memphismarshas

.com), 524 E. 12th Ave., Bowling Green. Open Thu.–Sat. 10–4. This impressive collection of paintings, photography, jewelry, and ceramics is worth browsing through. They feature award-winning art from regional artists.

Rickman Pottery (270-782-8550), 1121 E. 14th Ave., Bowling Green. Closed Sun. and Mon. Watch the potter's wheel spin to create bowls, vases, and dinnerware, and then see the kiln where it is all baked to perfection. This working pottery studio is right in the heart of Bowling Green and includes a retail shop, so you can take home your finds.

ANTIQUES Smith Grove Antique District (270-563-6444). This quaint community features 10 antiques shops and two historic B&Bs, just a few minutes from downtown Bowling Green. Antiques range from rare primitives to exquisite pieces.

Flea Land of Bowling Green/Antique Mall at Flea Land (270-843-1978; www.flealandbg.com), 1100 Three Springs Rd., Bowling Green. Antiques mall open daily 10–5, Flea Land open Sat. and Sun. 9–6. This is a fantastic combination of flea market and fine antiques. Kentucky's largest indoor, climate-controlled flea market, is more than 85,000 square feet. The antiques mall is huge, too, with 12,000 square feet of browsing space.

✱ Special Events

✿ ♿ ✸ *July:* **National Corvette Homecoming** (270-791-2117; www .nationalcorvettehomecoming.com). All corvettes are made at the GM plant in Bowling Green, so what better location could there be for a festival of all things 'Vette? Enjoy the all-Corvette parade, which stretches for miles, a Corvette car show, a Corvette parts swap meet, and a Corvette auction. There is also live music, festival food, and an arts and crafts show. Held at the Sloan Convention Center and Grounds.

✿ ♿ ✸ *August:* **Duncan Hines Festival** (www.duncanhinesfestival.com). Celebrating the life and times of Bowling Green native Duncan Hines. This name, synonymous with cake mixes, belonged to a man who had a storied career writing guidebooks and producing more than 250 products aimed to aid the life of a housewife. Although he sold his company to Proctor & Gamble in 1956, the company kept his iconic moniker. This festival features a dessert recipe contest, pageants, a street dance, and an art contest and auction.

✿ ♿ ✸ *September:* **Bowling Green International Festival** (www .bginternationalfest.com). Celebrate cultural diversity with music, food, games, and juried art. Held annually at downtown's Fountain Square Park Many nationalities come together to share their unique cultures.

CAMPBELLSVILLE, GREENSBURG, AND THE GREEN RIVER LAKE AREA

These tiny communities, situated just 10 miles apart on US 68, are both basking in history. The folks from the National Historic Register should consider opening a satellite office in this part of the state, with so many remnants of the past.

Once you've doused yourself in history, maybe it's time for some recreation. Head in the direction of the gigantic 8,200-acre **Green River Lake**. Known as one of the clearest in the state, Green River Lake lures (no pun intended) fishing enthusiasts in their quest for white, largemouth, smallmouth, and Kentucky bass, bluegill, crappie, and muskie. The sheer size of the lake and its surrounding wooded landscape makes it a favorite of houseboaters, hikers, and campers. Most of the lodging choices center on the water, so if you're staying in the area, consider a houseboat, a rustic cabin, or even a Floating Condo.

Campbellsville, the seat of Taylor County, is approximately 85 miles from Louisville, Lexington, Bowling Green, and Somerset. This central location in the middle of a heart-shaped county lets them boast that they are truly "the Heart of Kentucky."

This small town of about 10,000 people is filled with history. There are about 30 sites in the county on the National Historic Register. From the 1830s to the 1870s, Campbellsville served as a stagecoach stop on the national mail route between Zanesville, Ohio, and Florence, Alabama. As the railroad arrived in nearby Lebanon in the 1850s, a feeder route was created to Campbellsville, allowing the area to grow. With the start of the Civil War, the city was on the invasion route for both the Yankees and the Confederates. In 1963, the Battle of Tebbs Bend was fought on the Green River. After this huge victory for the North, homes and churches in Campbellsville were turned into makeshift hospitals, some of which you can see today.

You'll love the southern hospitality of the residents. They're glad to have you, and it shows.

Greensburg is a tiny speck on the map, but it has deep historical roots. Visit the 200-year-old Green County Courthouse, which is the oldest courthouse west of the Alleghenies and is listed on the National Register of Historic Places. Its claim to fame is that President Andrew Jackson once practiced law here. Currently a museum, the old limestone building houses mementos and artifacts from Greensburg and Green County history.

A stationary 445-foot-long, wooden plank footbridge, constructed in 1929, connects the town square to the historic L&N. Railroad Depot and the valley across the square. It's easy to picture turn-of-the-20th-century travelers disembarking the train and walking the bridge. The town square, which is full of historic buildings, still looks as it did then.

Originally established by John Glover and called Glover's Station, the town changed its name to Greensburg in 1794. In an effort to remember John, you can visit Glover's Station Antique Mall right on the town square. While you're on the square, stop in the shops and restaurants on the way. They're darling.

GUIDANCE **Taylor County Tourism Commission** (270-465-3786, 800-738-4719; www.campbellsvilleky.com), 107 W. Broadway, Campbellsville. Open weekdays 8–4. Nice place to stop for guidance, with a friendly staff who know the area well. **Greensburg–Green County Chamber of Commerce** (270-932-4298; www.greensburgonline.com), 110 W. Court St., Greensburg. Open Mon.–Fri. 8–4. Although this isn't really a visitors center, per se, they have brochures and welcome tourists. In fact, everyone working there is full of friendly advice.

GETTING THERE The closest commercial airport is about 75 miles away, in Louisville. The **Louisville International Airport** (502-368-6524; www.fly louisville.com) is served by most commercial airlines and has rental cars available.

GETTING AROUND Campbellsville and Greensburg are not located near an interstate highway or parkway. The main route through Taylor County is US 68, connecting Lexington and Bowling Green. Streets are well marked and easy to get around; parking in the downtown areas is free.

MEDICAL EMERGENCY **Taylor Regional Hospital** (270-465-3561; www .tchosp.org), 1700 Old Lebanon Rd., Campbellsville. This 90-bed hospital serves the 110,000 people who live in Campbellsville and the regional area. **Jane Todd Crawford Memorial Hospital** (502-932-4211), 202–206 Milby St., Greensburg. Named for Jane Todd Crawford, a patient of Dr. Ephraim McDowell who in 1809 became the first person to undergo abdominal surgery in Kentucky. This 44-bed hospital has been serving the needs of the community since 1962.

ALCOHOL Taylor County is a moist county with alcohol sales permitted in a few restaurants. The surrounding counties of Adair, Casey, and Green are all dry, with the sale of alcohol prohibited within the county borders.

✳ To See

In Campbellsville
1823 Jacob Hiestand House (270-789-4343), on KY 210. See the period furnishings and exquisite hand-tooled masonry of this German stone house. It is one of only 12 in the state. Open by appointment.

1840 Atkinson-Griffin Log House (270-465-4463), 544 Lake Rd. After the Civil War Battle of Tebbs Bend, this home served as a Confederate hospital. Open by appointment.

The Friendship Schoolhouse (270-465-5410), 300 Ingram Ave. Built around 1918, this one-room schoolhouse taught between 8 and 40 students at a time, in grades one through eight. Open by appointment.

In Greensburg

Green County Old Courthouse (270-932-4298), downtown Greensburg. One of the oldest public buildings still standing in Kentucky, the courthouse was built in 1802 and in use for 135 years. It is the oldest courthouse west of the Allegheny Mountains.

Foot Bridge at Courthouse Square (270-932-4298), 110 W. Court St. If you are not scared of heights, walk the 445-foot-long, 40-foot-high foot bridge, which connects the Greensburg public square to the early-1900s L&N Railroad depot.

✳ To Do

Miller Park (270-465-7011), KY 289, Campbellsville. This 65-acre park features an Olympic-sized swimming pool, tennis courts, a walking trail, and flower gardens. There is a 9-hole golf course, basketball courts, and ball fields.

🎬 🐾 ♿ **Skyline Drive-In** (270-932-2817; www.skylinedrivein.com), 5600 Hodgenville Rd., Greensburg. Watch first-run movies under the stars. With room for 300 cars, the Skyline Drive-In is the place to see a double feature for less than the cost of one movie at the theater.

GOLF Green County Golf Association (270-932-7031; www.greencountygolf .com), 158 Golf Course Rd., Greensburg. This 9-hole course is surrounded by mature trees and rolling hills. Go when you're short on time but want to get in a quick round of golf.

WALKING TOUR Greensburg Walking Tour. Start at the chamber of commerce (270-932-4298), 110 W. Court St., Greensburg. The best way to get acquainted with Greensburg is to take the one-hour walking tour that includes 24 historic homes, government buildings, the railroad depot, cemeteries, and other sites. Proudly demonstrates Greensburg efforts to preserve its rich and multilayered heritage.

✳ Green Space

American Legion Park (270-932-6562), 1099 Legion Park Rd., Greensburg. This park, which is adjacent to the Green River, has a ramp, perfect for canoes. They also have walking trails, a ball field, and a picnic area with grills.

✳ Green River Lake Marinas & Lodging

Emerald Isle Resort & Marina (270-465-3412, 888-815-2000; www.emeral disleresort.com), KY 372, Campbellsville. They can meet all your marina needs with gas, groceries, supplies, and pontoon- and fishing-boat rentals. They also have a very casual restaurant on site, cooking up breakfast and lunch daily. After a day of roughing it on the lake, rent a luxury condominium on the shore. Try out the large sunporches on the outside or the cozy fireplaces on the inside. With two or three bedrooms, they can accommodate up to eight people. All the amenities are included to make your stay perfect, like appliances, sheets, towels, and utensils. You can even park your boat right outside; a complimentary boat slip comes with every rental.

Green River Marina State Dock (800-465-2512; www.greenrivermarina.com), KY 55S, KY 1061, Campbellsville. All the things you need in a marina, like fuel, food, emergency assistance, and a gift shop with souvenirs. They have so many houseboats available for rent, you'll have a hard time choosing which one. All these houseboats feature modern necessities, like queen-sized beds, hot tubs, and slides off the back. This dock also offers Floating Cabins or, as they like to call them, Floating Condos. These homes on water were built in the hull of a houseboat. They are moored to the dock with a boat slip for you to park. Measuring about 1,100 square feet, some sleep up to 12 people.

✳ Where to Eat

EATING OUT Creek Side Restaurant (465-7777; www.creeksidecville.com), 1837 New Lebanon Rd., Campbellsville. Open daily for lunch and dinner. Named for a former restaurant that used to be alongside a creek, this new location isn't even near water. No matter what the name, though, this family restaurant offers a full-service menu with seafood, country ham, salads, and sandwiches, but the buffet is so good, you won't need a menu. On weekends you can get frog legs and shrimp as well as their famous chicken tenders on the buffet. $$

Anew Blend (270-932-5339), 105 N. Main St., Greensburg. Open 5 AM–3 PM Mon.–Fri. Look for the inviting red door when you're in the historic downtown area and you will be in for a real treat. They offer soups, salads, sandwiches, and specialty burgers. Try the pineapple teriyaki burger—regulars rave about it. The menu also has a huge array of coffee drinks. $

SNACKS A Taste Like Home Country Market (270-932-2766), 8217 Marshall Ridge, Greensburg. Closed Sun.–Mon. Stop in to get fresh-baked goods, like homemade pies and cookies. They also have a fantastic deli. $

✳ Selective Shopping

ANTIQUES Sapps Antiques (270-789-4192, 270-789-7497), 300 E. Main St., Campbellsville. Open Mon.–Fri. 10–4, or call when you're in town and they'll open up for you. Specializing in early American, Victorian, primitive, and oak furniture, as well as china and glassware.

SHOPS Glover's Station Antique Mall (270-932-5588), 121 S. Public Square, Greensburg. The mall is an antique itself. Built in 1900, it was formerly a department store. Have a look at the old-time manual elevator—it's no longer in use, but fun to see. They have a huge selection of antiques and collectibles.

Brenda's Flowers and Crafts (270-932-4053), 210 S. Main St., Greensburg. In addition to meeting all your floral needs, Brenda stocks a variety of locally made craft items. Nice selection of handmade bird houses, intricate jewelry, wind chimes, and soaps. Look for the yellow house with green shutters.

✳ Special Events

⅃ ✿ *July:* **Green River Lake Arts & Crafts Festival** (270-465-8601). Enjoy live music, clogging demonstrations, myriad food choices, and arts and craft items for you to browse and buy.

♪ ⅃ ✿ *September:* **Cow Days!** (270-932-4298). A salute to our bovine friends, this two-day street festival is held right in the middle of downtown Greensburg. Carnival games, live music, a talent show, a 5K run, and a pipe-smoking contest. But the real attraction is a life-sized plastic cow that kids can milk.

THE LAKE CUMBERLAND AREA, INCLUDING SOMERSET, JAMESTOWN, RUSSELL SPRINGS, AND MONTICELLO

With the creation of the gargantuan **Lake Cumberland** in the 1950s came the transformation of these sleepy rural communities that now surround the lake. An estimated 1.7 million vacationers head to the lake each year, and these towns, which could be easily zipped through on your way to the water, cater to this crowd. In fact, most of them make their livelihood from the lake, so you can find plenty of places to stock up on supplies. Yet there are also nice restaurants, shops, and even a few doses of history.

Known as the Houseboat Capital of the World, the Lake Cumberland area has the highest number of luxury houseboats of any lake in the United States, so there is no excuse not to rent one for a few days. See the lake as it was meant to be seen, as you float around in pure comfort.

The city of **Russell Springs** became known as a health resort in the 19th century because of a nearby chalybeate spring. The iron-laden chalybeate water was said to have health-giving properties. Tourists flocked there in the 1850s—and 100 years later, with the creation of Lake Cumberland, they are still coming.

So park the car, stretch your legs and take a look around.

GUIDANCE **Somerset-Pulaski Convention & Visitors Bureau** (606-679-6394, 800-642-6287; www.lakecumberlandtourism.com), 522 Ogden St., Somerset. Open Mon.–Sat. 8–4. Stop in the visitors center for free and friendly information about what to do in the area. **Russell Springs Tourism** (270-866-4333; www.lake cumberlandvacation.com), 650 S. Hwy. 127 just inside the Russell Springs city limits. Stop by for maps and directions—they've got everything you need. Open 8–4 in winter and 8:30–4:30 in summer.

GETTING THERE The closest commercial airport is the **Bluegrass Airport** in Lexington, which is about 100 miles away (859-425-3114; www.bluegrassairport .com). There are car rentals available. The nearest **Greyhound Bus** (606-864-2040) station is 30 miles away in London, 1938 London Shopping Center.

GETTING AROUND Although there is no formal public transportation, you can always call **Somerset's Taxi Express** (606-679-9944) if you need a ride. Otherwise, getting around by car is fairly easy. The major route through the area is the Cumberland Parkway, also known as Louie B. Nunn Parkway, and if you travel about 60 miles, east or west, you will hit major arteries I-65 and I-75.

photo by Deborah Kohl Kremer

RUSSELL SPRINGS VISITORS CENTER

MEDICAL EMERGENCY Lake Cumberland Regional Hospital (606-679-7441; www.lakecumberland hospital.com), 305 Langdon St., Somerset. Serving 42 surrounding counties and more than 300,000 people, they have 259 beds.

Russell County Hospital (270-866-4141; www.russellcohospital.org), Dowell Rd., Russell Springs. This 25-bed critical access hospital offers quality health care and round-the-clock emergency services.

ALCOHOL Although alcohol sales are prohibited in Pulaski County, alcohol sales by the drink are permitted in nearby Burnside.

Russell and Wayne County are dry, so there are no alcohol sales within the county borders.

✳ To See

&. **Mill Springs Battlefield, Cemetery, and Museum** (606-636-4045; www .millsprings.net), in the tiny burg of Nancy. Open every day 10–4. In the Union's effort to protect the Cumberland River, the Cumberland Gap, and the surrounding area, a Civil War battle broke out on this site on January 19, 1862. There were 671 total casualties, and the Union was declared the winner. The museum allows visitors to look out on the battlefield that once held the Union camps. During your visit, watch the 18-minute video and get a good overview of what took place. You can take a driving tour, which includes the cemetery where more than 100 unidentified Confederate troops are buried under one headstone. Also on the property is Brown-Lanier House, which was built in 1830. During the war it was used as both headquarters and hospital. It was originally the home of the miller who operated the adjacent gristmill. This mill has the largest operating overshot waterwheel in the country and is

MILL SPRINGS BATTLEFIELD MUSEUM
photo by Deborah Kohl Kremer

photo by Deborah Kohl Kremer

MILL SPRINGS BATTLEFIELD CEMETERY

powered by 13 springs. $4 adults, $3 seniors and military, $2 children.

Creelsboro Arch (270-866-4333). Near the deserted town of Creelsboro, you will find the largest natural arch east of the Rockies. With a span of 104 feet, it arches Jim Creek shortly before the creek enters the Cumberland River. Although located on private land, the bridge is open to the public. Getting there can be a bit confusing, involving unmarked gravel roads, so get a map from the tourist office or ask a local.

🐾 🐟 **Wolf Creek Dam Powerhouse and Overlook** (615-736-7161), US 27S. Enjoy the spectacular view from this mile-long construction marvel. Constructed in 1950 to generate hydroelectricity and prevent flooding, it's better known for creating Lake Cumberland, the largest human-made lake east of the Mississippi. Free.

🐾 🐟 **Wolf Creek National Fish Hatchery** (270-343-3797; www.fws.gov/wolf creek), 50 Kendall Rd., Jamestown. This hatchery raises about 800,000 rainbow and brown trout for the lakes, rivers, and streams of Kentucky each year. They welcome 100,000 people each year to their visitors center, where you can tour the hatchery and do some public fishing. Free.

✵ To Do

Lake Cumberland Speedway (606 561-8994; lcspeedway.net), 1 Racetrack Rd., Burnside. This 3/8-mile dirt oval features races for Late Models, Open Wheel Modified, Superdirt Roadhogs, Chevettes, and Frontwheel Drives. Call for race times and events.

The Links at Lily Creek (270-343- 4653; www.linksatlilycreek.com), 500 Lily Creek Resort Rd., Jamestown. This 18-hole public golf course is designed by PGA professional Dave Wilson. It also has a driving range, practice area, and fully stocked pro shop.

Kentucky Off-Track Betting (270-343-3939), 628 N. Main St., Jamestown. Place your bets without going to the track. They offer thoroughbred racing from Keeneland, Churchill Downs, Turfway Park, and other top tracks across the country.

🐾 ♿ **MOVIES 27 Twin Drive-in** (606-679-4738; www.27drivein.com), 5270 Hwy. 27S, Somerset. Not many left of this dying breed of entertainment. This drive-in has two screens; both show double features all summer. Pack up the station wagon and check the web site to see what's showing.

🐾 **MINIATURE GOLF Somerset Falls Miniature Golf Course** (606-451-2000; www.somersetfalls.com), 100 Family Fun Dr., Somerset. This 18-hole mini golf course has waterfalls, streams, and natural limestone.

✐ SCENIC TOUR **Big South Fork Scenic Railway** (606-376-5330; www.bsfsry
.com), 100 Henderson St., Stearns. Open Apr.–Oct.; call for reservations. Ride the
16-mile round trip through the Daniel Boone National Forest on the 100-year-old
Kentucky & Tennessee Railroad. Your rail ticket also includes admission to the
McCreary County Museum, which is located in the 1907 Stearns Coal & Lumber
Company headquarters. This museum exhibits artifacts of early Appalachian life.
$18 adults, $17 seniors, $9 ages 3–12.

✳ Green Space

✐ PARKS **General Burnside Island State Park** (606-561-4104), 8801 S. US 27,
Burnside. Named for Civil War general Ambrose Burnside, who patrolled the
Cumberland River. He and his troops circled this 400-acre island to protect it from
Confederate troops. Today the park includes a campground, a marina, a picnic
area, a swimming pool, and a golf course.

✐ **Big South Fork National River and Recreation Area** (bigsouthfork-
park.com). Established in 1974 by Congress to protect the free-flowing Big South
Fork of the Cumberland River and its tributaries. Encompassing 125,000 acres of
the Cumberland Plateau, Big South Fork National River and Recreation Area
boasts miles of scenery like gorges and sandstone bluffs. It also offers a huge range
of outdoor recreational activities, including hiking, horseback riding, paddling, and
hunting. While you are there, take the short, 1-mile loop hiking trail to Yahoo
Falls. It is Kentucky's highest waterfall, dropping 113 feet.

Pulaski County Park (606-636-6450), 1200 Hwy. 3189, Nancy. The park located
in western Pulaski County offers picnic areas, grills, shelters, camping, playground,
and 18-hole disk golf courses plus hiking trails.

LAKES

Dale Hollow Lake

About 50 miles southwest of Russell Springs, you'll find Dale Hollow Lake. This
enormous 28,000-acre lake straddles the Kentucky–Tennessee border, and was created in 1943 by damming the Obey River.
This massive dam provides flood control
and power to the area. It is 1,717 feet in
length and holds back Dale Hollow
Lake, which is 61 miles long, offers 653
miles of shoreline, and is 120 feet deep
at its deepest point. The entire lake area
offers the usual outdoor activities like
fishing, camping, boating, canoeing, hiking, waterskiing and tubing, and the
unique crystalline waters even allow for
snorkeling.

27 TWIN DRIVE-IN

photo by Deborah Kohl Kremer

With a lake of this size, you're sure to
find people casting a line. Dale Hollow
Lake is stocked with white bass,
bluegill, crappie, muskie, and rainbow
trout. The park has a marina that rents

boats of all sizes. With more than 3,398 acres of wooded forest area surrounding the lake and lodge, don't miss the 15 miles of trails that can be used for hiking, horseback riding, and mountain biking. In addition to all kinds of water sports, Dale Hollow has one of the best golf courses in the state. The 18-hole public course is situated within the lush rolling hills.

❝❡❞ ✑ ♿ **Dale Hollow Lake State Resort Park** (270-433-7431, 800-325-2282; parks.ky.gov), 6371 State Park Rd., Burkesville. Even though most of this lake is located in Tennessee, Kentucky could not pass up the opportunity to create a wonderful state resort park on the Frogue Peninsula, on the northern side of the lake. Here you'll find the 60-room **Mary Ray Oaken Lodge**, which sits high on a bluff overlooking the lake. They also have a 165-site campground, with a few sites set aside for campers who have horses. There are a few air-conditioned cabins scattered about the woods, too. Diners love the **Island View Restaurant**, which has phenomenal views of, you guessed it, the small islands that dot the lake. Serving three meals a day, seven days a week, the restaurant offers a huge variety that includes fried catfish, barbecue ribs, and char-grilled steaks. Don't forget to try the bourbon-laced bread pudding; it's the perfect ending to any meal. $–$$

Dale Hollow Marinas

Hendricks Creek Resort (800-321-4000; www.hendrickscreek1.com), 945 Hendricks Creek Rd., Burkesville. One-stop shopping for your weekend on the lake. Hendricks rents houseboats that can sleep up to 12 people. They have small runabouts and pontoons, too. The marina has a well-stocked store with everything from fuel to bait. You can also rent a furnished, family-sized fishing cottage with a nice lake view.

Sulphur Creek Resort (270-433-7272; www.sulphurcreek.com), 3498 Sulphur Creek Rd., Burkesville. Nice resort where you can rent boats of all sizes, including luxury houseboats. If you would rather sleep on shore, check out their selection of furnished cabins that are tucked into the wooded hillsides around the lake. They also have 22 lakeside campsites, each with a boat slip. **Mike's Landing**, a floating restaurant at the resort, is a fun casual place to relax after a day on the water. Open Apr.–late Oct., Mike's serves up all three meals.

Lake Cumberland

Created by the construction of Wolf Creek Dam in 1950, Lake Cumberland is a huge tourist destination for Kentuckians as well as those from neighboring states. With 1,225 miles of shoreline, it has more waterfront access than the state of Florida and is considered one of the best boating and fishing areas in the eastern United States.

❝❡❞ ✑ ♿ **Lake Cumberland State Resort Park** (270-343-3111, 800-325-1709; www.parks.ky.gov), 5465 State Park Rd., Jamestown. This Kentucky state park covers 3,000 acres and would be a nice place to vacation, even if they didn't have access to the adjacent 63,000-acre Lake Cumberland. They have two lodges, the 63-room **Lure Lodge** and the 13-room **Pumpkin Creek Lodge**. Tucked back in the woods a bit are 30 two-bedroom and chalet-style cottages. You can also camp at the 146-site campground. This resort has both indoor and outdoor pools, tennis courts, miniature golf, and horseback-riding stables. The grounds are perfect for hiking, but if you would rather hike on greens and fairways, they have a 9-hole par-3 golf course. Serving three meals daily, the **Rowena Landing Restaurant** has a nice view of the lake, as well as a varied menu featuring many locally grown ingredients.

photo courtesy of www.kentuckytourism.com

HOUSEBOATING ON LAKE CUMBERLAND

Lake Cumberland Marinas

Jamestown Resort and Marina (270-343-5253; www.jamestown-marina.com), 3677 S. KY 92, Jamestown. Offering a fleet of pleasure craft like deluxe houseboats and pontoon boats, they also have an easily accessible launch ramp, if you have your own boat. The houseboats are all fully equipped with modern-day features, but if you would rather sleep on land, they have an all-suite hotel, some rustic cabins, and three deluxe log homes. This marina also has a café offering sandwiches, burgers, and a buffet on the weekends.

Lake Cumberland State Dock (270-343-6000, 888-782-8336; www.statedock .com), 6365 State Park Rd., Jamestown. This dock has all you need to get your lake vacation started. Rent a luxury houseboat, or bring your own. They have pay-at-the-pump fuel docks for your convenience. There is a store with full line of grocery, apparel, footwear, novelty items, boating accessories, fishing licenses, and even live bait. Always looking out for your comfort, they have recently added a fitness center complete with men's and women's showers. Get your supplies at the store and stop in at the **Lakeside Grill Restaurant** for burgers before heading out to your favorite spot on the lake.

Popplewell's Alligator Dock #1 (270-866-3634), 6959 S. KY 76, Russell Springs. As the first commercial dock on Lake Cumberland, Popplewell's has loyal customers who have been coming for decades. They have a 200-slip rental dock where you can rent all sizes of boats and a Jet Ski if you want. They also have nice, furnished cabins that sit about 1,000 feet from the shoreline.

Alligator II Marina (270-866-6616; 877-363-9911), 2108 KY 1383, Russell Springs. Alligator II Marina was one of the original full-service marinas on Lake Cumberland, offering clothing, gas, and bait. Rent a boat—they have everything from a 16-foot fishing boat to a luxurious wide-body houseboat. If you are hungry, visit the **Gator II Grill**. You can sit on the floating deck and enjoy a big ol' country breakfast as well as burgers and sandwiches. They also have fully stocked, comfortable resort cabins that will sleep up to 12 people.

♈ **Lee's Ford Marina Resort** (606-636-6426; www.leesfordmarina.com), 451 Lees Ford Dock Rd., Burnside. As the only marina on Lake Cumberland that allows alcohol sales, this is a very popular watering spot. The surrounding county is dry, but the city of Burnside allows alcohol by the drink in restaurants. The **Harbor Restaurant and Tavern** has American and Mediterranean entrées. Sit on the deck and enjoy the view. Or take your order to go and relax in one of their cottages. Available with one to four bedrooms, these spacious cottages are well equipped and sit about 300 yards from the marina, tucked in among the trees. They are quiet and private but not far from all the action of the lake. At the marina, rent a 14-foot fishing boat, a ski boat and some skis, and a houseboat, too. They have all you need to enjoy Lake Cumberland.

Woodson Bend Resort (800-872-9825; www.woodsonbendresort.com), 14 Woodson Bend, Bronston. A true full-service resort, located 300 feet above Lake Cumberland, with breathtaking views of the lake and the limestone palisades. This is the answer to getting away from it all. Wonderful condos, some with up to four bedrooms, a Lee Trevino–designed 18-hole championship golf course, and an upscale restaurant are all right on site.

Conley Bottom Resort (606-348-6351; www.conleybottom.com), 736 KY 1275N, Monticello. With various lodging options, boat rentals, and a full-service restaurant, what more could you want? They have lake-view cabins that sleep up to 10 people, as well as lakeside campsites that can accommodate tents, campers, and boats. At the marina, rent a huge 12-person houseboat or a pontoon or ski boat. If you already have a boat, head to the marina to rent knee boards, skis, and tubes. The **Lighthouse Café** offers lake-view dining with a menu that covers everything from pancakes, to burgers, to deep-fried jumbo shrimp. Something for every appetite. Open daily 8–8. $

THE HARBOR RESTAURANT AND TAVERN AT LEE'S FORD MARINA

photo by Deborah Kohl Kremer

✳ Lodging

✐ ♿ **BED & BREAKFASTS Acorn & Fox Inn** (606-561-7755; 888-561-4704; www.acornandfoxinn.com), 85 Noble Oaks Dr., Bronston. A romantic upscale inn with an amazing view of Lake Cumberland. Amenities include a gourmet breakfast, king-sized beds, and antique furnishings throughout. $

∞ **Doolin House** (606 678-9494; www.doolinhouse.com), 502 N. Main St., Somerset. With a B&B owned by gourmet chefs Charles Sobiek and Allison Hahn-Sobiek, you know breakfast will be spectacular, but the home is a real gem too. This reproduction of an 1850s Somerset home has five guest rooms named for past Kentucky Derby horses. Rooms feature fireplaces, whirlpool tubs, and original hardwood flooring. $–$$

✐ **Farm House Inn B&B** (606-376-7383; www.farmhouseinnbb.com), 735 Taylor Branch Rd., Parkers Lake. On a secluded farm, surrounded by the Daniel Boone National Forest with babbling brooks, rock and cave formations, miles of hiking trails, and a few fishing ponds, too, you'll find this wonderful B&B. The three guest rooms are just down the road from the innkeeper's house, offering total privacy. The loft room is perfect for families, as it has a king and a double bed in one room and a full and twin bed in the adjoining room.

CAMPING Russell Springs KOA Campgrounds (270-866-5616; www.koakampgrounds.com), 1440 KY 1383, Russell Springs. This full-service campground is just a mile from the lakeshore, boat ramps, and boat rentals. They offer tennis and volleyball courts and an in-ground pool. The large recreation hall has cable TV and plenty of video games, too.

✳ Where to Eat

DINING OUT The Cove Restaurant (270-866-9191), 145 W. Steve Wariner Dr., Russell Springs. Open daily. This casual, family restaurant has delicious filet mignon, seafood, and pasta dishes, and the dessert menu fills the needs of anyone's sweet tooth. Try one of these homemade desserts: New York cheesecake, chocolate lava cake, fresh apple pie, or the delicious carrot cake. They also have live entertainment on weekends. $$

Guthrie's on the Square (270-343-6166), 310 Monument Square, Jamestown. Open for lunch and dinner Tue.–Fri. and for dinner only on Sat. Hip but casual, this restaurant recommends their steaks, seafood, and pasta. Known locally for serving really good food, but people just rave about the pecan-crusted chicken and the grilled rib eyes. $$

♿ **Bread of Life Café** (606-787-6110), 14 Belden Ave., Liberty. Open Mon.–Sat. 10–8. This buffet-style restaurant lets you get your fill of southern classics like fried chicken, catfish, and meat loaf. There is always a huge variety of vegetables and homemade desserts, too. The yeast rolls are worth the trip alone. This restaurant has ties to the Galilean Children's

BREAD OF LIFE CAFÉ

photo by Deborah Kohl Kremer

Home, a home for severely disabled children, so patronizing this restaurant is not only good for your appetite but also supports a worthy cause. $–$$.

The Meeting Place (270-343-4030), 340 N. Main St., Jamestown. Open daily for lunch and dinner. This is a family-style diner with choices like sandwiches and steaks. If you go on a weekend, be sure to get the all-you-can-eat catfish or butterfly shrimp. It comes with two sides for $9.99. Can't get a better deal. $

Giovanni's Pizza (270-343-5555), 628 N. Main Street, Jamestown. Open daily for lunch and dinner. A locally owned, casual pizzeria, serving up tasty Italian treats. You can't go wrong with a pizza—either thick or thin crust will impress you. They also have calzones, sandwiches, and salads. $

Mammy Frog's Diner (270-866-3813), 230 Steve Wariner Dr., Russell Springs. Open Mon.–Wed., 10–8, Thu.–Sat. 10–9. Closed Sun. They don't sell frog legs, but this diner has just about everything else. Stop in for a juicy burger or crispy chicken strips. The word *homemade* goes in front of everything on the menu. Casserole and vegetable choices change daily. Excellent pies, but don't think of leaving without trying their oatmeal pie. Owner Lisa describes it as a pecan pie with oatmeal instead of pecans. Add a scoop of vanilla ice cream and call it a day.

🍴 **SNACKS Amon's Sugar Shack** (606-678-4392), 523 S. US 27, Somerset. Open Mon.–Sat. 5 AM–5 PM, Sun. 6 AM–noon. Serving up hearty breakfast favorites, like eggs and country ham. Inexpensive lunch specials during the week. Good food, but the real draw is the huge variety of doughnuts; get there early for the best selection. They are also known for their coconut cake, so get a slice (or even a whole one) to take with you. $

🍴 **Haney's Appledale Farm** (606-636-6148; www.haneysappledalefarm.com), 8350 W. KY 80, Nancy. Call for hours. Come out to this fifth-generation farm, where you can pick your own apples. If you don't feel like exerting yourself, just pick out an apple pie from their bakery. They grow 25 varieties of apples and 10 varieties of peaches. They turn both into pies, jellies, sauces, and dressings that are for sale in their country store.

✳ Entertainment

The Star Theater (270-866-7827; www.startheater.org), 546 Main St., Russell Springs. Hosted in a vintage-1950s movie house, you can see entertaining community theater productions throughout the year. Check the web site to see what's showing.

✳ Selective Shopping

Junkyard Pottery (606-376-8959; www.junkyardpottery.com), 66 P. P. Walker Lane, Parkers Lake. Closed Mon. and Tue. Featuring the hand-thrown pottery of Carol Howe; stop in to see her amazing pieces.

The Mantle Florist and Gifts (270-866-8833), 3213 S. US 127, Jamestown. Located in midtown, what locals call halfway between Russell Springs and Jamestown, you'll find this cute shop. They carry all kinds of wreaths and silk flower arrangement as well as Kentucky souvenirs.

ANTIQUES Barrett's Antique Mall (270-343-5110; www.barnettsantiquemall.com), 150 W. Cumberland Ave., Jamestown. In business for more than a decade, this mall has more than 5,000 square feet of display space. They have everything from furniture, to lamps, handmade quilts, and jukeboxes.

✳ Special Events

🔌 ♿ 🐾 *July:* **The Jamestown Lakefest Celebration** (270-343-4594). Jamestown's annual Fourth of July weekend event, this fun gathering for locals and visitors features arts and crafts, food booths, free entertainment, and traditional fireworks. Good old-fashioned fun.

🔌 ♿ 🐾 **Somerset Master Musicians Festival** (www.mastermusiciansfestival .com). Bringing a wide variety of multicultural, multigenerational, and multiracial music to various stages, this festival has been around since 1994. It honors musicians who have devoted much of their lives and their resources to preserving their musical heritage, and whose contributions have had a significant and lasting effect in their genre. In addition to a weekend full of live music, the festival also features games, arts and crafts, and storytelling. It is held on the campus of Somerset Community College.

Lexington and the Bluegrass Region

3

BEREA AND RICHMOND

DANVILLE AND HARRODSBURG

FRANKFORT AND GEORGETOWN

THE LEXINGTON AREA

VERSAILLES, MIDWAY, AND
SURROUNDING WOODFORD COUNTY

photo by Deborah Kohl Kremer

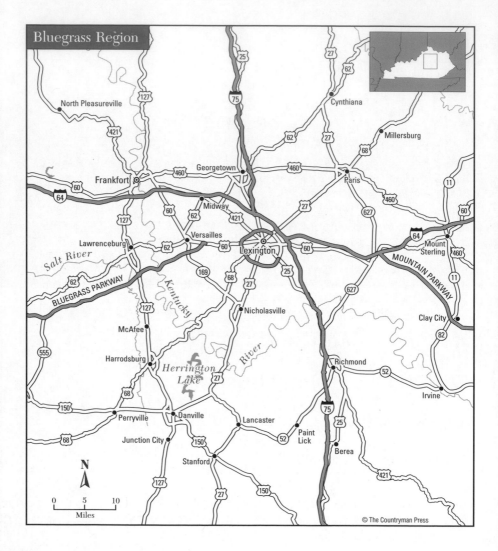

Bluegrass Region

North Pleasureville

Cynthiana

Millersburg

Frankfort

Georgetown

Paris

Midway

Lawrenceburg

Versailles

Mount Sterling

Lexington

MOUNTAIN PARKWAY

Salt River

BLUEGRASS PARKWAY

Clay City

McAfee

Nicholasville

Harrodsburg

Herrington Lake

Richmond

Irvine

Perryville

Danville

Lancaster

Paint Lick

Junction City

Stanford

Berea

N

0   5   10
Miles

© The Countryman Press

INTRODUCTION: LEXINGTON AND THE BLUEGRASS REGION

The Bluegrass Region is like a patchwork quilt of horse farms, tobacco farms, dairy farms, and, well, basic fruit-and-vegetable-type farms.

Its center core is **Lexington**, which is Kentucky's second largest city, and it offers a mix of modern downtown buildings, a scattering of museums, and a large dose of historical sites intermingled in the downtown streets. Although it is not all about horses, there is usually something horse-related on every block.

As you head out of the downtown core and into the suburbs and farming areas, that is where you'll likely see some glimpse of the famed Kentucky bluegrass, which, by the way, is not really blue; it's green like grass should be. It got its name because sometimes it has bluish buds that can be seen in the fields if the sun is just right. No matter what color it is, it thrives on the rich limestone in Kentucky's soil, and is credited for being the key ingredient to growing a fast thoroughbred.

This part of the state is also home to the state capital, Frankfort. The town is bursting with history and also has one of the most awe-inspiring domed capital buildings in the United States.

Also in the surrounding vicinity are the college towns of Berea, Danville, Georgetown, and Richmond. Each a charmer on its own, they offer opportunities for craft shopping, antiquing, and taking in historical sites.

Although this area is located in the Bible Belt, ironically, some of the largest industries are tobacco, bourbon, and gambling on horses. With the decrease in tobacco usage nationally, farmers are looking into other cash crops. Kentucky has seen an increase in wineries (that limestone-rich soil also grows plump and juicy grapes) and the push to legalize hemp. This outlawed plant has been used to make paper, rope, food products, cosmetics, and clothing but is verboten because it is a distant relative of marijuana.

KENTUCKY TOBACCO

photo by Nick Kremer

Although hemp is free of the drug-related chemicals that make up its next-of-kin, it is still shunned for its bloodline.

The Bluegrass Region was the first area of Kentucky that was settled as Daniel Boone and his followers came across the state. When they got here, they stayed. After visiting this part of the state and taking part in the dining, history, and southern hospitality of the people, you'll see why.

BEREA AND RICHMOND

Madison County is home to **Richmond**, the county seat, and **Berea**, which is about 12 miles south of Richmond. The county covers more than 440 square miles and has a population of about 81,000. That population swells during the school year as the county welcomes back students to both Eastern Kentucky University as well as Berea College.

Richmond was founded in 1798 by Colonel John Miller, a Revolutionary War soldier, and named for his hometown of Richmond, Virginia. The area is dripping in history as the home to Daniel Boone, who built and resided at a nearby fort in between exploring expeditions. A reproduction fort has been built on the site, Fort Boonesborough State Park. Visitors are invited to see what fort life was like, exploring cabins with artisans demonstrating candle making and weaving, but you can also camp and enjoy the sand beach along the Kentucky River.

Berea, which got its start around 1850, is named for a biblical town, and started out as a group of citizens sympathetic to emancipation. They quickly established a church, village, and Berea College, which is still the centerpiece of this charming, artistic community.

Madison County saw a few Civil War skirmishes, and today visitors can take a driving tour of the battlefields. To get a more personal feel for that era in Kentucky's history, tour the home of the prominent emancipationist Cassius Clay. The statesman's home, which he called White Hall, is furnished as it was in the mid-1800s. You don't have to wear a hoop skirt, but you'll definitely feel like you've gone back in time.

In the early 1900s, Richmond became the home to what is now Eastern Kentucky University. Although there are industries in the vicinity, the town relies largely on the university for its livelihood. The town has some storybook antebellum homes, a walk-able downtown chock-full of historic buildings, and a notable cemetery.

As Berea College grew over the years, the Appalachian artists who came to the area to hone their craft decided to stay. Today Berea bills itself as the Folk Arts and Crafts Capital of Kentucky. One visit to the city will tell you why. There are craft shops and working artists' studios scattered about, so not only can you purchase these fine items, but sometimes you can actually watch them being created.

Madison County is Kentucky at its best. Made up of rolling Kentucky farmland, and the charm of Berea and the small college-town feel of Richmond, it has all the good things you would want in a travel destination.

photo by Deborah Kohl Kremer

BEREA WELCOME CENTER

GUIDANCE Both Berea and Richmond have their own tourism commissions. You can contact them individually, but they work hand in hand and will both supply you with information about the other.

Berea Welcome Center (800-598-5263; www.berea.com), 201 N. Broadway, Berea. Open Mon.–Sat. 9–5, Sun. noon–5. Closed Sun. Jan.–March. Visit the Berea Welcome Center, which is housed in a restored 1917 L&N train station. You can't miss it, right in the middle of the Old Town Artisan Village. As you enter town, look for signs directing you to Old Town.

The Richmond Tourism Commission (800-866-3705; www.richmondkytourism .com) is located in the Irvinton House Museum, 345 Lancaster Ave., Richmond. Open Mon.–Fri. 8–4. Grab some maps and information and tour this amazing old home while you're there. They have exhibits on Richmond's past and feature a Revolutionary War uniform, one of only seven known to exist today.

RICHMOND'S VISITORS CENTER AT THE IRVINTON HOUSE MUSEUM

photo by Deborah Kohl Kremer

GETTING THERE The closest airport is about 30 miles away, Lexington's **Bluegrass Airport** (859-425-3114; www.bluegrassairport.com). There are car rentals available at the airport. There is also a **Greyhound** bus station (859-986-5840) at 301 W. Jefferson Street in Berea.

GETTING AROUND Kentucky **River Foothills** (800-819-7083; www.foothillscap.org) offers public bus service Mon.–Fri. 9–6. Richmond has two buses that run on 90-minute loops. One bus services Berea; it runs on a one-hour loop. Bus stops are well marked with signs, and schedules are available at each stop.

Both Richmond and Berea are easy to get around by car, with not much traffic and free parking available everywhere.

MEDICAL EMERGENCY **Saint Joseph Hospital Berea** (859-986-3151; www .bereahospital.org), 305 Estill St., Berea. Serving the residents of Madison, Jackson, Rockcastle, and Garrard Counties since 1898, Berea Hospital is a member of Catholic Health Initiatives, one of the largest Catholic health care systems in the United States. It has been continually recognized for outstanding patient care. In Richmond, the place to turn for care is **Pattie A. Clay Regional Medical Center** (859-623-3131; www.pattieaclay.org), 789 Eastern Bypass, Richmond. This short-term hospital has been serving Richmond and the surrounding community for more than 115 years. The facility has 105 beds and services range from diagnosing broken ankles to intensive care procedures.

ALCOHOL Madison County is considered a moist county. Although alcohol sales are prohibited through most of the county, the city of Richmond is wet, allowing package liquor sales and by-the-drink sales.

✳ To See

Eastern Kentucky University (859-622-1000; www.eku.edu), Richmond. "The Campus Beautiful," as it's known throughout the state, was founded in 1906 as a teachers' college. Today EKU offers over 164 degree programs in five colleges to about 15,000 students per year. Full of ivy-covered buildings and lushly landscaped grounds, there is always something to see or do on campus.

Berea College (859-985-3000; www.berea.edu), Berea. Founded in 1855 as the first interracial and coeducational college in the South, Berea charges no tuition and admits only students with limited financial resources. In addition to a full course load, all students are required to work 10 to 15 hours per week on campus. Berea offers bachelor's degrees in 28 fields, to approximately 1,500 undergraduates, 73 percent of which come from the Appalachian region and Kentucky. Take a walking tour of the handsome campus and you'll get a feel for how special it is.

& **Acres of Land Winery** (859-328-3000, 866-714-wine; www.acresoflandwinery .com), 2285 Barnes Mill Rd., Richmond. Closed Sun. and Wed. Owners Lowell and Katherine Land have transformed their former burley tobacco farm into an agritainment business consisting of a vineyard, winery, and restaurant. Tour the farm on their fun and comfortable tractor-pulled wagon ride. Tours are available on Fri. and Sat. at 1:15 and 3:45. Reservations are a good idea. Stop by the tasting room and gift shop before you leave to see their whole selection of wines and enjoy a sample, too.

Richmond Cemetery (859-623-2529), E. Main St., Richmond. This is the largest cemetery in the area. Kentucky's most famous emancipationist, Cassius M. Clay, is buried here as well as many soldiers from the Civil War Battle of Richmond. There is also a Veterans of Foreign Wars memorial. Get a map at the cemetery office.

✒ & **Daniel Boone Monument** (859-622-1000, 800-465-9191; www.eku.edu), University Dr., Richmond. On EKU's campus you'll find a huge bronze statue ded-

DANIEL BOONE MONUMENT

photo by Paul Kremer

icated to one of the first trailblazers of the Kentucky frontier. Boone, who traveled around Kentucky extensively in the 1770s, was a true Kentucky statesman. Make sure you rub his well-polished boot for luck, as so many students and visitors do as they pass.

🔭 **Hummel Planetarium and Space Theater** (859-622-1547; 800-465-9191; www.planetarium .eku.edu), Kit Carson Dr., EKU Campus, Richmond. This is the fourth largest planetarium of its kind—in the world, so make sure you tour the galaxy at one of their public shows. Check the web site for showtimes. Small admission fee.

🏺 **Bybee Pottery** (859-369-5350), 610 Waco Loop Rd., Bybee. Free tours are given on request. They are open 8–3:30 during the week, but plan ahead: They close every day for lunch noon–1. Although it is off the beaten path, 8 miles east of Richmond, Bybee is worth the trip. In operation since 1809, the weather-beaten, dirt-floor barn where they make the pottery is a reminder of this family's humble beginnings. Watch the potters throw pots as they have for more than 100 years and chat with these artists as they work. Bybee produces more than 100,000 pieces per year, and their easily recognizable bowls, plates, and pitchers are sold around the world. Pick up a few bargains at wholesale prices while you are there.

♿ **Kentucky Artisan Center** (859-985-5448; www.kentuckyartisancenter .ky.gov), 975 Walnut Meadow Rd., Berea. Open 8–8 every day. Right off I-75, you can't miss this 25,000-square-foot showroom where visitors can shop for authentic Kentucky products. You'll find superbly crafted glass, pottery, woodworking, metalwork, paper, jewelry, specialty foods, music, and books. They have a helpful visitors center too, loaded with brochures and information. Free.

HUMMEL PLANETARIUM

photo by Deborah Kohl Kremer

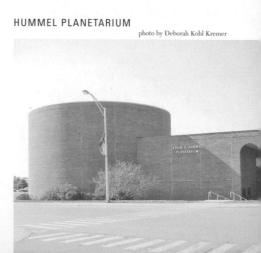

photo by Deborah Kohl Kremer

WHITE HALL, THE HOME OF CASSIUS CLAY

🌱 🐾 **Valley View Ferry** (859-258-3611; www.lfucg.com/trafficinfo/ValleyView Ferry.asp), 169 E. Kentucky Ave., Richmond. Forget the interstate. Drive aboard this old-time ferry and cross the Kentucky River from Madison to Jessamine County. In business since 1785 and Kentucky's oldest continuous business, your short ride will be a memorable one, as the view from down in the valley is fantastic. The ferry is free, but call ahead, as they sometimes close in times of bad weather or high water.

White Hall State Historic Site (859-623-9178; parks.ky.gov), 500 White Hall Shrine Rd., Richmond. Open Apr.–Labor Day 9:30–4. During the winter days and times vary, so call ahead to make sure they are open. This 44-room mansion with slave quarters and outbuildings was the home to Kentucky statesman Cassius Marcellus Clay. The restored Italianate mansion was built in 1798 and remodeled in the 1860s. Costumed guides will take you on a tour where you can take in the period pieces and artifacts of White Hall and the Clay family. Small fee.

♿ 🌱 **STATE PARK** **Fort Boonesborough State Park** (859-527-3131; www .parks.ky.gov), 4375 Boonesboro Rd., Richmond. Situated right on the banks of the Kentucky River, you can enjoy a sandy beach, nature trails, mini golf, and an outdoor pool with waterslides. Tour **Fort Boonesborough**, which is open daily Apr.–Nov. 9–5. This reconstructed fort sits on the site of Kentucky's second settlement, which Daniel Boone helped to establish more than 200 years ago. Each cabin of the fort is furnished to represent the time and features an artisan creating items that were used at the time, such as candle dipping, pottery turning, lye soap making and welding. Also on site is the Kentucky River Museum, which is housed in the former lock operator's home right on the banks of the river. The museum has exhibits depicting the lives of those who lived on the Kentucky River in the 1900s. Admission includes entrance to both the fort and museum. $7 adults, $5 ages 6–12; 5 and under free. **Fort Boonesborough Campground** is open year-round. It offers 167 sites, most with water and electric hookups; there are some primitive sites available, too. The campground is fairly famous for their over-the-

photo by Deborah Kohl Kremer

THE BEACH AT FORT BOONESBOROUGH

top Halloween decorating contest each fall. The campground management supplies their share of inflatable witches and ghosts, but the campers join in, too, marking their territory with pumpkins, bats, and all things scary. It's fun to see.

✳ To Do

GOLF **Gibson Bay Municipal Golf Course** (859-623-0225; www.gibsonbay .com), 2000 Gibson Bay Dr., Richmond. A driving and putting range, as well as a championship 18-hole public golf course.

The Bull at Boone's Trace (859-623-4653; thebullgolf.com), 175 Glen Eagle Blvd., Richmond. This 18-hole championship golf course was created on land that used to belong to Kentucky statesman Cassius Clay. The course winds its way along the high cliffs above the Kentucky River. Legend has it that Clay, who was struggling with a rowdy bull on this site, let go of the beast, which charged away. The bull plunged over the cliff and down the 200 feet to its death. Although this cliff is on the perimeter of the property, the 120-acre course is named in honor of the wayward bull.

Berea Country Club (859-986-7141; www.bereacountryclub.com), 104 Churchill Ct., Berea. Don't let the name scare you off. On the grounds of the country club is a 9-hole, par-36, regulation-length public golf course. It's a nice course, within walking distance of Berea College.

HUNTING/FISHING **Central Kentucky Wildlife Management Area** (800-859-1549), 638 Dreyfus Rd., Berea. Regulated hunting, fishing, and skeet and trapshooting are available on this 1,688-acre wooded preserve.

HORSEBACK RIDING **Deer Run Stable** (859-527-6339; www.deerrun stable.com), 2001 River Circle Dr., Richmond. Enjoy a relaxing day of horseback riding on their farm trails. They also offer hayrides and rustic camping.

TOURS **Battle of Richmond Driving Tour** (859-626-8474, 800-866-3705), 345 Lancaster Ave., Richmond. A part of the National Trust Civil War Discovery Trail, this driving tour with audio guide takes approximately two hours. The battle, which took place in 1862, covered about 17 miles of Madison County. Pick up the audio at the Richmond Tourism Center.

Richmond Downtown Walking Tour of Homes (859-626-8474, 800-866-3705), 345 Lancaster Ave., the Richmond Visitor Center, Richmond. Get a real feel for Richmond on a self-guided walking tour. The route features more than 70 historical buildings, homes, and churches in the downtown area.

✳ Green Space

John B. Stephenson Memorial Forest State Nature Preserve. Get a map at the Berea Welcome Center. Although this park is located in Rockcastle County, it is easiest to find by traveling through Berea. Enjoy the 124-acre wooded gorge that boasts a huge array of natural wildflowers and the pièce de résistance, the 75-foot **Anglin Falls**. The park also offers well-marked trails for nature study, hiking, and bird-watching.

PARK Lake Reba Recreational Complex (859-623-8753; parks.richmond.ky.us), Gibson Bay Dr., Richmond. This 450-acre complex has recreation for everyone. There are baseball and soccer fields as well as basketball and volleyball courts. You can also take advantage of the walking trails, and the huge lake for fishing.

✳ Lodging

⌗ & **Boone Tavern Hotel** (859-985-9358, 800-366-9358; www.boonetavern hotel.com), Main St., Berea. A true landmark in the area, Boone Tavern Hotel was built in 1909 as a guesthouse to accommodate visitors to Berea College. All 58 rooms feature modern amenities, as well as handcrafted cherry, oak, and pine furniture that has been made by Berea College student craftsmen over the past 100 years. The hotel, which is owned by Berea College, is staffed by college students. Berea College, which charges no tuition, mandates that all students must work at least 10 hours per week in addition to carrying a full course load to offset the costs of room and board. $$

The Glyndon Hotel (859-623-1224), 246 W. Main St., Richmond. In operation since 1892, this hotel features Victorian/European decor with an ornate staircase leading to the charming mezzanine level. You'll find original wood-

work, antiques, and nice chandeliers in the lobby. Recently updated, the hotel's 16 rooms are decorated in dark colors with charming features like antiques and old-fashioned braided area rugs. $

⌗ ❝❞ **B&BS The Bennett House Bed & Breakfast** (859-623-7876; www.bennetthousebb.com), 419 W.

BOONE TAVERN HOTEL

photo courtesy of www.kentuckytourism.com

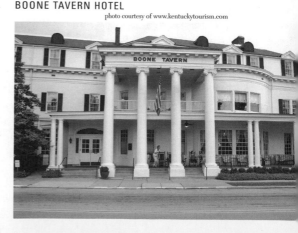

photo by Deborah Kohl Kremer

THE BENNETT HOUSE B&B

Main St., Richmond. Listed on the National Register of Historic Places, this restored 1880s Queen Anne–style residence with Romanesque detailing has three elegant guest rooms. $–$$

The Doctor's Inn Bed & Breakfast (859-986-3042), 617 Chestnut St., Berea. Dr. Bill Baker and his wife, Biji Baker, welcome you to their Greek Revival home located right in the heart of Berea. Guest rooms feature genuine Berea College antique furniture, Oriental rugs, and stained-glass windows. The full country breakfast specially cooked by Dr. Bill features country ham, biscuits and redeye gravy, eggs, and potatoes or grits. $$

The Great House Inn Bed & Breakfast (859-986-735; www .bbgreathouse.com/greathouse2), 317 Jackson St., Berea. This fully restored 1917 Arts & Crafts–style home has a scrumptious front porch with a wicker swing, rockers, and a view of the mountains. The home is a convenient walk from Berea College Square. Pat Greathouse (hence the name), your innkeeper, serves up biscuits, gravy, country ham, and eggs each morning. $

Snug Hollow Farm and Country Inn (606-723-4786; www.snug hollow.com), 790 McSwain Branch, Irvine. Situated about 20 miles east of Berea, this private inn is snuggled right in the heart of Red Lick Valley in Estill County on 300 acres of creeks, wildflowers, wildlife, and mountain views. You can stay in one of the two comfortable rooms in the farmhouse, or tuck yourself into a restored tin-roofed log cabin. Rates include breakfast, which usually consist of oatmeal pancakes with gingered bananas, crunchy oatmeal-cornmeal waffles, smoked cheddar omelets, and fresh fruit smoothies. With not many restaurants nearby, lunch and dinner are available on request. $$

CAMPING Walnut Meadow RV Campground (859-986-6180; www .walnutmeadowcampground.com), KY 21, Exit 76 off I-75 in Madison County. Boasting they are city close and country quiet, they have 103 sites that can accommodate small campers to big rigs. They also have free Wi-Fi.

OH! Kentucky Campground (859-986-1150; okcg2.homestead.com/okcg2.html), 1142 Paint Lick Rd. (KY 21W), Berea. This wooded campground offers 70 sites with water and electric hookups, tile showers, coin laundry, and two pools.

❋ Where to Eat

♿ **DINING OUT Boone Tavern Hotel Dining Room** (859-985-9358, 800-366-9358; www.boonetavern hotel.com), Main St., Berea. Breakfast 7–10, lunch 11–2, Sun.–Thu. dinner 5–8:30, Fri. and Sat. dinner 5–9, Sunday brunch 11–2. Known for its fine, elegant dining, this 100-year-old beauty offers traditional salads and entrées as well as southern favorites like spoonbread, a signature dish that inspired an annual three-day festival in its name. $–$$

♝ **JW's Fine Food and Spirits** (859-626-4767), 246 W. Main, Richmond.

Open 11–11 Mon.–Thu., 'til 2 AM Fri. and Sat. Adjacent to the Glyndon Hotel, this casually elegant dining room is known for their wood-fired grill, the only one in Central Kentucky. They have an assortment of steaks, salmon, burgers, and sandwiches all grilled up to perfection. $$

& ♈ **Acres of Land Winery Restaurant** (859-328-3000), 2285 Barnes Mill Rd., Richmond. Serving lunch and dinner every day. How about some regional cuisine and southern hospitality to go along with your wine? The restaurant specializes in using locally grown ingredients, some grown right outside in the vegetable and herb garden (how's that for fresh?). They offer soups, salads, and sandwiches for lunch. Supper entrées include catfish, pork loin, and grilled chicken options. For something different, try the veal stuffed with blue cheese and doused in Chardonnay cream sauce. Lunch $7–17; supper $$–$$$

& **EATING OUT Main Street Cafe** (859-986-0703; main-st-cafe-berea.com), College Square, Berea. Mon.–Sat. 11–8:30-ish, Sun. noon–3. This is a warm cozy neighborhood

photo by Ellie Kremer

PAPAPLENO'S ITALIAN

restaurant where you'll feel right at home. Their menu says they probably have the best salad in town, and they are probably right. With choices like signature goat cheese salad, as well as Greek, Asian, and Caesar, they've got salads covered. They also have choices like fried green tomato ciabatta, grilled yellowfin tuna steak, and a house recipe for crabcakes. Enjoy live music on Saturday nights. $

& **Papaleno's Italian** (859-986-4497; www.papalenos.com), 108 Center St.,

MAIN STREET CAFÉ

photo by Deborah Kohl Kremer

College Square, Berea. Serving lunch and dinner every day. Walk in and breathe the delicious garlic-scented air. When a restaurant smells this good, you know you're in for a real treat. This Italian, family-style eatery offers favorites like pizza, pasta, and even subs on homemade bread. $

🍸 **Madison Garden** (859-623-9720; www.madisongarden.net), 152 N. Madison Ave., Richmond. Tue.–Wed. 11 AM–1 AM, Thu. and Fri. 11 AM–2 AM, Sat. 10 AM–2 AM, Sun. 10 AM–9 PM. They also serve breakfast to the after-bar crowd on Thu., Fri., and Sat. nights 10 PM–2 AM. Fun sports bar with lots of televisions to watch the big game. The menu features, sandwiches, salads, burgers, bar food, and drink specials. $

SNACKS **Blondies Ice Cream** (859-986-6633), 634 Chestnut St., Berea. Closed Sun. The only ice cream shop in town, you'll have to stop here to get your fix. There's a huge assortment of flavors and ice cream treats like sundaes, banana splits, and shakes. Their waffle cones are homemade, which is a great way for you to enjoy a scoop or two. $

MADISON GARDEN

photo by Deborah Kohl Kremer

✷ Selective Shopping

In Richmond

Alley Cat Pottery (859-582-1148), 246 W. Main St. Featuring traditional and funky tableware and decorative items. The pottery is hand thrown and the glazes are hand mixed from old recipes. Shop located in the basement of the Glyndon Motel.

Big T's Gift Shop (859-623-0083), 2635 Lexington Rd. Owners Travis and Paula Timbrook invite you to look around at all their home furnishings, home decor goods, candles, jewelry, antique furniture, chimes, seasonal decorations, and decorative ornaments. Enjoy the park-like grounds and manicured landscaping there, too.

Jana Kappeler Studio (859-314-4595; www.janakappelerstudio.etsy.com), 106 S. 3rd St. Jana designs stunning pieces of fused glass, creating pieces of art in the form of bowls, vases, and platters. She also offers the works of her artist friends, who create soaps, pottery, and notecards.

The Country Place Antiques (859-623-0629), 2513 Lexington Rd. Situated on a gentleman's farm on the outskirts of town, this antiques store is full of all kinds of unique items. The shop is in a former horse-breeding barn that now breeds your love of antiques.

In Berea

Berea, known as the **Folk Arts and Crafts Capital of Kentucky**, is an artisan community full of craftsmen (and -women) and the studios where they create and sell their wares. Visitors can witness glassblowing, weaving, woodworking, and myriad other talents just by poking through the shops. Berea has three main shopping areas: Old Town Artisan Village, Chestnut Street, and College Square. In each of these areas you will find unique shops,

photo by Deborah Kohl Kremer

LOG HOUSE CRAFT GALLERY

working artists' studios, and galleries.

Log House Craft Gallery (859-985-3000; www.berea.edu/studentcrafts), 200 Estill St., College Square. As one of the oldest craft galleries in Kentucky and one of the best galleries in the nation, this is the place to find genuine handcrafted art. Find pottery, woodworking, wrought iron, and handmade furniture, all created by Berea college artisans. They also have a fine collection of quilts, baskets, and stained-glass pieces created by some of the finest artists in America.

Promenade Gallery (859-986-1609), 205 Center St., College Square. Offering the works of Kentucky artisans, this shop features handcrafted, one-of-a-kind items like pottery, jewelry, candles, art, and ceramics.

Warren May Woodworker (859-986-9293), 110 Center St., College Square. In business since 1977, Warren specializes in handmade furniture and Kentucky mountain dulcimers. You'll be amazed at the fine detail that goes into each piece.

Honeysuckle Vine Gallery and **Hot Flash Beads** (859-986-2411), Depot Circle in the Old Town Artisan Village. Two shops owned by two sisters. Stop by the gallery to see a huge assortment of Bybee Pottery and handcrafted home decor items. Then pop next door and watch Jimmy Lou Jackson as she

WARREN MAY WOODWORKER

photo by Deborah Kohl Kremer

photo by Deborah Kohl Kremer

HONEYSUCKLE VINE GALLERY AND HOT FLASH BEADS

creates glass beads and jewelry using the ancient art of lampworking.

✱ Special Events

✎ ♿ ♘ *September:* **Berea Annual Spoonbread Festival**. This festival honors Boone Tavern's famous spoonbread, a delicious warm, rich corn bread with almost a pudding feel to it, a comfort food for generations. The festival features free concerts all weekend, a balloon glow, a 5K run, a car show, and, of course, plenty of spoonbread.

✎ ♿ ♘ **Richmond Pottery Festival**. Features potters from across the state showing their wares and doing pottery demonstrations. There are also other arts and crafts vendors, food, and a kids' play area.

DANVILLE AND HARRODSBURG

I f you need a quick infusion of history, the towns of Danville and Harrodsburg ought to satisfy your needs. Although Native Americans roamed Kentucky for generations, it was in Harrodsburg that the first permanent settlement took root. Just about 10 miles away in Danville is the location where our forefathers dotted the *i*'s and crossed the *t*'s resulting in Kentucky's statehood.

Danville, a darling college town in Boyle County, looks like the setting for a heartwarming family TV show. It is picture perfect. In 2001, Danville received a Great American Main Street Award from the National Trust for Historic Preservation. It's just that perfect.

Along with claiming the first post office west of the Alleghenies and the first courthouse in Kentucky, Danville was also the site of the first surgery in the state. Today visitors can tour the home of Dr. Ephraim McDowell and see the actual room where this operation took place.

The town square is home to Constitution Square State Historic Site, which is the birthplace of Kentucky's statehood. Tour the centuries-old buildings and learn how Kentucky went from being a county in the western part of Virginia to becoming a state all her own.

THE MASSIVE OSAGE ORANGE TREE

photo by Deborah Kohl Kremer

Kentucky's oldest town, **Harrodsburg** was established in 1774 by James Harrod. Originally known as Harrod's Town or Harrodstown, it was the first permanent settlement west of the Allegheny Mountains. Today there is a full-scale replica of the original fort on the site.

Old Fort Harrod State Park, the centerpiece of town, is a formidable structure, complete with costumed craftspeople depicting the daily life of the settlers who lived here. On the grounds you'll also find a cemetery, a museum, and the Lincoln Marriage Temple, the cabin where Abraham's parents were wed. While you're there, don't miss the best climbing tree in the state. This colossal osage orange tree, which dates back to the late 1800s, is a massive tree full of low twisting branches. Usually full of kids, it's hard to resist.

A stop in Harrodsburg wouldn't be complete without a visit to the Beaumont Inn. This memorable inn and restaurant oozes Kentucky ambience and southern hospitality. If you can't stay there or eat, at least stop by their gift shop and have a look around. This 1840s-era former academy for girls is situated on luxuriant grounds amid centuries-old trees.

Not only was Harrodsburg home to the original Kentuckians, it was also where the religious sect the Shakers chose to put down roots. This community arrived in nearby Pleasant Hill around 1805 and prospered for about 100 years. Today you can tour the original buildings and farmland and learn about this simple religious group whose members were known to shake, shudder, and shiver as they worshipped.

GUIDANCE Contact the **Danville-Boyle County Convention & Visitors Bureau** (859-236-7794; 800-755-0076; www.danville-ky.com) or stop in to 105 E. Walnut St., Danville. **Harrodsburg/Mercer County Tourist Commission** (800-355-9192; www.harrodsburgky.com.), 488 Price Ave., Harrodsburg. Both visitors centers are full of maps, brochures, and helpful information.

GETTING THERE If you are traveling by car, both Danville and Harrodsburg are located just a few miles apart along the 127 Corridor. By air, Danville and Harrodsburg are both about 40 miles from Lexington's **Bluegrass Airport** (859-425-3114; www.bluegrassairport.com). There are car rentals available. **Greyhound** bus service is also available in Lexington (859-299-8804; www.greyhound.com).

DANVILLE VISITORS CENTER
photo by Deborah Kohl Kremer

GETTING AROUND Easily navigable by car, Danville and Harrodsburg offer pleasant driving with little traffic and plenty of free parking.

MEDICAL EMERGENCY The **Ephraim McDowell Regional Medical Center** (859-236-4121; www.emrmc.com), 217 S. 3rd St., Danville. Serving more than 146,000 residents from six counties in Central Kentucky, this medical center was established more than 120 years ago. This 222-bed, not-for-profit hospital is named in honor of Dr. Ephraim McDowell, a Danville doctor who performed the first surgery in Kentucky. **James B. Haggin Memorial Hospital** (606-734-5441), 464 Linden Ave., Harrodsburg. Named for Kentucky-born millionaire James Ben Ali Haggin, this 50-bed, full-service hospital serves Mercer County and more than 25,000 patients annually.

ALCOHOL Boyle County is a moist county, as they allow alcohol sales in the city of Danville, but prohibit the sales everywhere else in the county. Mercer County is technically a dry county, which prohibits alcohol. However, liquor is available by the drink at restaurants in Harrodsburg and Shakertown.

✳ To See

In Danville

✐ ✿ ⅙ **Constitution Square State Historic Site** (859-239-7089, 800-755-0076; www.parks.ky.gov), 134 S. 2nd St., Danville. Visit this site of the signing of Kentucky's constitution, which promoted Kentucky to statehood on June 1, 1792. Ten constitutional conventions were held in a log courthouse on this site, which hammered out the basics for the constitution. The park contains a number of buildings including a tavern, built in 1785, where many heated debates took place prior to ratifying the constitution. You can also tour a Presbyterian meetinghouse, a two-room schoolhouse, and the first post office west of the Allegheny Mountains. Don't miss the bronze statue depicting two friends embracing, representing the motto, "United we stand, divided we fall." Free.

CONSTITUTION SQUARE

photo by Deborah Kohl Kremer

photo by Deborah Kohl Kremer

DR. EPHRAIM MCDOWELL HOUSE

⚕ **McDowell House and Apothecary Shop** (859-236-2804; www.mcdowellhouse.com), 125 S. 2nd St., Danville. Mon.–Sat. 10–noon and 1–4, Sun. 2–4. Tour this home of Dr. Ephraim McDowell, the doctor who performed the first successful surgery in Kentucky in 1809. This surgery was performed without the use of anesthesia or sterilization, which gives you a true appreciation for modern medicine. The home is filled with furniture as it must have looked between 1790 and 1830. Visit the attached apothecary and see all sorts of jars and containers full of medicine and remedies and medical devices. $5 adults, $3 seniors, $2 ages 13–20, $1 under 12.

Centre College (800-423-6236; www.centre.edu), 600 W. Walnut St., Danville. First offering classes in the fall of 1820, this college was actually occupied by both Confederate and Union troops during the Civil War. Today Centre is home to about 1,200 students and offers 26 academic majors. On the 115-acre campus are 60 ivy-covered buildings, 13 of which are included on the National Register of Historic Places. Take a campus tour and see them for yourself.

Chateau du Vieux Corbeau Winery (859-236-1808; www.oldcrowinn.com), 471 Stanford Ave., Danville. They produce more than 5,000 gallons of wine each year, using berries and grapes bought from local farmers. Stop in to tour the winery and have a sample or two while you're there. Free.

JFC Museum (859-236-3442, 800-755-0076; www.bellsouthpwp.net/r/o/rock town), 1369 Stanford Ave., Danville. JFC Museum is open weekends 10–6. A private collection that is now open to the public. See fossils, rocks, minerals, war memorabilia, Native American artifacts, and distinctive items from the area. Small fee.

Kentucky School for the Deaf (859-239-7017), 303 S. 2nd St., Danville. Call for tour info. This groundbreaking school, the first of its kind in the nation, opened in 1823. Tour the restored Italianate structure, which features a re-created 1850s student dorm and classroom.

Perryville Battlefield State Historic Site (859-332-8631; www.perryville.net), 1825 Battlefield Rd., Perryville. Call for tour info. Perryville is the site of Kentucky's largest and most brutal battle. On October 8, 1862, 22,000 Union soldiers battled nearly 17,000 Confederates. The park includes burial grounds and monuments to both armies, plus a museum. Battle re-enactments take place in early October.

In Harrodsburg

⚕ **Old Fort Harrod State Park** (859-734-3314; www.parks.ky.gov), 100 S. College St. A full-scale replica of the fort that was built by James Harrod in 1774 is the centerpiece of this park. Huge stockade walls made of logs enclose the cabins and blockhouses where you'll find interpreters in period-correct clothing performing pioneer tasks such as woodworking, weaving, broom making, and blacksmithing. This park is also home to the Lincoln Marriage Temple, which protects the cabin where Abraham Lincoln's parents were married. While you are there, stop in the Mansion Museum, an 1830s Greek Revival home with artifacts from Native Americans as well as pieces of the Civil War. Look for the huge osage orange tree right outside the fort. It dates back to the late 1800s and is unofficially the largest and oldest tree like it in the nation. It is perfect for climbing. Small admission fee.

🔭 ♿ **Shaker Village of Pleasant Hill** (859-734-5411, 800-734-5611; www .shakervillageky.org), 3501 Lexington Rd. Open Apr. 1–Oct. 31, 10–5; Nov. 1–Mar. 31, 10–4:30. Visit America's largest restored Shaker community. This religious sect, named for the shaking and twitching they did while worshipping, lived in Kentucky from 1805 to 1910. The community thrived through the 1800s, but alas, with their celibate lifestyle, the community eventually died out. What's left now is a village made up of 34 restored buildings, 3,000 acres of preserved farmland, and 25 miles of handcrafted rock fences. Tour the buildings and learn as skilled craftspeople demonstrate techniques commonly used by the Shakers, including broom making, woodworking, spinning, and weaving. Apr. 1–Oct. 31: $14 adults, $7 ages 12–17, $5 ages 6–11. Nov. 1–Mar. 31: $7, $4, $3.

🔭 ♿ **Dixie Belle Riverboat at Shaker Village** (859-734-5411, 800-734-5611; www.shakervillageky.org), 3501 Lexington Rd., Harrodsburg. Mid June–early Nov. Board this authentic sternwheeler and travel the Kentucky River through a 400-million-year-old limestone canyon. Besides the beauty of the Palisades, you will view huge cliffs, towering waterfalls, and unbelievable scenery that can only be seen from the river. $6 per person.

Harrodsburg Historical Society Old Mud Meeting House (859-734-5985), 220 S. Chiles St., Harrodsburg. Call ahead to arrange a tour. This original pioneer-era log meetinghouse was home to the first Dutch Reformed Church west of the Alleghenies. Built in 1800, it is constructed from oak timbers; the walls are filled with mud mixed with straw and sticks.

OLD FORT HARROD

photo by Deborah Kohl Kremer

✳ To Do

DISK GOLF Henry Jackson Park (859-238-1233), Crosshill Dr. off Maple Ave., Danville. This 9-hole, par-30, regulation disk golf course has both amateur and professional tees. Free.

FISHING Herrington Lake (859-734-2364; www.harrodsburgky.com), KY 152E, Harrodsburg. This 3,600-acre lake was created in the 1920s by damming the Dix River. It is 32 miles long and is full of bass, bluegill, catfish, and crappie.

GOLF Old Bridge Golf Club (859-236-6051; www.oldbridgeinc.com), 1 Old Bridge Rd., Danville. This course features a premier, par-72, public, 18-hole golf course and driving range adjacent to Herrington Lake.

Bright Leaf Golf Resort (859-734-5481; 800-469-6038; www.brightleafgolf resort.com), 1742 Danville Rd., Harrodsburg. Duffers will love this 36-hole championship course, with a lighted 9-hole par-3 course. They also have a driving range and a pro shop.

HORSEBACK RIDING Big Red Stables (859-734-3118), 1605 Jackson Pike, Harrodsburg. Enjoy horseback riding on this huge farm, which covers about 1,000 acres.

MOVIES Twin Hills Drive-In Theatre (859-734-3474; 800-734-8011; www .drive-ins.com), 1785 Louisville Rd. (US 127N), Harrodsburg. One of the few remaining drive-ins in the state, it's a fun spot to watch first-run movies all summer long. Visit the concession stand or bring your own snacks.

RACING Lightning Valley Motor Sports Park (859-854-6535, 800-755-0076; www.lightningvalley.bizland.com), 6800 US 127, Stanford. Come watch all classes of go-carts race. Check the web site for race schedules.

SKATEBOARD PARK Danville-Boyle Millennium Skate Park (859-238-1233), off US 150, Perryville Rd., Danville. Skateboarders, in-line skaters, bikers, and remote-control car owners can enjoy this 10,000-square-foot skateboard park every day from dawn until dusk. Free.

✳ Green Space

Danville-Boyle Millennium Park (859-238-1233), off US 150, Perryville Rd., Danville. Created out of 124 acres of rolling pastureland, this park has all the ingredients for recreation. Spend some time on the hiking paths, baseball and soccer fields, playgrounds, concession areas, shelters, and fishing pond.

Anderson Dean Park (www.andersondeanpark.com), US 127, 3 miles north of Harrodsburg. This 213-acre recreational park was built in 1993 and has volleyball, basketball, and tennis courts, an aquatic center, playgrounds, picnic shelters, softball fields, an 18-hole disk golf course, a walking trail, and a skate park.

Central Kentucky Wildlife Refuge (www.ckwr.org), off KY 37 on Carpenter Creek Rd., near Parksville. A 500-acre preserve located 13 miles from Danville and open year-round from dawn to dusk. Visitors can walk the trails to enjoy nature in her purest form. Also a favorite of bird-watchers: Varieties of northern cardinal, blue jay, Carolina chickadee, American goldfinch, downy woodpecker, and white-breasted nuthatch, to name a few, can be seen throughout the year.

✳ Lodging

In Danville
Morning Glory Manor and Cottage (859-236-1888), 244 E. Lexington Ave. This Queen Ann–style home dates back to 1895 and is positively charming. They offer two guest rooms in the upstairs of the home, which share a bath. There is also a darling, and private, one-bedroom cottage out back amid a serene garden. $

Old Crow Inn (859-236-1808; www .oldcrowinn.com), 471 Stanford Ave. This English stone manor house dates back to 1780 and has three guest rooms. Wander the 27 acres of farmland, visit the working craft studio, sit on the patio, relax in the rose garden, or tour the on-site Chateau du Vieux Corbeau Winery. You can do it all, or you can do nothing. It's up to you. $

In Harrodsburg
The Beaumont Inn (859-734-3381, 800-352-3992; www.beaumontinn .com), 638 Beaumont Inn Dr. A true landmark in the area, the Beaumont Inn is the grande dame of Central Kentucky. It's the oldest family-run inn in the state, currently run by fourth- and fifth-generation members of the Dedman family. Offering hotel services with the charm of a B&B, this stately inn has 33 guest rooms in four distinct buildings. Originally built as a school for young ladies in the 1840s, it was turned into an inn around 1919. The main inn building, a true example of Greek Revival architecture, is on the National Register of Historic Places. Rooms are full of authentic antiques like four-poster beds and marble-top dressers. Throughout the property you will find southern-inspired artwork and mementos of past

residents. Walk the park-like grounds spread out over 33 acres, and enjoy the birds, fresh air, and 100-year-old trees. Check out some of books in the lobby area—they are still on the shelves from the inn's days as a girls' school. $$–$$$

♿ **Inn at Shaker Village of Pleasant Hill** (859-734-5411, 800-734-5611; www.shakervillageky.org), US 68E, 3501 Lexington Rd. Enjoy the simple, relaxing style of Shaker Village. Stay in one of the 81 rooms housed in several of the restored buildings on the property. The rooms have modern amenities, like air-conditioning and televisions, with Shaker-inspired furnishings, sparse on elaborate details but warm and homey. $$–$$$

Bright Leaf Golf Resort (859-734-5481, 800-469-6038; www.brightleaf golfresort.com), 1742 Danville Rd. Not just for golf, this resort includes a modern health club, swimming pool, and restaurant, in a casual and relaxing atmosphere. The resort offers a 65-unit motel and 40 private villas. $–$$

THE BEAUMONT INN

photo by Deborah Kohl Kremer

⊙ ♪ **Aspen Hall Manor** (859-734-5050, 888-485-8870; www.aspenhall manor.com), 558 Aspen Hall Dr. This huge 9,000-square-foot Greek Revival home, which dates back to 1840, is surrounded by lush magnolia trees. All four elegant guest rooms have king beds and fireplaces. You can walk downtown but you might not want to leave. $$–$$

Southern Charm B&B (859-734-9340; www.southerncharmbb.com), 363 N. East St. This B&B is housed in an elegant 1831 Greek Revival home and features three spacious rooms. Enjoy modern conveniences like the in-ground pool and the big-screen TV in the family room. Delicious continental breakfast each morning and desserts by candlelight each evening. $–$$

CAMPING Chimney Rock RV Park (859-748-5252; www.chimneyrockrv park.com), 220 Chimney Rock Rd., Harrodsburg. With huge mature trees and wonderful sites right on the edge of Herrington Lake, this campground offers sites for everything from the smallest tent to the largest RV. They have city water, electric, and sewer hookups as well as a bathhouse, laundry facilities, and a convenience store.

✳ **Where to Eat**

✿ **DINING OUT The Beaumont Inn** (859-734-3381, 800-352-3992; www.beaumontinn.com), 638 Beaumont Inn Dr., Harrodsburg. Wed.–Fri. 11:30–1:30 and 6–7:30, Sat. 6–8, Sun. 11–1:30. This dining room is so southern-inspired, it has a giant portrait of Robert E. Lee as well as an orange-lemon cake named in his honor. While hotel guests are welcomed for breakfast, the dining room is only open to the public for lunch and dinner. So if you must have their famous cheese grits, beaten biscuits, and a plate of griddle corncakes, you're going to need to book a room. But if you can hold out for lunch or dinner, you can enjoy house specialties like two-year-old Kentucky cured country ham, yellow-legged fried chicken, and their award-winning corn pudding. For dessert have the chocolate superfecta, three mini chocolate desserts with three shots of bourbon from Buffalo Trace Distillery. $$–$$

♿ ✿ **Shaker Village of Pleasant Hill** (859-734-5411, 800-734-5611; www.shakervillageky.org), US 68E, 3501 Lexington Rd., Harrodsburg. Lunch, weekdays 11:30–2:30, weekends noon–3, dinner every day 5:30–8:30. Reservations mandatory. The Shakers were known for their hard work and vigorous worshipping, which involved dancing, trembling, and, well, shaking. All of this must have worked up some powerful appetites, because they left behind some awesome recipes. The salmon croquettes and fried chicken are oft-requested favorites, but they also serve soups, sandwiches, and salads. If you're going to live like a Shaker, try the Shaker Lemon Pie. The recipe uses every part of the lemon, even the rind, because Shakers never wasted anything. The dining room, which is full Shaker-inspired furnishing, is a simple variety of elegant, but dress is more on the casual side. $$

EATING OUT Red Rooster Café (859-236-2394), 118 E. Main St., Danville. Weekdays 6 AM–8 PM, Sat. 6–3. Right in the heart of town, this is the place to go for a Mom-style home-cooked meal. Start your day with a huge country breakfast, as many locals do. Lunch and dinner choices run the gamut. They have delicious burgers, traditional hot brown, and meat loaf. They're also known for their creamy milk shakes; be sure to clean your plate so you can have one for dessert. $

The Village Inn Restaurant (859-748-5943; villageinn.org), 501 E. Main St., Burgin. Sun. 7–2, Mon. 6–2, Tue.–Thu. 6–8, Fri. 6–9, Sat. 6–8. While it might not be all that fancy, you might not want it to be when you're there for fried green tomatoes and the all-you-can-eat catfish on Sundays. Sit down and visit with the locals. $

Cloud's Country Cooking (859-734-0086), 1028 N. College St., Harrodsburg. Open seven days a week, 11–8. The restaurant is smoke-free on Sundays noon–2 PM. Get better home cooking than you can get at home. Specialties include country-fried steak and their famous dressing mound: corn bread stuffing with hidden pieces of chicken, covered in gravy. They also have a mouthwatering hash brown casserole and butterfly shrimp. $

Olde Bus Station (859-734-4202), 227 S. Greenville St., Harrodsburg. Mon. 6–2, Tue.–Fri. 6 AM–8 PM, Sat. 8–2, Sun. 11–2. Just like the name says, this hometown eatery is located in the former Greyhound bus station. You can still eat at the original soda fountain, or outside on the newly built covered deck. This is a very casual, mom-and-pop-type place with juicy cheeseburgers, plate lunch specials, and a daily assortment of homemade pies. Owner Lori Hill treats everyone who walks in the door like family. $

Aunt Gravy's and Family (859-734-2151), 419 E. Office St., Harrodsburg. Open Mon.–Sat. 6:30–2; Feb.–Aug. they serve dinner Tue.–Fri. 5–8. Nothing says home cooking like the biscuits at Aunt Gravy's. These delectable bites of homemade goodness are even better slathered in gravy. In fact, aren't most things better with gravy? Locals

photo by Deborah Kohl Kremer

KENTUCKY FUDGE COMPANY

come every day for the specials; whether it's meat loaf, spaghetti, or pork chops, it will all be good and inexpensive. Try the homemade butterscotch pie for dessert. $

✐ ᕒ **SNACKS Kentucky Fudge Company** (859-733-0088, 877-892-3657; www.kentuckyfudgecompany.com), 225 S. Main St., Harrodsburg. Closed Mon. Tue.–Fri 10–9, Sat. 8:30–9, Sun. 11–7. Starting out as Smith and Dedman's Drug Store in the 1860s, this old-time location still dispenses all things necessary in life: gourmet coffee, homemade pastries, ice cream, and handmade fudge. Browse the high shelves, once full of medical cures, now full of interesting memorabilia. They have sandwiches and soups, too.

ᕒ **Burke's Bakery** (859-236-5661), 121 E. Main St., Danville. Mon.–Sat. 7–5. Located right across the street from Constitution Square; you can pop over during your tour. This bakery has been around since 1936, and it's a true staple in the community. They offer fresh-baked pastries and sandwiches but are best known for their Salt Rising Bread. $

photo by Deborah Kohl Kremer

BURKE'S BAKERY

¶¶ & Hub Coffee Shop and Café
(859-936-0001; www.thehubcoffee
housencafe.com), 236 W. Main,
Danville. Mon.–Sat. 6:30 AM–10 PM.
Housed in an old department store,
this cute café is warm and inviting.
Stop in for a cuppa joe and some free
Wi-Fi and stay for a deli sandwich,
salad, or wrap. Live music on weekends.

PIONEER PLAYHOUSE

photo courtesy of www.kentuckytourism.com

✳ Entertainment

**Pioneer Playhouse Outdoor Din-
ner Theater** (859-236-2747; www
.pioneerplayhouse.com), 840 Stanford
Rd., Danville. Founded in 1950, this
theater is both rustic and inviting. It
was built with a hodgepodge of building materials that all add to its character. As the oldest outdoor theater in
Kentucky, the Pioneer Playhouse is
credited with starting the whole outdoor theater movement in the state.
Dinner is served on the adjacent patio
area, and choices are limited to fried
chicken or barbecue pork, served with
corn pudding, green beans, salad, and
a cookie. The theater itself is darling
but the shows are first-rate. The schedule includes plays, dramas, comedies,
and musical performances. During
summer a live performance takes place
every Tue.–Sat., come rain or shine.
It does move indoors in case of rain.
Check the web site to see what's
showing.

West T. Hill Community Theatre
(859-236-8607; www.westthill.com),
117 Larrimore Lane, Danville. Named
for the founding member and former
chairman of the Dramatic Arts Department at Centre College, West T. Hill,
the group was formed in 1980. This is
a very talented community theater
group, producing seven or eight shows
each year in their 125-seat auditorium.
Check the web site to see what's
going on.

✳ Selective Shopping

**The Wilderness Trace Art League
Gallery** (859-239-7089), 100 E. Main
St., Danville. Home to original arts and
crafts created by local artists. See
something new every time you stop by.

My Mapletree Gallery (888-666-
4331; mymapletreegallery.com), 225
W. Main St., Danville. Exclusive dealer

of Vietri pottery, Cranes Stationery, and Pomegranate merchandise, this cute shop has items for gifts and yourself.

ANTIQUES **Antiques in Danville** (859-239-0088; antiquesin-danville.com), 4070–80 S. Danville Bypass, Danville. This 8,000-square-foot multidealer gallery of fine antiques, art, and decorator items also has outside display of ornamental iron-work and yard statuary.

Old Kentucky Restorations and Cairn's Antiques (859-734-6237), 122 W. Lexington St., Harrodsburg. In business for 27 years, the Cairn family knows all about the antique furniture they sell. Their main business is antique furniture restoration and repair, but call for an appointment to see their 8,000-square-foot antiques gallery.

Harrodsburg Dish Barn (859-734-4763), 1108 N. College St., Harrodsburg. Set your table and someone else's with their huge variety of china and glassware. They can also decorate your home with lamps, shades, and parts, pottery, antiques, prints, and baskets.

Harrodsburg Flea Mall & Antique Center (859-733-9245), 900 S. College St., Harrodsburg. This is the largest antiques mall in Central Kentucky, with more than 300 booths. Not just antiques but flea-market treasures, too.

✳ Special Events

🖊 ᚛ ❀ *June:* **Great American Brass Band Festival**. This annual Danville event features a wide variety of brass bands, a hot-air balloon race, a parade, and live brass band concerts all weekend. Everyone loves the sound of an old-fashioned brass band.

🖊 ᚛ ❀ **Fort Harrod Beef Festival**. Held on the Mercer County Fair Grounds and at Old Fort Harrod State Park, this festival celebrates Kentucky's beef industry. There is a chili cook-off, a 5K run, called a stampede, juried arts and crafts, live music. There is also a beef grill-off, where teams compete to make the best brisket, steak, and burger.

🖊 ᚛ ❀ *September:* **Constitution Square Festival**. Located right on the grounds where Kentucky's forefathers met and signed Kentucky's constitution. This festival features arts and crafts exhibitors, living history reenactments, food, music, kids' activities, and guided tours of all the historical buildings on site.

🖊 ᚛ ❀ *October:* **Forkland Heritage Festival**. This festival is held annually at the Forkland Community Center, in southern Boyle County. Celebrating the county's heritage and rural past, the community comes together with a true folk festival with arts and crafts, games, educational displays, food, and live music.

FRANKFORT AND GEORGETOWN

These two delightful towns are just about 20 miles apart and connected by Frankfort Road, also known as US 460. The twisty country road is worth the trip itself, as you are privy to historic mansions on the Georgetown end, hand-laid stone fences and horse farms in the middle, and then the sights of Frankfort at the other end. Doesn't matter which town you start in, but both are must-sees.

Frankfort, a little storybook town on the banks of the Kentucky River, is filled with history-laden buildings and darling old Victorian homes. It also has an aura of elegance and importance, as it is the Kentucky state capital.

The town was established in 1786 as Frankfort, Virginia, and it became the capital when Kentucky became its own state in 1792. Today it boasts a population of approximately 28,000 permanent residents, but the daily population swells to about 50,000 based on the workforce of legislators, politicians, and state government employees who commute in each day.

Visitors can tour various state buildings, including the Kentucky State Capitol and Governor's Mansion. You'll wish the walls could talk but instead, and almost as good, you'll find knowledgeable tour guides available to fill you in on the details.

No trip to Frankfort is complete without a stop at the Frankfort Cemetery, where you can pay your respects to the grave of Daniel Boone, followed by a stop at Rebecca Ruth Candy for a free Bourbon Ball.

THE KENTUCKY STATE CAPITOL

photo by Gene Burch

Frankfort is enjoyable because of its unique balance. Although it is the center of Kentucky politics, which can seem somewhat glamorous, its small-town roots allow visitors to find homey restaurants and cute antiques stores and galleries along the downtown streets.

Prior to the 1980s, when Toyota arrived, **Georgetown** was a sleepy little college town with tree-lined streets that accented 100-year-old homes, complete with turrets and porch swings.

Although the downtown looks much today as it did then, the difference is the influx of money and people that came when Toyota opened their massive plant on the outskirts of town. You can visit Georgetown without even knowing there is a 200-acre building on the other side of I-75, but try to set aside time for a tour. It really is fascinating to see these cars coming through the assembly line.

Georgetown was first settled around 1785 by the Reverend Elijah Craig and a group of Virginia Baptists. Craig, who was quite an entrepreneur, settled near the ever-flowing Royal Branch Spring, where he manufactured cloth and paper. He founded a classical school in the town, which has evolved into today's Georgetown College. This wonderful spring was vital to Georgetown's growth. Craig used it for distilling and is credited with creating a little drink that became popular throughout the state, bourbon.

Named in honor of George Washington, Georgetown is known for its antiques district in the lovely downtown, as well as a variety of restaurants and shops scattered about. For die-hard shoppers, there is a 20-store outlet mall right off I-75.

Today Georgetown is an easy mix of industry and farming. You'll find thoroughbred farms just beyond the downtown area in any direction. Go for a drive and enjoy the scenery of horses in their bluegrass fields, acres of hand-laid limestone fences, and rolling countryside.

GUIDANCE Frankfort Tourism (800-960-7200; www.visitfrankfort.com), 100 Capital Ave., Frankfort. Mon.–Fri. 8–5. The darling Frankfort Visitors Center is in a Victorian home with gingerbread trim and a wraparound porch that has an inviting porch swing and rocking chairs. It fits right into the neighborhood of fine homes, so look for the sign out front. In addition to maps and brochures, they have craft items from area shops, as well as a sampling of displays you will find in the area museums. They also have a computer you can use to check your e-mail or make hotel reservations. Friendly staff make you feel like you have a friend in Frankfort. **Georgetown/Scott County Tourist Commission** (888-863-8600; www.georgetownky.com), 399 Outlet Center Dr., Georgetown. Open weekdays 9–5. Right behind the Cracker Barrel, you'll find the tourism office. They have all kinds of brochures and maps about Georgetown and other touristy areas of the state.

GETTING THERE The nearest airport is just south of Georgetown and Frankfort, in Lexington. Fly into **Lexington's Bluegrass Airport** (859-425-3114; www .bluegrassairport.com), which is about 20 miles away from each. There are car rentals available. **Greyhound** bus service is also available in Lexington (859-299-8804; www.greyhound.com).

GETTING AROUND The state capital seems to be the crossroads for every major artery in Kentucky. I-64, US 60, US 127, US 460, and US 412 all come through town, making you feel like all roads lead to Frankfort. Streets are well marked, but a map might not be a bad idea. The downtown area has parking lots and some parking meters, but you can easily park down a nearby residential street. **Frankfort Transit** (502-875-8565; www.frankfort-ky.gov/transit-division.html) runs three routes through the city Mon.–Sat.; see the web site for schedules. In Georgetown, you will find well-marked streets and friendly residents whom you can stop and ask directions from. It is easy to get around by car, with lots of free parking everywhere.

MEDICAL EMERGENCY The Frankfort area is served by **Frankfort Regional Medical Center** (502-875-5240; www.frankfortregional.com), 299 Kings Daughters Dr., Frankfort. This 173-bed hospital has been providing health care to Franklin, Anderson, Owen, Woodford, Shelby, and surrounding county residents since 1896. **Georgetown Community Hospital** (502-868-1100; georgetowncommunityhospital.com), 1140 Lexington Rd., Georgetown. This 75-bed acute care facility has won awards for its excellence in health care.

ALCOHOL Franklin County, which, by the way, is named for American statesman Benjamin Franklin, is a wet county, with alcohol sales permitted everywhere. Scott County, home to Georgetown, also allows alcohol sales, but only in restaurants.

✳ To See

In Frankfort

⚓ ♿ 🐾 **Kentucky State Capitol** (502-564-3449), 300 Capital Ave. Open weekdays 8–4:30, Sat. 10–2, Sun. 1–4. The capital, which opened in 1910, houses the three branches of government. It is highly ornate and very elegant. Created in the Beaux-Arts style, it includes many traditional French designs and elements of classical architecture. The first floor, or executive floor, is where you'll find the governor's office and the imposing seven-story dome and rotunda. This area is home to statues of Kentucky notables Abraham Lincoln, Jefferson Davis, Henry Clay, Alben Barkley, and Ephraim McDowell. Also on the first floor, don't miss "Kentucky's First Ladies in Miniature"—a display of dolls, one of each first lady dressed in her inaugural ball gown. The grand marble staircases take visitors to the judicial floor, where you will find Kentucky's Supreme Court. The third floor is the home of both the Kentucky House of Representatives and Senate. Stop to take in the oil-painted murals depicting Daniel Boone as he explored Kentucky. Free.

⚓ ♿ 🐾 **Floral Clock** (502-564-3449), 300 Capital Ave. Adjacent to the capitol building, this working clock is 34 feet in diameter and created from a variety of colorful flowers. The minute hand alone is 21 feet long.

⚓ ♿ 🐾 **Governor's Mansion** (502-564-8004; www.governorsmansion.ky.gov), 704 Capital Ave. Guided tours Tue. and Thu. mornings 9–11. Sitting on the east lawn of the capitol is the Beaux-Arts-style mansion that was modeled after Marie Antoinette's summer villa in France. It was constructed, trimmed, and finished with native stone produced from quarries in Kentucky. Although it has housed 24 governors since Governor James McCreary moved in during his 1914 term, most of the lighting fixtures, ornamental plaster, and mantels are original. Free.

GOVERNOR'S MANSION

photo by Ellie Kremer

⚓ ♿ 🐾 **Frankfort Cemetery and Daniel Boone's Grave** (502-227-2403), 215 E. Main St. This historic cemetery is situated on a hill high above the state capitol grounds, offering stunning views. It is most visited for the grave site of Daniel and Rebecca Boone, but it is also the final resting place for 17 Kentucky governors. Free.

Kentucky Military History Museum (502-564-3265; www.history.ky.gov), 125 E. Main St. at Capital Ave. Open Tue.–Sat. 10–5. Located in the old state arsenal, its displays include firearms, edged weapons, and artillery and weaponry from the Revolutionary War until today. $4 adults $4, $2 ages 6–18; under 5 free.

Kentucky Vietnam Veteran's Memorial, 300 Coffee Tree Rd. One of the nation's most original and unusual memorials, it is a huge sundial made of stainless steel and granite. The names of 1,103 Kentuckians lost in the war are engraved into the plaza, including 23 missing in action. Each name is placed so that the tip of the shadow touches the name on the anniversary of death.

✐ ⅙ 🍬 **Rebecca Ruth Candies & Tours** (502-223-7475, 800-444-3766; www .rebeccaruth.com), 112 E. 2nd St. Tours Mon.–Sat. (Jan.–Nov.) 9–noon and 1–4:30. Started by two teachers who enjoyed candy making more than instructing, Rebecca Gooch and Ruth Hanly, these ladies left their classrooms and opened a candy company in 1919. Credited with inventing the Bourbon Ball (every woman knows bourbon and chocolate go together), Rebecca Ruth offers all kinds of candy, not just those drenched with liquor. Stop in and take a tour of the factory and enjoy a free sample. No advance notice is needed. Tours $2.

Liberty Hall Historic Site (502-227-2560, 888-516-5101; www.libertyhall.org), 218 Wilkinson St. Tours Tue.–Sat. 10:30, noon, 1:30, and 3. Visit the two notable homes on the grounds. First is a Federal-style house built in 1796 by one of Kentucky's first two US senators, John Brown. The second is an 1835 Greek Revival home called the Orlando Brown House (John Brown's son). These homes are filled with remarkable pieces of the past, but don't forget to stroll the lovely gardens while you are there. $4 adults, $3 seniors, $1 ages 4–18; under 4 free.

✐ ⅙ **Thomas D. Clark Center for Kentucky History** (502-564-1792; www .history.ky.gov), 100 W. Broadway. Open Tue.–Sat. 10–5. Kids love the permanent $2.8 million exhibit A Kentucky Journey, which portrays 12,000 years of Kentucky with the help of 3,000 artifacts, hands-on activities, animatronics, and interactive exhibits. There is also a *huge* research library with rare books, maps, and manuscripts that bring Kentucky's past to life. If you have roots in Kentucky, save time to do a little genealogy research while you are there; the staff are really helpful. $4 adults, $2 ages 6–18; 5 and under free.

Vest-Lindsey House (502-564-6980), 401 Wapping St. Tours by appointment. One of Frankfort's oldest homes, dating back to the early 1800s, this Federal-style house with Victorian features was home to US senator George Graham Vest. Today it serves as a state meetinghouse for Kentucky government.

REBECCA RUTH CANDIES

photo by Deborah Kohl Kremer

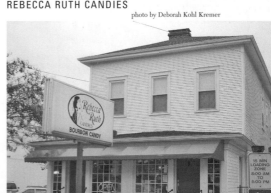

OLD STATE CAPITOL

photo by Ellie Kremer

&. **Old State Capitol** (502-564-1792; history.ky.gov), 300 W. Broadway. Tours Tue.–Sat. 10–5 on the hour. Completed in 1830, this building was used as the Kentucky state capitol for about 80 years. The architectural significance of the building is that this style of Greek Revival had just been introduced into Kentucky. Another architectural marvel is in the central rotunda: an amazing self-supporting marble staircase that is held together by pressure and precision. It splits halfway up to become a double circular staircase, which is quite remarkable. Upstairs, the Senate chamber is furnished in 1830s reproduction desks and chairs. Across the hall, the House of Representatives chamber is furnished mostly in reproduction desks and chairs used prior to the Civil War through 1909. The Old Capitol building still has some original furnishings, including 1840s chandeliers and hand-blown window panes. Free.

Kentucky State Police Museum (502-875-7625; www.ksppa.com), 633 Chamberlin Ave. Open weekdays. A museum dedicated to the rich tradition and proud past of the Kentucky State Police. Memorabilia, vehicles, photographs, and weapons are displayed. Free.

Kentucky State University (502-597-6000; www.ksu.edu), E. Main St. KSU is a small, unique liberal studies university founded in 1886 right in the heart of Frankfort. Two buildings on campus, Hume and Jackson Halls, are on the National Historic Register. Jackson Hall contains a public art gallery that features exhibits by KSU students and the Center of Excellence for the Study of Kentucky African Americans. Blazer Library contains over 350,000 volumes, has a special African American collection, and is open to the public.

In Georgetown

TRAM TOUR OF THE TOYOTA PLANT

photo courtesy of Toyota Motor Manufacturing

✈ &. ☕ **Toyota Motor Manufacturing Plant Tours** (502-868-3027, 800-866-4485; www.toyotageorgetown.com), 1001 Cherry Blossom Way. This tour, which lasts about an hour, includes a video depicting the story of Toyota and how it came to call Kentucky home. After the intro movie, board a tram and take a tour of the 8-million-square-foot plant floor, where you can watch as cars are actually being assembled. This plant produces 500,000 Camrys, Solaras, and Avalons each year. Children must be over eight years old, and you will need reservations for the tour. Visitors center open to the public. Free.

Georgetown College (502-863-8000; www.georgetowncollege.edu), 400 E. College St. This delightful campus, right in the middle of town, was established in 1787 and is the oldest Baptist college west of the Alleghenies. It's a small, Christian, liberal arts school home to 1,300 students. Stroll the campus and visit the Anne Wright Wilson Fine Arts building, which has one of Central Kentucky's largest art galleries.

Cardome Centre (502-863-1575; www.cardomecenter.com), 800 Cincinnati Pike. Cardome—the word is Latin for "dear home"—is a wonderful example of a public building constructed in the 1890s. It has a rich and varied past, serving as a residence for a private girls' academy. Take a tour and marvel in the colorful stained glass, intricate woodwork, and historical significance. Call to schedule a tour.

Ward Hall (502-863-2547, 888-863-8600; www.wardhall.info), US 460W. If you are interested in architecture, make Ward Hall, just a mile outside downtown Georgetown, your destination. Said to be the largest Greek Revival house in Kentucky and referred to as the finest example of this style of architecture in the South. Built in 1853, this home is magnificent in its own right, but take time to enjoy the attractive grounds, too. Call for tour information.

Georgetown and Scott County Museum (502-863-6201), 229 E. Main St. Enjoy displays of artifacts from prominent families of the region, as well as relics from the Civil War and Indian times.

✂ ♿ ❀ **Evans Orchard and Cider Mill** (502-863-2255; www.evansorchard.com), 180 Stone Rd. Open seasonally Tue.–Sat. 9:30–6. Enjoy a day on the farm, touring the orchards where they grow apples, peaches, and pears, plus 30 acres of vegetables. You can pick some yourself, too. They also offer a corn maze, a hay mountain with slides, and a rope maze.

QUILT SQUARE IN GEORGETOWN

photo by Nick Kremer

✎ ♿ ⚑ **T O U R Buffalo Gals Barn Quilt Trail** (502-863-2547; www.george townky.com). This driving tour through picturesque farmland is pleasant, but add the element of searching for quilt squares and it makes the ride doubly enjoyable. Quilt squares are roadside art, 8–by-4-foot squares painted to represent what is usually created with needle and thread. These works of art are painted onto the sides of barns and scattered about the area. The entire trail includes more than 100 barn quilt squares, so take a camera and "collect" them as you meander through the countryside. Contact the Georgetown tourism office for map of the trail.

✷ To Do

C A N O E I N G Canoe Kentucky (502-227-4492,888-226-6359; www.canoeky.com), 7323 Peaks Mill Rd., Frankfort. Offering canoe, kayak, and raft rentals year-round on Elkhorn Creek. Canoe Kentucky can set up a lazy float on the stream, a day of fishing for smallmouth bass, or a ride on the rapids. The choice is yours.

✎ **F A M I L Y F U N Starway Family Fun Park** (502-227-1864), 3350 Louisville Rd., Frankfort. Lots of fun on the 18-hole miniature golf course complete with waterfalls and bridges. They also have a go-cart course, with rookie carts for little ones. Don't forget to bring some change for the arcade room.

G O L F Ducker's Lake Golf Course (502-695-4653; www.duckerslakegolfcourse .com), 98 Buena Vista Dr., Frankfort. Nestled into the rolling hills and pasture land is an 18-hole championship public course.

Cherry Blossom Village Golf & Country Club (502-570-9849; www.cherry blossomgolf.com), 150 Clubhouse Dr., Georgetown. Voted the best public golf course in Kentucky by *Golfweek* magazine. Make sure you try this 18-hole, par 72, championship course.

Longview Country Club (502-863-2165) 3243 Frankfort Rd., Georgetown. This public, par-72 course has 18 holes, a driving range, and motorized cart and golf club rentals.

D I S T I L L E R Y T O U R Buffalo Trace Distillery (502-696-5926, 800-654-8471; www.buffalotrace.com), 1001 Wilkinson Blvd., Frankfort. Tours start on the hour, Mon.–Fri. 9–3, Sat. 10–2. This is the oldest continuously operating distillery in the United States. Tours include the fermenting room as well as the rickhouses where the bourbon barrels are stored while they age. Tastings and a free bourbon ball follow the tour. They also have a gift shop for souvenirs.

Four Roses Distillery (502-839-3436; www.fourroses.us), 1224 Bonds Mill Rd., Lawrenceburg. The 45-minute tours start on the hour, Mon.–Sat. 9–3. Closed most of the summer and major holidays. This distillery, built in a Spanish Mission style, looks like it should be in Southern California instead of on the banks of the Salt River. The beautiful building, constructed in 1911, is on the National Register of Historic Places. Guests over 21 can enjoy a small sample of this smooth and mellow bourbon.

Wild Turkey Distillery (502-839-4544), US 62E, Lawrenceburg. Offers free tours Mon.–Sat. at 9, 10:30, 12:30, and 2:30. Advance notice is requested for groups of more than 10. Closed all major holidays, the first full week of January, and the last two full weeks of July. Guests can view the process from grain delivery through barreling.

HORSEBACK RIDING A Little Bit of Heaven Riding Stables (502-223-8925; www.horses4u2.com), 3226 Sullivan Ln., Frankfort. Feel the Kentucky farmland under your hooves as you ride an Appaloosa horse along the trails of this family-run farm. The name fits.

Whispering Woods Riding Stables (502-570-9663; www.whisperingwoods trails.com), 265 Wright Ln., Georgetown. This 250-acre farm offers wooded trails as well as pastureland for your horseback ride. They have lots of friendly horses or ponies for you to choose from.

RECREATION Georgetown/Scott County Pavilion Recreation Center (502-863-7865), 140 Pavilion Dr., Georgetown. If you want to work out, head for this huge 55,000-square-foot rec center. They have a fitness center, aerobics room, gymnasium with two full-sized basketball courts, an elevated walking track, an eight-lane indoor lap pool, and an indoor leisure pool with a 108-foot slide.

✳ Green Space

✎ ⚐ ❧ **Salato Wildlife Education Center** (502-564-7863; www.kdfwr.state.ky.us/ salat01.htm), 1 Game Farm Rd., Frankfort. Operated by the Kentucky Department of Fish and Wildlife Resources, this 132-acre recreational and educational complex is an enjoyable way to learn about nature. Hiking trails, boating, and fishing are available on site. The indoor education center is full of fun, interactive displays, and even a few live animals. The paved (and handicapped-accessible) walking trail treats visitors to wildlife encounters with Kentucky natives like bear, bison, elk, and a wildcat named Blue, who is the official mascot of the University of Kentucky.

Leslie Morris Park (502-696-0607), 325 Ann St., Frankfort. Right in the middle of Frankfort is 124 acres of forest, virtually untouched since the Civil War era when locals protected the city from Confederate raiders in 1864. Two of these earthwork forts remain intact. The trail into the park, which starts right behind the Capital Plaza Tower, connects to trails with interpretive markers. Be sure to look for the dry-laid stone fences while you hike.

✎ ⚐ ❧ **Yuko-En on the Elkhorn, the Official Kentucky–Japan Friendship Garden** (502-316-4554), 800 Cincinnati Pike, Georgetown. Wonderful Japanese-style strolling garden with walking trails, waterfalls, bridges, and a Zen rock garden. Peaceful and serene; come here to rest and recharge.

✳ Lodging

⁙ ✎ **Meek House** (502-227-2566, 866-646-7650; www.bbonline.com/ky/ meek), 119 E. 3rd St., Frankfort. Located within walking distance of the state capitol, this Gothic Revival home offers comfortable rooms and a peaceful garden and pond area for you to relax. The home was built in 1869 by Benjamin F, Meek, a silversmith who helped develop the Meek and Milam Fishing Reel. $

⁙ **The Meeting House** (502-226-3226; www.themeetinghousebandb .com), 519 Ann St., Frankfort. This pre–Civil War home has plenty of fascinating stories in its past, and innkeepers Gary and Rose Burke love to share them with interested guests. The home still has original fireplaces, floors, and wood moldings to help you soak it all in. The five warm guest rooms are all richly decorated. They also have a charming little café and gift shop open to all. $

⁏⁏ ☉ **Bryan House Bed & Breakfast** (502-863-1060, 877-296-3051; www.bryanhousebnb.com), 401 W. Main St., Georgetown. This stately red brick Queen Anne–style home, features stained glass, 11-foot ceilings, original oak flooring, and walnut woodwork. Relax in one of the three guest rooms decorated with period furnishings. $$

✔ **The Inn at Old Friends** (502-863-1775; www.oldfriendsequine.org), 1841 Paynes Depot Rd., Georgetown. This B&B with two guest rooms is the perfect place to get up close and personal with horses. On the grounds of Old Friends Equine, a 52-acre thoroughbred retirement farm, guests can take part in the workings of a real horse farm as well as meet some former champions in the thoroughbred industry. $$

✔ **Pineapple Inn Bed & Breakfast** (502-868-5453; www.pineappleinnbed andbreakfast.com), 645 S. Broadway, Georgetown. This bright yellow 1876 Victorian home has inviting architecture with gables, a bay window, and poplar floors. Four large private rooms are all decorated with antiques to fit the theme. The Derby room makes you feel right at home. $

✔ ⁏⁏ ☉ ♿ **Capital Plaza Hotel** (502-227-5100; www.capitalplazaky .com), 405 Wilkinson Blvd., Frankfort. Experience gracious hospitality at this 189-room hotel. Within walking distance of the downtown district and 2

miles from the capital, you'll be close to everything. Capital Plaza has nicely furnished rooms, covered parking, interior corridors, an indoor pool, sauna, and exercise room. Check out the nice waterfall fountain in the lobby when you enjoy your complimentary breakfast. Ask for a room on the top floor, where you'll have an excellent view of the stunning Kentucky State Capitol. $

CAMPING Still Waters Campground, Marina & Canoe Trails (502-223-8896), 249 Strohmeier Rd., US 127N. You'll find Still Waters on the Kentucky River, at the mouth of Elkhorn Creek. Lots of RV and tent sites, with water, electric, and sewer. They also have primitive sites for those who are really gung-ho. Everything you need for outdoorsy recreation, like boat ramps, bait, canoeing, and kayaking, is available on site. They also have rugged trails for hiking. $

✸ **Where to Eat**

Υ **DINING OUT Serafini Italian Restaurant** (502-875-5599), Broadway & Saint Clair St., Frankfort. Mon.–Fri. 11–2 and 5–10. Fine dining, right in the heart of the historic downtown. This open, airy restaurant offers big roomy booths, white tablecloths, and upscale menu choices. Try the Kentucky bison flank steak, the ruby-red trout, or the Memphis dry-rubbed ribs, all culinary masterpieces. $$–$$$

Υ **Capital Cellars Wine & Spirits Café** (502-352-2600, capitalcellars.net), 227 W. Broadway, Frankfort. Mon.–Thu. 10–9, Fri. and Sat. 10–10. In addition to their huge wine selection, you can order an interesting mix of salads and sandwiches. Order an assortment of stuffed olives, or try the pimiento cheese and cucumber sandwich served on ciabatta bread with a

photo by Deborah Kohl Kremer

CAPITAL CELLARS

& Ÿ **Galvin's** (502-863-1909), 135 E. Main St., Georgetown. Open Mon.–Thu. 11–9, Fri.–Sat. 11 AM–midnight. Billing itself as a sports bar, Galvin's has great menu choices that exceed your standard bar-food expectations. The roomy restaurant has casual family favorites like burgers, sandwiches, pizza, and calzones. The servings are big, so plan accordingly. The owners are Pittsburgh Steelers fans, but you still might see one of the Cincinnati Bengals stop by when they are in town for training camp. $$

side of Chex Mix. Stop by on Thu. or Fri. night for free wine tastings. $

The Meeting House Café (502-226-3226; www.themeetinghousebandb .com), 519 Ann St., Frankfort. Call for hours. Enjoy soups, sandwiches, pastries, and gourmet coffees in this darling eatery attached to an 1840s-era home. Open for lunch only; you can eat indoors or outside in the inviting courtyard when the weather is nice. $

Ÿ **The Terrace** (502-227-5100), 405 Wilkinson Blvd. in the Capital Plaza Hotel. Open for all three meals, seven days per week. This is the place to go for classic fine dining, white tablecloths, and impeccable service. The menu features steaks, seafood, and traditional dishes. They are also known for their fantastic Sunday brunch. $$

Oasis Mediterranean Restaurant of Frankfort (502-227-3456), 334 Saint Clair St., Frankfort. Open Mon.–Sat. 11–9. The dining room has an upscale feel to it, but the service is warm and friendly. They offer pitas stuffed with favorites like hummus, falafel, and tabbouleh, but they also have more Americanized choices like Philly cheese steak sandwiches, chicken kebabs, and grilled salmon. Check out the Tuesday lunch buffet so you can try a little bit of everything. $$

EATING OUT Johnny Carino's Italian Kitchen (502-223-4401), 1303 US 127S, Suite 600, Frankfort. Open 11–10 every day. This is Frankfort's answer to excellent Italian food, and don't worry, you won't leave hungry. Sumptuous menu choices include spaghetti, ravioli, salads, and sandwiches. $

✎ & **Buddy's Pizza** (502-352-2920; www.buddyspizza.com), 212 W. Broadway, Frankfort. Open Mon.–Thu. 11–9, Fri. 11–11, Sat. noon–10. Named for a beloved dog; take a look at the wall of dog tribute photos. While you're there, enjoy the pizza, salads, and sandwiches, too. They make a traditional pizza, but their blanca pizza—which features a roasted garlic and olive oil base, covered with tomatoes, feta cheese and fresh basil—is outstanding. Try the Kettle Fried Wings for something different. $

Rick's White Light Diner (502-330-4262), 114 Bridge St., Frankfort. Open Tue.–Sat. 7–2. Frankfort's oldest restaurant, sometimes referred to as a hole-in-the-wall, is a favorite with locals and political types. Owner Rick Paul mans the stove and entertains customers at the same time. Enjoy the crazy signs posted all around, and try to sit at the counter so you'll be in the

BUDDY'S PIZZA

photo by Ellie Kremer

middle of everything. Paul serves up some southern favorites like pork barbecue, oyster po'boys, and crawfish pie, but he also has a juicy cheeseburger and fried potatoes that make an awesome meal. Save room for a bourbon ball. $$

Gibby's (502-223-4429), 212 W. Broadway, Frankfort. Open Mon.–Sat.

RICK'S WHITE LIGHT DINER

photo by Deborah Kohl Kremer

10:30–9. Nice family restaurant with a casual feel. Menu choices rival chain restaurants, with sandwiches, pastas, and gourmet salads, but the prices are reasonable. $$

Marshall's Backstretch Diner (502-223-5006), 232 W. Main St., Frankfort. Open Mon.–Fri. 6–3, Sat. 6–1, Wed.–Fri. 6–8. When you have a hankering for country ham, homemade biscuits, gravy, and made-to-order eggs, head for Marshall's. You can sit at one of their well-worn booths or at one of the four stools at the counter. If you're there at lunchtime, they make a good burger. $

Melanie's on Main Café (502-226-3322), 238 W. Main St., Frankfort. Although their official hours are Mon.–Fri. 11–3, they'll tell you they're "Open 'til we're closed and closed 'til we're open." This is a warm and inviting lunchtime spot where you'll find a kitschy decor of bumper stickers on the wall, daily specials written on the big dry erase board in the middle of the dining room, and pretty white tablecloths on each table. Fine selection of soups, salads, and sandwiches. Try the chicken salad sandwich for a real treat. $

Fava's Restaurant (502-863-4383; favasofgeorgetown.com), 159 E. Main St., Georgetown. Open 6:30 AM–9 PM every day except Sun. A part of downtown Georgetown since 1910, this cute family eatery offers a huge variety— everything from snow crab legs to tuna salad sandwiches. This restaurant, which started out as an ice cream shop, still has delectable milk shakes. Enjoy the kitschy collection of Disney memorabilia and coffee mugs. $

Fat Kats Pizzeria and Restaurant (502-570-0773; www.fatkatspizzeria .com), 3073 Paris Pike, Georgetown. Sun.–Thu. 11–9, Fri.–Sat. 11–10. Experience homemade freshness and flavor when you eat any of their award-winning pizzas, subs, pastas, and salads. Save room for their gourmet jumbo cupcakes or homemade cinnamon rolls for dessert. $

&. **Sam's Restaurant** (502-863-5872; www.samsrest.com), 1973 Lexington Rd., Georgetown. Open Mon.–Sat. 7–10, Sun. 7–2. What started out in 1952 as a truck stop diner has evolved into a family restaurant featuring Kentucky dishes like hot brown and sautéed chicken livers. Sam's has a hearty selection of burgers, salads, and sandwiches that still meet the expectations of their original trucker crowd. The cream pies are made fresh daily, and no trip to Sam's is complete without a slice. $

❝❡❞ **SNACKS Kentucky Coffeetree Café** (875-3009), 235 Broadway, Frankfort. Weekdays 9:30–6, Sat. 9:30–5, Sun. 12:30–5. Inside Poor Richards Books is a cozy place to grab a bite. They have a nice selection of coffees, like the delicious Banana Bread Latte. They also serve up soups, scones, and smoothies. Check out the dog bowls outside with snacks for your four-legged friend, who can sit outside and wait for you. $

Adelia's Bakery and Café (502-227-9492), 1140 US 127, Frankfort. Mon.–Fri. 10–5, Sat. 10–3. Located in a little strip mall on the city's west side, this is where locals know come for lunch. Their most popular items are the Cuban, Baja, or Italian sandwiches, which are not your run-of-the-mill deli fare. They also have a tempting array of pies and desserts whipped up from scratch. $

Granny's Goodies Bakery (502-570-0013), 143 S. Hamilton, Georgetown. Visit this cute shop located in an old home and try some of their homemade pastries or their famous sour cream pound cake. Granny also serves sandwiches; locals rave about the homemade chicken salad. $

TEAROOMS Candleberry Tea Room (502-875-0485; candleberry tearoom.com), 1502 Louisville Rd., Frankfort. Open for Mon.–Sat. 11–2. This upscale treat offers homemade selections of quiche, salads, and sandwiches in a cozy inviting atmosphere. Try the bread pudding with bourbon sauce. $

✶ Entertainment

Country Place Jamboree (502-223-3776; www.countryplacejamboree .com), 60 Old Sheep Pen Rd., Frankfort. Take the whole family out on Saturday nights for live entertainment and country music. It's down-home fun.

❝❡❞ **The Upbeat Café & Music Venue** (502-863-5445 www.upbeat cafe.com), 117 N. Broadway, Georgetown. Grab a coffee, dessert, or light meal in this cute eatery, right in the heart of town. The homemade dressings and fresh croutons make the salads fabulous. Come on weekends and enjoy live music.

Georgetown Community Theater (georgetowncommunitytheatre.moon fruit.com). In an effort to bring together actors in the community with Georgetown College faculty, students, and alumni, the Georgetown Community Theater was born. They produce five or six shows a year. Check the web site to see what's in store.

ART GALLERIES Capital Gallery of Contemporary Art (502-564-2649), 314 Lewis St., Frankfort. Open Tue.–Sat. Fantastic collection of original paintings, fine art prints, crafts, and small-press books by artists from Kentucky and across the country. The gallery also includes the studio of owner-artist Ellen Glasgow.

Jessie's Art Gallery (502-227-2495; www.jessiesartandframing.com), 39 Fountain Place, Frankfort. Find signed and numbered limited-edition prints and canvases as well as collectible reproductions by America's finest artists.

Fine Art Editions Gallery (502-863-2299; www.finearteditions.net), 146 E. Main St., Georgetown. See the latest by John Hockensmith, who specializes in equine art and photography, and Rosalind Trigg, an artist specializing in sporting dogs and hounds.

✳ Selective Shopping

Poor Richard's Books (502-223-8018; poorrichards.booksense.com), 233 W. Broadway, Frankfort. This independent bookstore, right across the street from the Old Capitol, specializes in Kentucky works but has all the popular favorites, too. Listen to Kentucky music as you browse the jam-packed aisles. Shelves are so high they have ladders on wheels that run the length of the store, just like an old shoe store. Stop and chat with owners Richard (a former poet laureate of

Kentucky) and his wife, Lizz Taylor. They can recommend good titles and know plenty about Frankfort, too.

The Irish Sea Celtic Shop (502-223-9946; www.leroygalleries.com), 333 W. Broadway. Unbelievable selection of Celtic goods from Scotland, Wales, and Ireland. It is the place to go for all things Celtic: food, china, jewelry, music, and home decor items. If you need a new pin for your plaid kilt, this is just the place.

1792 Store (502-564-1792; www .history.ky.gov), 100 W. Broadway, Frankfort. Named for the year Kentucky became a state, this is where you'll find Kentucky gifts and souvenirs. It is located inside the Thomas D. Clark Center for Kentucky History Center.

Completely Kentucky (502-223-5240, 800-457-1990; www.completely kentucky.com), 237 W. Broadway, Frankfort. Featuring the work of more than 450 of Kentucky's best artisans, they have a huge selection of Kentucky arts, crafts, and gourmet foods.

Stones Throw Artisans (502-867-5897), 116 N. Broadway, Georgetown. This shop caters to what they call yarn folk. You know the type: spinners, weavers, and knitters. The shop stocks all kinds of yarn, spinning wheels, and even looms. You can find works created by the yarn folk for sale, too.

ANTIQUES Georgetown Antique Mall (502-863-1891), 124 and 132 W. Main St., Georgetown. Spread out over two buildings and four floors, you'll find 15,000 square feet of antiques shopping. In business for 33 years, this mall has everything antique.

Glover's Bookery (502-863-1275), 134 W. Main St., Georgetown. They carry all kinds of unusual items. In addition to used and rare books, you'll find African artifacts and even old maps.

POOR RICHARD'S BOOKS
photo by Deborah Kohl Kremer

Heirlooms & Gretchen's (502-863-2538; www.heirloomsandgretchens .com), 136 W. Main, Georgetown. Specializing in stained glass and supplies, they also have lots of lamps and lamp parts, dollhouse supplies, and small antiques. Chances are good you'll find something you need.

OUTLET MALLS Factory Stores of American Outlet Mall (502-868-0682), 401 Outlet Center Dr., Georgetown. Conveniently located just off I-75, this outlet center has more than 20 stores. So you might want to plan some time to hit the outlets.

✳ Special Events

✦ ♿ ❀ *May:* **Governor's Derby Day Breakfast**. Hosted by Kentucky governors for 30 years, this annual rite of spring is held on the capitol grounds on the morning of the Kentucky Derby. All Kentuckians and their guests are invited to enjoy a free country-style breakfast of ham, sausage, scrambled eggs, cheese grits, and biscuits. After breakfast, tour the capitol and Governor's Mansion, visit Kentucky craft and food booths, or sit back and enjoy a variety of musical performances. Free.

✦ ♿ ❀ *June:* **Capital Expo**. Held the first weekend in June in downtown Frankfort, this annual event features juried crafts, live music on several stages, carnival rides and games. Free.

✦ ♿ ❀ *July:* **Cincinnati Bengals Training Camp** (502-868-6300; www .bengalscamp.com). The only NFL training camp in Kentucky is held each year on the campus of Georgetown College. The Cincinnati Bengals, who normally reside about 80 miles to the north, train July through mid-August. Fans can watch the workouts, practices, and scrimmage games, as well as take a peek at who could make the starting team.

✦ ♿ ❀ *October:* **The Festival of the Horse**. This festival celebrates Georgetown's rich heritage and the role that horses have played along the way. This downtown event, which has been going on for about three decades, features horse parades, midway rides and games, live entertainment, a 5K run, and a whole weekend full of fun.

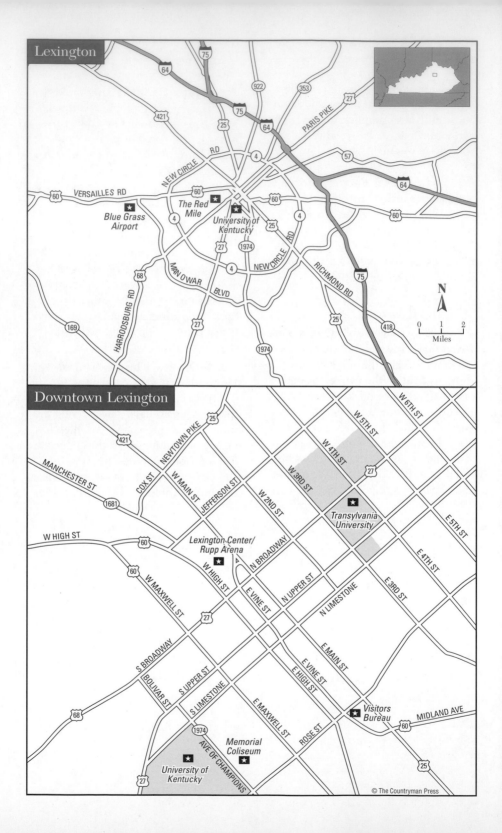

Lexington

Downtown Lexington

© The Countryman Press

THE LEXINGTON AREA

ounded in the late 1700s, **Lexington** quickly became the state's largest town. This growth is credited to the fact that most Kentucky trails and roads passed through the city, and therefore the travelers and the peddlers did as well. Early on, Lexington was known as the Athens of the West, as it was one of the largest and wealthiest towns in what was then considered the West. Unfortunately, with the coming of the steam engine, lots of Kentucky cities were able to enjoy the payload of growth in commerce, so people started heading in other directions. Then, in the 1820s, as river traffic increased, the growth shifted to Ohio River cities like Louisville and Cincinnati.

Lexington did achieve some firsts along the way. In the days long before political correctness, the Eastern Lunatic Asylum, one of the first psychiatric hospitals in the country, opened in Lexington around 1824. Also in the 1820s, Lexington's Transylvania University became one of the most notable schools in the country, specializing in law and medicine, drawing the attention and the admissions of some very notable families.

The city has a rich past, evident by museums and historical markers. It was home to the infamous John Hunt Morgan, a Confederate soldier known for his raids in Kentucky. You can tour his home as well as those of statesman Henry Clay and the girlhood home of Mary Todd, who grew up to be Mrs. Abraham Lincoln.

Today's population hovers around 275,000 in the urban county area. This population fluctuates somewhat when the 26,000 students at University of Kentucky are on campus. It also increases when the beloved UK Wildcats have a home game. For basketball, it is not uncommon for 24,000 fans to migrate to downtown's Rupp Arena to see the Cats in action. At Commonwealth Stadium, where the football team plays, you can find about 70,000 fans decked out in blue and white on Saturdays in fall. These people are serious tailgaters, holding pregame parties in parking lots, open fields, and front yards. Bring some fried chicken and make new friends on your way to the game.

If you want to spend some time with horses, Lexington's your place. It is home to the Kentucky Horse Park, Keeneland Race Track, the Red Mile Race Course, and loads of horse farms. In 2010 it will be the site of the FEI World Equestrian Games. This is the first time this prestigious event, held every four years, will take place outside Europe. Expected to draw more than 500,000 people, it will be the largest equestrian sporting event ever held in the United States.

Lexington is the heart of Kentucky with miles of bluegrass farmland, an active

photo by Deborah Kohl Kremer

TAILGATING AT THE UK GAME

urban center, amazing examples of the past, and modern-day amenities that all mix together nicely.

GUIDANCE Right in the center of town, you'll find the **Lexington Convention & Visitors Bureau** (859-233-7299, 800-845-3959; www.visitlex.com), 301 E. Vine St., Lexington. They are available to help seven days a week.

GETTING THERE If you fly into the **Bluegrass Airport** in Lexington (859-425-3114; www.bluegrassairport.com), be sure to look out the window as you come in for a landing. The airport is located very close to the famous Calumet Horse Farm and Keeneland Race Track. Seeing a bird's-eye view of these world-renowned facilities devoted to horses, just as you arrive—well, it makes a wonderful welcome mat to the Horse Capital of the World. If you travel by bus, **Greyhound** service is available in Lexington (859-299-8804; www.greyhound.com), 477 W. New Circle Rd.

GETTING AROUND Although Lexington is close to both I-64 and I-75, neither of these highways runs through the city. The downtown area is made up of roads that run from downtown to a suburban community and are named for the community—Richmond Road, Nicholasville Road, and Harrodsburg Road, for instance—so you always know where you are headed. There is also an inner beltway, New Circle Road, which connects these roads that head out of town and make up the spokes of the wheel. Sometimes rush-hour commuters refer to it as "New Circus Road," as drivers get a little nutty on their way to the suburbs.

For public bus service, **LexTran** (859-253-4636; www.lextranonthemove.org), 200 E. Vine St., Lexington, operates eight routes 5:30 AM–11:20 PM seven days a week from the Lexington Transit Center along Vine Street in downtown. Taxicab service is also available through **American Taxi Cab Company**, 859-381-1010.

MEDICAL EMERGENCY If you are going to get sick, Lexington is the place to do it. The city is served by some of the nation's most respected hospitals.

University of Kentucky Healthcare (859-257-1000; www.ukhealthcare.uky.edu), 800 Rose St., Lexington. The largest health care system in the commonwealth, with facilities that include UK Chandler Hospital, Kentucky Children's Hospital, UK HealthCare East, Kentucky Clinic, Polk-Dalton Clinic, Kentucky Clinic South, and 80 specialized clinics. They have been chosen as one of America's Best Hospitals by *US News and World Report*.

Central Baptist Hospital (859-260-6100; www.centralbap.com), 1740 Nicholasville Rd., Lexington. This 371-bed major medical center is well respected for advances in cardiac research.

St. Joseph Hospital (859-313-1000; www.sjhlex.org), 1 Saint Joseph Dr., Lexington. Nationally recognized for treatment in the areas of cardiology, orthopedics, and stroke, this 468-bed medical center is known as Lexington's Heart Hospital.

ALCOHOL Fayette County is a wet county, meaning alcohol sales are permitted everywhere.

✳ To See

𝒮 ⅋ **Kentucky Horse Park** (859-233-4303, 800-678-8813; www.kyhorsepark .com), 4089 Iron Works Pike, Lexington. Open every day, year-round, because horses are always in-season. This 1,200-acre working horse farm is the place to go to learn about horses and see them in their natural setting. The park features nearly 50 different breeds, and in the daily Parade of Breeds visitors get to see several varieties. Don't miss the award-winning 23-minute film called *Thou Shall Fly Without Wings*—a perfect introduction to the dynamic world of the horse. The park features museum exhibits, demonstrations, and shows. They also offer horseback riding for an additional fee. This is a park that you can tour at your own pace, where you can relax and just enjoy the surroundings. You'll know you're there when you see the 30 miles of white plank fencing that surrounds it. Mar. 15–Oct. 31: $15 adults, $8 ages 7–12; 6 and under free. Nov. 1–Mar. 14: $9, $6, free.

University of Kentucky (859-257-3595; www.uky.edu), Lexington. What started in 1865 as a land-grant institution near downtown Lexington, UK now has a campus that covers more than 716 acres and is home to over 26,000 students. Stroll the grounds of the campus and stop by the William T. Young Library, a massive 365,000-square-foot, six-story octagonal building. If you need something to read, maybe you could find something among its 1.2 million volumes.

Transylvania University (859-233-8300; www.transy.edu), 300 N. Broadway, Lexington. In 1780, when Transylvania opened, it was only the 16th college in the

KENTUCKY HORSE PARK

photo by Deborah Kohl Kremer

United States. Famous alumni include Steve Austin and Cassius Clay, as well as 50 US senators, 101 US representatives, and 36 governors. Today this liberal arts college, with approximately 1,100 students, has a warm, inviting campus right in the downtown area. Make an appointment to see the Monroe Moosnick Medical and Science Museum, a rare collection of anatomical models and science artifacts from the early 1800s. It will make you appreciate modern medicine. Also on campus is one of the first log cabins built in Lexington. This home, built around 1775, belonged to Robert Patterson, one of the founding fathers of Lexington and Transylvania. Another option while you're in the area is to grab your sweetheart and steal a kiss under the famous Kissing Tree. Transy's answer to mistletoe, this 250-year-old white ash tree is said to be the most romantic place on campus.

photo by Deborah Kohl Kremer

TRANSYLVANIA U

♂ ও **Headley-Whitney Museum** (859-255-6653; www.headley-whitney.org), 4435 Old Frankfort Pike, Lexington. Tue.–Fri. 10–5, Sat.–Sun. noon–5. Visit the former home of George W. Headley III, a famous designer of jewelry and unique ornate objects called bibelots. See amazing displays of gemstones, shells, and miniatures. As an affiliate of the Smithsonian Institution, a wing has been added to feature revolving exhibits from Washington, DC. $7 adults, $5 ages 62 and up, $5 students; ages 5 and under free.

Ashland, The Henry Clay Estate (859-266-8581; www.henryclay.org), 120 Sycamore Rd., Lexington. Open Mar.–Dec., Tue.–Sat. 10–4, Sun. 1–4. Home of the famous Kentucky statesman Henry Clay. Said to be a mentor to Abraham Lincoln, Clay lived here from 1806 until his death in 1852. This 600-acre plantation grew hemp, tobacco, and grains and was home to about 50 slaves. Clay named the property Ash Land for the huge number of massive ash trees that stood on the property. The one-hour tour includes the 18-room Italianate-style main house, outbuildings, and lush garden area. You can grab a sandwich or snack at the **Ginkgo Tree Cafe** (open mid-Apr.–mid-Oct.). $7 adults, $3 ages 6–18; 5 and under free.

ASHLAND, THE HOME OF HENRY CLAY
photo by Deborah Kohl Kremer

♂ ☕ **Ale 8 One** (859-744-3484; www.ale-8-one.com), 25 Carol Rd., Winchester. Kentucky is known for another drink besides bourbon: Ale 8 One is a carbonated citrusy drink that Central Kentuckians are raised on. When locals say the name, it comes out sounding like *A Late One*, and you might not know what they are referring to. You'll catch on quickly when you pull up to any shopping center, where you'll likely see five Ale 8 One vending machines and just one for Coke or Pepsi. This is definitely the soft drink of choice for the region. You can take a 30-minute tour of the factory in Winchester every Friday at 10:50. Don't forget to call ahead to make a reservation. At the end of the tour you can shop their company store, where you can buy a few cases of this fizzy drink and even a T-shirt to wear home.

photo by Deborah Kohl Kremer

HUNT MORGAN HOUSE

Hunt Morgan House and Civil War Museum (859-233-3290; www.bluegrass trust.org), 201 N. Mill St., Lexington. Open for tours Wed.–Sun. mid-April–mid-Dec. Call for hours. Built in 1814, this Federal-style home was an architectural wonder of its time. Home to John Wesley Hunt, the first millionaire of the New West, John Hunt Morgan, a radical soldier of the Confederacy, and Nobel Prize winner Thomas Hunt Morgan. This home features artwork and furnishings that once belonged to this notable family. The second floor has an extensive collection of Civil War memorabilia. $7 adults, $5 students.

✎ **Explorium of Lexington** (859-258-3253; www.explorium.com), 440 W. Short St., Lexington. Tue.–Sat. 10–5, Sun. 1–5. Formerly known as the Lexington Children's Museum. Kids of all ages will enjoy the hand-on exhibits. See what it feels like to be inside a bubble, explore the human brain, or learn all about dinosaurs. $6 per person over the age of 1.

& ❦ **Lexington History Museum** (859-254-0530; www.lexingtonhistorymuseum .org), 215 W. Main St., Lexington. Call for hours and exhibits. Housed in the former Fayette County Courthouse, this museum offers rare peaks into Lexington and Kentucky history. Free.

Lexington Cemetery (859-255-5522; www.lexcem.org), 833 W. Main St., Lexington. Established in 1849 and encompassing 170 acres of fully landscaped gardens, this feels more like a park than a cemetery. It is the final resting place of many Civil War soldiers and famous Kentuckians.

MARY TODD LINCOLN HOUSE

Mary Todd Lincoln House (859-233-9999; www.mtlhouse.org), 578 W. Main St., Lexington. Open Feb. 18–Nov. 30, Mon.–Sat. 10–4. The first museum in America to honor a first lady. Tour the girlhood home of Mary Todd, who became the wife of Abraham Lincoln. This two-story brick Georgian home was built in 1806 and is filled with period pieces, some original to the home. The Lincolns and their children spent time in this

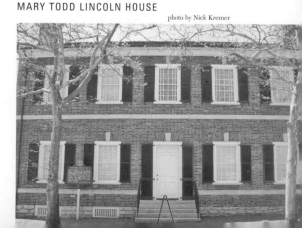

photo by Nick Kremer

photo by Deborah Kohl Kremer

LEXINGTON HISTORY MUSEUM

magnificent home, and there are some artifacts from the 16th president on the third floor. $7 adults, $4 ages 6–12; under 6 free.

Waveland State Historic Site (859-272-3611; parks.ky.gov), 225 Waveland Museum Ln., Lexington. Mar. 1–Dec. 15, Mon.–Sat. 10–5, Sun. 1–5. Dec. 16–end of Feb., Tue.–Sat. 10–3. Tour the home of the Joseph Bryan family, who followed Daniel Boone through the Cumberland Gap and became early settlers of Kentucky. The site includes the 1848 Greek Revival antebellum home, three original outbuildings, slave quarters, smokehouse, and icehouse. $7 adults, $6 seniors, $4 children.

✐ **The Thoroughbred Center** (859-293-1853; www.thethoroughbredcenter .com), 3380 Paris Pike, Lexington. Guided tours at 9 AM. Experience a day in the life of a thoroughbred in training. At this 240-acre site, you can tour the various tracks, barns, and paddocks, and talk to trainers who hope their young colts get to experience the Run for the Roses someday. Learn about the cost of training a thoroughbred, how much exercise is required, and even how they teach a horse to go into the starting gate. This tour is suitable for all ages but does involve getting on and off a bus a few times. Reservations recommended, especially in spring and fall. $10 adults, $5 children.

THOROUGHBRED CENTER

photo by Deborah Kohl Kremer

KENTUCKY HORSE FARMS

Horse racing has been a part of the human culture as far back in time as ancient humans who drew hieroglyphics of such races on cave walls. It has deep roots into Kentucky history, too.

As early as the 1775 Transylvania Convention, Daniel Boone introduced the first bill "to improve the breed of horses in the Kentucky territory." As forts transformed into cities, many Kentucky towns had a "Race Street" used for, yes, racing horses. And according to history books, the Lexington Jockey Club was formed in 1809 with famous Kentucky statesman Henry Clay as a founding member.

As home to the infamous Kentucky Derby, which first ran in 1875, the Bluegrass State became known for fast horses and beautiful women, although sometimes the adjectives are swapped if the speaker has had one too many bourbon-laced mint juleps.

The horse industry progressed in Kentucky, probably due to the rolling acres of pasture, the limestone-rooted bluegrass—or, most likely because religious reformers were shutting down tracks in the East. Lexington always had a nice track, with plenty of affluent fans ready to make a wager.

Nonetheless, thoroughbreds from Kentucky took on a pedigree status, and people came from all over the world to witness Kentucky horse racing. The tradition continues today, as Kentucky is home to famous tracks like Churchill Downs and Keeneland and more than 450 horse farms in the Bluegrass Region, with nearly 150 in Lexington's Fayette County alone.

Witnessing a Kentucky horse race is something all visitors should do while in the state, but if schedules and itineraries don't match up, maybe you could take in a horse farm tour while in the area.

Several tour companies operate in the Lexington area. They will pick you up at your hotel and give you a great overview of horses, farms, tracks, and the area. They stop at a few farms where you can actually see where the horses are raised, trained, and bred.

If you are more interested in just heading straight to a farm for your own tour, that's fine, too, but you must remember to call ahead and schedule an appointment, as well as remember to tip your groom (somewhere in the $5-per-person range) when your tour is complete.

There is much involved in the life of a thoroughbred, and in the Lexington area, you can learn about each step of a horse's life. Visit Three Chimneys Farm, where they specialize in breeding, the Thoroughbred Center, where they specialize in training, and Old Friends, a farm where they specialize in horse retirement.

At **Three Chimneys Farm** (859-873-7053; www.threechimneys.com) in

Versailles, one-hour walking tours are given Tue.–Sat. at 1. These tours are by reservation only and they do fill up fast, so call well in advance of your trip. This farm, owned by Robert Clay, began as a small 100-acre site in 1972. It is the former home of infamous Seattle Slew; today Kentucky Derby winners Smarty Jones and Big Brown live comfortably there.

"When the Clays started this farm, they had the ambition of being a worldwide name, but never imagined that someday they would have more than 2,000 acres and welcome more than 25,000 visitors per year," said Ann Hays, director of tours.

THREE CHIMNEYS

photo by Deborah Kohl Kremer

The tour covers aspects of the thoroughbred business as well as breeding. "Sometimes in the spring, the visitors actually get to witness the breeding," Hays added. "Although it is very interesting, it is sometimes a little much for children."

Just like five-year-olds go to kindergarten, prospective race horses go to the **Thoroughbred Center** (859-293-1853; www.thethoroughbredcenter.com) in Lexington when they are about two. It is here that they live and learn to run the track, get used the starting gate, and train to race.

Taking advantage of the daily one-hour tours is a great way for visitors to see what goes into the making of a racehorse.

"It is a behind-the-scenes look at racing," said Ann Wilson, who arranges the tours. "It's not a place to come to ride or pet horses, but a place to learn about the racing profession."

This 200-acre facility has two training tracks and can board and train about 1,000 horses at a time. Wilson noted that you can see the horses up close but you also get a taste for their workouts and the training involved. "Our visitors are usually just in love with horses when they come, and they have so much respect for horses when they leave."

After a few years of racing, a horse usually becomes a breeder. They head back to the farm and have a pretty nice life filled with, uh, well, breeding. But that chapter, too, closes on a horse's life, and the future is retirement.

Although you won't find shuffleboard or bingo games at this retirement home, the old folks here can spend their days as they please. Based in Georgetown, **Old Friends, A Kentucky Facility for Retired Thoroughbreds** (502-863-1775; www.oldfriendsequine.org) is a welcoming place for horses to live out their golden years.

"When we bring horses here, you can just see them unwind," said Michael Blowen, president and founder. "They go from being competitive and high-strung athletes to laid-back, relaxed horses."

Specializing in stallions (because they typically require a little more care and separate paddocks), the facility is one of a kind. They welcome all retired horses here, however, and go above and beyond to keep older animals out of the slaughterhouse.

"If we hear of a stallion in Japan that has finished his breeding career, we begin fund-raising to bring him home," said Blowen. "We've brought five back to Lexington from Japan, and we are willing to bring more."

Free, hour-long tours are given daily so visitors can get to know the residents. As you hear each horse's story, you begin to feel you are in the presence of celebrities, and rightly so. Horses such as Sunshine Forever, the 1988 Turf Horse of the Year, and Williamstown, who held the 10-year record for the mile at Belmont Park, call Old Friends home.

Incorporating an aspect of the horse industry into your trip to the Bluegrass is a must. But the good news is, the opportunities are limitless. Whether you visit one of the establishments listed above or spend a day at the huge **Kentucky Horse Park** (www.kyhorsepark .com), tradition-steeped **Keeneland Race Track** (www.keeneland.com), or history-rich horse farms like **Claiborne Farm** (www.claiborne farm.com) and **Gainesway Farm** (www.gainesway.com), your trip is sure to be a winner.

photo by Deborah Kohl Kremer

CREATOR, A RETIRED HORSE AT
OLD FRIENDS

photo by Deborah Kohl Kremer

KEENELAND RACE TRACK

✳ To Do

 ⛶ **HORSE RACING Keeneland Race Track** (859-254-3412, 800-456-3412; ww2.keeneland.com), 4201 Versailles Rd., Lexington. Conducting live race meets in Apr. and Oct. since 1936, this thoroughbred track is steeped with tradition. The fieldstone grandstand looks as stunning when the surrounding cherry blossom trees are in bloom as it does when it is wrapped in the dramatic colored leaves of fall. Come for the racing but stay for the scenery. You'll also find a gift shop and track eateries where you can try famous Kentucky burgoo as well as the heady bread pudding with bourbon sauce.

⛶ **Red Mile Harness Track** (859-255-0752; www.theredmile.com), 1200 Red Mile Rd., Lexington. It's not just about thoroughbred racing in Kentucky. Come to the Red Mile and watch the harness racing, where horses pull two-wheeled carts called sulkies. The track, the second oldest in the country, is open year-round for simulcasting. Check the web site for live racing dates.

GOLF Tates Creek Golf Course (859-272-3428), 1400 Gainesway Dr., Lexington. This par-72, 18-hole public course has been around since 1958 and is a true favorite of Lexington golfers.

Meadowbrook Golf Course (859-272-3115), 370 Wilson Downing Rd., Lexington. an inexpensive 18-hole, par-55 course. Greens fees include a golf cart.

Peninsula Golf Resort (859-548-5055, 877-249-4747; www.penisulagolf.com), 200 Clubhouse Dr., Lancaster. Just south of Lexington, but worth the drive, is this 18-hole championship course. Stay at the furnished two-bedroom condos right alongside the course for a perfect golf-weekend getaway.

MINOR-LEAGUE BASEBALL Lexington Legends (859-252-4487; www
.lexingtonlegends.com), 207 Legends Ln., Lexington. This minor-league baseball
team is an affiliate of the Houston Astros. The games are fun, so if the Legends
are in town when you are, try to take in a game. Their home field, Applebee's
Park, is not too far from downtown.

TOURS Blue Grass Tours (859-252-5744, 800-755-6956; bluegrasstours.com),
817 Enterprise Dr., Lexington. See the sites of Lexington and the region on one of
their bus tours. It's a great way to take in all the sites of Lexington in just a few
hours.

Lexington Livery Horse-Drawn Carriage Tours (859-259-0000; www.lexing
tonlivery.com), 171 Saunier Ave., Lexington. Enjoy the clippity-clop of horse
hooves as you relax for a carriage ride. Tours depart each evening from Broadway
and Vine St.; both 30-minute and one-hour tours are offered.

✳ Green Space

Raven Run Nature Sanctuary (859-272-6105; www.lfucg.com/parks/raven.asp),
5888 Jacks Creek Rd., Lexington. Enjoy 11 miles of hiking trails along the Kentucky River Palisades in this 734-acre nature preserve. Raven Run is home to
over 56 species of trees, 600 species of plants, 200 species of birds, and other
wildlife.

University of Kentucky Arboretum (859-257-6955; www.ca.uky.edu/arboretum),
500 Alumni Dr., Lexington. Spread out over 100 acres, this arboretum lets you
enjoy nature at her finest. Open year-round so you can learn about native trees,
grasses, and flowers, but plan your visit to coincide with the blooming of the 1,500
varieties of roses.

PARKS McConnell Springs (859-
225-4073) 416 Rebmann Ln., Lexington. You might think you're lost as you
enter this industrial park, but keep
going and you'll end up at McConnell
Springs. Hike the 2 miles of trails that
surround the natural springs on this
26-acre park. It's a combination of
nature and history, as it was the original campsite for the first settlers in the
Bluegrass Region.

♪ Thoroughbred Park (859-288-
2900) E. Main St. at Midland Ave.,
Lexington. Not really a park, more like
a drive-by attraction. See seven life-
sized bronze racehorses that appear to
be galloping along the sidewalk to the
finish line. Located right downtown.

THOROUGHBRED PARK

photo by Deborah Kohl Kremer

✳ Lodging

♿ **Gratz Park Inn** (859-231-1777, 800-752-4166; www.gratzparkinn.com), 120 W. 2nd St., Lexington. This luxury boutique inn offers 42 rooms, each decorated in 19th-century antique reproductions, exquisite mahogany furniture, and local artwork. $$$

Bed & Breakfast at Silver Springs Farm (859-255-1784; www.bbsilver springsfarm.com), 3710 Leestown Pike, Lexington. This farm operated as a distillery from 1867 to Prohibition, and although those days are over, the natural spring still runs through the property. The Federal-style home has all the modern-day features, as well as the original floors and woodwork and period antiques. Book a room for yourself and one for your horse, too, as they have comfy accommodations for both of you. $$

✐ **Lyndon House Bed and Breakfast** (859-420-2683; www.lyndonhouse .com), 507 N. Broadway, Lexington. This fascinating home was built in 1883 and features five guest rooms. Each themed room honors a different aspect of Kentucky. $$–$$$

THE MANSION AT GRIFFIN GATE
photo by Deborah Kohl Kremer

✳ Where to Eat

♉ **DINING OUT Giuseppe's** (859-272-4053; www.giuseppeslexington .com), 4465 Nicholasville Rd., Lexington. Lunch weekdays 11:30–2:30, dinner every day 5–10, Sun. brunch 11–2:30. Venture down the hidden, wooded, gravel driveway off busy Nicholasville Road to find this secluded, romantic Italian fine-dining establishment. In business since 1994, this wonderful combination of upscale dining and award-winning entrées features Italian favorites like manicotti, lasagna, and fettuccine. But in an attempt to please everyone, they offer veal, chicken, seafood, and Black Angus beef dishes, too. With more than 100 Italian wines on the list, have a glass with your tiramisu, homemade cannoli, Italian cream cake, spumoni, or gelato dessert. $$–$$$

♿ ♉ **The Mansion at Griffin Gate** (859-288-6142; www.mansion restaurant.com), 1720 Newtown Pike, Lexington. Dinner Tue.–Sat. 6–10. Dine in this spectacular pillared antebellum mansion while surrounded by crystal chandeliers and priceless antiques. French-based menu with Asian influences and plenty of familiar choices like king salmon and boneless rack of lamb. $$–$$$$

♉ **Jonathan at Gratz Park Inn** (859-231-1777, 800-752-4166; www.gratz parkinn.com), 120 W. 2nd St., Lexington. Open for lunch 11–2 and dinner 5–10 every day. For an upscale dining experience in the heart of Lexington, Jonathan is the place. The menu features American fare like filets and seafood, but some dishes have a southern twist, like the sea scallop hot brown and the pimiento cheese grit fries. Sunday brunch lets you try lots of favorites like the southern eggs Benedict made with fried green tomatoes and country ham, and Kentucky burgoo. $$$

Y **Dudley's Restaurant** (859-252-1010; www.dudleysrestaurant.com), 380 S. Mill St., Lexington. Lunch Mon.–Sat. 11:30–2:30; dinner Sun.–Thu. 5:30–10, Fri.–Sat. 5:30–11. Sun. brunch 11:30–2:30. Tucked inside this old school, which was built in 1881, you'll find a cozy, inviting restaurant. Walk on the creaky wood flooring and enjoy the intricate woodwork as you choose from the steaks, lamb, pasta, and seafood dishes. $$–$$$

Y **Bellini's** (859-388-9583; www.bellinis.us), 115 W. Main St. Lexington. Lunch weekdays 11:30–2:30, dinner every night starting at 5. Offering fine Italian dining right in the center of downtown, this upscale eatery serves traditional dishes that are as enticing to look at as they are to eat. They have all your pasta favorites as well as steaks, chops, and seafood. $$–$$$

Natasha's Bistro (859-259-2754; www.beetnik.com), 112 Esplanade, Lexington. Mon.–Sat. 11–10. This artsy restaurant has a far-reaching menu and an eclectic decor. Enjoy soups, salads, wraps, or even Hungarian goulash. The choices are vast but the ingredients are all fresh and flavorful. Live music acts range from accordions to sax solos; check the web site to see who's on stage. This funky restaurant is fun every time. $$

Y **Merrick Inn** (859-269-5417; www.murrays-merrick.com), 1074 Merrick Dr., Lexington. Serving dinner Mon.–Sat. A part of Lexington's dining scene for more than 30 years, this upscale but casual restaurant is the place to go for a nice evening out. Their southern-inspired menu features crabcakes, fried chicken, and the locals' favorite: pecan-crusted pork tenderloin topped with Maker's Mark apple chutney. The dining room is warm and welcoming, but eat outside on the patio if you can. It continually wins awards for the best outdoor dining in the state.

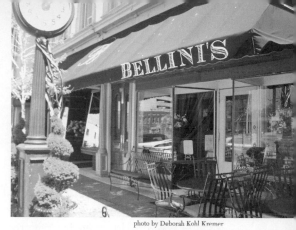

BELLINI'S

photo by Deborah Kohl Kremer

Y **Malone's** (859-335-6500; www.malonesrestaurant.com), 3347 Tates Creek Rd., Lexington. Open 11:15–11:15 every day. In business since 1998, it is the place to go for steak. They also have seafood, pork chops, and burgers, but why bother? This is a steak restaurant, and Malone's knows how to do it right. All entrées are served with Malone's bottomless Lexingtonian salad, which could be a meal on its own. $$–$$$

Y **A la Lucie** (859-252-5277), 159 N. Limestone, Lexington. Open for lunch and dinner every day. This hip place with funky decor verges on elegant but doesn't feel stuffy. They have white tablecloths and an upscale menu, but servers are relaxed so it's not so hoity-toity. A wide variety of steak and chicken dishes are available, but also unusual choices like buttermilk-fried quail. $$

Y **EATING OUT Cheapside Bar & Grill** (859-254-0046; www.cheapsidebarandgrill.com), 131 Cheapside, Lexington. Open for lunch and dinner every day. This is the kind of place where you go for happy hour and end up staying for last call. The relaxed, casual atmosphere and tropical-inspired patio usually bring in a fun crowd. Menu choices range from appetizers (they call it Social Grazing) to rare entrées like a duck enchilada, chipotle meat loaf, and a real backyard burger. $$

Hall's on the River (859-527-6620; www.hallsontheriver.com), 1225 Athens-Boonesboro Rd., Winchester. Serving lunch and dinner weekdays 11:30–9, weekends 11:30–10. One of the only restaurants to sit right on the edge of the picturesque Kentucky River; you can see why this has been a bar or restaurant since 1783. Known for their beer cheese appetizer, which you should order, they also have steaks, seafood, and regional favorites. If the weather is warm, eat on the deck; it's tucked into the rocky cliffs of the river valley. $$

Ÿ **Winchell's Restaurant and Bar** (859-278-9424), 348 Southland Dr., Lexington. Mon.–Sat. 8 AM–1 AM, Sunday 8 AM–11 PM. A casual restaurant with a sports bar feel. They have an extensive sandwich menu that includes an open-faced beef brisket, a country-fried steak and egg, and a pulled pork barbecue topped with vinegar slaw. As if that weren't enough, their dinner entrées include country-fried steak, grilled chicken cordon bleu, blackened salmon, and Kentucky hot brown. Unbeatable variety at reasonable prices. $–$$

Stella's Kentucky Deli (859-255-3354; www.stellaskentuckydeli.com), 143 Jefferson St., Lexington. Mon.–

HALL'S ON THE RIVER

Fri. 8:30–4, Sat. (brunch buffet only) 10–2. Inside this cute yellow house is a wonderful restaurant where everything is made from scratch. Committed to using fresh, local ingredients, they can tell you how to get to the farm where the cheese was made and where the tomato on your sandwich was grown. Open for breakfast and lunch. $

& Ÿ **The Atomic Café** (859-254-1969), 265 N. Limestone, Lexington. Open for lunch and dinner. With the spicy smell of island cuisine mixed with the Latino music and wall and ceiling murals of beaches, waves, and palm trees, you'll wonder if you are still in the Bluegrass. The menu features such island favorites as jerk chicken and coconut shrimp, but you can also find comfort foods like mac-n-cheese and chicken potpie. Homemade salad dressings like green onion coconut, honey papaya vinaigrette, and orange sesame add to the island ambience. In summer, live bands play on the patio out back. $$

& Ÿ **Joe Bologna's** (859-252-4933; www.joebolognas.com), 120 W. Maxwell St., Lexington. Open every day 11–11. Eat in this restored Jewish temple, surrounded by priceless stained-glass windows and chandeliers that were original to the 1890s building. It's probably the only pizza place listed on the National Register of Historic Places. Casual dining in an energy-charged environment. Pizzas and pastas are delectable, but the reason locals keep coming back to Joe B's is the garlic breadstick. Each entrée is served with a small loaf of bread that is served, literally, swimming in garlic butter. Put your napkin on your lap, because it will drip. $$

Ÿ **Buddy's Bar and Grill** (859-335-1BUD; www.buddysbarandgrill.com), 854 E. High St., Lexington. Mon.–Thu. 11:30–10, Fri.–11:30–11,

Sun. 11:30–9, with brunch available 11:30–3. Billed as a "neighborhood joint," this laid-back restaurant is a little more upscale than that. Although it is named for the owner's dog, the decor is hip and funky—and the menu is, too. They have the regular assortment of burgers and bar-food appetizers but they also have some not-so-common dinner entrées. For something different, try the Baja fish tacos, the pepper bacon mozzarella chicken, or the lump crabcakes. $–$$

◢ ◰ **Parkette Drive In** (859-254-8723; www.theparkette.com), 1216 E. New Circle Rd., Lexington. Open every day except Sun., for lunch and dinner. You can eat inside at the '50s-inspired diner, but to get the real feel for the place, order from your car and have the carhop serve you there. That's right: This place is the real deal. Parkette is a genuine drive-in restaurant that has been part of Lexington's history since 1952. The most popular item on the menu is the poor-boy burger and fries, but the onion rings are stellar, too.

◢ ⍩ **Ramseys** (859-259-2708; ramseysdiners.com), 496 E. High St., Lexington. Three other locations throughout Lexington, but this is the original. Open weekdays 11–11, weekends 10–11. Don't let the creaky wood floors and mismatched tables and chairs scare you away. This highly casual restaurant is where you'll find a bonanza of comfort-food choices. Try the open-faced pot roast sandwich with a side of kale, or southern-style catfish with creamed corn and apple fritters. Portions are huge, but save room for a piece of Mile-High Meringue Pie: The flavor choices change, but the pies are legendary. $$

⍩ **Two Keys Tavern** (859-254-5000), 333 S. Limestone, Lexington. Open seven days for lunch and on into the wee hours. This legendary bar, a staple of any University of Kentucky grad or fan, has been part of UK's party scene for as long as anyone can remember. Wildcat memorabilia creates the decor, and Wildcat fans fill the seats. Typical bar food makes up the menu, which tastes good and is inexpensive. Go for lunch when the college crowd is presumably in class, or go to watch a UK game on one of their dozens of TVs for the full experience. $

◰ **Alfalfa Restaurant** (859-253-0014; www.alfafarestaurant.com), 141 E. Main St., Lexington. Open every day for breakfast and lunch. Open for dinner Wed.–Sat. only. Notable for their vegetarian choices like eggplant burritos and hoppin' john, they also have wonderful salads, soups, and country ham sandwiches. Everything on the menu is fresh; the ambience is artsy

ALFALFA RESTAURANT

photo by Deborah Kohl Kremer

and eclectic. Check out the daily specials on the chalkboard when you come in the door. $–$$

Wheelers Pharmacy (859-266-1131), 336 Romany Rd., Lexington. Open for breakfast and lunch. Wheelers opened in 1958 with a full variety of pharmaceuticals and two U-shaped counters and three booths where you could order a milk shake. And that's what you'll find today, except in the 1960s they added a grill so you could get a burger or bacon and eggs to go along with your ice cream. They open at 9 AM and there is usually a line of regulars waiting to get in, which tells you a lot about this homey place.

∅ **SNACKS Ruth Hunt Candies** (859-268-1559; www.ruthhuntcandy.com), 2313 Woodhill Dr., Lexington. The original location is in Mount Sterling, but you don't have to drive all the way there to get this awesome candy. Although they produce about 70 varieties of candy, Ruth Hunt is best known for Woodford Reserve bourbon balls and Kentucky pulled cream candy. Don't forget to order a Blue Monday—a candy bar made of cream candy dipped in dark chocolate.

& **Magee's Bakery** (859-255-9481; www.mageesbakery.com), 726 E. Main St., Lexington. Open weekdays 6:30 AM–5:30 PM, Sat. 6:30 AM–2 PM, Sun. 8 AM–2 PM. Proudly meeting Lexingtonians' bakery needs for more than 50 years. The glazed doughnuts are like eating sweetened air. They are simply perfect. Have one while you choose the rest of your order. Make sure that order includes at least one transparent pie, their number one best seller. These come in traditional 9-inch and convenient 3-inch tart sizes. They are also famous for their homemade mallowbars. Yes, they are as amazing as they sound. They have a wide array of

photo by Deborah Kohl Kremer

MAGEE'S BAKERY

doughnuts, cakes, cookies, and pastries, too. They also have a coffee bar and a deli offering fresh sandwiches, salads, soups, or quiche.

❋ **Entertainment**

Actors Guild of Lexington (859-233-7330; www.actorsguildoflexington.org), 141 East Main St., Lexington. Professional theater company offering a wide variety of performances featuring both local and world renown actors. Check the web site to see list of upcoming shows.

❋ **Selective Shopping**

Third Street Stuff (859-255-5301; www.thirdstreet.stuff.com), 257 N. Limestone, Lexington. You can't walk past this shop; it looks so cool and funky on the outside, you'll want to know what's inside. Even the outside electric meter is painted purple with stripes! This fun shop has novelty gifts and hand-painted jewelry, artwork, and crafts.

Kentucky Korner (859-231-8899; www.lexingtoncenter.com/shops/kykorner). Adjacent to Rupp Arena, home of the Kentucky Wildcats, this is the place to grab your UK fan wear and Kentucky souvenirs.

Artique (859-233-1774, 859-272-8802; www.artiquegallery.com). Two locations: Civic Center, 410 W. Vine St. and the Lexington Green (closed Sun.); and 161 Lexington Green Circle, Lexington, open every day. Featuring the work of more than 1,000 artists, Artique is a fun, funky, colorful store. More than an arts and crafts gallery, it is the place to find distinctive works of art, intricate jewelry, handblown glass, and fabulous pottery.

Keeneland Gift Shop (859-254-3412; www.keeneland.com), 4201 Versailles Rd., Lexington. Although this prestigious track only runs in April and October, the shop is open for your equestrian-themed gift needs all year round. Fabulous selection of horse-related home decor, clothing, and jewelry items. They also have Keeneland logo hats, shirts, and jackets.

Fayette Cigar Store (859-252-6267), 137 E. Main St., Lexington. If you are looking for a fine selection of cigars, head for the walk-in humidor in the back. Cigar aficionados know this is the place to find rare cigars and a friendly, knowledgeable staff. But there is more to this shop than cigars. You will also find a newsstand with an enormous selection of newspapers and magazines. A word of caution to those traveling with small children: In the back corner of the store is quite a selection of X-rated magazines. Although these are discreetly displayed away from the general-interest publications, you might want to keep little eyes near the front of the store. Fayette Cigar Store also sells candy, books, gift items, and artwork.

photo by Deborah Kohl Kremer

FAYETTE CIGAR STORE

Peggy's Gifts and Accessories (859-255-3188; www.peggysgifts.com), 112 Clay Ave., Lexington. Located in a renovated old home, Peggy's offers a full line of purses, jewelry, and baby and wedding gifts; most can be personalized. They also have an assortment of customized sorority gift items.

Black Swan Books (859-252-7255; www.blackswanbooks.net), 505 E. Maxwell St., Lexington. Closed Sun. Close to the University of Kentucky's campus, you'll find Lexington's finest

PEGGY'S GIFTS

photo by Deborah Kohl Kremer

WoodSongs Old Time Radio Hour (859-252-8888; www.woodsongs.com), 214 E. Main St., Lexington.

When Michael Johnathon began broadcasting a small radio show comprising a mix of folk and bluegrass music a few years ago in his friend's studio in Lexington, he never dreamed that he would soon have fans from around the globe, with faithful listeners from Thailand to Topeka.

WoodSongs Old Time Radio Hour, which is available on local radio and the web, also airs on PBS channels nationwide. Viewers get to see not only the artists but also the technical crew, the audience, the incredible performances, and all the WoodSongs action from the stage of the historic Kentucky Theatre in Lexington, Kentucky.

Johnathon and his guests hope the national broadcast of this show does for Kentucky what *Austin City Limits* has done for Texas and *Prairie Home Companion* has done for Minnesota.

Broadcasting acoustical, genre-free shows with a blues or bluegrass feel, Johnathon explains that WoodSongs is not about famous stars. "A real artist has a passion for their art, and their goal is to bring it to an audience," he said. "They are not interested in their pocketbook, which is good because no one on the show earns a dime."

Not only are the performers unpaid, the entire crew are volunteers. Luckily the show is financed through donations of listeners, the $10 ticket price, and corporate sponsors.

Each show is archived on the web site (www.woodsongs.com). It is available for downloading, so that each show can be heard in its entirety, no matter where in the world you are. The average show gets about 125,000 full-view streams worldwide the first five weeks it is posted, which explains why Johnathon gets e-mails from people in Australia and Asia asking questions about the show.

"Our global audience loves folk music," he said. "They care more about the art than the marketing. They are not interested if the artist has signed with a national recording company, which is why we say on the show, 'Our artist don't have to be famous, they just have to be good.'"

Each Monday night the Kentucky Theater in Lexington is packed with music fans who come to enjoy good folk music. They do not know who they will be listening to or what instruments will be played, but the venue sells out week after week. Johnathon explained, "Our audience trusts us to supply the talent. The fact that they are unknown is what keeps them interested."

photo courtesy of www.kentuckytourism.com

WOODSONGS OLD TIME RADIO HOUR

Johnathon, a songwriter, folksinger, and playwright, is the host of the show. Although he is not a native of Kentucky, he feels he is a Kentuckian by now. With a love of Appalachian music in his heart, he moved to rural Knott County, where he went around knocking on doors, going house to house, learning music and songs from people who lived there. As his talents grew, he eventually moved to Lexington, where he now lives.

Years ago Johnathon was having his banjo repaired in the basement workshop of Homer Ledford, who is known for his Appalachian dulcimers. Surrounded by all the beautiful wooden instruments, he coined the term *WoodSongs* as a better alternative to *folk music*. Sometimes *folk music* conjures up a negative image, and Johnathon did not want his warm, peaceful shows to ever conjure up anything negative. Featuring artists who specialize in everything from the cello, the mandolin, and the banjo to a laptop dulcimer, *WoodSongs* takes the audience to a wonderful place with the music.

Johnathon believes *WoodSongs* has such a large audience because folk music is what gave birth to rock and country music. "Lexington is the global crossroads of bluegrass, blues, and folk music," he said. "It is perfect that *WoodSongs* comes from Kentucky."

collection of used books. They also carry new books, but it's the stacks and stacks of used books that really put Black Swan on the map. In business for more than 25 years, they claim to specialize in history, horses, military, and Kentucky literature, but they really have everything.

The Paperweight (859-252-8106), 109 Clay Ave., Lexington. Specializing in custom-designed invitations and stationery, this elegant store also stocks fine photo albums and picture frames. The knowledgeable staff can also help you with all your etiquette questions.

Dandelion Bead Connection (859-335-9600; www.dandelionbeads.com), 209 Rosemont Garden, Lexington. Jewelry makers and bead collectors will think they've died and gone to heaven when they enter this darling shop. In business for about 20 years, owner Mark Lightfoot knows his beads. The shop is stocked with semi-precious stones, freshwater pearls, and hard-to-find glass beads as well as clasps, thread, and supplies.

ART GALLERY Loudoun House Gallery (859-254-7024, 800-914-7990; www.lexingtonartleague.org), 209 Castlewood Dr., Lexington. Providing exhibit and educational arts programs,

this organization does all it can to support local artists. Ever-changing gallery; stop by to see what's on display.

Cross Gate Gallery (859-233-3856; www.crossgategallery.com), 509 E. Main St., Lexington. Specializing in equine and sporting art, this gallery has some breathtaking pieces. They are located in a massive Greek Revival home that was built in 1901, so enjoy the art and historic building at the same time.

ANTIQUES Belle Maison Antiques (859-252-9030; www.bellemaison antiques.com), 525 W. Short St., Lexington. Owner Debbie Chamblin scours the famous Marché aux Puces, also known as the Paris Flea Market, and the small towns of France looking for antiques she can bring back to Lexington. Furniture and home decor items as well as lots of urns and planters for your garden.

Ardery's Antiques (859-987-8180), 627 Main St., Paris. Taking you back to the days of the dime store, this 6,000-square-foot former Newberry's store is filled to the walls with antiques. They even renovated the soda fountain area, where you can order homemade sandwiches, soups, and pies. Closed Sun. and Mon.

Forest Hill Antiques Fine Art & Collectibles (606-365-2929), 55 Hubble Rd., Stanford. Visiting this 1840s home—listed on the National Register of Historic Places—is alone worth the trip, but take a stroll and you'll also find antique furniture, linens, and toys as well as fine art collectibles and paintings. Open Wed.–Sun.

Athens Schoolhouse Antique Show (859-255-7309; www.bigblueantiques .com), 6270 Athens Walnut Hill Rd., Lexington. Located 1 mile east of I-75. This antiques show, featuring 150 to 170 dealers, takes place in an old school

THE PAPERWEIGHT

photo by Deborah Kohl Kremer

building the second weekend of every month. Hours are Fri. 9–5, Sat. 9–5, Sun. 11–5. This place is huge, so allow yourself plenty of time to make the rounds. A snack shop on site is called **Back Door Café**. They offer soups and sandwiches if you need a break from all that antiquing. Admission $2.

✳ Special Events

⚘ ᕐ April: **Rolex Kentucky Three Day Event** (www.kyhorsepark.com). Held the last weekend in April at the Kentucky Horse Park, this is the premier event for equestrian riding in the United States. The event, which draws thousands of spectators from around the world, includes competitions in dressage, cross-country, and show jumping.

Ⴤ May: **Kentucky Wine & Vine Fest** (www.kywineandvine.com). Kentucky's list of wineries grows each year, keeping up with the plump grapes that are flourishing on the former tobacco farms around the state. Nicholasville (just 8 miles south of Lexington) has created a festival to celebrate all things vino. This weekend event, held in the historic downtown, includes bus tours of local vineyards and wineries, a grape stomp-off, and a winemaking competition. You can also enjoy the live Dixieland and jazz music featured all weekend. Although the weekend is lots of fun, it is, obviously, not for children.

⚘ ᕐ June: **The Festival of the Bluegrass** (www.festivalofthebluegrass .com). A whole weekend committed to the enjoyment of Kentucky bluegrass music. Held on the grounds of the Kentucky Horse Park, there are three stages hosting well-known acts as well as local artists.

⚘ ᕐ 🌺 September: **Roots & Heritage Street Festival** (www.rootsand heritagefestival.com). Capturing the powerful spirit of Lexington's African American culture, this festival features live music with internationally known acts, an African marketplace, and a wide variety of exciting, culturally enriching activities.

VERSAILLES, MIDWAY, AND SURROUNDING WOODFORD COUNTY

V ersailles is a darling community in the heart of thoroughbred country in Woodford County. The area is filled with rolling countryside and horse farms tucked inside familiar white plank fencing. The town is named for a city in France—but when you're here, you have to say it like a Kentuckian, and Kentuckians say *ver-SAILS* (as opposed to the French version, *ver-SIGH*).

The area has many ties to the railroad. The nearby town of Midway was actually built by the L&N Railroad, and the tracks run right through the shopping district. In Versailles you can visit the Bluegrass Railroad Museum, located in a former L&N railroad station, which was built in 1911.

The breezy countryside and winding back roads, sometimes lined with hand-

DOWNTOWN MIDWAY, KENTUCKY

made stone fences, make it a glorious place to drive. Along the way you can shop for antiques in the Versailles downtown area, stroll around Midway College, Kentucky's only all-women's college, dine at the fabulous Holly Hill Inn, and take a tour of a horse farm or two.

GUIDANCE **Woodford County Chamber of Commerce** (859-873-5122; www.woodfordchamber-ky.com), 141 N. Main St., Versailles. Open weekdays 9–4:30. You'll find lots of brochures, regional information, and recommendations right in downtown Versailles.

GETTING THERE Versailles is just 14 miles from downtown Lexington, so the **Bluegrass Airport** is your best bet (859-425-3114; www.bluegrassairport.com). There are car rentals available at the airport. **Greyhound** bus service is available in Lexington (859-299-8804; www.greyhound.com), 477 W. New Circle Rd., Lexington.

GETTING AROUND Located about halfway between Lexington and Frankfort, this small country town has an unhurried feel to it. Streets are well marked. Getting around by car is a pleasure.

MEDICAL EMERGENCY **Bluegrass Community Hospital** (859-873-3111; www.bluegrasscommunityhospital.com), 360 Amsden Ave., Versailles. This 25-bed hospital consistently ranks above the 95th percentile in national patient, employee, and physician satisfaction surveys.

ALCOHOL Woodford County is a wet county, allowing alcohol sales throughout the area.

✳ To See
✒ **Bluegrass Scenic Railroad and Museum** (859-873-2476, 800-755-2476; www.bgrm.org), 175 Beasley Rd., Versailles. Grounds open year-round. The gift shop and ticket office hours are open 12:30–4 every Sat. and Sun. from mid-May until the end of Oct. Train rides at 2. Enjoy a one-hour train ride aboard coaches built in the 1920s and '30s. Visit the museum full of railroad memorabilia. You can even send a message with their working telegraph. Brush up on your Morse code before you get there. $10 adults, $9 ages 65 and over, $7 ages 2–12; under 2 free. Locomotive cab rides $25.

✒ **Nostalgia Station Toy & Train Museum** (859-873-2497), 279 Depot St., Versailles. Open Wed.–Sat. 10–5, Sun. 1–5. The train exhibits, housed in a restored 1911 L&N Railroad passenger station, include vintage toys and toy trains that date back to 1900. There is also a gift shop full of fun train-related merchandise.

Equus Run Vineyards (859-846-9463, 877-905-2675; www.equusrunvineyards .com), 1280 Moores Mill Rd., Midway. Take a guided tour of the tobacco-barn-turned-winemaking-facility, or spend time walking the vineyard area on your own. Equus Run also has a nice amphitheater where they host concerts in summer.

Jack Jouett House (859-873-7902), 255 Craigs Creek Rd., Versailles. Open Wed.–Sun., Apr.–Oct., or call for an appointment. This house was built in 1793 by Captain Jack Jouett, a prominent leader for Kentucky statehood and Revolutionary

War hero. This Federal-style cottage is well preserved and furnished with period pieces. It fact, it looks much as it did when Jack and his wife, Sally Robards, were raising their 12 children here, except it's a lot less noisy.

Pisgah Presbyterian Church (859-873-4161; www.pisgahpresbyterian.org), 710 Pisgah Rd., Versailles. Call for tour information. This church was established in 1784 as the first Presbyterian church west of the Allegheny Mountains. Originally made of logs, the current facility, built in 1812, is constructed of fieldstone. It is home to priceless stained-glass windows and an immense pipe organ. There is also a cemetery on site, in which lies the remains of seven Revolutionary War soldiers.

Woodford County Historical Society Library and Museum (859-873-6786; www.woodfordkyhistory.org), 121 Rose Hill Ave., Versailles. Open Tue.–Sat. 10–4. Housed in the restored 1819 Big Spring Church and Meeting House, the museum has artifacts, data, and genealogy information from people who have lived in the Woodford County area. Free.

Woodford Reserve (859-879-1812; www.woodfordreserve.com), 7855 McCracken Pike, Versailles. Open Tue.–Sat. 9–5, Sun. 12:30–4:30. Tour the distillery of Labrot & Graham, home of Woodford Reserve Bourbon. The limestone buildings reflect the traditions of the area and the distiller, where they still use the time-honored copper pot method to make their fine bourbon. $5 adults (18 and up); under 5 free.

✳ To Do

GOLF The Brook Golf Course (859-873-8404; www.thebrookgc.com), 2260 Lexington Pike, Versailles. This 18-hole championship public golf course is a favorite of locals and visitors due to its central location and lush setting.

RECREATION Falling Springs Recreation Center (859-873-5948; fallingsprings.net), 275 Beasley Dr., Versailles. Go have some fun at the indoor and outdoor pools, three-court gym, and fitness center.

✳ Green Space

Buckley Hills Wildlife Sanctuary 1305 Germany Rd., Frankfort. Open Wed.–Sun. This 374-acre wildlife haven encompasses parts of Woodford and Franklin Counties. It is operated by the National Audubon Society and offers a 2-mile loop nature trail, bird-watching, and special events.

✳ Lodging

∞ "1" **Castle Post Luxury Tourist Home** (859-879-1000; www.the castlepost.com), 230 Pisgah Pike, Versailles. Royalty never had it so good. This Lexington landmark, which was once a private home, has been transformed into an off-the-charts upscale getaway. Complete with turret rooms, 30-foot ceilings, and 12–foot wooden doors, the massive structure is surrounded by a solid stone wall. It's not all cold and castle-like, though, and the owner describes it as a castle on the outside and a palace on the inside. Imported chandeliers, million-dollar woodwork, and impeccable furnishings create a truly one-of-a-kind lodging experience. The guest suites include

photo by Deborah Kohl Kremer

CASTLE POST

oversized bathrooms, well-appointed sitting rooms, and extravagance at every turn. A night's stay includes a three-course gourmet dinner and breakfast the next morning. Tours are not offered. $$$$

⊕ "I" **Montgomery Inn Bed and Breakfast** (859-251-4103; www .montgomeryinnbnb.com), 270 Montgomery Ave., Versailles. Offering 10 guest suites, each with a two-person Jacuzzi tub, this spectacular Victorian home dates back to 1911. Enjoy fresh baked cookies and snacks in the evening and a hearty gourmet breakfast in the morn. $$

$ "I" **A Storybook Inn** (859-879-9993; www.storybook-inn.com), 277 Rose Hill Ave., Versailles. This 1840s home is just as darling on the outside as on the inside. Featuring three guest rooms and a private two-bedroom cottage, this cute inn has been compared to a small European luxury hotel. Small extras like fresh-squeezed orange juice and premium roasted fresh-ground coffee make the apple-cinnamon bourbon breakfast pudding that innkeeper Elise Buckley-Snoddy whips up even better. $$$

"I" **1823 Historic Rose Hill Inn** (859-873-5957; www.rosehillinn.com),

233 Rose Hill Ave., Versailles. There are seven guest rooms in this lovingly renovated and preserved home. Enjoy the stained-glass windows, original ash floors, and intricate woodwork. Some rooms have kitchens, some sleep families, and some have room for your dog, so you are sure to find a room to meet your needs at this large home. Breakfast, served on lace-covered tablecloths and delicate china, offers southern choices like Rose Hill grits, ham with redeye gravy, or orange cream French toast. $$–$$$

"I" **The Woodford Inn** (859-879-9466; www.woodfordinn.com), 140 Park St., Versailles. Originally built as the Versailles Female College in 1876, this 10-room inn has been updated with modern amenities. They also have a nice sit-down restaurant and a tavern. $$

✳ Where to Eat

⅄ DINING OUT Holly Hill Inn (859-846-4732; www.hollyhillinn.com), 426 N. Winter St., Midway. Dinner Wed.–Sat. beginning at 5:30. Sat. and Sun. brunch served 11–2. Owners Chris and Ouita Michel invite you to dine with them in their 1830s Greek Revival inn. The white tablecloths and impeccable service only enhance the three- or six-course meal. Chef Ouita's menu changes seasonally to maximize the local fresh ingredients. Try the corn bread soufflé or the bourbon country lamb for a real southern-style treat. $$$

The Glitz Restaurant at Irish Acres (859-873-6956; www.irishacresgallery .com), 4205 Ford's Mill Rd., Nonesuch. Their famous three-course lunch is served Tue.–Sat. Reservations required. Housed in the basement of a former school, although you'd never know it, this fine-dining experience lives up to its name as a glitzy, glamorous place to eat lunch. $$

The Woodford Inn (859-879-9466; www.woodfordinn.com), 140 Park St., Versailles. Open Tue.–Sat. Lunch 11–2, Dinner 5–9. Eat in the dining room of the main house, which was built in 1876, the four-season sunporch, or outside on the patio. Sandwiches and salads as well as steaks, pasta, and grilled salmon choices fill the menu. $$–$$$

EATING OUT Darlin' Jean's Apple Cobbler Café (859-846-9485), 137 E. Main St., Midway. Open Mon.–Sat. 11–2. Also open for dinner Wed.–Sat. 5–9. You can't miss this place with the giant silo out front. This is a family-run restaurant, and the menu reflects generations of recipes. Notable dishes are Kentucky hot brown, bagel melt sandwiches, and coconut chicken salad. Don't even think about leaving without ordering some cobbler. Although the apple kind of started it all, they have delicious peach, blackberry, chocolate, and pecan cobblers, too. $$

& Y **Heirloom Restaurant** (859-846-5565), 125 Main St., Midway. Open Tue.–Sat. 11:30–2. Also open for dinner Tue.–Sat. beginning at 5:30. Reservations strongly recommended. This is a cool restaurant with a discriminating, upscale feel to it. The lunch menu features salads with unusual ingredients like anchovies, arugula, and goat cheese. They have burgers and sandwiches, but all with a funky twist. The BLT, for example, is a fried green tomato BLT, served on toasted sourdough with lemon aioli and cracked pepper chips. For dinner, entrées run the gamut from chile-roasted tiger prawns, to seared duck breast, to seared Alaskan halibut with kumquat relish. If you are looking for some new and exciting taste combinations, this is the place. $$–$$$

Debbie's Café (859-576-8120), 110 S. Main St., Versailles. Open Mon.–Fri. 6–2, Sat. 6–12. Some locals come every morning, so it must be good. Debbie is known for her breakfast choices, especially the homemade biscuits. For lunch she offers sandwiches and salads that bring people back each day. $

Wallace Station Country Store, Bakery and Deli (859-846-5161), 3854 Old Frankfort Pike, Versailles. Mon.–Sat. 8–5, Sun. 11–4. Mon. night fried chicken dinners 5–8. Stop at this homey place for lunch or dinner. You'll have a hard time deciding which giant sandwich to go with, but rest assured, they are all delicious and made on their own homemade bread. If you are there on a Monday night for the fried chicken dinner, you'll enjoy the black-eyed peas and cheesy grit side dishes as much as the main dish. $$

Quirk Café and Coffee (859-846-4688), 131 E. Main St., Midway. Serving lunch Mon.–Sat. Tucked inside Le Marche gift shop, this lunch spot has fresh scones, deli sandwiches, and weekly quiche specials. $

Y **Wilson's Pool Room** (859-879-0277), 131 Lexington St., Versailles. Open Mon.–Sat. 7:30 AM–10 PM. Although they serve up eggs, bacon, and country ham for breakfast, everyone goes to Wilson's for the giant ½-pound Willy Burger. They'll make one for you any time of day, just ask. Shoot a game of pool with the regulars while you are there.

🍴 **SNACKS Cornerstone Pharmacy** (859-873-3007), 100 Main St., Versailles. Weekdays 9–6, Sat. 9–3. Pull up a stool and enjoy some ice cream at the old-time soda fountain. They also serve lunch specials. Monday is broccoli soup day, and there is usually a crowd for it. Cornerstone has been around for about 50 years, and Versailles residents treasure it. $

✳ Entertainment

The Woodford County Theatrical Arts Association (859-873-0648; www.woodfordcountytheater.com), 275 Beasley Dr., Versailles. Producing several Broadway-style shows and plays each season, this community theater group is big on talent and fun. Check the web site to see when the curtain will rise next.

✳ Selective Shopping

Damselfly Studio and Gallery (859-494-8759), 126 E. Main St., Midway. This cute, colorful shop features lots of photography and watercolors of local artists. They also have lampwork beads and jewelry, and sometimes offer bead-making demonstrations. It's kind of a whimsical place that you'll enjoy browsing around in. Owner Mary Thoreson loves roosters, and you'll see a wide variety of these colorful creatures reflected in the artwork and craft items.

🍴 **Boyd Orchards Fresh Produce & Potted Plants** (859-873-3097; www .boydorchards.com), 1396 Pinckard Pike, Versailles. Enjoy farm-style fun

like hayrides, apple picking, and corn mazes. Get some fresh-from-the-field produce while you are there.

Freedman's Harness and Saddlery (859-846-9674; www.freedmanharness .com), 136 E. Main St., Midway. Closed Sun. and Mon. Whether you need a saddle for your horse or a finely made purse, Freedman's can help you out. They've been making fine leather goods since 1802, so you can trust them for quality and craftsmanship.

Lil Amish Mercantile (859-846-9438), 113 E. Main St., Midway. Once you sit in an Amish-made rocking chair, no other kind will do. Here at Lil Amish, you can test out (and purchase) these famed rockers. They also carry a full line of Kentucky crafts, old-fashioned candy, and a huge assortment of locally made jams, jellies, and relishes.

ART GALLERIES Heike Pickett Gallery & Sculpture Garden (859-233-1263; www.heikepickettgallery .com), 110 Morgan St., Versailles. Surrounded by century-old boxwoods, this outdoor sculpture garden is worth the trip alone, but don't miss the adjacent Carter House, built around 1792. It is loaded with a fantastic collection of art from both new and established artists.

ANTIQUES Irish Acres Gallery of Antiques (859-873-7235), 4205 Fords Mill Rd., Nonesuch. This antique hunter's dream features 32,000 square feet of American and European furniture, antiques, and collectibles. It's housed inside an old school, so it's huge. Plan accordingly.

Farm House Antiques and Gifts (859-873-5100; www.fhantiques.com), 825 Scotts Ferry Road, Versailles. With rare antiques and a wide range of gift lines, this is the place to come for yourself or someone on your gift list. They carry hard-to-find lines like Rowe

Pottery, Makers Mark products, Aspen Spice, and Elmwood Inn Teas.

✳ Special Events

✐ ♿ ❦ *June:* **Francisco Farm Art Festival**. Held on the campus of Midway College each year. The festival is named for the original landowner, John Francisco, who sold his 216 acres of farmland to the Lexington & Ohio Railroad in 1835. They, in turn, built the town of Midway. Award-winning fine arts and crafts festival with music, food, and juried art vendors.

Northern Kentucky

4

MAYSVILLE, OLD WASHINGTON,
AND AUGUSTA

COVINGTON, NEWPORT, AND
SURROUNDING SUBURBS

CARROLLTON

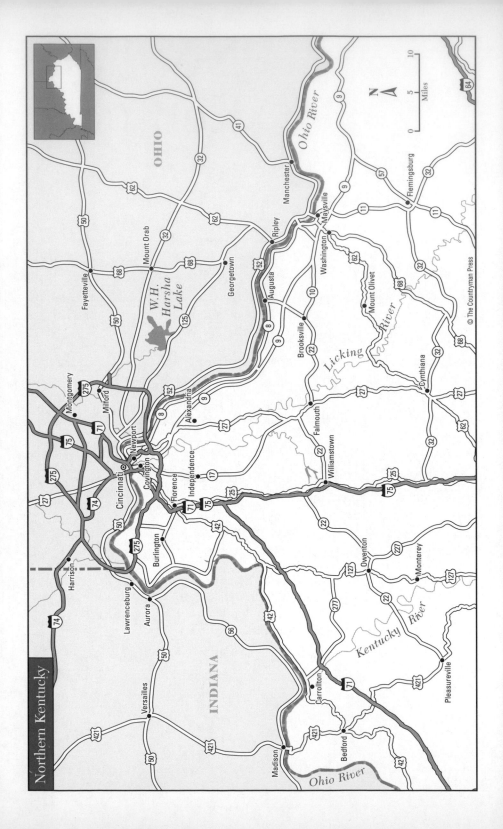

Northern Kentucky

INTRODUCTION:
NORTHERN KENTUCKY

Northern Kentucky is anchored by the Ohio River. Its communities all draw their history from this 981-mile-long waterway. Most of these small towns got their start as trading settlements catering to the many flatboats that made their way downriver from Pittsburgh during the westward expansion of the early 1800s.

Starting at the eastern end of the region, the town of Maysville is doused with history, as it has ties to early Kentucky frontiersmen like Daniel Boone and Simon Kenton, and later was a famous depot on the Underground Railroad. Today's Maysville and nearby Augusta are just sweetheart little towns with walkable main streets, an assortment of homegrown restaurants, shops, and fun festivals throughout the year.

The river makes its huge arc around the northernmost point of Kentucky, hugging the counties of Boone, Kenton, and Campbell, where you will find the area that locals refer to as Northern Kentucky. In most parts of the state, when you ask someone where they are from, they will answer with the name of a county. But here, "Northern Kentucky" generally covers all three counties; the suburbs blur together, making it feel like all one place.

Kentuckians sometimes refer to Northern Kentucky as simply Southern Cincinnati, but that is simply not the case. Northern Kentucky draws the best from the large midwestern city to the north, as well as the time-honored traditions of the South, and blends them together to form a culture like nowhere else.

Although you might not always hear a southern drawl in the voice of locals, you will hear very good manners. Northern Kentuckians are notorious for using the word *Please* when they really mean *What?* So if you ask directions, and the resident misunderstands you, there is a good chance she'll look at you and say "Please?" Translation: "What did you say?"

Another thing you will only find in this part of the country is goetta. Usually served for breakfast, this sausage-like dish, with German roots, is fried up crisp and served alongside eggs at many local restaurants. It is a must-eat while you are here.

Following the river south- and westward will lead you to Carrollton and, heading inland, to the rural town of Owenton. Both offer interesting attractions and unmatched family-style dining. In nearby Sparta, you'll find the Kentucky Speedway, one of the finest motor speedways in the country. This 1.5-mile oval track hosts NASCAR events throughout the year. Even though the location is out in the country, the track is first-class.

Northern Kentucky really has it all. You will find riverfront communities, historic and vibrant downtowns, scenic farmland, multicultural dining opportunities, and a unique mix of North and South that will make anyone feel right at home, wherever you are from.

MAYSVILLE, OLD WASHINGTON, AND AUGUSTA

Cuddled up alongside the Ohio River is the delightful city of Maysville. Although the area is a history lover's dream, there are attractions for all interests, including eclectic shops, phenomenal architecture, and golf and fishing opportunities.

Maysville, originally known as Limestone, was established in 1775 by frontiersman Simon Kenton. The villagers were forced out by some western battles of the American Revolution, but Kenton resettled the area in 1784. Around that same time, Daniel Boone established a trading post and tavern nearby, and the city of Maysville took root.

As a popular river trading stop, the city grew. It became known for local craftsmen who created intricate wrought iron. This ironwork can still be seen in the historic downtown and, more notably, downriver in the French Quarter of New Orleans, Louisiana. The trading of burley tobacco, once a staple to the area, also added to the growth.

Maysville's favorite daughter, Rosemary Clooney, established the Rosemary Clooney Music Festival, which is held each year just outside the historic Russell Theater. The festival brings in big-name entertainers as well as folks from all over who want to enjoy the music under the stars.

This theater was close to Rosie's heart, as it was the location of the 1953 world premiere of her first film, *The Stars Are Singing*. In 2008, Hollywood came to town again as Rosie's nephew, Hollywood heartthrob George Clooney, followed in her footsteps by bringing the premiere of the movie *Leatherheads*, which he starred in and directed, to the theater.

Travel just 4 miles south of Maysville proper and you will find **Old Washington**, where the original fieldstone streets and authentic log cabins makes you feel like you have gone back in time. The village is on the National Register of Historic Places and features original 18th-century buildings where slaves lived and were sold. Several of the buildings were reputedly stops on the Underground Railroad— probably one of the slaves' final stops before crossing the nearby Ohio River into freedom.

About 20 miles downriver is picture-perfect **Augusta**. With its darling homes, adorable shops, and lovely river walk, you'll not only want to visit but might want to live here. It is so perfect that in 2005, Kentucky's most famous historian, Dr.

Thomas Clark, included Augusta in his list of top 11 places to see in the state. It ranks right up there with the Cumberland Gap, Mammoth Cave, and Shaker Village. While it may seem to be somewhat off the beaten path, go ahead and take that path so you can breathe the clean air, slow down, and unwind in Augusta.

GUIDANCE Stop for guidance at the **Maysville Welcome Center** (606-564-6986), 115 E. 3rd St., next to the Simon Kenton Bridge. They are open weekdays 10–4 and Sat. 10–1. For information about Old Washington, head for the **Old Washington Visitors Center** (606-759-7411; www.oldwashington.com), 2215 Old Main St. Their address is in Maysville, but the center is in the Washington Historic District. Open Mon.–Sat. 10–4:30 and Sun. noon–4; the office is closed Dec.–Mar. The **Augusta Welcome Center** is located inside the red caboose parked on the corner of Main St. and Riverside Dr. Open during the summer months only, Thu.–Sun. 11–4, it is stocked with all the information you'll need for a good, neighborly visit. During the rest of the year, stop by the tourism office in **Augusta City Hall** (606-756-2183; www.augustaky.com), 219 Main St., Augusta. They are open weekdays 8:30–5 and are well stocked with brochures, maps, and advice.

GETTING THERE The nearest airport is about an hour from Augusta: the **Cincinnati/Northern Kentucky International Airport** (859-767-3151; www .cvgairport.com). Car rentals are available at the airport, and you will need a car. Augusta is approximately a one-hour drive. The river cities of Augusta and Maysville are about 22 miles apart. They are connected by the direct AA Highway, which is also known as KY 9. They are also linked by the more scenic KY 8, which hugs the river between the two.

GETTING AROUND It is easy to get around the Maysville and Old Washington area by car, with well-marked streets and ample off-street parking available everywhere.

MEDICAL EMERGENCY In the heart of Mason County is **Meadowview Regional Medical Center** (606-759-5311; www.meadowviewregional.com), 989 Medical Park Dr., Maysville.

ALCOHOL Both Mason County, home of Maysville, and Bracken County, home of Augusta, are wet, which means alcohol is available in restaurants and stores throughout the area.

✳ To See

In Maysville

✐ ⛭ **Kentucky Gateway Museum Center** (606-564-5865; www.kygmc.org), 215 Sutton St. Tue.–Fri. 10–5, Sat. 10–4, Sun. 1–4. Three distinct collections housed under one roof, the center has something for everyone. Whether you are interested in genealogy and research, regional history, or a 1/12-scale miniatures collection, you can see it all and take in the pioneer graveyard next door at the same time. The collection of miniatures (calling them dollhouses does not seem to do justice) is amazing. See these teeny-tiny homes, apartments, and shops filled with even teenier and tinier furniture and household items. The whole museum is well done, but the miniatures collection is a must-see. $10 adults, $2 students.

Maysville Floodwall Murals (606-564-9419; www.cityofmaysville.com), 25 E. McDonald Pkwy. Nine murals depict the history of Maysville along the city's floodwall. They illustrate the four centuries of the city and Maysville's connection to the Ohio River.

✧ Magee's Bakery (606-759-4882; www.mageesbakeryfarm.com), 8188 Orangeburg Rd. This bakery, a Maysville landmark in business since 1941, is best known for transparent pudding and transparent pie. Also known as poor man's pie in the South, this is a treat you can make—as owners Judy and Ron Dickson explain—with limited ingredients, just eggs, milk, and butter. And if you have some flour, you can make a crust, too. While there, tour the home (it dates back to 1790) and take a hayride around the working farm. Stay for lunch and you can help make it. Don an apron and hat and make some country ham sandwiches, corn pudding, and scalloped cabbage. A wide variety of from-scratch bakery items is available, too.

National Underground Railroad Museum (606-564-9419; www.cityofmaysville.com), 115 E. 3rd St. Call for appointment. This river city played a key component in the operation of the Underground Railroad, as it is located right on the border between slavery and the free state of Ohio. See slavery artifacts, documents, and memorabilia, and learn how abolitionist helped enslaved people reach freedom.

Hickory Hill Plantation and Nursery (606-742-2596; www.bramelshickoryhillnursery.com), 6037 Mill Creek Pike, Mays Lick. Tours by appointment only. Tucked away in the Mason County countryside is the authentic 1861 Greek Revival plantation home, which was once a part of American statesman John Marshall's estate. Tour the family home, carriage and icehouse, and combination dairy-smokehouse. Don't forget to walk through the lovely nursery and grounds.

In Old Washington

Carriage Museum (606-759-7305), Old Main St. Call for hours. This museum portrays the history of transportation prior to the car. Their time frame starts with a basic farmer's wagon and moves forward to an elegant four-seat carriage. They also have interesting exhibits and memorabilia relating to carriage travel.

Harriet Beecher Stowe Slavery to Freedom Museum (606-759-4860), 2124 Old Main St. Call for hours. Visit this early antebellum home, which once hosted Harriet Beecher Stowe. In 1833, she witnessed a slave auction that touched her so deeply, she included a description of it in her 1850s classic *Uncle Tom's Cabin*.

Mefford's Fort (606-759-7411; www.washingtonkentucky.com), Old Main St. Call for hours. Get a real feel for history as you tour this rustic 1787 log cabin. From an era when nothing went to waste, Mr. Mefford transformed a flatboat into his home. After traveling down the Ohio River from Pittsburgh, Mefford and his 13 children used the planks to build their log cabin.

Paxton Inn (606-759-7411; www.washingtonkentucky.com), 2030 Old Main. Call for hours. The circa-1810 inn, a popular early-19th-century hangout for local lawyers and citizens, has a secret stairway between the first and second floors where runaway slaves could be hidden as they traveled along the Underground Railroad.

In Augusta

Rosemary Clooney House (www.rosemaryclooneyhouse.com), 106 E. Riverside Dr. Open Wed. 11–3, Fri. and Sat. 11–5, Sun. 1–5. You can't miss this bright yellow riverfront house where Rosemary Clooney lived for more than 20 years. The home, owned by former lieutenant governor Steve Henry and his wife, former Miss America Heather French Henry, is loaded with the largest known private collection of memorabilia from the 1954 holiday movie classic *White Christmas*. There are also exhibits dedicated to Augusta's other famous residents George Clooney, Nick Clooney, and Heather French Henry. A $5 donation is requested.

Augusta River Walk (606-756-2183; www.augustaky.com), Riverside Dr. Stroll along the Ohio River and past many of Augusta's historic homes. The river is very calm through this area, so pull up a park bench, rest your legs, and watch the water glide by.

Augusta's Historic Jail (606-756-2183), City Park, W. 2nd St. Open by appointment. Contact Bracken County Historical Society at 606-735-3337 to make tour arrangements. Built in 1811, this is the oldest jail in Kentucky that still sits on its original foundation. See the first-floor prisoner's quarters and the second-floor living quarters of the jailer.

Lavender Hills of Kentucky (606-735-3355; www.lavenderhillsofkentucky.com), 229 Conrad Ridge Rd., Brooksville. Breathe in the sweet scent as you tour the first commercial lavender farm in Kentucky. Covering 100 acres of farmland, you can see (and smell!) more than 600 lavender plants. They have 15 different varieties in pink, white, yellow, and all shades of purple. Peak bloom time is in mid-June, but the family offers tours and workshops year-round. There's a nice gift shop on the farm where you can find soaps, sachets, cleaning products, and recipes.

✳ To Do

BOATING Augusta Boat Dock and Marina (606-756-2183; www.augustaky .com), River and E. 2nd Sts., Augusta. If you are boating on the Ohio, this is a convenient place to stop for gas, snacks, and supplies. They do not rent boats, but if you bring your own, they have rental slips available.

GOLF Laurel Oaks Golf Course (606-759-5011), 808 US 62, Maysville. Visit this 18-hole, par-72 public course with generous fairways and greens. The course was designed to make the best use of the gently rolling terrain.

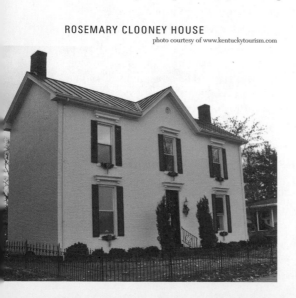

ROSEMARY CLOONEY HOUSE
photo courtesy of www.kentuckytourism.com

Wells Creek Golf Course (606-759-5604), Old Main St., Maysville. You can enjoy 9 holes on this picture-perfect course located at the Maysville–Mason County Recreation Park.

RACING Earlywine Racing Inc. (606-883-3098; www.earlywine racing.com), 4248 Walton Pike, Maysville. Here at the nation's largest permanent indoor motocross racing facility, visitors can race ATVs, dirt bikes, and remote-control trucks. Check the web site for schedules.

Big Rock Off Road Park (606-759-9106; www.bigrockoffroadpark.com), 8157 Stonelick Rd., Maysville. This 2,000-acre ATV and dirt bike park is slightly off the beaten path, but for fans it is worth the drive.

WALKING TOURS Downtown Maysville Walking Tour (606-564-9419; www.cityofmaysville.com), 216 Bridge St., Maysville. Tour the historic downtown area on this 1½-hour excursion in which you will explore the floodwall murals, St. Patrick's Church, Russell Theater, Mason County Courthouse, First Presbyterian Church, Museum Center, and Pioneer Graveyard. Call the visitors center to reserve your spot.

Old Washington Walking Tour (606-564-9419; www.washingtonkentucky.com), 2215 Old Main St. in Old Washington. Tours originate from the visitors center. The village was established in 1786 and is home to several authentic log cabins as well as early-1800s buildings. This is a real gem for history enthusiasts; there aren't many places left where you can take in so many genuinely historic structures on one tour.

Augusta Walking Tour (www.augustaky.com/tourism/tours). Go online (most of Augusta is Wi-Fi, you know) and print out a walking tour brochure to get started. This is the perfect way to see all that Augusta has to offer. The tour map has some interesting facts about the historic homes, some dating back as early as 1790. The tour also points out examples of Colonial, Italianate, and Victorian architecture that are prevalent throughout the town.

⊘ ⚹ "↑" **Blue Licks State Resort Park** (859-289-5507, 800-443-7008; parks.ky .gov), US 68, Mount Olivet.

Kentucky history, which is inundated with Civil War references, sites, and memorials, actually has one state park dedicated to preserving the memory of the Revolutionary War: Blue Licks State Resort Park, found 25 miles south of Maysville. On the site of the Battle of Blue Licks—sometimes referred to as the Last Battle of the American Revolution—stands a memorial to all who perished in a terrible battle among American Indians, Kentucky settlers, and the British that took place on August 19, 1782. The park features a museum full of Indian artifacts, dinosaur bones, and exhibits that depict the history of the Blue Licks area. Several short historic walking trails offer sights of buffalo paths as well as the location of Daniel Boone's capture by Shawnee Indians. **The Lodge**, which sits right on the Licking River, has 32 hotel rooms, two modern executive cottages, which have two bedrooms, and 51 campsites with utility hookups. For fine dining at the resort, **Hidden Waters Restaurant** is open seven days a week for breakfast 7–10, lunch 11:30–2, and dinner 5–9. While the spot is known for Kentucky country ham dinners and fried catfish, all menu items feature locally grown products whenever possible. $–$$

❋ Lodging

Magnolia Inn of Maysville (606-564-5857 or 606-564-0055), 222 Lee St., Maysville. Owner Sherry Rice welcomes you to her three-room B&B situated in the historic district of Maysville. Choose the Railroad Room, the Outdoorsman's Room, or the Horse Room, each with private bath. The 100-year-old home has current-day amenities, and Sherry can give you ideas of things to do and places to see while she serves up a southern breakfast of homemade biscuits and gravy with sausage and eggs. $

✎ & **French Quarter Inn** (606-564-8000; www.frenchquarterinn.com), 25 E. McDonald Pkwy., Maysville. Get a taste of New Orleans along with Kentucky hospitality at this 63-room inn. Guests compare it to a large B&B due to the warm, homey feel. The New Orleans–inspired decor features lots of wrought iron, verdigris accents, molding, and even a bronze statue right in the middle of the lobby fountain. Ask for a room overlooking the river for an unforgettable view. $

& ∞ **The Parkview Country Inn** (606-756-2603; www.parkviewcountry inn.com), 103 W. 2nd St., Augusta. This inn features 10 cozy guest rooms, outfitted with a mix of antiques and modern-day amenities. Built in the early 1800s, the home is on the National Historic Register. Enjoy your home-cooked country breakfast in the on-site Parkview Inn Restaurant. $

∞ **Asbury Meadow B&B** (606-756-2100; www.asburymeadow.com), 3737 Asbury Rd. This stately antebellum home features southern details like majestic columns and a widow's walk. Inside you'll find two guest rooms, one with a Murphy bed that tucks up into the wall. Out in the backyard, you can stay in the cottage, which was formerly the slave quarters of the plantation.

The cottage has come a long way since those early days: It now boasts a Victorian soaking tub, a wood ceiling, and a kitchenette. $

❋ Where to Eat

& ♼ **DINING OUT** **Caproni's** (606-564-4321), 320 Rosemary Clooney St., Maysville. Open Mon.–Thu. 11–9, Fri. 11–10, Sat. 3–10, Sunday 11–3. Enjoy an upscale but casual Italian meal with a glorious view of the Ohio River. Meals are complemented with homemade garlic bread and pies, cakes, and cheesecakes. The signature dish is Chicken Caproni made with linguine, but American fare like steaks, chops, and seafood is also on the menu. $$–$$$

♼ **The Beehive Restaurant** (606-756-2202), 101 W. Riverside Dr., Augusta. Open for lunch and dinner Wed.–Sun. This legendary restaurant has been the icon of Augusta for more than 20 years. Housed inside a 200-year-old building right along the river, the restaurant is full of period-piece antiques and a wood floor that has obviously lived through a few floods. The ever-changing menu features upscale cuisine at reasonable prices. The black bean soup and homemade rolls and desserts are fabulous. $–$$

Chandler's On Market (606-564-6385), 212 Market St., Maysville. Open Mon.–Sat. for lunch and dinner. Tucked into the historic district of downtown Maysville is a local favorite. This sit-down, upscale restaurant is known for their tomato soup, as well as their steaks and chops. Owner Chan Warner has filled his restaurant with antiques and an inviting warm decor so that everyone feels welcome. $$

& **EATING OUT** **Parkview Country Inn Restaurant** (606-756-2667; www .parkviewcountryinn.com), 103 W. 2nd

St., Augusta. Open daily for lunch and dinner. Enjoy the comfortable surroundings of this inn, built in the early 1800s, while dining on a big country meal. They have a popular buffet available at every meal, so you can get your fill of tasty fried chicken, smoked country ham, and maybe even some spiced catfish. Don't forget to order some potato soup; that seems to be everyone's favorite. $–$$

The Augusta General Store (606-756-2525), 109 Main St., Augusta. Open daily 6–9. This is a countrified version of those chain restaurants you see just off the interstate with rocking chairs on their porch. It looks like an old-fashioned general store, complete with gift shop in the front and good eats in the back. The menu features hearty breakfasts, juicy burgers, and toasted sub sandwiches. Save room for dessert; the assorted homemade pies, cobblers, and cookies are the best. $

Carota's Pizza (606-756-2343), 115 Main St., Augusta. Open daily for lunch and dinner. This is *the* place to get pizza in Augusta, and luckily the Carota family has been making fantastic pizza for generations now. They have salads and hoagies, too, but the pizza will make you ask for more. $–$$

Delites (606-564-7047), 222 Market St., Maysville. Open Mon.–Sat. 8–5. Nothing fancy, mind you, just the best burgers in Maysville. Run by John and Erato Kambelos, a darling couple who make everyone feel welcome. The menu features mostly classic diner food, but it is sprinkled with options like gyros from the Kambelos' home country of Greece.

Margie's Southern Café (606-563-9424), 130 Market St., Maysville. Open Mon.–Thu. 5 AM–9 PM, Fri. and Sat. 5 AM–2 AM. Margie's is where you'll find a home-cooked meal just like Mom used to make. Owner Margie Zimmer,

who is originally from New Orleans, adds a hint of Cajun spice to some of her hometown favorites. This Maysville staple has been around for more than a decade. $

SNACKS Hutchison's Grocery (606-564-3797), 1201 E. 2nd St., Maysville. Open weekdays 9–5, Sat. 9–4. A visit to Maysville isn't complete until you stop at this little grocery that has been in business for more than 150 years. Yes, Micajah Hutchison hung out his shingle in 1850, and they've been going strong ever since. Not much to look at on the outside, or the inside for that matter, but go in and try one of their legendary Kentucky ham sandwiches and maybe an order of onion rings. They have a full menu of burgers, sandwiches, and even pork tenderloin, but you'll have to order it to go, as they don't have any tables. Still worth a stop.

✳ Entertainment

The Maysville Players (606-564-3666; www.maysvilleplayers.com), at the Washington Opera House, 116 W. 2nd St., Maysville. The oldest theater group in Kentucky, the Maysville Players present such Broadway classics as *Once Upon a Mattress*, *Our Town*, and *Nunsense*. Check the web site for this year's shows.

✳ Selective Shopping

In Maysville
Steve White Art Gallery (888-266-6220; www.stevewhitefineart.com), 225 Market St., features the watercolor and oil paintings of world-renowned artist Steve White. An award-winning landscape and portrait painter, Steve had one of his paintings featured as the cover for Rosemary Clooney's CD *Still on the Road*.

The EAT (Exquisite Art Treasures) Gallery (606-564-5578; www.eat gallery.com), 46 W. 2nd St. Specializing in art created from nature, this gallery has an amazing collection of amethysts, geodes, crystals, and wood carvings. The selection is remarkable.

Market Street Bookstore (866-571-5036), 224 Market St. Glenn and Carol George are the proud owners of this bookstore, which features new and used books of all genres. They also sell the watercolor paintings of local artist Barb Clark, who specializes in scenes of Maysville.

Tierney's Antiques (606-564-4104), 51 W. 2nd St. Stop by and visit with Jim and Martha Tierney in their shop that specializes in Depression glass and traditional and primitive furniture. It's housed in a building that dates back to the early 1800s and still has the original tin ceiling.

In Old Washington

Keepsake Treasures (606-759-0505; www.keepsaketreasures.biz), 2116 Old Main St. Find the perfect antique, collectible, or gift at this little shop in a historic 1900s home.

Phyllis' Antique Lamp Shop (606-759-7423; phyllisantiques.com), 2112 Old Main St. In business 40 years, these people know lamps. Specializing in antique lighting and restoration, Phyllis' is the place to go for lamp parts, specialty shades, and antique lusters. They also stock dollhouse supplies, Blue Bird china, and collectibles.

The Strawberry Patch Country Store (606-759-7001), 2109 Old Main St. Wander through this old country store and find antiques, teddy bears, wreaths, and collectibles.

The Irongate (606-759-7074), 2103 Old Main St. Pottery lovers will be thrilled to find such a nice selection of Bybee and Hadley Pottery under one roof. They have rare books, silver, and collectibles, too.

In Augusta

Barbara's Art Studio and Gallery (606-756-2787), 210 Riverside Dr. Features the working studio and gallery of artist Barbara Kelsch in historic early-1800s digs. The gallery, located in the family home of Kelsch's husband, is situated on the banks of the Ohio. Sumptuous landscapes, dynamic abstracts, and richly detailed portraits are some of the subjects of her works in oils, watercolors, charcoals, and pastels.

Folk Art Shop (606-756-3077), 114 Main St. Out-of-the-ordinary collection of gift items housed in a rustic log cabin that dates back to the late 1700s.

Small Town Gift Shop (606-756-2747; www.smalltowngiftshop.home stead.com), 129 Main St. This appropriately named shop is a perfect addition to Main Street. It is the kind of place where locals pop by regularly to see what's new. They feature crafty items like comforters, throw pillows, china, homemade toys, and floral arrangements, but the merchandise changes frequently so you never know what you'll find. Everything in this darling shop was created in or near Augusta, so it is all home grown.

✳ Special Events

In Maysville

 ♿ *June:* **Maysville Uncorked**. This is a *really* festive festival featuring Kentucky wine. The event includes wine tastings, music, art, and locally made products for sale.

♿ *September:* **Rosemary Clooney Music Festival**. Maysville's premier annual event is held at the Russell Theater where Rosie spent her childhood looking up at the big screen and later returned to for the premiere of her first major movie, *The Stars Are Singing*. Guests are treated to a night of music including Grammy Award–winning performers. Past years have featured Linda Ronstadt, Michael Feinstein, and Smokey Robinson.

In Old Washington

&. ✍ ❦ *April:* **Chocolate Festival**. Chocolatiers from all over the region gather to offer all things chocolate, including fudge, ice cream, funnel cakes, and even chocolate-covered cream candy and bourbon balls. Chocoholics get to enjoy live entertainment, games, and rides while they nosh.

&. ✍ ❦ *September:* **Simon Kenton Festival**. See historical reenactments and demonstrations of frontier life. It is also a family reunion of sorts for the descendants of the famous frontiersman who fought off Indians, once saved Daniel Boone's life, and helped found the cities of Washington and Maysville.

&. ✍ ❦ *December:* **Frontier Christmas in Old Washington**. The historic log cabins of Old Washington are decked out in fresh greenery, nuts, and fruits as the village celebrates the holidays.

In Augusta

&. ✍ ❦ *June:* **Art in the Garden**. Spend an enjoyable day browsing the work of local and regional artists while you stroll along picturesque Riverside Drive.

&. ✍ ❦ *July:* **The Augusta Riverfest Regatta**. A true celebration of the river, Augusta welcomes stern-wheelers, paddle-wheelers, and all types of boats to the riverfront. Not just about boats, the festival offers juried arts and crafts, live entertainment, a beauty pageant, a 5K run, and kids' games.

&. ✍ ❦ **The Germantown Fair**. This regional fair includes Mason, Bracken, Robertson, Pendleton, Harrison, Nicholas, Fleming, and Lewis Counties and is the longest-running fair in the state. They have all the typical events of a county fair, like livestock competitions, food contests, beauty pageants, and horse shows.

&. ✍ ❦ *September:* **Heritage Days**. This annual Labor Day weekend festival is held downtown on West 2nd and Parkview. Enjoy live music, a huge flea market, festival food, crafters, and a car show.

&. ✍ ❦ *December:* **Rivertown White Christmas**. Come see all the shops of Augusta dressed up for Christmas. The event is usually held the first weekend in December; shops feature extended hours and holiday sales. Stick around for the lighting of the Augusta Christmas tree.

COVINGTON, NEWPORT, AND SURROUNDING SUBURBS

The Northern Kentucky region that encompasses Covington, Newport, and surrounding suburbs is a unique part of the state. Due to its close proximity to Cincinnati, Ohio, it is mainly an area made up of urban and suburban neighborhoods, but visitors are minutes away from rural Kentucky, just on the fringes of town.

It is in **Covington** and **Newport** where you will find the historical remnants of the German and Italian immigrants who flooded to the area during the early 1900s. These markings are evident in neighborhoods with names like Mutter Gottes in Covington and Spaghetti Nob in South Newport. You will find evidence in the architecture and churches in these communities as well. Traipse through a few old cemeteries; the family names will clearly show which motherland these residents hailed from.

Covington, which is Kentucky's fifth largest city, sits on the western corner of the Licking River, where it meets the Ohio. On the eastern shore of the Licking is Newport, Kentucky. Both Covington and Newport have attractions on their own, but together with the nearby cities such as Bellevue, Fort Mitchell, Highland Heights, Crestview Hills, and Florence they make up the regional area known as Northern Kentucky.

The city of Newport, which was once known as Sin City due to the number of seedy businesses with ties to gambling, prostitution, and organized crime, has seen an about-face in the last 30 years. Today it is home to a growing downtown, Newport on the Levee, an all-ages entertainment complex, and the state's multimillion-dollar aquarium.

Over in Covington, the Main Strasse Village is an area comprising restaurants, bars, and shops, most with a German flavor. This little neighborhood is located near the Goose Girl Fountain and Carroll Bell Chimes, two landmarks reminiscent of the Old Country.

As you head out of the urban core, you'll enter newer suburban communities where you can find excellent shopping and dining opportunities. Although there are plenty of the big-box chains and mall stores you'll find anywhere, don't miss the opportunity to explore the mom-and-pop places that give Northern Kentucky a personality you won't find anywhere else in the state.

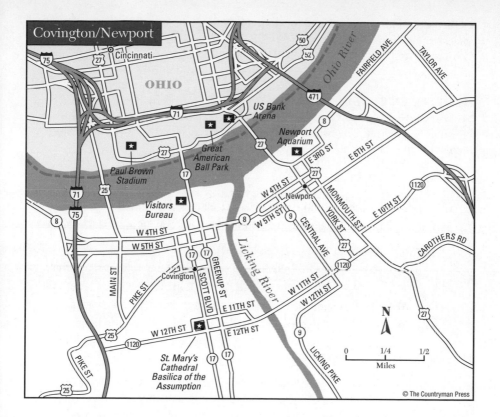

GUIDANCE **Northern Kentucky Convention and Visitors Bureau** (800-STAY-NKY; www.staynky.com), 50 E. River Center Blvd., Suite 200, Covington. Open weekdays 9–5. They have racks of brochures and maps for attractions in Northern Kentucky, and beyond.

GETTING THERE The area is served by the **Cincinnati/Northern Kentucky International Airport** (859-767-3151; www.cvgairport.com). Car rentals are available at the airport. Yes, the Cincinnati, Ohio, airport is in the Bluegrass State and is credited for phenomenal growth and prosperity in the area. If you are on a plane landing at this airport, watch the faces of your fellow travelers as the flight attendant announces "Welcome to Kentucky." These travelers, who thought they were on their way to Ohio and have no idea about geography, get a panicked look as they momentarily think they are on the wrong plane.

For bus and rail service, the nearest stations are across the river in Cincinnati. **Greyhound Bus** (513-352-6012; www.greyhound.com) is located at 1005 Gilbert Ave., Cincinnati. The **Amtrak** station (800-872-7245; www.amtrak.com) is located at 1301 Western Ave., in Union Terminal, Cincinnati.

GETTING AROUND **Transit Authority of Northern Kentucky** (859-331-TANK; www.tankbus.org). With 27 routes through Boone, Kenton, and Campbell Counties, TANK buses operate 365 days a year. **Southbank Shuttle** (859-578-

6943; www.tankbus.org). Watch for these well-marked buses and trams, which follow a loop encompassing the attractions and entertainment districts of Newport, Covington, and downtown Cincinnati. The shuttles appear about every 10 minutes and cost a small fee. Check the web site for exact route information.

MEDICAL EMERGENCY Northern Kentucky is served by the highly respected **St. Elizabeth Medical Center** (859-301-2000; www.stelizabeth.com). With five locations Covington, Edgewood, Ft. Thomas, Florence and Grant County, fine medical help is always nearby.

🔖 ♿ **Behringer-Crawford Museum** (859-491-4003; www.bcmuseum.org), 1600 Montague Rd., Covington. Open Tue.–Fri. 10–5, Sat.–Sun. 1–5. $7 adults, $6 seniors, $4 ages 3–18.

The Behringer-Crawford Museum, once known as an oddities museum, tells the story of Northern Kentucky history. The museum, which is located in Covington's picturesque Devou Park, uses the theme "History in Motion: Rivers, Roads, Rails and Runways." It is dedicated to relating the tales of Northern Kentucky's settlement and development through the unique lens of transportation. Not the modes of transportation, per se, but instead how these modes played a part making Northern Kentucky what it is today.

What would Northern Kentucky be without the mighty Ohio River? In the Rivers section, guests are treated to a re-creation of the famous Roebling Suspension Bridge that has spanned the river between Covington and Cincinnati since 1866, as well as a huge interactive packet boat. As immigrants from Germany, Ireland, and Italy disembarked in Cincinnati, some crossed the river into Northern Kentucky and found it to be just like home. They sent word back to the Old Country, and future immigrants made Covington and Newport, Kentucky, their destination.

In a tribute to Roads, the museum invites guests to sit in a 1959 Buick Electra that has been reformatted to simulate a trip to the drive-in movies. A doctored rendition of a '50s-era movie, *Radar Men from the Moon*, is playing on the big screen. Visitors can choose to watch a video, *Today's America*, which is narrated by Northern Kentucky's own Nick Clooney.

The growth of Northern Kentucky would never be complete if the Greater Cincinnati/Northern Kentucky International Airport was not included. In the Runways section, guests can learn more about the humble beginnings of an airstrip in Boone County that eventually became a world-class airport. One of the gems on display is the actual telegraph sent from Senator Alben Barkley to the city of Covington alerting them that funding for the airport had been approved.

Train tracks and streetcar lines play the starring role in the Rails sec-

ALCOHOL The three main counties comprising this region of Northern Kentucky—Boone, Kenton, and Campbell—are all wet, which means alcohol is available at restaurants, bars, and liquor stores.

✷ To See

✧ ♿ **Newport Aquarium** (859-261-5888, 800-406-3474; www.newportaquarium .com), 1 Aquarium Way, Newport Open 365 days per year. Located at Newport on the Levee, this aquarium features 200 feet of seamless acrylic tunnels where you can walk under and through the massive tanks holding killer sharks, fish, stingrays,

tion of the museum. The Greenline streetcar system is credited with populating the suburbs. The centerpiece is an actual street car, The Kentucky, sitting on actual tracks, right as you enter the museum. In keeping with the rail theme, a beautiful train display, complete with scale-sized local landmarks, allows visitors to go under the tracks and come up in the middle of the exhibit for a 360-degree view. There are also several toy train sets, perfect for little hands, available for play.

"We made this as interactive as possible," said Laurie Risch, executive director. "Small kids will enjoy all the hands-on features, and adults can take in all the historical memorabilia on the walls."

So the Behringer-Crawford has grown up as a museum, but even grown-ups need to have some fun. The famous oddities, the beloved two-headed calf, the big hairball, and the shrunken head, are still there. "Those are our beginnings," said Risch. "We will always have a place for them, too."

DRIVE-IN MOVIE AT THE BEHRINGER-CRAWFORD MUSEUM   photo by Deborah Kohl Kremer and sea turtles. Get up close and personal with American alligators, playful penguins, a relaxing jellyfish exhibit, and thousands of other varieties of sea creatures from around the world. $19 adults, $12 ages 2–12; under 2 free.

⊚ ⚹ **St. Mary's Cathedral Basilica of the Assumption** (859-431-2060; www .covcathedral.com), 1140 Madison Ave., Covington. Open daily 10–4. After 21 years of construction, this immense Roman Catholic cathedral was completed in 1915. Recognized as a French-Gothic replica of Notre Dame in Paris, France, it is home to the world's largest church stained-glass window as well as 26 gargoyles that were hand carved in Italy. Fascinating arched ceilings and fluted columns are architectural marvels protecting more than 80 stained-glass windows, murals by famed Covington artist Frank Duveneck, sculptures by Clement J. Barnhorn, and a massive Aultz-Kersting pipe organ. Self-guided tours are free; call for an appointment for a docent-guided tour.

✏ ⚹ ♿ **World Peace Bell** (859-581-2971; www.verdin.com), 4th and York Sts., Newport. The world's largest free-swinging bell rings every day at noon. The 66,000-pound bell was built in France and brought to Newport to celebrate the new millennium. It is huge; you can't miss it.

♿ **James A. Ramage Civil War Museum** (859-344-1145; www.fortwright.com), 1402 Highland Ave., Fort Wright. Open Fri. and Sat. 10–5, Sun. noon–5. This museum, which is housed in a former residence, has interesting artifacts and memorabilia from the Civil War. It sits high atop a hill in Northern Kentucky, which was known as Battery Hooper during the Civil War. The location was a pristine spot for the Union army to be on the lookout for any Confederates who were planning to attack Northern Kentucky and Cincinnati.

✏ ♿ **Creation Museum** (859-727-2222, 800-778-3390; www.creationmuseum .org), 2800 Bullittsburg Church Rd., Petersburg. Mon.–Thu. 10–6, Fri. 10–9, Sat. 9–6, Sun. noon–6. This 70,000-square-foot museum brings the pages of the Bible to life. It was designed by a former Universal Studios exhibit director, and visitors experience animatronics, murals, and computer-generated special effects that explain the origins of the universe according to the Book of Genesis. They have a lush garden area, restaurant, and gift shop, too. $22 adults (ages 13–59), $17 seniors (over 60), $12 ages 5–12; 4 and under free.

WORLD PEACE BELL

photo by Paul Kremer

✏ **Vent Haven Museum** (859-341-0461; www.venthaven.com), 33 W. Maple, Fort Mitchell. Open May–Sept. Tours by appointment only. As the world's only museum dedicated to the art of ventriloquism, this is the one place to see more than 700 ventriloquial figures and memorabilia under

photo by Deborah Kohl Kremer

COVINGTON FLOODWALL MURALS

one roof. The collection is amazing to see, but do not call them dummies, or you might look like one. Admission $5.

✏ ♿ ✿ **Covington Floodwall Murals** (859-655-4159). Along the river, at the foot of Madison Ave., Covington. Learn about Northern Kentucky history by viewing the 40-by-25-foot murals painted on the concrete floodwall in Covington. Each depicts a different historical event from the area. These hand-painted murals, the work of nationally renowned artist Robert Dafford, cover 700 feet of floodwall. Individually they are gems, and as a group they're stunning. Viewers feel like they are observing snippets of history as they gaze at John Roebling, builder of the Suspension Bridge, conferring with Amos Shinkle, Covington banker, about construction plans. Another mural invites us to watch as escaped slave Margaret Garner struggles to cross the frozen Ohio River with her children. Take time to view all 18 panels, each one a chapter in Northern Kentucky's past.

✏ ♿ ✿ **Carroll Chimes Bell Tower** (859-655-4159), W. 6th St. at Philadelphia St. in Covington. This 100-foot bell tower, a replica of an authentic German glockenspiel, contains a 43-bell carillon that chimes on the quarter hour. At the top of each hour, watch as automated puppet-like figures carry out a performance of the Pied Piper of Hamelin, a German folktale.

✿ **Monte Casino Chapel** (859-341-5800), 333 Thomas More Pkwy., Crestview Hills. This tiny fieldstone chapel is just 6 by 9 feet. It was built by Benedictine monks in 1878 on the grounds of a nearby monastery. The monks left town and the property was sold, but the owner donated the tiny chapel to Thomas More College. In 1965, locals spearheaded a campaign to restore and move the wee chapel 6 miles to the campus. In 1922, *Ripley's Believe It or Not* named it the "Smallest Church in the World." You can't go inside, but you can look in the windows and admire it from the surrounding patio. Free.

MONTE CASINO CHAPEL

photo by Nick Kremer

✳ To Do

BOATING BB Riverboats (859-261-8500, 800-261-8586; www.bbriverboats.com), 1 Riverboat Way, Newport. The area's oldest and largest riverboat company. Cruise the Ohio River on an authentic paddle-wheeler and enjoy a delicious meal while enjoying your excursion. Various dinner and themed cruises are available year-round, but the schedule is cut back a bit Nov.–Apr.

GOLF Devou Park Golf Course (859-431-8030; www.golffusion.com/devoupark), 1344 Audubon Rd., Covington. This 18-hole public course is open year-round, with postcard-style hilltop views high above Covington and Cincinnati.

Twin Oaks Golf & Plantation Club (859-581-2410; www.golfattwinoaks.com), 450 E. 43rd St., Covington. Built in 1927, this public course features a serene course with massive mature trees, right along the Licking River. They have a full-service pro shop and a somewhat upscale bar and grill.

World of Sports (859-371-8255), 7400 Woodspoint Dr., Florence. Open weekdays 8–11 and weekends 7–11. They have an 18-hole, par-72 golf course. Easy to find, right off I-75, in the middle of a shopping mecca, it's the place to go if you want to get in a quick game. This course is right on the flight path of the nearby Greater Cincinnati International Airport, so you might feel like you have to duck your head as the overseas flights come in for a landing. They also have a lighted and covered driving range, a full-service pro shop, and a fun miniature golf course that is lighted so you can play at night.

The Golf Courses of Kenton County (331-371-3200; www.kentoncounty.org), 3908 Richardson Rd., Independence. With three courses at one location, golfers have a chance to try out all 54 holes. The rolling hills and tree-lined fairways offer challenges for all levels of golfers.

Meadowood Golf Club (859-586-0422), 1911 Golf Club Dr., Burlington. This 9-hole, par-35 public course is fairly flat and easy to walk. Although most holes are par 3, locals claim several of them are fairly difficult.

HORSE RACING Turfway Park Race Course (859-371-0200, 800-733-0200; www.turfway.com), 7500 Turfway Rd., Florence. Home to the Derby prep race known as the Lanes End Stakes in spring and, in fall, the Breeder's Cup prep race called the Kentucky Cup. Turfway Park is a well-respected track in the thoroughbred world. Catch a live race or bet on a race at a faraway track through the beauty of simulcasting. Turfway hosts three live meets per year, the Fall Meet, the Holiday Meet, and the Winter/Spring Meet. Lucky for you, the entire grandstand is indoors, so you can enjoy racing year-round. When the weather is nice, go outside and stand right at the track's edge where you can feel the wind as the horses charge past. Call for exact dates and times. The track is dark on Monday and Tuesday, which is horse-talk for "not open." Free admission and free parking year-round, except on the days of the big prep races mentioned above.

MINOR-LEAGUE BASEBALL Florence Freedom (859-594-4487; www .florencefreedom.com), Champion Window Field, 7950 Freedom Way, Florence. Good old-fashioned baseball games, without the major-league salaries or ticket prices. The Freedom plays in the independent Frontier League and is not affiliated with the pros. They usually play about 50 home games each summer, packing each one with exciting baseball mixed with silly promotions, giveaways, and contests.

RACEWAY Florence Speedway (859-485-7591; www.florencespeedway.com), 12234 US 42, Walton. Built in the 1950s, this 0.5-mile high-banked clay oval is one of the premiere Dirt Late Model tracks in Kentucky. Open on Saturdays Mar.–Oct., this track is the place to go for a regular racing program of Late Models, Modifieds, Super Dirt Stocks, and Pure Stocks.

TOUR **Ride the Ducks** (859-815-1439; newportducks.com), 1 Aquarium Way, Newport. Open 9–9 daily during summer. See the area aboard a reproduction World War II–era amphibious motor vehicle. Operating on land and sea, or in this case river, the vehicle is part bus, part boat. Tours last about an hour, taking in all the hot spots on both sides of the river. Then, just in case they missed anything, the vehicle drives right into the river for a floating tour of the skylines. The tour guides are funny, and everyone on board gets a Wacky Quacker, a sort of kazoo shaped like a duck's bill. Passengers can make lots of quacking noises and grab the attention of passersby, as if cruising the streets in a giant boat weren't enough. $13 adults, $10 children.

ROEBLING SUSPENSION BRIDGE

photo by Deborah Kohl Kremer

WALKS Riverside Drive–Licking River Historic Area & Riverwalk Statue Tour (859-655-4159), Riverside Dr., Covington. Located at the confluence of the Ohio and Licking Rivers, Riverside Drive is home to Civil War–era homes, carriage houses, and serene gardens. Take a self-guided tour and admire the J. A. Roebling Bridge, a true Covington landmark, and visit with the seven life-like bronze statues of prominent Northern Kentucky historical figures: Simon Kenton, Mary B. Greene, James Bradley, Chief Little Turtle, John Roebling, John James Audubon, and Daniel Carter Beard.

✳ Green Space

PARKS Devou Park (859-292-2151), Western Ave., Covington. The grande dame of Covington parks, this 550-acre recreation area was a gift to the city from the Devou family in 1910. Full of rolling hills, wooded trails, and scenic vistas, it is perfect for year-round fun. It features an 18-hole golf course, playgrounds, a fishing lake, walking, hiking, and biking trails, and a breathtaking overlook of the Covington, Newport, and Cincinnati riverfronts. A historic amphitheater is home to the summer series of the Northern Kentucky Symphony Orchestra and other outdoor productions. It is also home to the Behringer-Crawford Museum, where you can learn millions of years' worth of information about the history of Northern Kentucky.

🐾 ♿ 🐾 **Big Bone Lick State Park** (859-384-3522; www.parks.ky.gov), 3380 Beaver Rd., Union. About 15,000 years ago, this area was populated by mammoths, mastodons, ground sloths, and bison that were attracted by the warm salt springs. They lived and died here, making the grounds a smorgasbord of paleontology fossils. The 546-acre park includes a museum that exhibits some of these fossils as well as a life-sized diorama that shows how some of the animals died while in the marsh bog. There are also walking and hiking trails, playgrounds, bass and bluegill fishing, and a herd of live bison.

BIG BONE LICK STATE PARK

photo by Nick Kremer

Split Rock Conservation Park (859-689-9999; www.splitrockpark.org), 4503 Belleview Rd., Petersburg. This outdoor education facility offers programs on ecology, archaeology, geology, and the history of the local area. Named for the glacial formations created on the site during the ice ages thousands of years ago, Split Rock Park is an educational experience for both young and old. Call for guided tour.

✴ Lodging

⊗ ✎ ⁗ᵀ⁗ BED & BREAKFASTS

Amos Shinkle House (800-972-7012; www.amosshinklebnb.com), 215 Garrard St., Covington. Built in 1854 and listed on the National Historic Register, this magnificent home features 16-foot ceilings and intricate woodwork. The six antiques-filled rooms have private baths, modern-day amenities like phones, cable television and wireless Internet access. It is located in Covington's Licking-Riverside Historic District, just a block and a half from the Ohio River. Breakfast is made to order, so try some goetta, a hometown favorite, and live like a local. $$

Christopher's B&B (859-491-9354, 888-585-7085), 604 Poplar St., Bellevue. Named for the patron saint of travel. You'll love spending the night in this former church built in the mid-1800s. The comfy rooms feature the breathtaking original stained-glass windows and well-maintained hardwood floors. The whirlpool tubs and warm welcome from the Guidugli family will make you want to stay. $$–$$$

⊗ ✎ 🐾 **First Farm Inn** (859-586-0199; www.firstfarminn.com), 2510 Stevens Rd., Idlewild. Get away from it all without being very far. This 1870s farmhouse is surrounded by 200-year-old trees and 21 acres of farmland, but really only about 20 minutes from Florence or Cincinnati. Owner Jen Warner invites her guests to go horseback riding, soak in an outdoor hot tub, or simply sit on the porch swing and breathe in the clean air. If you are traveling with your horse, they have overnight stalls available. $$

⁗ᵀ⁗ **Gateway House Bed and Breakfast** (859-581-6447; www.gatewaybb.com), 326 E. 6th St., Newport. This Italianate town house, which dates back to 1878, is located right in the heart of Newport's East Row Historic District. It has been restored to its original grandeur with intricate woodwork and plaster moldings, but modern-day conveniences like private baths have been added. Innkeepers Ken and Sandy Clift have filled it with Victorian-era antiques, musical instruments, and artwork. The home has three guest rooms, all with queen-sized bed, private bath, and a fireplace. $

⁗ᵀ⁗ **Willis Graves Bed and Breakfast** (859-689-5096; www.burligrave.com), 5825 N. Jefferson St., Burlington. You'll feel like you are so far out in the country, but really you're only minutes from the hustle and bustle. Rooms and suites are available in both the 1850s William Rouse log cabin and the 1830s Willis Graves Federal brick homestead. All the rooms are wonderfully appointed with authentic antiques and accessories to make you feel right at home. Even though the surroundings are old and authentic, you might not want to get out of the modern steam showers found in each room. Innkeepers Nancy and Bob Swartzel know how to make everyone feel welcome. Their attention to detail will amaze you. Don't miss the gourmet breakfast of crème brûlée French toast. $$

✎ 🐾 ⁗ᵀ⁗ **Weller Haus Bed and Breakfast** (859-431-6829; www.wellerhaus.com), 319 Poplar St., Bellevue. Just a stone's throw from the attractions of Newport, this B&B is actually two side-by-side Victorian Gothic homes. There are five guest rooms, all with private bath, and three with two-person Jacuzzi tub. Guests choose when breakfast is served and order off a menu. If you are stumped, try the banana walnut French toast. $

ꝼ **Wallace House Bed and Breakfast** (859-261-2717; www.wallacehouse bb.com), 120 Wallace Ave., Covington. This 1900s Colonial Revival home is tucked right in the heart of Covington's historic Wallace Woods neighborhood. Surrounded by Victorian mansions, Queen Anne–style homes, and huge Tudors with Palladian-inspired gable windows, fish-scale shingles, gingerbread accents, and stained-glass windows and transoms, it is an architectural dream. Each of the three guest rooms has a queen-sized bed, private bath, cable television, and high-speed Internet access. Enjoy a gourmet breakfast by candlelight; the main attraction is innkeeper Jenni Woodruff's maple croissant soufflé. $

✳ Where to Eat

⚹ ꝼ **DINING OUT Greyhound Tavern** (859-331-3767; www.greyhound tavern.com), 2500 Dixie Hwy., Fort Mitchell. Open every day for lunch and dinner; Sunday brunch 10–2. This landmark eatery is the upscale yet casual place to eat delicious food and see old friends. Northern Kentucky's oldest continuous operating restaurant has been serving up their signature dishes like Kentucky hot slaw and huge, really huge, onion rings since 1921. You have your choice of dining in the Williamsburg Room, with a colonial decor, the Knotty Pine Room with a rustic, comfortable atmosphere, or even outside on the front porch. Crowd pleasers are the fried chicken dinners and the Kentucky hot brown. $$–$$$

⚹ ꝼ **The Argentine Bean** (859-426-1042; www.argentinebean.net), 2875 Town Center Blvd., Crestview Hills. Open daily for lunch and dinner. Tucked into a corner of an upscale shopping center is a gem of a restaurant. It feels like a coffeehouse, with a comfy couch, bistro-style tables, antiques scattered about, and fun Argentine music playing. The tapas-style menu features small entrées made for sharing and noshing. Order a few so you can try the various choices like skirt steak with chimichurri, pepper-crusted tuna, or a panzanella salad. It's all fresh and delicious. Live music on weekends. $–$$

ꝼ **Behle Street Café** (859-291-4100; www.behlestreetcafe.com), 50 E. RiverCenter Blvd., Covington. Open every day 11 AM–2 AM. The menu covers all the bases, with comfort food like meat loaf and shepherd's pie along with fajitas and the very popular Capellini Behle Street, a garlic-enhanced sautéed pasta dish. Salads are big and served with a wide variety of dressings. The menu also offers stuffed-full sandwiches, homemade soups, and wonderful appetizers. $$

ꝼ **Vito's** (859-442-9444; www.vitos cafe.com), 654 Highland Ave., Fort Thomas. Serving dinner at 5 every day. Enjoy upscale dining, authentic Italian recipes, warm and cozy ambience, all while being serenaded by singing waiters. Feast on wheel of Parmigianno while enjoying an aria from a classic opera like *Carmen*. Owners Vito and Mary Ciepiel don't want you to stop by on your way out for the evening; they want Vito's to be your evening. $$–$$$

ꝼ **Jeff Ruby's Waterfront** (859-581-1414; www.jeffruby.com/waterfront), 14 Pete Rose Pier, Covington. Mon.–Thu. 5:30–10 PM, Fri. 5:30–10:30, Sat. 5–11. Known for their steak, lobster, and sushi, the Waterfront is a floating restaurant and nightclub offering an unmatched view of the Cincinnati skyline. This is upscale dining, with impeccable service, in a highly charged atmosphere. Kind of the place to see and be seen, it is frequented by TV and sports celebs, as well as the pretty people who usually surround them. $$–$$$

Ŷ **Dee Felice Café** (859-261-2365; www.deefelice.com), 529 Main St., Covington. Open daily with dinner served at 5. Sunday brunch 10:30–3. Nestled in the heart of Covington's German Main Strasse Village, you will find Dee Felice Café, a restaurant known not for sausage and strudel, but for Cajun and Creole specialties. This New Orleans–inspired restaurant is elegant but relaxed and fun. Their most popular entrée is Dee's Filet—a blackened filet served on shrimp cream sauce and surrounded by shrimp. Ease into your Sunday morning with an omelet-of-the-day or gourmet French toast. To add to the ambience, diners get to enjoy live jazz or Dixieland music every night. $$–$$$

Ŷ **Tousey House Tavern** (859-586-9900; www.touseyhouse.com), 5963 N. Jefferson St., Burlington. Serving dinner Tue.–Sun. at 5. Reservations suggested. Dine in the extraordinary home Erastus Tousey built for his family in 1825. The restaurant is full of period pieces, like antique furnishings and handmade cross-stitch samplers that enhance the original woodwork, mantels, and staircases in this home. This upscale dining establishment offers varied menu options like limestone Bibb salad, Tousey hot brown, and glazed pork chops. $$–$$$

Ŷ **Indigo Casual Gourmet Cafe** (859-331-4339; www.myindigogrill .com), 2053 Dixie Hwy., Fort Mitchell. Open daily 11–10. Eclectic menu features salads, pasta dishes, sandwiches, and pizzas, all with fresh and not-so-common ingredients like hummus, artichokes, shiitake mushrooms, and Asiago cheese. Try the Indigo Idaho appetizer—much like traditional potato skins, with bacon and sharp cheddar

on a pizza crust. If the weather is cooperating, dine outside on their front patio. $$

Ŷ **Knotty Pine on the Bayou** (859-791-2200), 1802 Licking Pike, Cold Spring. Serving dinner seven days per week. This isn't Louisiana, but you might think you've died and gone to Cajun Heaven once you've arrived at this out-of-the-way gem. Menu features include garlicky frog legs, crispy crabcakes, extraordinary gumbo, and fried oysters; on Thursday nights, they even have a crawfish boil. $$–$$$

Ŷ **Molly Malone's Irish Pub and Restaurant** (859-491-6699; www .mollymalonesirishpub.com), 112 E. 4th St., Covington. Open for lunch and dinner every day. A true Irish pub and eatery in the heart of downtown Covington. The rich wood decor and huge authentic bar make the restaurant warm and inviting. The bar serves up Irish brews, and the menu features favorites like bangers and mash, fish-and-chips, and traditional lamb stew straight from the Emerald Isle. $–$$

Ŷ **Oriental Wok** (859-331-3000; www.orientalwok.com), Buttermilk Pike, Fort Mitchell. Open Sun.–Thu. 11–9:30, Fri. 11–10:30, Sat. 4–10:30. Mike and Helen Wong immigrated to the United States from Hong Kong in the 1970s and opened their upscale Chinese restaurant in 1977, counting on the American Dream to be their reality. Today the Oriental Wok is Northern Kentucky's answer for where to go for an elegant evening of fine dining and impeccable service. Fountains, waterfalls, and even a stream with goldfish running through the spacious and warm dining room make the experience incomparable. $$–$$$

Ŷ **Pompilios** (859-581-3065), 6th and Washington Ave., Newport. Open for lunch and dinner every day. Pompilios,

Ⓨ **Hofbräuhaus Newport** (859-491-7200; www.hofbrauhausnewport.com), 3rd and Saratoga at the Levee, Newport. Open 11–9 daily. $$–$$$

Northern Kentucky's German roots run deep. So when you are hungry for some authentic German beer and some Wiener schnitzel, well, just grab your lederhosen and head for the Hofbräuhaus in Newport. The giant dining hall and brewery is a re-creation of the famous haus in Munich.

The beer made on site is not some fancy new brew created to compete with microbreweries. The Hofbräu brand was created in 1589 when Duke William V of Bavaria wanted to provide beer to his royal family. It's brewed on site according to the German Purity Law using water, hops, malt, and yeast only. In keeping with tradition, Newport has a Brew Master on site to supervise the production of the Hofbräuhaus beer. You can also supervise production yourself: The brewing area is surrounded by windows, and for a closer view you can ask for a tour.

Hofbräu beers are a little more potent than typical American brews, so consider yourself warned. Some good ones to sample are the Hofbräu Premium Lager and Hofbräu Maibock, which is 7.2 percent alcohol. Munich's favorite, the Original Hofbräu Dunkel, is still directly imported from Munich.

The Hofbräuhaus produces seasonal brews as well. The spring beer, Maiboch, is tied to the German tradition of Maifest. In November and December, they brew Winterfestbier, to coincide with the chilly weather.

The company wanted its US version to have the same feel as the original in Munich, so the Beer Hall has imported benches, chairs, and tables, as

which has been a local favorite for nearly 70 years, is famous for two things: traditional Italian food and the toothpick scene from the movie *Rain Man*. Yes, Dustin Hoffman and Tom Cruise filmed that scene right there in the corner of the bar area. Once you get past that star-crossed moment, grab a menu. Italian food makes up 98 percent of their offerings, and once you taste their handmade meat and cheese ravioli, or their linguine cacciatore, you will know why. Start your meal with the homemade minestrone soup and wrap it up with the home-made cannoli for dessert. Don't forget to order a Coca-Cola. It's served in little 8-ounce bottles like you used to get when you were a kid. $$

✐ ⚲ **EATING OUT Anchor Grill** (859-431-9498), 438 W. Pike St., Covington. The neon sign in the window proudly proclaims, WE MAY DOZE, BUT NEVER CLOSE, and that's how regulars remember the Anchor Grill's hours. Some may call this a greasy spoon, but to locals, that's quite an insult. The compliment is that chain restaurants try to copy this hometown diner feel, well as woodwork and brewing artifacts. It's certainly not fancy, but the giant hall is festive and feels like you're attending a party.

With seating for about 720, chances are good you'll find a table. You can dine in the rowdy Beer Hall and listen to the "Haus band" play old-fashioned oom-pah-pah; or in the beer Stubbe, a quiet dining area for families and those who would like a more relaxing meal. The Bier Garden is out back and attracts a large after-work crowd in summer.

Although the brew is straight from the Old Country, the menu is straight from a German kitchen, with a few American favorites thrown in as well. The most popular menu item is the Pretzels and Bier Cheese. The pretzels are imported from Germany, but the Bier Cheese is created locally. Other German items that are imported are the red cabbage and sauerkraut. Not everything comes from Germany; they import Holtzhofenbrot, a nutty rye bread for Reuben sandwiches, from Canada.

Menu options like Sauerbraten, Fritierte Gurken (fried pickles), and Hofbräuhaus Gulaschsuppe (a type of beef stew with Hungarian paprika) all add to the German ambience. How about some Leberkäse—Bavarian meat loaf served with German potato wedges and topped with a fried egg? Certainly not your run-of-the-mill menu items.

Don't skimp on dessert. What's a traditional German meal without Apfelstrud'l (apple strudel) or Windbeutel (a traditional Bavarian creampuff)?

For those not so daring, the menu also features New York strip, chicken tenders, and glazed salmon. Looks like whatever you choose, it will be wunderbar!

but you just can't re-create 60 years of history. The food, simple meals like pork chops, meat loaf, and burgers (order yours deluxe if you want lettuce and tomato), is always good. Round-the-clock breakfast, like eggs, goetta, hash browns, and fried egg sandwiches are always in high demand, especially on weekends around 2 AM when it's hard to find a table. To add to its charm, instead of a smoking section, the restaurant is all-smoking. While you're there, don't miss the band in the back room. Whenever a song is played on the jukebox (Don Ho's "Tiny Bubbles" is a popular favorite), the disco ball spins and a 2-foot-tall enclosed stage in the corner lights up. A curtain opens and a small band made up of mechanical figures "plays." One of the band members malfunctioned years ago, so now a Barbie Doll fills in. $

Y **Barleycorns** (859-331-6633 Lakeside location, 859-442-3400 Cold Spring location; www.barleycorns.com), 2642 Dixie Hwy., Lakeside Park, and 1073 Industrial Rd., Cold Spring. Open for lunch and dinner every day. There is always something fun going on at Barleycorns. This neighborhood sports bar and restaurant is the perfect place to bring a family or to come watch the big game on one of the many TVs scattered about. They are known for their bar food, like wings, skins, and nachos. But go for lunch or dinner and enjoy entrées like grilled salmon, Kentucky hot brown, and grilled rib eyes. The Lakeside Park location is housed in a former tollgate along Dixie Highway, with creaky hardwood floors and walls loaded with memorabilia and even a few stuffed wild animals. The Cold Spring location, loaded with sports paraphernalia, is the place to be when the Kentucky Wildcats are on TV. Both sites have fantastic outdoor patios, complete with umbrella tables. $$–$$$

Montoya's Mexican Restaurant (859-341-0707), 2507 Chelsea Dr., Fort Mitchell. Open for lunch and dinner every day. Stop in for authentic, casual, Mexican dining at reasonable prices. Owner Socorio Ramirez moved to the United States from Mexico more than 30 years ago, bringing with her the recipes and the know-how of a Mexican kitchen. Her most popular entrées are the enchilada plate and Montoya's Plato, which is made of bite-sized pieces of seasoned pork tenderloin. Entrées are delicious and generous in size, but locals know it is the homemade salsa that makes their mouths water. $

LaRosa's Pizza (859-347-1111; www.larosas.com), nine locations in Northern Kentucky. Serving up authentic Italian pizza for more than 50 years, LaRosa's is the best. Their pizza, calzones, wings, and hoagies make the national chains pale in comparison. Try the Philly cheese steak calzone or the baked Buddy hoagy, named for founder Buddy LaRosa. It's a delectable combination of capicola ham, pepperoni, salami, and provolone, baked and covered in pizza sauce, onions, and pickles. Before you go, you might want to buy some LaRosa's Italian salad dressing or spaghetti sauce to take with you. Everybody does. This is the perfect place to bring a family, but they also deliver more than 40 menu items in a timely fashion. $–$$

Colonial Cottage (341-4498), 3140 Dixie Hwy., Erlanger. Open daily 7 AM–9 PM. If you haven't had your mandatory-while-in-Northern-Kentucky serving of goetta yet, head for the Cottage and get yourself some. They serve breakfast all day long in their warm and inviting dining room. The centerpiece is a huge fieldstone fireplace, which makes you feel like you are in someone's living room. Owner Matt Grimes and his waitresses, some of whom have worked at the Cottage for more than 20 years, are glad to have you and will probably remember your name next time you're there. In addition to their loosen-your-belt-a-notch breakfasts, they features southern favorites like hand-breaded catfish, cottage ham, and fried chicken. They also offer five hot vegetables each day and unbelievable meringue pies. $–$$

Kremer's Market (859-341-1067; www.kremersmarket.com), 755 Buttermilk Pike, Crescent Springs. In business since 1913, the Kremer family was known locally for their homegrown vegetables like hothouse tomatoes, sweet Silver Queen corn, and crispy Bibb lettuce, all grown on their farm in nearby Villa Hills. The business has come a long way since then. Now run by fourth-generation Kremers, they still offer seasonal homegrown vegetables but also have a full-service deli, garden center, and unique gift items. There's no room for seating, so you'll have to get yours to go. Stop by the giant side-by-side red barns and try some famous chicken salad, home-made breads, chicken and wild rice soup, and butter cream fudge. $–$$

Green Derby Restaurant (859-431-8740), 846 York St., Newport. Serving three meals a day, every day. A local favorite for home-cooked meals, the Green Derby has been making people feel at home for more than 50 years. Because the spot has been repeatedly voted Best Fish Sandwich in the Tris-tates, you may feel obligated to try the wonderful fried halibut sandwich—but you'll be equally satisfied with a burger and fries or some pork chops. They are also known for their Derby salad: shredded iceberg lettuce served like hot slaw. For dessert, don't miss their homemade pies—apple, coconut cream, lemon meringue, among others. $–$$

Walt's Hitching Post (859-331-0494), 3300 Madison Pike, Fort Wright. Open daily 11 AM–midnight. There's some-thing about a working smokehouse out in the parking lot that tells you this is the place to go for ribs. Walt's has been a Northern Kentucky institution for about 50 years, serving smoked, dry-rubbed ribs with plenty of their own tangy sauce for generations. This casu-al family restaurant offers steaks, chops, and burgers, too, but it's the ribs that make them famous.

Ⴤ **Stringtown Restaurant** (859-371-8222), 255 Main St., Florence. Open Mon.–Sat. 8–8, Sun. 9–2. Housed in a building that dates back to 1869, Stringtown used to be a stagecoach stop for weary travelers on their way between Lexington and Cincinnati. Today it is a casual stop for locals look-ing for homemade food at reasonable prices. World-renowned chef Rick Pot-ter keeps favorites like sandwiches, meat loaf, and liver and onions on the menu but introduces more exotic

dinner specials to show off his culinary dexterity. $$

Ⴤ **York Street Café** (859-261-9675), 801 York St., Newport. Open for lunch and dinner every day. On the National Historic Register, this building—which once housed a pharmacy—dates back to the 1880s. In the first-floor dining area you'll be drawn in by the floor-to ceiling cabinetry that once held elixirs and tonics, now jam-packed with funky collectibles for your enjoyment. The warm woodwork, some stained glass, and mismatched light fixtures all add to the show. It is a mix of restaurant, art gallery, and lounge. Enjoy an entrée or a homemade dessert or settle in to a comfy couch and order a con-versation platter like the Mediter-ranean board, a sampling of Greek favorites including hummus, tab-bouleh, Greek salad, and spanakopita, created for sharing. $$

Ⴤ **Herb and Thelma's** (859-491-6984), 718 Pike St., Covington. Mon.–Sat. 11–11, Sunday 1–7. This is a neighborhood bar with cheap, as well as excellent, cheeseburgers. Owner Chip Boemker is behind the bar all the time, serving up drinks and burgers and chatting with everyone who comes in. The tavern has been in business since the 1930s and hasn't changed much over the years, which is quite an asset. Watch your step as you open the door: The concrete stoop has started to wear away, evidence of the 80 years of foot traffic going in and out. $

Spare Time Grill (859-635-5542), 7807 Alexandria Pk., Alexandria. Open Mon.–Sat. 6 AM–2 PM, Sun. 8–2. This is one of those landmark places, some-times referred to as a "dive." This 50-plus-year-old diner has just two tables and 15 stools at the counter . . . but what it lacks in luxury, it makes up for in charm. There is usually a lively con-versation going on with the regulars to the tune of bacon, eggs, burgers, and potatoes sizzling on the grill. $

Rima's Diner (859-331-6444), 2520 Hazelwood St., Crescent Springs. Serving lunch and dinner every day. If you can walk past the dessert case without stopping to ogle the giant servings of cakes and pies that are slowly spinning their tempting way, well, you've made it farther than most people. Seems most customers know what they are ordering for dessert before they even get their menu. But take time to read the menu. Rima's has southern-influenced offerings like fried chicken, pinto beans, and lots of side dishes covered in gravy. Sandwiches, salads, and lunch specials are all good options. This family-style diner features old-time movie posters and memorabilia. $–$$

✑ **SNACKS Graeter's** (859-341-3005, 859-261-3160; www.graeters .com), 301 Buttermilk Pike, Fort Mitchell, and 342 Monmouth St., Newport. Open daily. A Cincinnati favorite with two locations in Northern Kentucky. This is what ice cream is all about. Following a family recipe that dates back to 1870, Graeter's ice cream is so dense and creamy, it can only be made 2 gallons at a time. Of course they have vanilla and butter pecan, but do yourself a favor and order a flavor with chips, like black raspberry chip or chocolate chip. Calling it a chip is sort of a misnomer: Hidden inside the ice cream are gigantic chunks of deep dark solid chocolate. It's like finding a prize in every bite. $

✳ **Entertainment**

Monmouth Theatre (859-655-9140; www.monmouththeatre.com), 636 Monmouth St., Newport. This truly eclectic entertainment venue in downtown Newport features a huge variety of live performances. Check the web site to see what's showing; expect anything from live theater to jazz shows and everything in between.

♈ **Shadowbox Cabaret** (859-581-7625, 888-887-423,; www.shadow boxcabaret.com), 1 Levee Way, Newport. Lunch and dinner shows daily. Newport's answer to stuffy dinner theater is the eclectic Shadowbox Cabaret at Newport on the Levee. The high-energy show featuring comedy, monologues, and live rock 'n' roll, is often compared to *Saturday Night Live* on a local level. All shows go for the outrageous, over-the-top performance, to surprise the audience and make them come back for more. Although there is no age requirement to get into the shows, Shadowbox rates them R—this is adult comedy, full of mature themes, an occasional four-letter-word, and a full dose of double entendres. This is a theater that serves food and drinks, not a bar with a show. Menu choices like pizzas, salads, and nachos, along with a full bar, are available before the show and at intermission. During the show, all the employees are in the production, so they can't be waiting tables.

Southgate House (859-431-2201; www.southgatehouse.com), 24 E. 3rd St. Newport. Built in 1814, this historic mansion, which is said to be haunted, has had many notable owners and visitors. One such resident was Brigadier General John Taliaferro Thompson, the inventor of the Thompson machine gun, better known as a Tommy gun, who was born here on December 31, 1860. Today it is a nationally recognized music venue featuring a different act on each of its four cozy floors. They are hugely supportive of the local music scene; check the web site for a list of bands, acts, and performances.

✳ Selective Shopping

Kentucky Haus Craft Gallery (859-261-4287; www.kentuckyhaus.com), 411 E. 10th St., Newport. Find the finest works of Kentucky artisans in this unique shop. They have a huge collection of Louisville Stoneware, Bybee Pottery, and various Kentucky foods, baskets, candles, and books.

Donna Salyers' Fabulous Furs (859-291-3300, 800-848-4650; fabulousfurs.com), 25 W. Robbins St., Covington. You've probably seen these impeccable wraps, throws, and fake-fur coats on stars and models, but you just assumed they were real. They certainly look like they just came off a mink, fox, or rabbit, but they are actually made of the finest acrylic you can find. Visit the showroom and wrap yourself in the lap of luxury, without the guilt. Donna invites you to feel everything in the store. You won't believe it's faux.

Rabbit Hash General Store (859-586-7744; www.rabbithash.com), 10021 Lower River Rd., Rabbit Hash. Step back in time when you enter the doors of this authentic general store that has been in operation since 1831. Located right in the heart of the historic river town of Rabbit Hash, it is the centerpiece for the whole town. Stop in and shoot the breeze with some locals while you browse an assortment of antiques, handcrafted goods, collectible pottery, and organic products. Stick around for the barn dances and impromptu concerts usually held on weekends. You might even get to meet the town mayor, Lucy Lou, a Border collie, who beat out her competition with the slogan "A bitch you can count on."

✪ **The Blue Marble Children's Bookstore** (859-781-0602), 1356 S. Fort Thomas Ave., Fort Thomas. What little one hasn't wondered what it would be like to go into the great green room from the book *Good Night Moon*? Well, at the Blue Marble, you'll see a reproduced great green room so authentic, it even has a bowl full of mush. This independent bookseller has been around since 1979, and they are the authority on children's books. The staff are amazingly helpful and seem to know something about all 30,000 titles they have in stock.

The Village Gallerie (859-331-5965), 1870 Ashwood Circle, Fort Wright. Specializing in the works of local and regional artists, this gallery has a fine collection of equestrian art and Cincinnati and Northern Kentucky scenes. They also do excellent framing.

ANTIQUES Florence Antique Mall (859-371-0600; www.florenceantique mall.com), 8145 Mall Rd., Florence. This is an antiques collector's dream: a one-level, air-conditioned 50,000-square-foot showroom with the finest wares of over 300 quality dealers. They have a wonderful selection of fine antiques, collectibles, furniture, and art.

SHOPPING DISTRICTS Historic Fairfield Avenue (www.shopbellevue ky.com), Bellevue. Historic Fairfield Avenue is still the main thoroughfare in Bellevue, but the once abandoned downtown has been revitalized into a cool retail mix. The **Bellevue Beadery** (859-292-0800) carries thousands of beads from all over the world. You can take a jewelry-making class or just stock up on beads for your own creation. Also, while you are on The Avenue, don't miss **Saponi Soaps** (513-253-1488), where you'll find handcrafted natural soaps made from vegetable oils, herbs, spices, fruits, and even mud from the Dead Sea. Everyone needs a little chocolate after a day of browsing the stores, so swing into **Schneider's Sweet Shop** (859-431-

3545) and order a piece or two of their famous Opera Cream Candy. This is a little piece of rich, creamy, delectable heaven, dunked in milk or dark chocolate. You can only find them in this area, so try one of each. Then pick up a box to take home with you. They also have mouthwatering caramels, truffles, and chocolates, all made from scratch. Walk along the old storefronts and see all the charming shops. Call ahead or check the web site for hours.

Newport on the Levee (859-291-0550, 866-538-3359; www.newporton thelevee.com), 1 Levee Way, Newport. Sitting high atop the floodwall, or Levee, you'll find this hip entertainment destination. Full of trendy nightclubs, mall stores, and a variety of restaurants, the complex is anchored by the Newport Aquarium, the Shadowbox Cabaret, GameWorks, and a 20-screen movie theater.

✳ Special Events

April–October: **Burlington Antique Show**. Held on the third Sunday of the month at the Boone County Fairgrounds, this show usually draws about 250 vendors from around the region. The show officially begins at 8 AM, but the early birds start bargaining about 5 AM. Get there early, wear comfortable shoes, and dress for the weather, because the show goes on regardless of rain, shine, frost, or scorching heat.

&. ✿ *May:* **Maifest at Main Strasse**. Modeled after the German tradition that welcomes spring, Maifest is held annually on the streets of Main Strasse, the German-inspired neighborhood of Covington. There are plenty of libations to quench a thirst, as well as a huge variety of foods. Try a German egg roll—just like its Asian counter-

part, except this one is filled with goetta. This festival brings together unique arts and crafts booths and a variety of musical entertainment, from oom-pah-pah German bands to Kentucky bluegrass.

&. ✿ *June:* **Newport Italianfest**. Held alongside the Ohio River, adjacent to Newport on the Levee. Celebrating Newport's Italian heritage, this weekend festival draws thousands to enjoy authentic Italian food, music, and even a pizza-eating contest.

&. ✿ *August:* **Goettafest**. The celebration of all things goetta, which is Northern Kentucky's answer to breakfast sausage. This German concoction of pork, beef, steel-cut or pinhead oats, and seasonings is fried up to crispy perfection and has been enjoyed for generations. This festival, held annually on Newport's riverfront, brings together food vendors who must provide a few goetta choices, a non-goetta choice, and a dessert. Since no two vendors can offer the same dish, you'll find some pretty creative uses of goetta. If you are new to the dish, try it plain. If you are a connoisseur, try the goetta pizza or goetta Reuben. Goettafest features rides, music, and fun goetta games, too.

&. ✿ *September:* **Octoberfest at Main Strasse**. Held the weekend after Labor Day, this festival is comparable to the annual celebration in Munich. Grab a mug of German beer and a Limburger cheese sandwich and watch men in lederhosen do a polka. There are rides for the kids, live music, and unique crafts at this annual fall festival.

CARROLLTON

Situated almost halfway between Cincinnati and Louisville is the river city of **Carrollton**. Although today's visitors may find it a convenient stopping point for gas and snacks when commuting between the two cities, it was this location that put it on the map back in the late 1700s. Located right at the mouth of the Kentucky River, where it connects to the Ohio, Carrollton became a stopping point, almost an exit ramp, in those early years as river travelers decided which route to take.

Named in honor of Charles Carroll, whose signature you will find on the Declaration of Independence, Carrollton is a perfect example of small-town America. The historic downtown offers a few antiques shops, hometown eateries, and excellent views of the Ohio River. High on a hill overlooking the town, you'll find General Butler State Resort Park, offering a combination of recreation with a splash of history mixed in for good measure.

Although it's hard to call Carrollton a destination city, it is definitely worth a stop as you commute down I-71. Or, if you happen to be traveling by keelboat, there are plenty of docks available, too.

GUIDANCE Carrollton/Carroll County Tourism and Convention Commission (502-732-7036, 800-325-4290; www.carrolltontourism.com), 515 Highland Ave., Carrollton. Open weekdays 9–5. The welcome center here is fully stocked with brochures and maps. The helpful staff can also assist with advice and historical questions.

GETTING THERE As Carrollton is located about halfway between Louisville and Northern Kentucky, the area is served by both the **Cincinnati/Northern Kentucky International Airport** (859-767-3151; www.cvgairport.com) and the **Louisville International Airport** (502-368-6524; www.flylouisville.com), which is located at the intersection of I-65 and I-264. Check both to compare airfares. Car rentals are available at both airports.

GETTING AROUND Carrollton has no public transportation, so you will need a car. It is easy to get around the area, as streets are well marked and parking is free.

MEDICAL EMERGENCY Carroll County Hospital (502-732-4321), 309 11th St., Carrollton, is a 25-bed critical care facility. About 17 miles away across the river in Madison, Indiana, is the larger **King's Daughters Hospital** (812-265-5211; www.kingsdaughtershospital.org), 1 King's Daughters' Dr., Madison. This 115-bed hospital includes a full range of services.

ALCOHOL You can get a drink in the area, depending on which area you're in. Carroll County and Gallatin County are wet, meaning you can purchase alcohol most anywhere. Neighboring Owen County is dry, meaning no alcohol sales, except for the Elk Creek Winery (see the sidebar). And farther east, Grant County is moist, which means no liquor sales except in restaurants in the cities of Corinth and Williamstown. Call ahead if you want a drink with dinner and see what the law is there.

✳ To See

Butler-Turpin State Historic House is located inside General Butler State Resort Park (502-732-4384; www.parks.ky.gov), KY 227, Carrollton. Tours of the home and the outdoor summer kitchen are available. Tours Wed.–Sat. on the hour 9–4 (except for noon–1, when the house is closed for lunch). Originally owned by Phillip Turpin and his wife, Mary Ellen Butler Turpin, this Greek Revival home served this politically connected family well through the mid-1800s. The house is loaded with original family pieces and has been restored to its original splendor. Don't miss the pianoforte (which has never been removed from the home) or the drop-leaf table in the parlor, which still bears the claw marks of the family cat. $5 adults, $3 children; under 6 free.

The Masterson House (502-732-7036, 800-325-4290; www.carrolltontourism .com), Highland Ave., Carrollton. Call for tour hours. Visit what is thought to be the first two-story brick house built between Louisville and Cincinnati. An engineering marvel of its time, it was constructed by slaves around 1790 with bricks that were created on site.

The Old Stone Jail (502-732-7036, 800-325-4290; www.carrolltontourism.com), Highland Ave. and Court St., Carrollton. You won't believe that this primitive jail

THE BUTLER-TURPIN STATE HISTORIC HOUSE

photo by Deborah Kohl Kremer

was still in use as late as 1969, but it was. The two-story stone structure was built in 1880, with just a few barbaric-looking cells, a potbellied stove for warmth, and small, glassless windows for light. Contact the tourism office for a tour.

♂ ❦ **Markland Locks and Dam**, located 3 miles south of Warsaw. This concrete dam also serves as a bridge over the Ohio River. An observation tower high above lets you watch as boats and barges make their way through the locks.

♂ "¶" ♿ **STATE PARK General Butler State Resort Park** (502-732-4384; www.parks.ky.gov), KY 227, Carrollton. Named for General William Orlando Butler, who was a recognized army general, a congressman, and a vice presidential candidate in 1848. Although he owned slaves, he was staunchly in favor of the preservation of the Union and the gradual emancipation of slaves. Today the park in his name offers a welcoming lodge with 53 guest rooms and 24 cottages, some with up to three bedrooms. The lodge's wood-paneled common area has a cozy fieldstone fireplace, and soaring windows that take in the view high above the Ohio River Valley. Dine at **Two Rivers Restaurant**, a nod to the lodge's location at the confluence of the Kentucky and Ohio Rivers. The dining room is decorated with fun and interesting fishing paraphernalia like rods, reels, driftwood, and old tackle boxes. They serve three meals a day, including a lunch buffet so popular, it brings in people from downtown Carrollton. Sandwiches, burgers, and salads are always on the menu, but entrée choices include Kentucky hot brown, fried catfish, and southern pecan chicken, which is dripping with a sauce that is both sweet and sour at the same time. For recreation, the park has a 9-hole, par-35 golf course located high along the ridges of the mountaintops. The 30-acre lake is perfect for fishing for crappie, catfish, bass, and bluegill. The boat dock rents canoes and pedal boats in the summer. They also have miniature golf, tennis and basketball courts, and playgrounds. The Park Overlook, which is the highest point on the property, offers a breathtaking view of both rivers and the tiny town of Carrollton down below.

✳ To Do

GOLF Sugar Bay Golf Course (859-567-2601), 957 Dry Creek Rd., Warsaw. This 18-hole par-71 public golf course has 13 lakes that come into play on 6 holes.

Perry Park Country Club (502-484-2159), 595 Springport Ferry Rd., Perry Park. Open to the public, this club offers a 27-hole, par-72 championship course.

RACING Kentucky Speedway (888-652-RACE; www.kentuckyspeedway.com), I-71 Exit 57, Sparta. NASCAR lovers can get their fill of the industry's hottest races at the Kentucky Speedway. This enormous track seats more than 66,000 fans. Races are scheduled throughout the year and draw some big-name drivers. The web site will keep you up to date.

Richard Petty Driving Experience (859-743-5745; www.1800bepetty.com), Kentucky Speedway, I-71 Exit 57, Sparta. Whether you want to ride shotgun at speeds up to 165 mph—or actually do the driving yourself—this is the ultimate experience for race fans.

WALKING TOURS Historic Downtown Carrollton Walking or Driving Tour (502-732-7036, 800-325-4290; www.carrolltontourism.com). Pick up a map

photo courtesy of www.kentuckytourism.com

KENTUCKY SPEEDWAY

and begin at the welcome center at 515 Highland Ave., Carrollton. Take in all the sites, including historic and stately Carroll County Courthouse, proud Victorian homes, and the cute storefronts of Carrollton and the surrounding area.

✳ Green Space

Point Park (502-732-7060), 1st and Main Sts. in downtown Carrollton. This 15-acre park sits right at the convergence of the Ohio and Kentucky Rivers. Throughout the year it is used for city and county festivals, but on a daily basis it has a nice playground for kids, a boat ramp for easy access to the rivers, and relaxing places to just sit and enjoy the waterways.

Kleber Wildlife Management Area (502-535-6335), 5005 Cedar Creek Rd., Owenton. Kleber is a 2,575-acre preserve and trail system about halfway between Frankfort and Owenton off US 127. Trail maps are available on site. Hike these rugged trails through woods and grasslands, which often result in wildlife encounters. Kleber is home to plenty of deer, raccoons, and squirrels, but it is also a favorite place for bird-watchers.

✳ Lodging

⊙ BED & BREAKFASTS

The Poet's House Bed & Breakfast (502-347-0135; www.bbonline.com/ky/poetshouse), 501 Main St., Ghent. Sleep in one of the two inviting guest rooms, or for a little more privacy book the next-door River Dance Cottage, which sleeps four. The Federal-style brick home was built in 1863 and is listed on the National Historic Register. Innkeepers David Hendren and Rick Whitfill invite guests to eat their delicious breakfast in the formal dining room or outdoors on a deck overlooking the beautiful Ohio River.

⊙ **Highland House B&B** (502-732-5559; www.bbonline.com/ky/highland), 1705 Highland Ave., Carrollton. This beautiful home, once part of an 800-acre farm, is listed on the National Register of Historic Places. It was built in the early 1920s in an architectural style called Creative Eclectic. The three guest rooms, all furnished with king-sized beds, are spacious and overlook the Ohio River. The home is surrounded by 5 acres of lush gardens complete with walking paths and blossoming landscape. $$

✳ Where to Eat

Welch's Riverside Restaurant (502-732-9118), 505 Main St., Carrollton. Open Mon.–Sat. 5–8, Sun. 6–3. This is Carrollton's only restaurant offering dining with a river view, so grab a good table and enjoy the Ohio River. This is the kind of restaurant that serves breakfast all day and has a little bit of everything on the menu. The dining room consists of several different building additions, and the decor has been created out of a mishmash of booths, old photos of customers, and hotel-going-out-of-business chairs. There is *not* a nonsmoking section, but the locals swear by this place. Sandwiches like country ham, BLTs, and grilled cheese are in just as much demand as the daily specials, which include meat with side dishes like stewed tomatoes and pinto beans. $

Cooper's Restaurant (502-732-4990), 1420 Gillock Ave., Carrollton. Open daily 10–10. Stop in if you're in a hurry. It's like a fast-food restaurant, without all the bells and whistles of a national chain. The menu features choices like burgers, fries, fried chicken, and cod sandwiches. Order at the counter and they'll bring it to your table. They call everyone "honey," so relax and enjoy it. $

✳ Selective Shopping

Purse Heaven (502-732-1121), 509 Highland Ave., Carrollton. This shop specializes in purses inspired by high-priced designer bags. They are not fakes or knockoffs, which are illegal, but purses that look similar to the bags by Prada, Gucci, Vera Bradley, and other big names that carry a big price tag. Buy a whole wardrobe of purses for the price of one designer bag.

Cornerstone Floral and Gift (502-732-9912), 519 Highland Ave., Carrollton. With the heady collection of fresh flowers and scented candles, you'll want to just stand in the doorway and breathe, but do go in and look around. It's a cute shop with country and folk art home decor items, as well as hard-to-find collectibles from Boyd Bears and Willow Tree.

Shandio Valley Winery (502-732-4744), 108 Court St., Carrollton. This shop features fine wines, all made with North American grapes and fermented right in Carroll County. Try a Riesling, which they claim absolutely dances in your mouth. The storefront also sells Kentucky food products and home winemaking supplies.

The Classy Boutique (502-732-0826), 103 Parkland Shopping Center. Open Mon.–Fri. 10–8, Sat. 10–5. This is a consignment shop and craft boutique, full of one-of-a-kind items, collectibles, and handmade art.

ANTIQUES/FLEA MARKETS
Betty's Family Collectables (no phone), 109 5th St., Carrollton. This store is packed with all kinds of antiques: large pieces of furniture, handmade model ships, Civil War memorabilia, and lots of old pictures, bottles, and knickknack items.

Traderbakers Flea Market & Antique Mall (502-732-4173), KY 227, Carrollton. A hodgepodge of antiques and flea-market merchandise makes this the perfect place to spend some time poking around.

OUTLET MALLS
Butler Outlet Mall (502-732-6666), KY 227, Carrollton. Open daily. Shops include the VF (Vanity Fair) Outlet, Banister Shoes, Bon Worth, Dress Barn, Van Heusen,

and Wang's Jewelry. Get factory discounts on clothes and shoes for the whole family.

✳ Special Events

♦ ♿ ♣ *June:* **Carroll County Fair** (502-732-8005, 502-732-7036). This all-American County Fair is held on the Carroll County Fairgrounds each year. They have all the fixings of a traditional fair, like rides, games, demolition derbies, lots of 4-H exhibits, and plenty of food and music. You'll enjoy this good, old-fashioned county fair.

♦ ♿ ♣ *July:* **Bluegrass Festival** (502-732-8516). Held on the grounds of General Butler State Park, this festival offers a weekend of down-home bluegrass music, food, and fun.

♦ ♿ ♣ *September:* **Blues to the Point** (502-732-6960; www.bluestothepoint .net). Held at the confluence of the Ohio and Kentucky Rivers, at Carrollton's Point Park. Offering two days full of headlining blues music on two stages.

♦ ♿ ♣ **Two Rivers Fall Festival** (502-255-7054; www.tworiversfest .com). Enjoy some small-town fun at downtown Carrollton's Courthouse Square. The festival always has an assortment of rides and games, flea-market finds, arts and crafts, and plenty of food and fun.

♈ ELK CREEK

Located about an hour from Northern Kentucky, Louisville, and Lexington, in the tiny town of Owenton, you'll find Elk Creek. Home to a resort, winery, art gallery, and hunt club, this off-the-beaten-path locale makes for a perfect respite while traveling, but is actually a destination on its own.

Elk Creek Vineyards (502-484-0005; www.elkcreekvineyards.com), 150 KY 330. During the summer months, you can tour the fields where the grapes are growing, then come inside and learn about the ages-old process of winemaking. Wine-tasting packages are available. Summer also brings live entertainment, sometimes national acts, to the outdoor amphitheater here, so check the web site to see if anyone interesting is appearing. This is Kentucky's largest winery, so if you can only stop at one, Elk Creek is your place.

Elk Creek Resort (502-484-4569, 502-484-0005; www.elkcreekvineyards.com), 150 KY 330. Don't let the rustic log cabin appearance fool you. This is a new resort, which actually feels elegant inside. The high beamed ceilings, giant fieldstone fireplace, and large, welcoming guest rooms are enchanting. Book one of the four queen-sized bedrooms, or bring a group and rent the whole house. $$

Elk Creek Hunt Club and Sporting Clays (502-484-4569; www.elkcreekhuntclub.com), 1860 Georgetown Rd. Open year-round Tue.–Sun. 9 AM–dark. Throwing more than 1.5 million sporting clays per year, Elk Creek is one of the top-ranked clubs in the country. The three separate courses cover 2,500 acres of rolling woods and meadows of prime hunting land.

Louisville and the Derby Region

5

BARDSTOWN, LEBANON, AND
SPRINGFIELD

ELIZABETHTOWN, HODGENVILLE,
RADCLIFF, AND FORT KNOX

THE GREATER LOUISVILLE AREA

SHELBYVILLE, LAGRANGE, AND THE
SURROUNDING AREA

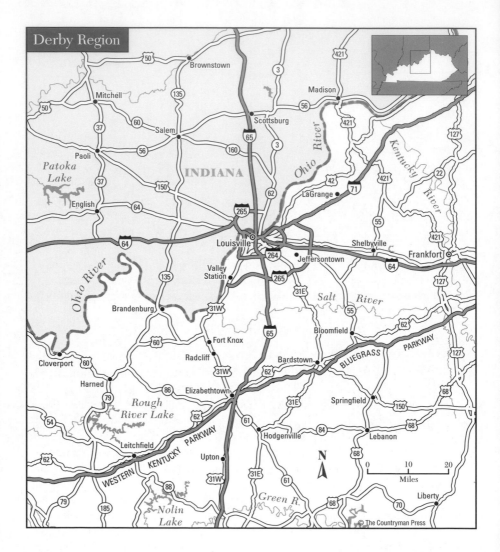

Derby Region

INTRODUCTION:
THE DERBY REGION

Blend the urban sophistication of Louisville, Kentucky's largest city, with small, hometown-y places like Bardstown and LaGrange, and you come up with the Derby Region. Travelers can get a taste for thoroughbreds, bourbon, and tobacco farms while enjoying the artsy magnetism of a major metropolitan area.

The whole region claims ties to bourbon distilleries, and with good reason. As you drive through the area, you'll see the rickhouses, full of aging barrels of bourbon, that dot the countryside. This ages-old process is a well-respected craft, and Kentuckians claim bourbon as our own. Whiskey can be made anywhere, but bourbon comes from the Bluegrass State. If your trip brings you to this region, a distillery tour is a must. Even if you don't imbibe personally, the painstaking process is interesting to see. And if bourbon is your drink of choice, remember the saying "When in Rome . . .'"

Just as Kentuckians are proud of their bourbon, we are equally proud that Abraham Lincoln was born here. In this Land of Lincoln you'll find his birthplace, as well as his boyhood home. There are also cabins, monuments, tributes, and ties to our 16th president throughout the state. Lincoln is quoted as saying that his earliest memories are of Kentucky, a fact that Kentuckians relish.

The Louisville metropolitan area is a perfect mix of historic and hip. The Bardstown Road and Frankfort Avenue corridors are an eclectic combination of cool shops and happening restaurants. You'll see bumper stickers and T-shirts proclaiming, KEEP LOUISVILLE WEIRD, all that funky culture oozing out. The vibrant downtown has modern office buildings, a museum district, recreation-filled waterfront parks, and cute eateries and antiques shops.

You can't mention Louisville without a nod to the first Saturday in May, the biggest day in the region . . . yes, the Kentucky Derby. It's the day the world's eyes are on Louisville, at least for two minutes, as this year's top thoroughbreds break out of the starting gate and seem to fly around the historic oval track. On the top floor of the grandstand is Millionaires' Row, a Who's Who of horse people, corporate bigwigs, and the occasional Hollywood star. Down in the infield, you'll find rowdy college kids acting like they're on spring break, along with normal folks who couldn't get grandstand seats. And those lucky enough to have seats are a wonderful mix of fancy-hat-wearing women, families, and just about everyone in between. Besides the thrill of the bets and the race, Churchill Downs is a people-watcher's dream.

The Louisville region is the place to go for a colorful snapshot of Kentucky: an urban core surrounded by suburbs, which are infused with farms, lakes, and nature. Although betting on a horse race and drinking a shot of bourbon seems like a stereotypical thing to do, it's just a small part of all the offerings of Kentucky's Derby Region.

BARDSTOWN, LEBANON, AND SPRINGFIELD

H ead south, and slightly east, away from Louisville, and latch on to the Bourbon Trail, an imaginary path that connects all things bourbon to the rest of the state. Although Lebanon and Springfield aren't quite as saturated in the fire-water as Bardstown, they are appealing communities with their own share of restaurants, shops, and historical attractions.

Breathe deep and if the wind is blowing in the right direction, you might get a whiff of the official drink of the Bluegrass State, bourbon. **Bardstown** is the Bourbon Capital of the World, and it is here that you will find several distilleries and even a museum dedicated to these fine spirits.

There's a lot to do in Bardstown besides drink bourbon, which is recommended but not mandatory. Kentucky's second oldest city, home to about 10,000 people, is also swimming in history. My Old Kentucky Home State Park, where Stephen Foster got the idea for the state song, a ballad that brings a tear to most Kentuckians' eyes, depicts life in the commonwealth during the era of plantations and hoop-skirted ladies. On the not-to-be-missed list is Old Talbotts Tavern, which has been serving weary travelers since the late 1700s. Join the ranks of famous historical figures who have stopped here for a good meal and a sampling of southern hospitality. There are several historical museums, streets lined with antebellum-style homes, and even a monastery where you can learn about the life of the Trappist monks who have dedicated their lives to serving God. To get the most out of your visit, it is advised that you tour first, drink bourbon second.

Situated right smack-dab in the middle of the state is **Lebanon**, the seat of Marion County. It was incorporated in 1815 and was once considered as the site of the state capital. Alas, Frankfort won out. That didn't stop Lebanon from growing, however, while still maintaining its small-town way of life and peaceful rural qualities. True rolling bluegrass, historic landmarks, and quaint villages like Gravel Switch make Lebanon a destination that is certainly worth the trip.

Lebanon served as a Union stronghold during the Civil War and was a major recruiting center for newly freed slaves. More than 2,000 men were recruited and joined the Union army here.

The notorious Confederate general John Hunt Morgan came through Lebanon with his Raiders on three occasions. In 1863, he burned down 20 of Lebanon's buildings in retribution for the death of his brother, but Lebanon carried on and today the downtown historic district is on the National Register of Historic Places. This city played many important roles during the Civil War, and you can follow several trails that transverse Lebanon. The tourist commission has maps guiding you to the actual sites, buildings, and travel routes that help tell the story.

Lebanon is home to about 6,000 residents, all very proud of their past and even more proud of the city they have become. The unique shops and restaurants will remind you that you really are in the heart of Kentucky.

Springfield, the small town of about 3,000 people, tries to bill itself as the home to Bart and Homer and the rest of the Simpsons, stars of the Fox Network's longest-running cartoon. Although they don't actually have a Moe's Bar or a Quickie Mart, the downtown is cute just the same.

GUIDANCE Bardstown/Nelson County Tourist Commission (502-348-4877, 800-638-4877; www.visitbardstown.com), 1 Court Square, Bardstown. Open weekdays 8–5, Sat. 9–5, and Sun. 11–3. This charming building, which is situated along a roundabout right in the center of town, is hard to miss. It has a tall steeple, complete with bell. Stop in for some excellent advice and tips. **Lebanon Tourist & Convention Commission** (270-692-0021; www.visitlebanonky.com.), 239 N. Spalding Ave., Suite 200, Lebanon. Located in an old school in the downtown Centre Square. You'll find friendly advice, maps, and brochures. Lebanon loves to have company.

GETTING THERE Bardstown and Lebanon are located less than an hour's drive from Louisville and Lexington, easily accessible from I-65 or the Bluegrass Parkway. The area is serviced by both the **Louisville International Airport** (502-368-6524; www.flylouisville.com), and **Lexington's Bluegrass Airport** (859-425-3114; www.bluegrassairport.com). Car rentals are available at the airport. **Greyhound** bus service is available in Louisville, Lexington, and Elizabethtown (www.grey hound.com).

GETTING AROUND Neither Bardstown nor Lebanon has public transportation, but both are easily navigated by car, with free parking everywhere.

The Heaven Hill Distilleries Trolley (800-638-4877; www.visitbardstown.com), 1 Courthouse Square, Bardstown. Tue.–Sat. 10, 1:30, 3; Sun. noon, 1:30, 3. Tours last approximately an hour and 20 minutes. This is an easy way to see Bardstown if you are short on time. Hop aboard this bourbon-colored trolley for a narrated tour of downtown Bardstown as well as a tour of Heaven Hill's Bourbon Heritage Center. Get your ticket at the Bardstown visitors center. $7 per person.

MEDICAL EMERGENCY With a modern, state-of-the art facility, **Flaget Memorial Hospital** (502-350-5000; www.flaget.com), 4305 New Shepherd Villa Rd., Bardstown, is available for any medical need. If you need medical help in Lebanon, turn to **Spring View Hospital** (270-692-3161; www.springviewhospital .com), 320 Loretto Rd., Lebanon.

ALCOHOL Since Bardstown is the Bourbon Capital of the World, it only seems fitting that Nelson County is a wet county, where alcohol sales are permitted everywhere. Lebanon is located in Marion County, also wet. Springfield is sopping up alcohol in the moist county of Washington, where the county is dry but they allow alcohol sales in the downtown area and at wineries.

In Bardstown

⚓ ♿ **My Old Kentucky Home State Park** (502-348-3502; www.parks.ky.gov), 501 E. Stephen Foster Ave. Tours are given 9–5, June–Aug.; open daily 9–4:45 the rest of the year. Visit the Bardstown mansion, called Federal Hill, that was the inspiration for Stephen Foster's song "My Old Kentucky Home." The home, a former plantation, dates back to the late 1700s. The stately brick Georgian-style mansion has 13 rooms full of family heirlooms and authentic furniture. Your guided tour of the home will be led by a genuine southern belle complete with hoop skirt. $6 adults, $5 seniors, $4 ages 6–12; under 6 free.

Abbey of Gethsemani (502-549-4406; www.monks.org), 3642 Monks Rd., Trappist. The welcome center is open Mon.–Sat., 9–5. Home to America's oldest order of Cistercian monks. The order, which arrived in 1848 from France, settled into these hills of Central Kentucky and made it their home. Visitors can walk the grounds, attend a church service, and enjoy the peaceful chanting of the monks. Stop in to the welcome center to view a film on the order, go through the archives, and shop. The monks support themselves by selling cheese, fruitcake, and bourbon fudge.

🍴 ♿ **Basilica of St. Joseph Proto-Cathedral** (502-348-3126; www.stjoechurch .com), 310 W. Stephen Foster Ave. Weekdays 9–5, Sat. 9–3, Sun. 1–5. This cathedral was home to the first Catholic diocese west of the Allegheny Mountains. This church opened its doors in 1819, before advances in modern construction. Bricks were baked on the grounds, and solid tree trunks cut from the wilderness were lathed in a circular pattern to form the stately columns supporting the building. Stop in for a tour and see this architectural marvel.

OLD KENTUCKY HOME

photo courtesy of www.kentuckytourism.com

✐ ᕐ **Civil War Museum/Old Bardstown Village/Natural History Museum/Women of the Civil War Museum** (502-349-0291; www.civil-war-museum .org), 310 E. Broadway St. Open Mar. 1–Dec. 15, Mon.–Sun. 10–5. The state's largest collection of artifacts focusing on the war's Western Theater. It is the fourth largest Civil War museum in the United States. See genuine military items used during the war, including uniforms, weapons, and other personal belongings. Old Bardstown Village is an authentic village of nine log cabins from the county that date from 1776 to 1820. Each one has a different theme. Also on the property is the Wildlife/Natural History Museum, which features an extensive collection of North American animals in natural habitats, along with fossils and minerals from around the world. Don't miss the Women of the Civil War Museum while you are there. They have a fascinating collection of documents, photos, and original clothing of the women who stayed home to protect the property, nurse the injured soldiers, spy on the enemy, and, in some cases disguise themselves as young men to fight with the soldiers. $6 adults, $5 ages 7–12; under 7 free. Packages are available if you are visiting more than one attraction.

Oscar Getz Museum of Whiskey History (502-348-2999; www.whiskeymuseum .com), 114 N. 5th St. Open Mon.–Fri. 10–5 (May–Oct.); Tue.–Fri. 10–4 (Nov.–Apr.); Sat. 10–4, Sun. noon–4 (year-round). Dripping with history, this museum is housed in a building that was used as a hospital during the Civil War. But have a look around at all the whiskey-related memorabilia like antique bottles, Abraham Lincoln's liquor license, and even a moonshine still. It's free to look around, but they would appreciate a donation.

Wickland (502-348-4877, 800-638-4877), 550 Bloomfield Rd. Open May–Labor Day, Fri.–Sun. 10–2. This Federal-style house, built between 1825 and 1828, features antique furniture of the period, and examples of fabulous Georgian architecture. Throughout history Wickland was home to three of Kentucky's governors and contains exhibits about each one, as well as local Civil War and African American history. Wickland is open for self-guided tours. $4 adults, $3 seniors, $2 ages 6–14; under 6 free.

In Lebanon

Historic Penn's Store (859-332-7706, 859-332-7716; www.pennsstore.com), 257 Penn Store Rd., Gravel Switch. Open Fri. and Sat. 11–4, Sun. 1–4. Visit this oldest country store in America, which has been run by the Penn family since 1845. This is not a restored landmark—it's authentic, and it looks about as it did when they opened. The store still sells groceries, sandwiches, and dry goods as it always has, but features gifts and handmade crafts. Don't miss the annual Great Outhouse Blowout, a celebration in honor of the privy. Held the second week of September, the festival features drag races with outhouses on wheels, live music, and food.

Lebanon National Cemetery (270-692-3390), KY 208. Open daily sunrise–sunset. Closed federal holidays except Memorial Day and Veterans Day. Designated a national cemetery in 1867. The first to be buried here were the Union soldiers who perished in the Battle of Perryville. There were 865 total original interments, including 281 unknowns. The cemetery, which is on the National Register of Historic Places, still holds military funerals today.

Sisters of Loretto Motherhouse (270-865-5811; www.nerinxhs.org/LKYhist), 515 Nerinx Rd., Nerinx. The Sisters of Loretto Motherhouse is home to one of the oldest religious communities of women in the United States. The sisters put down roots in the area in 1824, dedicating their lives to God and the education of poor children of the area. Today you can visit this working farm situated in a park-like setting. It is the residence of active and retired members, but visitors are welcomed daily. Please call ahead.

Holy Cross Catholic Church (270-865-2521; www.sf-hc.org). Church open Sun. at 8 AM for Mass only. Vestibule open daily 24 hours a day. Glass doors allow for viewing into the church. This is the site of the first Catholic Mass and Catholic church west of the Allegheny Mountains. Originally it was a log cabin, completed in 1792. But the current building was completed in 1823, which almost makes it seem modern.

Scott's Ridge Lookout (270-692-0799). Get a map at the Lebanon Tourist Commission. On a clear day, visitors can see more than 100 square miles from this mountaintop. Enjoy the peaceful drive along the way.

❋ To Do

CARRIAGE TOURS Around the Town Carriage (502-348-0331; www.visit bardstown.com/tourism), 223 N. 3rd St., Bardstown. Open daily, 9 AM–10 PM. Enjoy this narrated tour through historic Bardstown aboard a carriage, buggy, or stagecoach.

FISHING Fagan Branch Reservoir (270-692-2491). Located in Calvary, just 10 minutes from Lebanon. A fisherman's dream, stocked with large- and smallmouth bass, bluegill, and catfish.

Marion County Sportsman's Lake (800-858-1549). Created by the Kentucky Department of Fish and Wildlife, this old lake was drained and reconstructed to improve fish habitat, making the fish population swell. Hunting is permitted on the grounds; look for squirrel, deer, and waterfowl.

GOLF Kenny Rapier Golf Course at My Old Kentucky Home State Park (502-349-6542, 800-323-7803), 668 Loretto Rd., Bardstown. Golf in the shadow of My Old Kentucky Home on this par-71, 18-hole course. They have a pro shop with a snack bar, rental clubs, pull carts, and riding carts.

Rosewood Golf and Country Club (270-692-0506; rosewoodgolf-course.com/clubhouse/restaurant), 520 Fairway Dr., Lebanon. Carved out of rolling pastureland, this 18-hole golf course has mature trees, streams, lakes, and wooded areas.

HISTORIC TRAILS Civil War Historical Trail (270-692-0021). The National Turnpike runs from Maysville to Nashville. The Lebanon portion is full of historical sites, including homes and buildings that date back to the 1800s. Get more information at the Lebanon Tourism office.

William Clark Quantrill Trail (270-337-3796, 270-692-6507), 202 W. Main St., Bradfordsville. Relive the route taken by one of the most vicious renegades of all time, William Clark Quantrill. During the Civil War, Quantrill, a Confederate soldier, took it upon himself to attack Union camps and pro-Union sympathizers in

THE BOURBON TRAIL

One of Kentucky's fastest-growing tourist attractions is the famed Bourbon Trail. As the maker of 95 percent of the entire world's supply of bourbon, Kentucky is proud to show you how it all happens. See for yourself how pure limestone water, an abundance of sweet corn, charred oak barrels, and an aging process that makes the most of the Commonwealth's cold winters and hot summers can produce the silky lightning blend that the world knows as Kentucky Bourbon.

The following distilleries are in the Bardstown area:

🖉 ♿ 🌿 **Heaven Hill Distilleries Bourbon Heritage Center** (502-337-1000; www.bourbonheritagecenter.com), 1311 Gilkey Run Rd. Open year round. Tue.–Sat. 10–5, Sun. noon–4; closed Sun. in Jan. and Feb. Learn all about the history of bourbon as well as the history of Heaven Hill in this state-of-the-art center. The tour includes entrance to a working rickhouse and a sample tasting. Free.

🖉 ♿ 🌿 **Jim Beam's American Outpost** (502-543-9877; www.jimbeam.com), KY 245 in Clermont. Open year-round. Mon.–Sat. 9–4:30, Sun. 1–4. Closed Sun. Nov.–Mar. Offers up-close views of the distilling process. The tour includes a short film about the Beam family and how their brand grew to become the world's top-selling bourbon. See the Jeremiah Beam home that traces the family's heritage back to 1775 and founder Jacob Beam's first barrel of "Old Jake Beam Sour Mash." Sample a selection of their small-batch bourbons. Free.

🖉 ♿ 🌿 **Maker's Mark Distillery** (270-865-2099; www.makersmark.com), 3350 Burks Spring Rd., Loretto. Open year-round. Tours hourly on the half hour, Mon.–Sat. 10:30–3:30, Sun. 1:30–3:30. Closed Sun. in Jan. and Feb. Although it's slightly off the beaten path, getting there is half the fun. Enjoy the Kentucky countryside along the way and watch for Maker's Mark signs letting you know you're on the right track. Maker's Mark is the only distillery operating in America that has been designated a National Historic Landmark. The historic buildings on the grounds really tell a story of aging and traditions. If you purchase a bottle of Maker's while you're there, you get to dip it yourself in the famous red wax. Free.

Historic Tom Moore Distillery (502-348-3774) 300 Barton Rd., Bardstown. Free tours 9:30 and 1:30, Mon.–Fri. Bardstown's newest tour comes from one of its oldest distilleries. Tom

MAKER'S MARK DISTILLERY
photo courtesy of www.kentuckytourism.com

Moore founded the distillery in 1879 and produces 1792 Ridgemont Reserve, a premium brand named for the year Kentucky became a state. They also make Kentucky Tavern and Very Old Barton brands. The two-hour tour covers all parts of the distilling process, and they are quick to point out that the building was built to distill, not give tours—it's sort of a bare-bones excursion, without the bells and whistles of the other bourbon-making tours. Plans are under way for a visitors center in 2010. You must be 21 and able to walk stairs. Reservations required one day in advance.

The following distilleries are near Frankfort, Kentucky:

🖉 ♿ 🐾 **Buffalo Trace Distillery** (502-696-5926, 800-654-8471; www.buffalotrace.com), 1001 Wilkinson Blvd., Frankfort. Tours start on the hour, Mon.–Fri. 9–3, Sat. 10–2. This is the oldest continuously operating distillery in the United States. Tours include the fermenting room as well as the rickhouses where the bourbon barrels are stored while they age. Tastings and a free bourbon ball follow the tour. They also have a gift shop for souvenirs.

🖉 ♿ **Woodford Reserve** (859-879-1812; www.woodfordreserve.com), 7855 McCracken Pike, Versailles. Tue.–Sat. 9–5, Sun. 12:30–4:30. Tour the distillery of Labrot & Graham, home of Woodford Reserve Bourbon. The limestone buildings reflect the traditions of the area and the distiller, where they still use the time-honored copper pot method to make their fine bourbon. $5 adults (18 and up); under 5 free.

Four Roses Distillery (502-839-3436; www.fourroses.us), 1224 Bonds Mill Rd., Lawrenceburg. The 45-minute tours start on the hour, Mon.–Sat. 9–3. Closed most of the summer and major holidays. This distillery, built in a Spanish Mission style, looks like it should be in Southern California instead of on the banks of the Salt River. The beautiful building, constructed in 1911, is on the National Register of Historic Places. Guests over 21 can enjoy a small sample of this smooth and mellow bourbon.

Wild Turkey Distillery (502-839-4544) US 62E, Lawrenceburg. Offers free tours Mon.–Sat. at 9, 10:30, 12:30, and 2:30. Advance notice is requested for groups of more than 10. Closed all major holidays, the first full week of January, and the last two full weeks of July. View the process from grain delivery through barreling.

FOUR ROSES DISTILLERY
photo courtesy of www.kentuckytourism.com

brutal and barbaric ways. By 1862 he had more than 100 followers, including out-laws Frank and Jesse James. He and his band of raiders wreaked havoc through the Central Kentucky area, burning buildings and murdering civilians. Follow the trail of devastation from New Market, near Lebanon, to Hustonville, near Danville.

John Hunt Morgan Trail (270-692-0021). The infamous Confederate Raider vis-ited town in all three of his raids into Kentucky, and he once burned 20 buildings here in his effort to devastate the Union troops. The tour includes Myrtledene. Now a bed & breakfast, the site was once taken over by Morgan for his headquar-ters; here, in his grief over the death of his brother, he rode his horse right through the front door and started up the stairs.

✳ Green Space

Bernheim Arboretum and Research Forest (502- 955-8512; www.bernheim .org), Clermont. Open dawn–dusk daily except Christmas and New Year's Day. Successful bourbon distiller Isaac W. Bernheim established Bernheim Arboretum and Research Forest in 1929 and gave it to the people of Kentucky as a gift and a thank-you for his business triumphs. The 14,000 lush acres are available for hiking, biking, geocaching, picnicking, or just relaxing in its beauty. Free admission week-days. $5 per vehicle on weekends and holidays.

PARKS Graham Memorial Park (270-692-9358), 525 Graham Memorial Park Dr., Lebanon. Open Mon.–Fri. 5:30–8, Sun. 1–6. Walk the 3.5-mile blacktopped track; it's well lit, so you can walk at dusk. The park also offers tennis and basket-ball courts, baseball and football fields, and a disk golf course. They even have a model airplane runway. The adjacent **Lebanon Aquatic Center** has a heated indoor pool with lap lanes and an open area for splashing around.

Cecil L. Gorley Trail (270-692-2491), 120 S. Proctor Knott Ave., Lebanon. This 3.2-mile walking trail surrounds Fagan Branch Reservoir.

Lebanon Civil War Park (270-692-6272), corner of Spalding and Walnut, Lebanon. A depiction of Major General George H. Thomas, also known as the Rock of Chickamauga, who, in 1862, led Union forces from Lebanon to Mill Springs in the first major battle in Kentucky.

✳ Lodging

🖋 **BED & BREAKFASTS The Jail-er's Inn Bed & Breakfast** (800-948-5551; www.jailersinn.com), 111 W. Stephen Foster Ave., Bardstown. Although this jail, which was in opera-tion from 1797 until 1987, probably didn't seem all that inviting to the rowdy bunch of prisoners who stayed here, today it is a delightful mix of his-tory and kitsch. Five of the now ele-gant rooms are in located in the former warden's home, and are rich in luxury and antiques. But if you go, try to book the Jail Cell Room, an actual cell com-plete with bunks and a waterbed. Breakfast served outside in the court-yard when weather permits. $–$$

🖋 ∞ ✿ **The Historic Maple Hill Manor** (800-886-7546; www.maple hillmanor.com), 2941 Perryville Rd., Springfield. This beautiful Greek Revival plantation home, built in the mid-1800s, is one of Kentucky's best-preserved antebellum homes. Sur-rounded by farmland, the home, with its 14-foot ceilings and massive 12-foot doors, also boasts a stunning cherry staircase that seems to be floating. The seven large guest rooms are full of antiques, some with fireplace and/or Jacuzzi tub. $$

⁰ᵀ⁰ Myrtledene Bed & Breakfast (270-692-2223; www.myrtledene.com), 370 N. Spalding Ave., Lebanon. This home has a wild history: It was once used by Confederate general John Hunt Morgan as headquarters during his raids on Lebanon. Luckily, Myrtledene is much calmer now. The historic house is just dripping in antiques. The four guest rooms all offer modern amenities, and the large yard with gardens, fishpond, and swings is a wonderful retreat. The Kentucky Heritage Committee has designated Myrtledene a Kentucky Landmark. $

⊗ ⁰ᵀ⁰ ✎ Rosemark Haven Inn (502-348-8218; www.rosemarkhaven.com), 714 N. 3rd St., Bardstown. A magnificent spiral staircase draws you into this historic 1830s home. They offer seven cozy rooms in the mansion, all with king-sized bed, some with fireplace and whirlpool tub. They also have accommodations in the adjacent Federal House, which offers two bedrooms and a gathering room. The inn is a restaurant, too, so even though breakfast is included with the price of your room, you might want to arrive early and have dinner in their stately dining room. The menu is primarily Italian, but they have regional, bourbon-infused favorites as well. $$

✎ Merrywood Bed and Breakfast (270-337-3082), 301 Main St., Bradfordsville. Stay with innkeepers Ron and Linda Owens in their darling home, which was built around 1900. It has been designated a Kentucky Landmark by the Kentucky Historical Society. It has two comfy rooms and a wonderful swing on the big front porch. $

RV PARKS Country View RV Park (270-692-0408), 690 E. Main St., Lebanon. Located just three blocks from the heart of downtown Lebanon, so it's easy to find. It's a nice park, with about 14 sites that can accommodate big rigs as well as small tents. They have separate electric and water for each space. Well-stocked convenience store right on the property.

✳ Where to Eat

Ⴤ DINING OUT My Old Kentucky Dinner Train (502-348-7300; www.kydinnertrain.com), 602 N. 3rd St. Call for schedule. When the conductor yells "All aboard" and you take your seat on the vintage-1940s train, your mouth may start to water. The luxurious accommodations include fine dining while you enjoy the ever-changing scenery of Kentucky for the two- to three-hour excursion. In addition to the delicious meal, passengers are privy to the 1860s-era depot and the remarkable Jackson Hollow Trestle made completely of timber. By reservation only, and it fills up fast—call early. Lunch $$$, dinner $$$$

Ⴤ Old Talbott Tavern (800-482-8376; www.talbotts.com), 107 W. Stephen Foster Ave., Bardstown. Open for lunch and dinner every day. This famous tavern and inn, which dates back to 1797, was once a stagecoach stop in Kentucky's wilderness. The list of historical figures that have slept here looks like a Who's Who of Kentucky's past. The likes of Daniel Boone, a young Abe Lincoln, and George Rogers Clark have all sought shelter here. Today there is still a reminder of Jesse James, who, after possibly partaking of too much Bardstown bourbon, mistakenly thought there was an intruder in his guest room. So he whipped out his gun and shot right through the beautiful hand-painted murals that are still in the room today. Ask to see the bullet holes. Today Old Talbott Tavern offers five elegant guest rooms, but is better known for their restaurant. The menu features Kentucky comfort food, like hot brown and fried chicken, in a slightly upscale dining room with creaky wood floors. The tavern room is also the perfect place for a nightcap. Order a shot of bourbon; you're in the Bourbon Capital of the World, for goodness' sake. Rooms $, entrées $$–$$$

In Lebanon

Ŷ **Oak Barrel** (270-692-1295; www .theoakbarre1202.com), 202 Main St. Open for lunch Mon.–Fri. 11–2, and dinner Tue.–Sat. 4–midnight. Located in a historic building right in the heart of town. Bourbon-accented menu choices in a slightly upscale setting. $$

Big Jim's Steakhouse & Buffet (270-692-3970), 212 W. Main St. Serving dinner only Mon.–Sat. They are known for their scrumptious steaks and huge buffet of choices. Don't miss the live music and karaoke on weekends. $$

Ŷ **Mordecai's On Main** (859-336-3500) 105 W. Main St., Springfield. Open Tue.–Sat. 11 am–midnight, Sunday for brunch. Housed in a historic building in the middle of town. The warm decor is on the upscale side and extremely inviting. Mordecai's menu runs the gamut from salads and home-made soups to frog legs, bourbon-marinated pork chops, and New York strip steak dinners. On Friday and Saturday nights, they feature a loaded buffet where you can sample all the menu favorites. $–$$

Ŷ **Blues On Tap Restaurant & Bar** (270-402-2583; www.tastebourbon .com), 110 N. Proctor Knott Ave. Call for hours and reservations. The place to go for steaks, gumbo, and pulled pork dishes. Also home to the Ken-

tucky Bourbon Tasting Room. Sample a wide variety Kentucky spirits in the state's only tasting room. $$

Los Mariachis (270-692-9746), 119 W. Main St. Open every day 11–10. Authentic Mexican food prepared fresh each day. Los Mariachis' specials include fajitas, steak Mexicano, and enchilada rancheras. $

EATING OUT Mammy's Kitchen (502-350-1097), 114 N. 3rd St., Bardstown. Mon.–Tue. 6:30 AM–3 PM, Wed.–Sat. 6:30 AM–9:30 PM. This tiny diner offers down-home southern cooking served amid an assortment of signs and knickknacks that create a kind of homey decor. The food is just good and cheap, which is why you'll find a cast of regulars there every time you go in. Mammy's claims to have the "best grilled cheese in the world"—a pretty heady claim, so you might want to give it a try. Enjoy with a side of tater tots. $

Kreso's Family Restaurant & Mozart Café (502-348-9594; www .kresosweb.com), 218 N. 3rd St., Bardstown. Whether you want to catch a UK game or settle down for a sophisticated meal, Kreso has a place for you. Owners Dzevad and Merima Kreso, natives of Bosnia, have created a beautiful restaurant with a decor and menu that offer a taste of their homeland. Order anything from a burger and fries to goulash, Wiener schnitzel, or Chilean sea bass. Wide range of choices to match your mood. $

Kurtz Restaurant (502-348-8964), 418 E. Stephen Foster Ave., Bardstown. Serving lunch and dinner Tue.–Sat.; there's a fantastic Sunday brunch, too. A part of Bardstown since 1937, this family-owned restaurant sits just across the street from My Old Kentucky Home. The menu features stick-to-your-ribs entrées like casseroles, fried chicken, and homemade cobbler. For a "spirited" treat try the biscuit pudding, which is soaked in bourbon sauce. $

The Backyard BBQ and Grill (859-336-9090), 1007 Lincoln Park Rd., Springfield. Open Mon.–Thu. 11–9, Fri. 11–10, Sat. 4–10, Sun. brunch 10–2. Make sure to get some napkins, and maybe ask for a bib. This barbecue is simply smothered in the tasty sauce, and you *will* get some on your shirt. But it's worth it. Try the BBQ sampler platter so you can compare the brisket to the baby back ribs and the pulled pork, and then you'll know what to order next time. They also have burgers, salads, and corndogs for the kids, which are all good, but dig into the barbecue and make a real mess. $

𝒮 **SNACKS Adams Pharmacy** (270-692-9115), 125 W. Main St., Lebanon. Open weekdays 8:30–4, Sat. 8:30–noon This is a real old-fashioned soda fountain where you can sit on a stool and enjoy a cherry Coke. Browse the store's cute gift items, too. $

ⁱ⅂ⁱ **Java Joint Café** (www.thejava jointcafe.net), 126 N. 3rd St., Bardstown. Serving up mochas and more, Mon.–Sat. 7:30–5:30, and Sunday brunch 9:30–2:30. This warm and inviting café is the perfect place to stop to rejuvenate and enjoy a delicious soup, salad, quiche, or sandwich. Filled with funky Kentucky artwork and knickknacks; you'll want to stay awhile and relax. $

Hadorn's Bakery (502-348-4407), 118½ W. Flaget Ave., Bardstown. Although this full-service bakery offers cakes, pies, and breads, locals swear Hadorn's doughnuts are the best there is. Comparable to a famous southern doughnut chain, these little beauties are best when warm, but delicious anytime of day. $

𝒮 **Hurst Drug Store Soda Fountain** (502) 348-9261); 102 N. 3rd St., Bardstown. Pull up a stool and order a chicken salad sandwich, a glass of homemade lemonade, and a hot fudge sundae for dessert, and they'll swear you must be a regular. $

✳ Entertainment

𝒮 ♿ *The Stephen Foster Musical* (502-348-5971, 800-626-1563; www .stephenfoster.com), My Old Kentucky Home State Park, 501 E. Stephen Foster Ave., Bardstown. Productions during summer months only. Enjoy live theater under the stars, in this charming amphitheater. This musical, which is perfect for all ages, has been continuously running for more than 50 years. It focuses on the life of Stephen Foster, composer of famous American tunes like "Oh! Susanna," "Camptown Races," and "Jeannie with the Light Brown Hair." But it was the song "My Old Kentucky Home" that forever endeared him to the commonwealth, as this became the state song. Sing along to the tunes everyone knows by heart and enjoy the dazzling costumes that reflect life in the 1850s.

✳ Selective Shopping

In Bardstown

Bardstown Booksellers (502-348-1256), 129 N. 3rd St. This shop is simply packed with books, magazines, and music. It is so inviting, you just want to curl up with a book and stay all afternoon. They have a wide variety of Kentucky gifts, too.

Mary's Art and Antiques (502-350-9009; www.atmarys.com), 214 N. 3rd St. Seems like everything in this store is happy and fun. Bright-colored home decor items, eclectic accessories, as well as art, antiques, and floral arrangements.

Fergie's Now and Then (502-348-2779), 213 W. Stephen Foster Ave. Giant selection of antiques, furniture, and gifts, spread out over two floors.

In Lebanon
These Precious Things (270-692-1085; www.thesepreciousthings.com), 112 N. Spalding Ave. Mon.–Fri. 7:30–5, Sat. 8–1. Stop in for a cappuccino or latte and enjoy the cool selection of handcrafted wonders, like hand-painted scarves and the handmade jewelry of local artisans.

Goodin View Farm Country Store (270-692-0165), 569 KY 208. Get a taste of the country, where they offer fresh produce and hard-to-find farm-raised shrimp, catfish, and hybrid striped bass. They also have an enormous selection of baskets and candy. Stop by in fall and try to conquer the giant corn maze shaped like Kentucky.

Finders Keepers (270-699-2828), 148 W. Main St. Closed Sun. and Mon. What a nice gift shop. They have antiques, as well as new prints, candles, candy bouquets, blankets, jewelry, and purses. Don't miss the Kid's Corner with toys, nursery items, and gifts for newborns.

Mary's Place (270-692-3670), 4410 Danville Hwy. Open Wed.–Sun. This is a huge antiques store where you can browse to your heart's content.

✳ Special Events
✎ ♿ ♟ *January:* **Lebanon's Blue Grass Music Kick Off** (270-692-0021). Bands from across Kentucky compete in the Battle of the Bluegrass Bands. Workshops for banjo, fiddle, dobro, mandolin, vocals, and guitar are held, and there are areas designated just for jamming.

✎ ♿ ♟ *July:* **Jets Over Kentucky.** Lebanon's annual competition among and demonstrations of remote-controlled airplanes are really a sight to see. Cast your eyes to the sky and watch these daredevils. It is called the thoroughbred of radio-controlled jet shows.

✎ ♿ ♟ *September:* **Marion County Country Ham Days** (270-692-9594). Just like a good old-fashioned country fair, Ham Days features a parade, a 5K run, a car and truck show, a juried arts and crafts show, games for adults and kids, and live entertainment.

♿ **Bardstown's Kentucky Bourbon Festival** (www.kybourbonfestival.com). Paying homage to the spirit as well as the fine distillers who helped Bardstown become the Bourbon Capital of the World, this annual five-day event features fun for all ages.

ELIZABETHTOWN, HODGENVILLE, RADCLIFF, AND FORT KNOX

South of Louisville and heading into Western Kentucky, visitors will find themselves in the communities of Elizabethtown, Hodgenville, Radcliff, and Fort Knox.

In the Elizabethtown area, you can immerse yourself in Abraham Lincoln history by visiting his birthplace and boyhood home. Although Lincoln spent most of his life in Illinois, he still loved Kentucky and had many ties to the commonwealth. During the Civil War, he was quoted as saying, "I hope to have God on my side, but I must have Kentucky."

Just up US 31W, you will find the military base Fort Knox and its suburb, Radcliff. Fort Knox is famous as the home of the US Bullion Depository, the keeper of all the gold. They don't give tours, ever. So set your sights on touring the fort and the community surrounding it and keep all those visions of gold in your dreams.

With pioneers in the area as early as 1779, settlement consisted of small forts used as stockades for defense against Native Americans. One of these early settlers was Andrew Hynes, who, in 1797, had his 30 acres of land surveyed and marked off into lots and streets to establish **Elizabethtown**, which he named in honor of his wife.

E-town, as it's known to locals, is located 35 miles south of Louisville on I-65 at the crossroads of the Western Kentucky Parkway and the Bluegrass Parkway. Because Elizabethtown is so conveniently and centrally located, tourist do not have to travel far to see attractions in surrounding cities. The warm, country feel of the town welcomes you back after a day of easy sightseeing.

But Elizabethtown is a star in its own right. In 2005, Hollywood came calling, filming a major motion picture titled *Elizabethtown* right in the downtown area. The movie, directed by Cameron Crowe and starring Orlando Bloom and Kirsten Dunst, makes E-town look as darling on film as it does in person.

Learn about Elizabethtown by taking the Downtown Walking Tour, which is available in summer months. Follow the map and you may just bump into some historical figures (or costumed actors portraying them) who are scattered about town, full of stories about the buildings and the people who lived and worked there.

A perfect marriage of nature and history is available at Freeman Lake Park. You can hike, fish, canoe, and picnic on the picture-perfect grounds, as well as take in Lincoln-era log cabins and buildings right in the park.

Come to Elizabethtown to relax and wind down. You'll feel like a local as soon as you arrive.

A true military community, the **Radcliff and Fort Knox** area comprises Fort Knox, Fort Duffield (which overlooks the town of West Point), and Radcliff.

Dating back to the Civil War, both Fort Knox and Fort Duffield saw action as the Union and Confederate armies occupied the area. Around the time of World War I, the US military established a field artillery training center, which was named for Major General Henry Knox, chief of artillery for the Continental army during the American Revolution and later the nation's first secretary of war.

In the 1930s Fort Knox became known for the mechanized cavalry—otherwise known as the use of tanks in battle. One of the first American soldiers to distinguish himself in this revolutionary form of warfare was a 33-year-old cavalry captain named George S. Patton.

In his honor, the General George S. Patton Museum of Cavalry and Armor is located on Fort Knox. The museum contains personal artifacts of the fine general, as well as one of the most extensive collections of tanks and armored vehicles in the world.

Fort Knox is also home to the US Bullion Depository. The Gold Vault opened in January 1937. Inside you would find $100 billion worth of gold bullion, if you could go in. Access is so restricted a presidential order is required to get in. In fact, only two presidents have ever seen the place: Franklin Roosevelt and Harry S. Truman.

During World War II, Fort Knox trained thousands of new recruits and served as home base to military families. Today it encompasses 109,000 acres in three Kentucky counties. This respected military base has a population of over 23,000 soldiers, family members, and civilians.

As the army expanded the size of Fort Knox in the 1930s and '40s, by purchasing surrounding land, residents who were displaced moved to Radcliff. This small burg became home to civilians who worked on the base and a second home to thousands of soldiers who spent their leisure hours at the USO there.

Today Radcliff is a city of approximately 22,000 citizens. They play host to hundreds of military reunions every year and pride themselves on their military roots. Several festivals are held annually as a tribute to our men and women in service.

It's not all military, all the time, though. Kentucky's terrain has given way to biking, hiking, and walking trails as well as historical landmarks to round out your visit.

GUIDANCE Elizabethtown Tourism & Convention Bureau (270-765-2175, 800-437-0092; www.touretown.com), 1030 N. Mulberry St., Elizabethtown. The office is open Mon.–Fri. 8–6, Sat. 10–2, Apr.–Sept.; Mon.–Fri. 8–5 Oct.–Mar. Visitors looking for guidance should look for the giant mulberry-colored arch on the top of this building, which sits right on Mulberry Street. The staff just can't wait to share E-town with you. In addition to maps and brochures, there is also a small gift shop full of Kentucky crafts and souvenirs. **Radcliff/Ft. Knox Tourism & Convention Commission** (270-352-1204, 800-334-7540; www.radclifftourism .com), 562 A1 N. Dixie, Radcliff. Open weekdays 8:30—4:30. Look for this little tourism office, right downtown, right next to Stithton Baptist Church and directly across the street from a BP station. It's full of information on both local and regional attractions, and they even have free postcards of the area.

GETTING THERE Elizabethtown is located 35 miles south of Louisville, just off I-65 at the crossroads of the Western Kentucky Parkway and the Bluegrass Parkway. The **Louisville International Airport** (502-368-6524; www.flylouisville.com) is the closest airport; it's located at the intersection of I-65 and I-264. Car rentals are available at the airport. **Greyhound Bus** also serves Elizabethtown and Radcliff (270-765-4777; www.greyhound.com). The station is located at 2022 N. Mulberry St. in E-town.

GETTING AROUND Elizabethtown is easy to navigate by car. Off-street parking is available everywhere. You'll need a car to get around the Radcliff/Fort Knox area, but there is plenty of parking available.

photo by Deborah Kohl Kremer

ELIZABETHTOWN VISITORS CENTER

MEDICAL EMERGENCY Hardin Memorial Hospital (270-737-1212; www.hmh.net), 913 N. Dixie Ave., Elizabethtown. A 300-bed hospital providing care to citizens in Hardin and 10 surrounding counties. Ireland Army Hospital is located on Fort Knox but is only open to the military. There is also a **Carefirst Urgent Care Center** (270-351-1150) on Rogersville Rd. in Radcliff.

ALCOHOL Elizabethtown is the seat of Hardin County, a moist county. This means that alcohol sales are prohibited in the county, but they allow by-the-drink sales in E-Town and Radcliff restaurants that seat more than 100 people.

✳ To See

The Brown-Pusey House (270-765-2515), 128 N. Main St., Elizabethtown. Open Tue.–Sat. 10–4. Tour the Georgian mansion, which was built in 1825, and view artifacts and memorabilia from the residents' history. Free.

Black History Gallery (270-769-5204), 602 Gallery Place, Elizabethtown. Open weekends noon–5, or call for an appointment. A museum dedicated to the historical and cultural heritage of Black Americans. Displays include many untold stories, pictures, articles, biographies, and prints from magazines. Free.

The Cannonball (800-437-0092), corner of Public Square and W. Dixie Ave., Elizabethtown. Not a lot to see, but there is an actual cannonball embedded in the side of a building. During the Civil War, 3,900 Confederates attacked 652 members of the Union army right in downtown E-town. Many cannon balls struck homes and businesses nearby. This one had been stuck in the side of the Depp Building and was retrieved from the rubble when that building burned down in 1887. When the current building was under construction, the ball was placed back in the wall, close to its original location.

✐ **Kentucky Railway Museum** (502-549-5470, 800-272-0152; www.kyrail.org), 136 S. Main St., New Haven. Mon.–Sat. 10–5, Sun. noon–5. Train rides Tue.–Fri. at 2, Sat. 11 and 2, Sun. 1 and 3:30. Closed Sun. and Mon. in Jan., Feb., and Mar. Enjoy a 22-mile ride through the historic Rolling Fork River Valley on a restored passenger train. The museum houses all kinds of railroad memorabilia and equipment, a 3,000-square-foot model train display, and a museum of railroad memorabilia. Train rides: $15 adults, $10 ages 2–12; under 2 free.

Hardin County History Museum (270-763-8338; www.hardinkyhistory.org), 201 W. Dixie Ave., Elizabethtown. Guided tours by appointment only. The history of Hardin County from its early Indian inhabitants to modern times is portrayed in easy-to-follow exhibits.

✐ ♿ **Schmidt Museum of Coca-Cola Memorabilia** (270-234-1100; www .schmidtmuseum.com), 109 Buffalo Creek Dr., Elizabethtown. Open Mon.–Sat. 10–6, Sun. 1–5. With more than 8,000 square feet of space, you're going to need a Coke to see this, and you can get one at the old-time soda fountain. See one of the largest privately owned collections of Coca-Cola memorabilia in the world. $5 adults, $4 seniors, $2 students; preschoolers free.

A TASTE OF LOCAL HISTORY

A side trip to **Freeman Lake Park** (270-769-3916), 140 Freeman Lake Park Rd., Elizabethtown, will whet your appetite with authentic log cabins and a state-of-the-art recreation area. This giant lake could be the attraction on its own, but tucked over on the side of the lake are three historic buildings that have ties to the area. The park is open year-round, but the historic buildings are only open June 1–Oct. 1, Tue.–Sun. 10–5.

photo by Deborah Kohl Kremer

SARAH BUSH JOHNSTON LINCOLN CABIN

Sarah Bush Johnston Lincoln Cabin. This tiny, one-room log cabin is a replica of the 1819 home of Sarah Bush Johnston Lincoln, before she became the second wife of Thomas Lincoln and stepmother to Abraham Lincoln.

One Room Schoolhouse. See the schoolhouse that opened in 1892 and taught local children for 50 years. The white frame building housed about

⚷ ⚿ Swope's Cars Of Yesteryear Museum (270-765-2181; www.swope museum.com), 1100 N. Dixie Ave., Elizabethtown. Open Mon.–Sat. 10–5. See a 1910 Brush Runabout, a 1928 Packard Sedan, and about 50 other antique and classic cars. Free.

⚷ ⚿ ✿ Abraham Lincoln Birthplace National Historic Site (502-358-3137), Hodgenville. Open daily. An early-19th-century cabin is preserved in a memorial building in honor of our 16th president's humble beginnings. It is on 116 acres of the original Sinking Springs Farm and includes a visitors center with lots of information about Honest Abe. Free.

photo courtesy of www.kentuckytourism.com

SCHMIDT MUSEUM OF COCA-COLA MEMORABILIA

100 children when it opened, all in one room.

The Lincoln Heritage House. This is the former home of Hardin County resident Thomas Lincoln, father of our 16th president, Abraham. Made up of two log cabins,

photo by Deborah Kohl Kremer

LINCOLN HERITAGE HOUSE

one built in 1789 and a second, larger home built in 1805. The second cabin is the home that Thomas and Nancy Lincoln lived in when Abe's sister Sarah was born in 1807. See actual woodwork, mantels, and staircases built by the elder Lincoln.

Bring a picnic lunch and spend some time at this huge park. They have 7 miles of walking trails, an 18-hole disk golf course, volleyball courts, paddleboats, playgrounds, a 170-acre lake, and 93 acres of nature. It's a nice way to spend an afternoon.

✐ ♿ 🐾 **Abraham Lincoln Boyhood Home** (270-358-3137; www.nps.gov), US 31E, Hodgenville. Open daily Apr.–Oct. Visit this re-created cabin on the land where the Lincolns lived from the time Abe was two until about he was about eight years old. Free.

Fort Duffield (502-922-4574) Located at US 31W (Dixie Hwy.) at Salt River Dr. in West Point. Open dawn to dusk daily. General William Tecumseh Sherman ordered this earthen fortification built in 1861 to protect the Union supply route to Louisville. It still stands, and is probably Kentucky's best-preserved blockade, now listed on the National Register of Historic Places. Take a short hike from the parking lot to see the actual fort. Although reenactments are held on Memorial Day weekend, the park is open year-round. They have 10 miles of mountain bike and hiking trails, a nice garden area, and Memorial Hill Cemetery, which is a tribute to the 61 soldiers who died building the fort.

✐ ♿ 🐾 **Patton Museum of Cavalry and Armor** (502-624-3812; www.general patton.org) in Keyes Park near the main entrance to Fort Knox. Open 9–4:30 holidays and weekends, 10–6 May 1–Sept. 30, and 10–4:30 Oct. 1–Apr. 30. Closed Thanksgiving, Dec. 24 and 25, and Dec. 31 and Jan. 1. Named for the infamous general George S. Patton Jr., who led American troops through World War II, this museum exhibits artifacts from every conflict America has ever been involved in. Learn about the cavalry and the evolution of armor, and see many of the general's personal belongings. Free.

✳ To Do

DRIVING TOUR Self-Guided Elizabethtown Driving Tour (270-765-2175; www.touretown.com), See historic homes, churches and even the Elizabethtown City cemetery where there is a panoramic view of the city, without leaving your car.

GOLF American Legion Park (270-765-4030), 801 N. Miles St., Elizabethtown. A 9-hole, par-3 public golf course with tennis courts, playground, and clubhouse.

Pine Valley Golf Resort (270-737-8300, 800-844-1904; www.pinevalley golfandresort.com), 850 Pine Valley Dr., Elizabethtown. This 18-hole, par-4 golf course offers a driving range, two bars, a pro shop, and a restaurant. They also have several two-bedroom condos, making it a perfect place for a golf getaway weekend.

Lindsey Golf Course (502-624-4218, 502-943-9929 tee times; www.knox mwr.com/Rec/golf.asp), 4024 Bullion Blvd., Fort Knox. This challenging course features a par-5 18th hole—something to keep in mind as you wind your way through the fairways. Open daily.

PATTON MUSEUM

photo courtesy of www.kentuckytourism.com

SHOOTING RANGE **Knob Creek Gun Range** (502-922-4457; www.machine gunshoot.com), 690 Ritchey Lane, West Point. Offers recreational shooting as well as full line of guns and gun-related supplies and equipment.

TRAILS **Bridges to the Past** (270-352-1204), at the road junction of the old L&N Turnpike and old Dixie Hwy. Pick up a brochure and map at the visitors center. Travel along the original route of the L&N Turnpike on this walking tour, which takes about an hour. Cross stone bridges and enjoy the babbling brooks as you wander through a historic wooded area. You can even pretend to travel back in time, as you won't see any electric lines or signs of progress along the way. A peaceful way to commune with nature.

Tioga Falls Hiking Trail (270-352-1204), 8 miles north of Fort Knox off US 31W. Open at designated times, as it crosses into Fort Knox and is sometimes used for training. But when it is open to the public, it's worth your time to try out this trail. Allow yourself about two hours so you can take your time and see the 33 points of interest, like the hand-laid stone walls, fossil formations, and 130-foot Tioga Waterfall. Parts of this trail are nearly 200 years old; while it's very well preserved, it is rugged, and in some places the terrain is rough. Make sure all your hikers are up to it.

WALKS **Elizabethtown Greenbelt** (270-765-6121). More than 18 miles of walking trails surrounding Freeman Lake, Buffalo Lake, and Fisherman's Lake. Maps are available at the Elizabethtown Tourism Bureau.

Self-Guided Downtown Elizabethtown Walking Tour (270-765-6121). Enjoy a leisurely stroll past 25 historic sites and buildings varying in age and architectural style. Pick up your map at the tourism bureau.

✳ Green Space

Elizabethtown Nature Park (270-765-6121), 1916 Ring Rd. E., Elizabethtown. Created as a passive park. Visitors can enjoy the 104 acres of gently rolling terrain and beauty.

Saunders Spring Nature Preserve (270-351-1875), located between US 31W and Fort Knox (entrance off N. Wilson Rd.). Open dawn–dusk year-round. This nature preserve offers scenic hiking trails through 26 forested acres that show examples of the many sinkholes, caves, and natural springs that are abundant in this region. They also have a handicapped-accessible trail that winds through the woods and past a few waterfalls.

✳ Lodging

✎ ⁛¶⁙ ⴘ **Yongray's B&B Inn** (270-769-1301), 905 N. Mulberry St., Elizabethtown. Similar to big chain motels, this 36-room, locally owned inn is less expensive than competitors and offers warm, friendly service. Complimentary continental breakfast available daily. $

✎ ⴘ **Gold Vault Inn** (800-266-2104; www.goldvaultinn.net), 1225 N. Dixie Blvd., Radcliff. Radcliff's largest hotel features 94 rooms, a continental breakfast, and an indoor pool. Special rates available for military personnel. $

✎ ⴘ ❀ ⁛¶⁙ **Fort Knox Inn** (270-351-3199, 800-852-6164; www.fortknox

inn.com), 1400 Dixie Blvd., Radcliff. Located about a mile from Fort Knox, this clean, 40-room hotel is perfect for extended stays as they offer free guest laundry, as well as microwaves and refrigerators in the rooms. $

♂ ⁹ᵀ⁹ ♿ **Radcliff Inn** (270-351-8211, 800-421-2030; www.radcliffinn.com), 438 S. Dixie Blvd., Radcliff. Specializing in serving both military and civilians, they have 83 rooms, some with Jacuzzi tub. They also have a nice outdoor pool, fitness center, and game room. $

✳ Where to Eat

DINING OUT ♉ **Stone Hearth** (270-765-4898; www.stonehearthetown .com), 1001 N. Mulberry, Elizabethtown. Lunch Sun.–Fri. 11–2, dinner Mon.–Sat. 5–9. For an elegant gourmet meal or just a light lunch, locals have been going to Stone Hearth for more than 30 years. Dinner menu ranges from Mediterranean shrimp, to crab-crusted salmon, to slow-roasted prime rib. Save room for the house specialty pie, which tastes like a thick, warm chocolate chip pecan cookie, piled high with whipped cream. $$–$$$

Back Home Restaurant (270-769-2800; www.backhomerestaurant.com), 251 W. Dixie, Elizabethtown. Sun.–Mon. 11–3, Tue.–Sat. 11–9. You'll feel like you are back home when you order a pimiento cheese sandwich, fried green tomatoes, or a chicken-fried chicken dinner. Try these country meals and enjoy the comforts of this historic home, which dates back to 1872. $$

Uncle Franks German Food (270-352-4444), 821 N. Dixie Blvd., Radcliff. Open weekdays 11–2 and 5–9:30, Sat. noon–9:30. Closed Sun. The menu is so authentic, Uncle Franks has become a favorite for members of the military who have been stationed in Germany. Regulars order the Jaegerschnitzel, a breaded pork chop with mushroom gravy, that tastes like it was prepared in Munich. $$

⁹ᵀ⁹ **EATING OUT Cobbler Café** (270-982-2233; www.cobblerscafe .com), 125 E. Dixie Ave., Elizabethtown. Weekdays 7–3:30, Sat. 10–2. Housed in a historic downtown building that was once home to a shoe repair shop, this cute café now serves pastries, wraps, and sandwiches. There's a warm inviting interior—and nice patio dining is available, too. $

♉ **Back Stage Café** (270-234-1686), 109 N. Mulberry, Elizabethtown. Tue.–Thu. 11–4, Fri. 11–11, Sat. 11–4. Stop in for deli-style lunches during the week and local music on the weekends. Enjoy the very artsy atmosphere. $

Asian Buffet of Golden House (270-351-6888), 1225 N. Dixie Blvd., Radcliff. Open for lunch and dinner every day. With a 75-item buffet, you know you will find something you like. Locals swear by this place for great Asian specialties. $

Los Nopales Mexican Restaurant (270 -352-2230), 440 S. Dixie Blvd., Radcliff. Mon.–Thu. 11–10, Fri. 11–10:30, Sat. noon–10:30, Sun. noon–9:30. Tex-Mex fare using authentic Mexican recipes. Try the fajitas, quesadillas, and popular combo meals. $

⁹ᵀ⁹ **COFFEEHOUSES Arnold's Coffee Café** (270-982-4400; www .arnoldscoffeecafe.com), 2626 Ring Rd., Elizabethtown. Mon.–Fri. 7–9, Sat. 8–9, Sun. 8–2. Come in for some of the world's finest coffees—but stay for the made-to-order panini sandwiches, brick-oven pizzas, and mouthwatering pastries. $

"1" Seasons—The Bistro (270-982-2837; www.seasonsthebistro.com), 614 E. Dixie Ave., Elizabethtown. Open 7–3 Mon.–Thu.; until 7:30 PM on Fri. This little pastry and coffee bar also offers tasty sandwiches for lunch. $

✳ Entertainment

Hardin County Playhouse (www.hardincountyplayhouse.com), 209 W. Dixie Ave. Located in the Historic State Theatre's Plum Alley, this community theater stages an ambitious lineup of productions that has included *The Wizard of Oz, Steel Magnolias, A USO Christmas*, and other shows. Shows change seasonally, so check the web site to see what's showing.

Historic State Theatre Complex (270-234-8258; www.thestatetheater .org), 209 Dixie Ave., Elizabethtown. An art-deco-inspired movie theater that opened in 1942 and kept Elizabethtown entertained for 40 years, this regal facility has been restored and completely resurrected. Patrons can now enjoy live music, art displays, and drama and comedy shows. Check the web site for a list of performances.

Hardin County Schools Performing Arts Center (www.thepac.net), W. A. Jenkins Rd., Elizabethtown. Presenting a variety of programming, including live theater, gallery showings, and curriculum-based teaching units tied to the arts. The center was designed and is operated by theater professionals but owned by the public school system. Check the web site for featured shows.

✳ Selective Shopping

Rider's Fine Traditional Clothing (270-765-2233; www.ridersclothingky .com), 136 W. Dixie Ave., Elizabethtown. Surrounded by antiques and housed in a building that dates back to 1836, you'll know this isn't your typical clothing store. Kentuckians have been coming here since 1969 for the personal service and fine selection of elegant and stylish clothing.

Cottage Charm (270-765-7084; www .cottagecharm.biz), 532 W. Dixie Ave., Elizabethtown. With a wide variety of Vera Bradley purses, Waterford crystal, and everything in between, you'll find something for everyone on your gift list here.

The Red Brick Cottage (270-351-1224; www.theredbrickcottage.com), 776 S. Dixie Blvd. Radcliff. A nice little shop specializing in Kentucky gift baskets. You'll also find a wonderful selection of items like candles, soaps, purses, and gourmet food items.

The US Cavalry Store (800-777-7172; www.uscav.com), 2855 Centennial Ave., Radcliff. Not an army surplus store, but a store that focuses on outfitting individual soldiers. Complete line of military, law enforcement, and homeland security equipment.

ANTIQUES Buried Treasurer (270-982-4404), 516 N. Main St., Elizabethtown. Open Wed.–Sat. 10–4. They have a large selection of all kinds of antiques.

Goldnamers (270-766-1994), 210 N. Main St., Elizabethtown. Open weekdays by chance and appointment. Antiques and other treasures are available in this cute house in the heart of E-town.

Touch of the Past (270-765-2579), #9 Houchens Plaza on Sycamore St., Elizabethtown. Open Wed.–Sat. 11–4. They carry all kinds of antiques, collectibles, jewelry, and quilts. Stop in this cute shop to see what's new.

Somewhere In Time Antique Mall (270-352-0055), 332 N. Dixie Blvd., Radcliff. Spend an afternoon browsing around the thousands of antiques and collectibles.

SHOPPING DISTRICT **Historic Glendale** (270-369-6188; www .historicglendale.com). Located about 10 miles south of Elizabethtown is another darling little burg to visit. Glendale is a true old-fashioned rail-road country town. It boasts more than a dozen antiques and gift shops and unique dining all within two blocks. Most notable is the **Whistle Stop Restaurant** (270-369-8586), where you will find scrumptious fried green tomatoes, homemade soups, and their legendary fried corn bread.

✳ Special Events

✐ ಓ ❀ *May:* **Hooray for Heroes!** (www.radcliffchamber.org). This festi-val shows appreciation for members of the military, both past and present. It features live band music, games for children, clowns, and prizes.

✐ ಓ ❀ **Civil War Days at Fort Duffield**. This annual event held on Memorial Day weekend pays homage to those who fought in the Civil War. Union and Confederate reenactors make you feel like you were there.

✐ ಓ ❀ *September:* **Golden Armor Festival**. This weeklong event pays tribute to the Armored Force and Fort Knox personnel with a parade through town. They also have country-fair-type offerings like horseshoe-pitching con-tests, food competitions, and reunions.

✐ ಓ ❀ *Wednesday before Thanksgiv-ing–January 1:* **Christmas in the Park** (270-737-6568), Freeman Lake Park. Open 6–11 PM. With over a mil-lion lights, on more than 100 holiday displays, spread out over a mile of illu-minated park roads, you'll be in the holiday spirit before you leave. Free.

THE GREATER LOUISVILLE AREA

Souvenir T-shirts are available all around the city, proclaiming:

LOO EY VILLE
LOO A VUL
LOU IS VIL
LUH VUL

Making you wonder, how many ways can you say Louisville? Apparently several, and after spending some time there, hearing the different dialects, you'll understand the shirts. So choose your favorite pronunciation, they all work, but use *lou-is-vil* if you want everyone to know you are from out of town.

Kentucky's largest city, home to more than a million people in the metro area, was founded in 1778 by George Rogers Clark. He promptly named it in honor of King Louis XVI of France who was, at that time, sending troops to help American hold back the British during the Revolutionary War.

This river city credits its development to the Falls of the Ohio, a 2-mile stretch of rapids and shallow water that made boat navigation nearly impossible. It was the only such obstruction between Pennsylvania and mighty Mississippi, on the Ohio River; boaters had to remove their loads onto the shore and pull the vessel carefully through. All this loading and unloading created a powerful thirst, so taverns, inns, and restaurants started springing up to meet the demand. Next thing you know, Louisville was a bona fide city. The Falls of the Ohio was a legitimate landmark, noted in the writings of Clark, Daniel Boone, and Native Americans who used it as a reference point. With the completion of a canal system, and later locks and dams, the falls are no longer a problem for river travelers.

Louisville offers some swanky lodging options. From the glam of downtown's Seelbach or Brown Hotel to the opulent 100-year-old mansions-turned-B&Bs that line the neighborhood of Old Louisville, you will be living the high life. If you will be staying during Derby Week, plan ahead. Way ahead. With so many people descending on the city, the rooms fill up fast. They are not impossible to get, but the closer it gets to Derby Week, the farther out of town you will be staying.

As for dining, Louisville, quite an artsy city, has a wide array of, well, artsy restaurants. You'll find not only traditional southern cuisine but also a smattering of international favorites like Greek, Italian, and even Brazilian, which well repre-

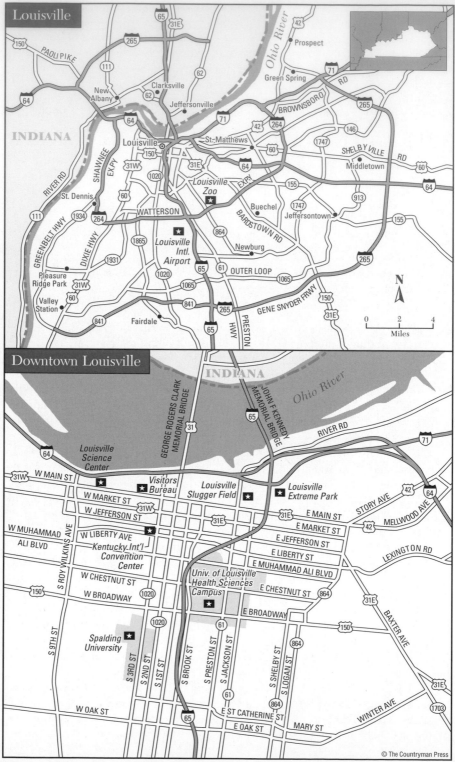

Louisville

PAOLI PIKE
Ohio River
Prospect
Green Spring
New Albany
Clarksville
Jeffersonville
BROWNSBORO
INDIANA
Louisville
St. Matthews
SHELBYVILLE RD
Middletown
Louisville Zoo
Buechel
Jeffersontown
WATTERSON
BARDSTOWN RD
St. Dennis
Louisville Intl. Airport
Newburg
Pleasure Ridge Park
OUTER LOOP
GENE SNYDER FRWY
Valley Station
Fairdale
PRESTON HWY

GREENBELT HWY
SHAWNEE EXPY
DIXIE HWY
RIVER RD

N

0   2   4
Miles

Downtown Louisville

INDIANA
Ohio River
GEORGE ROGERS CLARK MEMORIAL BRIDGE
JOHN F KENNEDY MEMORIAL BRIDGE
RIVER RD
Louisville Science Center
W MAIN ST
Visitors Bureau
Louisville Slugger Field
Louisville Extreme Park
STORY AVE
MELLWOOD AVE
W MARKET ST
W JEFFERSON ST
E MAIN ST
E MARKET ST
E JEFFERSON ST
W MUHAMMAD ALI BLVD
W LIBERTY AVE
Kentucky Int'l Convention Center
E LIBERTY ST
E MUHAMMAD ALI BLVD
LEXINGTON RD
S ROY WILKINS AVE
W CHESTNUT ST
W BROADWAY
Univ. of Louisville Health Sciences Campus
E CHESTNUT ST
E BROADWAY
BAXTER AVE
Spalding University
S 9TH ST
S 3RD ST
S 2ND ST
S 1ST ST
S BROOK ST
S PRESTON ST
S JACKSON ST
S SHELBY ST
S LOGAN ST
W OAK ST
E ST CATHERINE ST
E OAK ST
MARY ST
WINTER AVE

© The Countryman Press

KYEG#1 Louisville

sent the city's melting pot of cultures. Speaking of melting, Louisville is the home to the famous Kentucky hot brown, an open-faced turkey-and-bacon sandwich oozing with creamy warm cheddar cheese. This sandwich, which was obviously invented before cholesterol tests, was first introduced in 1926 at The Brown Hotel, hence the name. Visitors will find this dish on menus all over the state, but if you want the authentic recipe, head for The Brown.

Louisville, which is sometimes referred to as the northernmost city of the South, or the southernmost city of the North, draws the best features of both regions and presents itself as a world-class city, no matter how you pronounce it.

GUIDANCE For information, contact the **Louisville Convention & Visitors Bureau** (502-584-2121, 800-626-5646; www.gotolouisville.com), 301 S. 4th St., Louisville. Right downtown, you'll find this helpful visitors center. They have exhibits honoring Colonel Harland Sanders and a little restaurant he started, called Kentucky Fried Chicken. Another exhibit showcases the Bourbon Trail, where you can learn about all the nearby distilleries and where to find them. They have brochures for any direction you are headed. If you need Louisville T-shirts and souvenirs, they have all shapes and sizes. Architecture and history buffs may want to set aside time to tour Old Louisville, a spectacular 50-block area of the city. You can also get information at the **Visitors Center in Historic Old Louisville** (502-637-2922), 218 W. Oak St., Louisville. This center is open Tue.–Sat 10–5. Although they have information about the whole city, this center specializes in helping visitors to see the architectural gems of the Old Louisville neighborhood.

GETTING THERE The area is served by the **Louisville International Airport** (502-367-4636; www.flylouisville.com). Car rentals are available at the airport. **Greyhound Bus** (502) 561-2805; www.greyhound.com) is located at 720 W. Muhammad Ali Blvd., Louisville. The **Amtrak** station (800-872-7245; www.amtrak.com) is also located at 720 W. Muhammad Ali Blvd.

GETTING AROUND Public transportation is run by the Transit Authority of River City, also known as TARC (502-585-1234; www.ridetarc.org). The city buses serve all parts of downtown Louisville and Jefferson County, as well as Kentucky suburbs in Oldham and Bullitt Counties. For quick transportation within the downtown hotel and shopping districts, try the motorized trolleys, which run about every 20 minutes.

MEDICAL EMERGENCY Norton Healthcare (www.nortonhealthcare.com) is Kentucky's largest health care system, with four hospitals in Louisville, including Kosair Children's Hospital, Kentucky's only freestanding full-service children's hospital.

ALCOHOL Jefferson County is a wet county, so alcohol sales are permitted everywhere.

✱ To See

⚐ & Kentucky Derby Museum

(502-992-5905; www.derbymuseum
.org), 704 Central Ave., Louisville.
Mon.–Sat. 8–5, Sun. 11–5. Tours given
at various times throughout the day.
Even though the Derby is called the
greatest two minutes in sports, you can
spend the whole day learning about its
history and traditions. Watch film
footage of Derbies dating back to
1919. View historic memorabilia,
including hats worn on Millionaires'
Row and silks worn by jockeys. Speaking of jockeys, capture a whole new
appreciation for the sport when you
mount a simulated horse and try to
stay in the jockey's stance for the two

photo by Deborah Kohl Kremer

KENTUCKY DERBY MUSEUM

minutes it takes to run the 1.25-mile Derby route. Don't leave without attending
the film *The Greatest Race*, a 360-degree multimedia presentation that uses 96
projectors to tell the story of the Kentucky Derby. If you have time, sign up for a
walking tour or backside tour of Churchill Downs. Café and gift shop on site, too.
$10 adults, $9 seniors (55-plus), $8 ages 13–18, $5 ages 5–12; under 5 free.

LOUISVILLE SLUGGER MUSEUM & FACTORY

photo by Deborah Kohl Kremer

⚐ & **Glassworks** (502-584-4510, 800-
795-9429; www.louisvilleglassworks
.com), 815 W. Market St., Louisville.
Guided tours Sat. 10, 11, 1, and 3. Self-
guided tours weekdays 10–4. Learn
about the art of glassblowing in this
one-of-a-kind gallery. Watch glassblow-
ers pull molten glass from a 2,200-
degree furnace and transform it into
stunning works of art. Attend a glassblowing workshop or just mosey into
their walk-in studio, where you can
make awesome suncatchers and other
glass pieces. Before you leave, don't
forget to go to the on-site gallery
where you can purchase some of the
professionally made, breathtaking (no
pun intended) art. Guided tour $6.

Kentucky Museum of Art and Craft
(502-589-0102; www.kentuckyarts.org),
715 W. Main St., Louisville. Mon.–Fri.
10–5, Sat. 11–5. Featuring the work of
more than 200 artists, the museum
offers art in all media, folk art to furniture. There is also a galley shop so you
can bring some of these treasures
home with you.

🔗 ♿ **Louisville Slugger Museum & Factory** (502-585-5226, 877-775-8443; www.sluggermuseum.org), 800 W. Main St., Louisville. Hours vary slightly through the year. Typically open Mon.–Sat. 9–5, Sun. noon–5. There is no bat production on Sunday. Please call or check the web site for exact times. Since 1884, Louisville Slugger has been practicing the craft of baseball-bat making. They make the Official Bat of Major League Baseball, and you can watch. Take a tour through the factory and learn how they do it. In the museum, enjoy a short movie called *The Heart of the Game* featuring some of baseball's greatest hits, and view bats used by baseball greats such as Ty Cobb, Babe Ruth, Pete Rose, Hank Aaron, and Jackie Robinson. Lots of memorabilia and interactive features about America's favorite pastime as well as the bats that make it happen. Not sure if you're at the right place? Just look for the World's Biggest Bat, a six-story bat (it weighs 68,000 pounds!) propped up against the building. $9 adults (ages 13–59), $8 seniors (60-plus), $4 ages 6–12; 5 and under free.

🔗 ♿ **Louisville Science Center and IMAX Theater** (502-561-6100; www.louisvillescience.org), 727 W. Main St., Louisville. Mon.–Thu. 9:30–5, Fri. and Sat. 9:30–9, Sun. noon–6. Visit Kentucky's largest hands-on science center, with more than 120 exhibits covering all areas of science in a fun, exciting kid-friendly way. Don't miss the IMAX theater with a screen that is four stories tall. Call to find out what's showing. Prices range $6–15.

🔗 ♿ **Muhammad Ali Center** (502-584-9254; www.alicenter.org), 144 N. 6th St., Louisville. Mon.–Sat. 9:30–5, Sun. noon–5. This six-story, 96,750-square-foot museum is devoted to the life and values of Louisville's native son Muhammad Ali. See all his boxing memorabilia, a film about his life, and a full-sized boxing ring where a large projector shows Ali in his signature fight. $9 adults (ages 13–59), $8 seniors (65-plus), $4 military, $4 ages 6–12; 5 and under free.

🔗 ♿ **Frazier International History Museum** (502-753-5663; www.frazier museum.org), 829 W. Main St., Louisville. Mon.–Sat. 9–5, Sun. noon–5. Cover 1,000 years of history, with a focus on military artifacts like armor and weaponry. The entire third floor is an actual branch of the United Kingdom National Museum. Don't miss the Royal Armories, a collection of British arms, armor, and artillery dating from antiquity to the present day. Artifacts from American history, such as the Daniel Boone family Bible and Geronimo's bow, are also on display. On weekends you might just run into characters from history, like a former slave or a suffragette campaigning for women's right to vote as they mill about the museum. $9 adults, $8 military, $7 seniors, $6 under 14; under 5 free.

FRAZIER MUSEUM

photo by Deborah Kohl Kremer

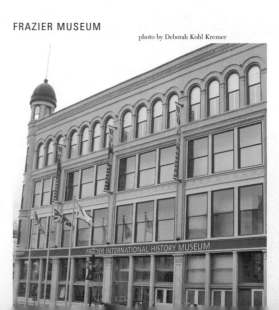

University of Louisville (502-852-5555, 800-334-UofL [8635]; www.louisville.edu). Just 3 miles from downtown, you'll find the 287-acre campus of U of L. Home to more than

20,000 students, the campus is steeped in history and tradition. Tour the campus to see one of the original castings of Rodin's *The Thinker* on the front steps of Grawemeyer Hall. If you are there in the fall, deck yourself in red and white and attend a football game at Papa John's Cardinal Stadium with 42,000 of your closest friends. On game day, everyone is a Cards fan.

Speed Art Museum (502-634-2700; www.speedmuseum.org), 2035 S. 3rd St., Louisville. Tue., Wed., and Fri. 10:30–4, Thu. 10:30–8, Sat. 10:30–5, Sun. noon–5. Impressive, to say the least, this is the oldest and largest art museum in Kentucky. See more than 12,000 pieces in the permanent exhibit that spans 6,000 years, ranging from ancient Egypt to the modern day. Free admission, although a donation of $4 is recommended.

Spirit of Jefferson/Belle of Louisville (502-574-2355; www.belleoflouisville.org), 609 W. Jefferson St., Louisville. Call for cruise times and reservations. Take a lunch, dinner, or sightseeing cruise aboard a National Historic Landmark, the *Belle of Louisville*, or her sister paddle-wheeler, the *Spirit of Jefferson*.

🎣 ♿ 🐾 **Callahan Museum of the American Printing House for the Blind** (502-895-2405; www.aph.org), 1839 Frankfort Ave., Louisville. Open weekdays 8:30–4:30, Sat. 10–3. This printing house published its first raised-letter embossed book, *Fables and Tales for Children*, in 1866 and has been bringing the written word to blind and visually impaired people ever since. Visit the museum where you can use a mechanical Braille writer and use your sense of touch to read Braille and raised-letter books. You will have a whole new appreciation for the services this printing house has given to the blind community. Free.

🎣 ♿ **Louisville Zoo** (502-459-2181; www.louisvillezoo.org), 1100 Trevilian Way, Louisville. Open daily Sept.–Feb. 10–4, Mar.–Labor Day 10–5. Open evenings in summer months. Check the web site for exact hours. Visit with 1,300 animals, living in their natural habitats. Don't miss the 4-acre Gorilla Forest Exhibit, where you can get really close to the gorillas and watch them play. Crowd favorites are Scotty, the zoo's youngest elephant, and King Louie, a rare white alligator. They also have a splash park for an additional fee. $12 adults (ages 13–59), $9 seniors (60-plus), $9 ages 3–11; 2 and under free.

🎣 ♿ **Louisville Underground Mega Cavern** (502-855-6342, 877-614-6342; www.louisvillemegacavern.com), 1841 Taylor Ave., Louisville. Open 7 days a week 9–5. Tour this former limestone quarry hidden under the Louisville Zoo. Covering 100 acres with 17 miles of roads, all underground, this massive cavern is a sight to see. The 70-minute tram tour covers areas of interest, including the geological aspects of the cavern, the green initiatives of building underground, and the fact that in 1962 it was designated an official bunker for the Cuban Missile Crisis. $14 adults, $12 seniors, $8 ages 3–11.

THE BELLE OF LOUISVILLE
photo courtesy of www.kentuckytourism.com

✒ **Louisville Stoneware Factory Tour** (502-582-1900, 800-626-1800; www.louisvillestoneware.com), 731 Brent St., Louisville. Mon.–Sat. 10–6. Tour one of the oldest and best-known pottery-manufacturing sites in the country. Watch the potters hand make and then hand paint each piece. There is also a museum, a paint-your-own pottery shop, and a factory retail store. $5 per person.

TOURS Old Louisville Tours (502-637-2922; www.oldlouisville.net/vc), the Visitors Center in Historic Old Louisville, 218 W. Oak St., Louisville. Open Tue.–Sat. 10–5. This 50-square-block section of the city is home to 1,400 structures built between 1885 and 1905 and includes practically every style of architecture prevalent during the Victorian era. It is a virtual open-air museum for lovers of architecture and old homes. As one of the

photo courtesy of www.kentuckytourism.com

OLD LOUISVILLE

largest National Register Historic Districts in the country, it is also one of the largest contiguous collections of Victorian mansions you'll ever see. A guided tour is worth your time. Both walking and motorcoach tours are available and are led by guides who are knowledgeable and passionate about Old Louisville. Tours last approximately 90 minutes. Ghost tours offered every Fri. night. Tours range $15–25 per person. Reservations required.

✷ To Do

✒ **FAMILY ENTERTAINMENT Kart Kountry** (502-543-9588; www.gokart kountry.com), Paroquet Springs Dr., Shepherdsville. Home of the world's longest go-cart track, this 1.5-mile course is fun for the whole family. They have five sizes of carts so everyone can take a spin. While you are there, take in 18 holes on their miniature golf course, ride the bumper boats, or take a few swings in the batting cage.

GOLF Nevel Meade Golf Course (502-228-9522; www.nevelmeade.com), 3123 Nevel Meade Dr., Prospect. A well-known, privately owned 18-hole golf course with a pro shop, clubhouse, and snack bar.

Quail Chase Golf Course (502-239-2110; www.quailchase.com), 7000 Cooper Chapel Rd., Louisville. With 27 holes, this public course has achieved a 4-star rating from *Golf Digest* magazine.

HORSE RACING Churchill Downs Race Course (502-636-4400; www.churchilldowns.com), 700 Central Ave., Louisville. Historic Churchill Downs, home to the Kentucky Derby, and the famous twin spires situated high above the grandstand, is a place legends are made. Although it is best known for the Derby, on a daily basis it's a thoroughbred racetrack featuring live racing and simulcasting. The **Fall Meet** runs from the end of October to the end of November. The **Spring Meet** runs from the end of April through early July. The track is usually dark—track-talk for "not running"—on Mon. and Tue. Call for exact dates and times.

MINOR-LEAGUE BASEBALL The Louisville Bats (502-212-2287; louisville.bats.milb.com), Louisville Slugger Field, 401 E. Main St., Louisville. The Louisville Bats are the Triple-A affiliate of the Cincinnati Reds. Modern Louisville Slugger Field can hold about 13,000 fans and is about a block from the river, right downtown.

✳ Green Space

Olmsted Parks (502-456-8125; www.olmstedparks.org). Created by famed landscape designer Frederick Law Olmsted, who also created Central Park in New York City, this system of parks, including 3 flagship parks and 15 smaller ones, is a true gem in the layout of the city of Louisville. Olmsted began working with Louisville in 1891, and his concept of creating a system of parks connected to tree-lined parkways was instrumental in the expansion of the city and the protected green space within it. This park system is one of only five nationwide designed by Olmsted. The flagship parks, Cherokee, Iroquois, and Shawnee, include charming vistas, rolling open plains, mature trees, and thousands of varieties of plants and wildlife.

Louisville Waterfront Park (www.louisvillewaterfront.com). Right on the banks of the Ohio, this park offers a grand view of the river, space for concerts and festivals, and green space for kids to run and families to picnic. Spread out over 85 acres, there are walking trails, a playground. and a water park open in summer months. The park is made up of three phases, two of which have been completed. The third phase is scheduled to be completed in 2011.

✳ Lodging

✮ ⁘ **HOTELS The Brown Hotel** (502-324-1389; www.brownhotel.com), 335 W. Broadway, Louisville. On the National Register of Historic Places, The Brown Hotel has been providing upscale accommodations to visitors for almost 100 years. The 293 guest rooms boast 5-inch pillow-top featherbeds with 310-thread-count Egyptian cotton linens and European white goose-down comforters for superior comfort. Just walk through the lobby and take note of the ornate hand-painted plaster relief ceilings, intricately carved railings, decorative crown moldings, and other classic architectural details of this grand English Renaissance hotel. $$$–$$$$

⁘ ✎ ✮ **Galt House Hotel & Suites** (502-589-5200, 800-843-4258; www .galthouse.com), 140 N. 4th St., Louisville. As the city's only riverfront hotel, fabulous views are available from some of the 1,291 guest rooms. Full of history, the Galt House originally opened in 1835 and over the years offered shelter to notable visitors, such as presidents, politicians, and celebrities. During the Civil War, Generals Grant and Sherman met here to plan the capture of

Atlanta. Although the original building no longer exists, today's visitors can enjoy modern conveniences, six restaurants, a rooftop fitness center, and 2,500 covered parking spaces. $$$–$$$$

⚑ ♿ **The Seelbach Hilton Louisville** (502-585-3200; www.seelbach hilton.com), 500 4th St., Louisville. A Kentucky tradition since 1905, The Seelbach is one of Louisville's premier hotels. Having played host to nine US presidents in its first 100 years, it's a glorious combination of glamour and southern hospitality. The 300 guest rooms have an understated elegance. Many notable characters have ties to this grande dame. Gangster Al Capone stayed there so frequently that he had access to secret passages where he could hide in case of a raid. He once donated a large mirror that still hangs in an alcove of the Oakroom dining room. It wasn't just a generous gift; the mobster used it to watch his back during card games. Another claim to fame is the mention of The Seelbach in *The Great Gatsby*, a 1925 novel by F. Scott Fitzgerald, who was known to frequent the hotel. $$$–$$$$

⚑ ♿ **21C Museum Hotel** (502-217-6300, 877-217-6400; www.21cmuseum .org), 700 W. Main St., Louisville. Ironically, you will find this contemporary hotel located right in the heart of the historic Museum Row on Main in the downtown area. Stay in one of the 91 modern rooms and enjoy the surrounding art and luxurious amenities. $$$–$$$$

⚑ **BED & BREAKFASTS DuPont Mansion** (502-638-0045; www.dupont mansion.com), 1317 S. 4th St., Louisville. Built in 1879, the mansion reflects the Victorian era Italianate-Renaissance Revival style that is prominent in this Old Louisville neighborhood. With soaring 10-foot doors

and windows, marble fireplaces, and crystal chandeliers, the architecture is something to behold. Each of the eight perfectly appointed guest rooms comes complete with fireplace and whirlpool tub, making the DuPont a fabulous place to unwind. Innkeeper Mary Pat acts as a personal concierge ready to help their guests with any need. $$–$$$$

⚑ **Inn at the Park** (502-638-0045; www.innatpark.com), 1332 S. 4th St., Louisville. Located right in the heart of Old Louisville you will find the massive 7,400-square-foot mansion that originally was home to Russell Houston, president of the Louisville & Nashville Railroad. Built in 1884, this Richardsonian Romanesque mansion features a stunning staircase. The eight guest rooms with original hardwood floors, intricate woodwork, and fine furnishings are simply the icing on the cake of this spectacular home. $$–$$$$

✿ **The Columbine Bed and Breakfast** (502-635-5000, 800-635-5010; www.thecolumbine.com), 1707 S. 3rd St., Louisville. Unique Greek Revival architecture in the heart of historic Louisville. The Columbine's white columns and portico make it truly memorable. Unwind in one of the six guest rooms. Filled with antiques and reproductions, the rooms also feature in-room fireplaces, 12-foot ceilings, and original hardwood floors. Breakfasts range from omelets to caramelized apple French toast. $$

Inn at Woodhaven (888-895-1011; www.innatwoodhaven.com), 401 S. Hubbards Ln., Louisville. This historical Gothic Revival mansion, which was built in 1853, features eight guest rooms. Listed on the National Register because of its architectural wonders, the home still boasts diamond window-panes with trefoil decorations, delicate plasterwork on the ceilings, interior shutters, and 14-foot arched Gothic doors. Enjoy your breakfast with fresh flowers, flickering candlelight, soft music, white tablecloths, and fine china. $$–$$$

❝⑂❞ **1888 Historic Rocking Horse Manor B&B** (502-583-0408; www .rockinghorse-bb.com), 1022 S. 3rd St., Louisville. Built in 1888 out of stone, this mansion still features glorious architectural treats such as stained-glass windows, claw-foot soaking tubs, and original woodwork. The six guest rooms are decorated in period furnishings but have all the modern amenities that today's travelers expect. Enjoy your gourmet breakfast in the fabulous dining room surrounded by lace tablecloths, crystal, and massive chandeliers. $$–$$$

❝⑂❞ **Pinecrest Cottage and Gardens** (502-454-3800; www.bbonline.com/ky/ pinecrest), 2806 Newburg Rd., Louisville. This one-bedroom guesthouse provides complete privacy. Guests will enjoy a fully stocked kitchen, a living room with a pullout couch, and a bedroom with a king-sized bed. The cottage sits on 6.5 luscious acres of carefully tended perennial beds and 100-year-old trees. There is also a pool and tennis court on the property. $$

✳ Where to Eat

⑂ **DINING OUT The English Grill at The Brown Hotel** (502-736-2996), 4th and Broadway, Louisville. Dinner Mon.–Sat. 6–10. Immerse yourself in fine elegance by dining at this landmark restaurant. The decor looks as it must have when they opened in the 1920s, with dark wood paneling, stately upholstered armchairs, and china- and crystal-covered tables. This sophisticated restaurant is tailored to diners with discriminating tastes. You won't find chicken nuggets on the menu, but a blend of choices like roasted venison, New York strip steak, and fresh

grouper with leeks and Dungeness crab. The service is impeccable, complete with palate cleansers between courses and never-ending home baked breads to accompany your meal. Leave the kids at home and enjoy this grown-up indulgence. $$$–$$$$

⑂ **Oakroom at The Seelbach Hilton** (502-807-3463; www.seelbachhilton .com), 500 4th Ave., Louisville. Tue.–Sat. 5:30–10, Sunday brunch 10–2. Arguably the finest dining experience you can have in Kentucky. This glamorous restaurant has been awarded the prestigious Five Diamond Award from AAA for more than 10 years. Its Kentucky's only Five Diamond Restaurant, so make reservations and enjoy the fabulous cuisine and flawless service. Their wine list, if you can call 1,200 choices a list, is the most expansive in the state. $$$–$$$$

⑂ **August Moon Chinese Bistro** (502-456-6569; www.augustmoonbistro .com), 2269 Lexington Rd., Louisville. Open for lunch and dinner every day. Chef Peng Looi serves up a menu right from the Orient, mixing together flavors and countries, with Malaysian, Indonesian, and Chinese dishes all promising a delicious meal in a cool contemporary dining room. $$

⑂ **Baxter Station Bar and Grill** (502-584-1635; www.baxterstation .com), 1201 Payne St., Louisville. Mon. 11:30–2, Tue.–Thu. 11:30–10, Fri. 11:30–11, Sat. 4:30–11. Closed Sun. This fun, casual restaurant has an international and regional American menu. From the crabcakes to the warm goat cheese salad to the fajita burritos and salmon croquettes, there really is something for everyone. Large selection of import and specialty beers on tap, too. Eat outdoors year-round and don't miss the adorable train that runs around the restaurant—it's up near the ceiling. $$

Ÿ **Buck's in the Mayflower** (502-637-5284; www.bucksrestaurantandbar.com), 425 W. Ormsby, Louisville. Lunch Mon.–Fri. 11–3, dinner Mon.–Thu. 5–10, Fri.–Sat. 5–11. Right in the heart of Old Louisville, Buck's offers upscale, romantic dining with a full array of menu choices. The dim lights, fresh flowers, and Victorian accents show the elegance, but the chic mishmash of china and utensils reveals Buck's eclectic side. $$–$$$

Ÿ **Come Back Inn** (502-627-1777; www.comebackinn.net), 909 Swan St., Louisville. Open for dinner Tue.–Sat. A favorite of locals, this is a cozy place to relax with tasty food and a full bar at very reasonable prices. The menu features Italian American food like Chicago-style Italian roast beef sandwiches and tortellini with prosciutto in a garlic cream sauce. Don't forget to try the pizza; it's award winning. $$

Ÿ **De La Torres Spanish Restaurant** (502-456-4955; www.delatorres.com), 1606 Bardstown Rd., Louisville. Open for dinner Tue.–Sat. Classic Spanish menu and Madrid accents make you think you're in Spain. This is fine dining with dishes like paella, marinated meats, and chorizo (traditional Spanish sausage) on the menu.$$

Ÿ **Limestone Restaurant** (502-426-7477; www.limestonerestaurant.com), 10001 Forest Green Blvd., Louisville. Lunch weekdays 11:30–2, dinner Mon.–Sat. 5–10, Sun. 10–2. Menu is a true taste of southern-style cooking. With appetizers like fried chicken livers and shrimp 'n' grits, and entrées of beef short rib on braised collard greens, or white beans and country ham, you'll know you're in the South. So try it while you're here. $$

Mayan Café (502-566-0651; the mayancafe.com), 813 E. Market St., Louisville. Lunch weekdays 11:30–2:30, dinner Mon.–Thu. 5–10, Fri. and Sat. 5–10:30. Each dish looks like a work of art, and the not-so-common ingredients combine to make a one-of-a-kind meal. Mayan recipes are very flavorful; try the Veracruz duck mole—sautéed duck with chocolate sauce—or the smoked salmon crêpe topped with light pumpkin seed cream sauce. $$

Ÿ **Napa River Grill** (502-893-0141; www.napariverlouisville.com), 1211 Herr Lane, Westport Village, Louisville. Lunch weekdays 11–2, dinner every night beginning at 5. Upscale casual dining featuring Northern California–inspired dishes as well as a few Pacific Rim menu choices. Weather permitting, you can eat outside on the fieldstone, vine-trellised patio near the oakwood grill. This cool bistro has plenty of drink choices, too. Check out the custom-built wine rack with more than 1,000 bottles to choose from. $$–$$$

Ÿ **Palermo Viejo** (502-456-6461; www.palermoviejo.info), 1359 Bardstown Rd., Louisville. Open for dinner Mon.–Sat. at 5. The owners, the Elbl brothers, chose the name for a vibrant neighborhood in Buenos Aires that is an eclectic mix of quirky shops, restaurants, and Tango Houses; Louisville's version is Bardstown Road, minus the Tango Houses. The menu is country cooking, just from another country. Most entrées come from Spanish or Italian roots. Several of the entrées are served on small hibachi-style grills that are brought right to the table. Don't miss the extensive list of Argentine wines. Never had Argentine food? Try a beef dish, all of them are marinated and served with chimichurri sauce, a blend of oil, vinegar, and herbs. The Elbl brothers claim this sauce is so good, diners have suggested they turn it into a drink. $$–$$$

Ỿ **Saffron's Restaurant** (502-584-7800; www.saffronsrestaurant.com), 131 W. Market St., Louisville. Lunch weekdays 11:30–2:30, dinner Mon.–Thu. 5:30–9:30, Fri.–Sat. 5–10. Serving authentic Persian cuisine in a relaxed but upscale atmosphere, this restaurant is very inviting. Since Persian recipes are not always familiar, the staff work extra hard to make sure you know what you will like, the personal service is unmatched. For dessert, order some Persian ice cream, with hints of saffron, pistachio, and rosewater. $$

Ỿ **Vincenzos** (502-580-1350; www .vincenzositalianrestaurant.com), 150 S. 5th St., Louisville. Lunch every day beginning at 11:30, dinner every day beginning at 5:30. Reservations recommended. Owned by brothers Agostino and Vincenzo Gabriele, who grew up in Palermo, Sicily, their menu reflects European specialty dishes in an elegant but yet relaxed setting. In addition to traditional pasta dishes, Vincenzos also has a nice variety of seafood, lamb, beef, and chicken dishes. Try the pesce spada con capperi e olive schiacciate—swordfish with capers. $$–$$$

Ỿ **EATING OUT Café Lou Lou** (502-893-7776; www.cafeloulou.com), 106 Sears Ave., Louisville. Open Sun.–Thu. 11–10, Fri.–Sat. 11–11. They have an amazing variety of calzones, pizzas, pastas, and sandwiches. The Cajun fries are so hot, they seem to numb your taste buds. The chef has ties to New Orleans—hence the name, for Lou(iville) and Lou(isiana). Most menu items have Cajun, Greek, or Italian influences. The bright, funky walls and artwork seem to make this hip place buzz. $–$$

Ỿ **J. Graham's Café at The Brown Hotel** (502-736-2996; www.brown hotel.com), 4th and Broadway, Louisville. Open weekdays 6:30–3, weekends 7–3. Home of the legendary Kentucky hot brown, a sandwich that has been a favorite since it first appeared on the menu in the 1920s. This open-faced combination of turkey, bacon, cheese sauce, and toast points is worth the indulgence. The casual café also features a daily breakfast and lunch buffet that draw crowds. $–$$

Ỿ **Captain's Quarters Riverside Grille** (502-228-1651; www.cqriverside .com), 5700 Captain's Quarters Rd., Harrods Creek. Open for lunch and dinner every day, Sunday brunch 10:30–2:30. Just north of Louisville, you'll find a welcoming place for outdoor dining right on the Ohio. The menu offers everything from appetizers to steaks, chops, and chicken favorites. They have sandwich and pizza selections too. This casual restaurant has an upscale feel to it. If you can't eat outside, curl up next to the giant stone fireplace and enjoy the river view out the window. $–$$$

Ỿ **Cunningham's Restaurant** (502-587-0526), 630 S. 4th St., Louisville. Open for lunch and dinner every day. Part of Louisville's history for more than 100 years, with photos on the walls to prove it. Everyone seems to know that this is the place for turtle soup and a generous-sized fried fish sandwich. Although those are the hometown favorites, Cunningham's also serves up burgers, hot brown, and even pan-fried oysters. It's a casual place with very reasonable prices. $–$$

Tony BoomBozz Pizza (www.tony boombozz.com). Open every day. With four locations around Louisville, you're always close to one of Louisville's favorite pizza places. Pizza maker Tony Palombino named his restaurant *BoomBozz* because it is Italian slang for "wild, crazy, and fun." So stop in for some gourmet pizza and have some *boombozz* while you're there. $–$$

Grape Leaf Restaurant (502-897-1774), 2217 Frankfort Ave., Louisville. Mon.–Thu. 11:30–9, Fri.–Sat. 11:30–9:30, Sun. 12:30–8:30. Recommended by vegetarians and fans of Mediterranean- and Middle Eastern–style cuisine, this is Louisville's answer to where to go for gyros, falafel, and hummus. $–$$

♪ **Lynn's Paradise Café** (502-583-3447; www.lynnsparadisecafe.com), 984 Barret Ave., Louisville. Mon.–Fri. 7–10, Sat.–Sun. 8–10. If you look up *eclectic* in the dictionary, there ought to be picture of Lynn's Paradise Café there. This is a nutty restaurant with a giant coffeepot and a huge moose that looks like a zebra in the parking lot, a life-sized metal bear dressed like Elvis to greet you, and a dining room full of wacky, kitschy things to look at while you eat. The menu is equally entertaining. Breakfast is available all day, so you might want to try the French toast, but the dinner menu's meat loaf and Paradise hot brown are good choices too. Stop in Lynn's attached gift shop, the World of Swirl, for hip gift items that you've never seen before. Bring a donation for the Ugly Lamp contest that Lynn's Paradise sponsors at the Kentucky State Fair each year. Look around the restaurant for this year's nominees. $–$$

Mike Linnig's Place (502-937-9888; www.mikelinnigsrestaurant.com), 9308 Cane Run Rd., Louisville. Tue.–Thu. 11–10, Fri. and Sat. 11–11, Sunday noon–10. Around since 1925, the Linnig family continues to dish up fish sandwiches and seafood plates the way they have since they started serving food at their small roadside market. In addition to crawfish, alligator, and swordfish steaks, Linnig's has juicy burgers, turtle soup, and onion rings.

Even the homemade tartar sauce is worth coming back for. This casual place is a local favorite, and their back-to-basics menu has something for everyone. Eat outside at a picnic table alongside the Ohio River, or eat in the front room where you are surrounded by mounted animals who have made a trip to the taxidermist. $–$$

Toast on Market (502-569-4099; www.toastonmarket.com), 736 E. Market St., Louisville. Open Mon.–Sat. 7–3. This cool place to eat breakfast and lunch is housed in a former theater downtown. Check out the huge stained-glass window on the front of the building with the word EMPIRE in the middle. No one seems to know what it means, but it looks really hip. You know the food is really good when you find that you have to wait for a table, no matter what time you go. They have hearty breakfast specials, as well as huge sandwiches and salads. Smells like homemade bread as soon as you open the door. Try a grilled cheese sandwich; they have four varieties to choose from. $–$$

WW Cousins Restaurant (502-897-9684), 900 Dupont Rd., Louisville. Open every day for lunch and dinner. Locals swear this is the place to go for the best burger in Louisville. The buns are homemade, and they have a huge fixin's bar where you can dress up your burger just the way you want it. This is a casual, family-style restaurant where everyone can find what they want. In addition to making buns every day, they also make some iced cookies that are simply wonderful. $

♀ **Wick's Pizza** (www.wickspizza.com). Open every day. Several locations around town. Michael and Meredith Wickliffe are the proud owners of four Louisville locations, all offering comfortable dining, their well-known pizza, and more than 60 foreign and domes-

tic beers and 75 blends of liquor. Sure, the pizza is awesome, but so are the aptly named Stuffed Breadwick and the Hot Sicilian Sandwich. $

Wagner's Pharmacy (502-375-3800), 3113 S. 4th St., Louisville. Open Mon.–Sat. 8–3. Given the prime location, just across the street from Churchill Downs, you'll be eating with authentic horse people. It's a favorite of jockeys and trainers who know you don't need fancy accommodations to get a good fried egg sandwich or burger. In business for about 100 years, Wagner's is a staple in the community. Listen up, you might just hear a tip about an upcoming race.

SNACKS Homemade Ice Cream and Pie Kitchen (www.homemadeice creamandpiekitchen.com). Open Mon.–Thu. 10–10, Fri.–Sat. 11–11, Sunday noon–10. They are easy to find because they have nine locations

MUTH'S CANDIES, HOME OF THE MODJESKA

photo by Deborah Kohl Kremer

around Louisville. What started out as a lunch counter that served pie turned into a pie restaurant that served homemade ice cream. They claim that the Caramel Iced Dutch Apple is their signature pie, but with flavors like Key Lime, Sweet Potato, and Red Raspberry Cream, who could choose? Make sure you order your pie à la mode— the fresh-churned ice cream is made of 14 percent butterfat and tastes like your mom just made it. People come from miles around when the pumpkin ice cream is in season.

❦ **Muth's Candies** (800-55MUTHS; www.shop.muthscandy.com), 630 E. Market St., Louisville. Closed Sun. In business since 1921, Muth's has been treating locals to fine candy for generations. The confectionary has a huge selection of sweets like bourbons, creams, and jellies, but they are known for the Modjeska. This caramel marshmallow wonder, as it is referred to, is a heavenly combination of soft marshmallow dipped in chewy caramel. It was named for a famous Polish actress, Helena Modjeska, who appeared in Louisville several times during the late 1800s and was quite fond of the city. Maybe she liked caramel, too.

✳ Entertainment

🍸 **4th Street Live** (502-584-7170; www.4thstlive.com), 420 W. Liberty St. Louisville. This entertainment district, covering more than a block of the downtown, is chock-full of bars, restaurants, live entertainment, a comedy club, and even a high-tech bowling alley. You'll find all the major clubs, a few retail chains, and cool eateries. During summer months they have free outdoor concerts featuring big-name county entertainment. Kick off your shoes and dance in the street, everyone else does.

photo by Jodi Karem

4TH STREET LIVE

Louisville Palace Theater (502-583-4555; www.louisvillepalace.com), 625 S. 4th St., Louisville. A true palace in the heart of downtown, this magnificent showplace was rumored to cost more than $2 million when it opened in 1928. Today you can see rock concerts, comedians, and Broadway shows in this Spanish Baroque–inspired 2,700-seat theatre. Even if you aren't there to see a show, poke your head into the lobby and admire this gorgeous Louisville treasure.

✍ ও **Six Flags Kentucky Kingdom** (800-727-3267; www.sixflags.com). At the crossroads of I-65 and I-264, this popular amusement park has 44 rides, a huge water park, and fun for all ages. Thrill seekers can ride coasters such as Greezed Lightnin' and Himalaya while little ones can enjoy tamer rides in the Belgian Village area of pint-sized rides.

Queen of Rags (502-454-7769), 1036 Bardstown Rd., Louisville. This vintage resale shop sells one-of-a-kind clothes, shoes, jewelry, cards, and dishes. You can also order a custom-made Derby hat.

Dot Fox (502-452-9191; www.dotfox clothingculture.com), 1701 Bardstown Rd., Louisville. You'll find a wide selection of progressive and independent lines of men's and women's clothing, shoes, and accessories.

Scout (502-584-8989; www.scouton market.com), 801 E. Market St., Louisville. An eclectic mix of home accessories, giftware, artwork and jewelry located in the downtown East Market Street Business District.

Hadley Pottery (502-584-2171; hadleypottery.com), 1570 Story Ave., Louisville. Hadley Pottery, known throughout the world, has been a Louisville mainstay since around 1940. You can see the entire collection and get a deal on a piece of Mary Alice Hadley's fine pottery at this warehouse store. The somewhat whimsical pieces, which are all hand painted, each features Mary Alice's logo M. A. HADLEY written on the back.

Zappos Shoe Outlet (502-921-4949; www.zappos.com), 376 Zappos.Com Blvd., Shepherdsville. If you've ever shopped this mega online retailer, you might want to head 20 miles south of Louisville and see what you can find at their outlet. The prices are not rock-bottom as you might expect with the word *outlet* in the name, but the selection is huge and the prices are lower than you'll find online. So swing in— it's right off I-65—and see what they have.

✐ ♿ *The Kentucky Show!* (502-562-7800; www.kentuckyshow.com), 501 W. Main St., Louisville.

Now appearing at the Kentucky Center for the Performing Arts is a one-of-a-kind tribute to the commonwealth of Kentucky. Called *The Kentucky Show!*, this fast-paced, 30-minute film, shown on a gigantic screen, takes you to all corners of Kentucky. With a combination of fantastic photography, compelling music, and the sheer size and pace of the show, that exclamation point is there for a reason.

Encompassing the state's history, people, culture, traditions, and economy, *The Kentucky Show!* melds together 75 hours of video and 125 hours of interviews that took 18 months to produce. The result is phenomenal.

Narration is by Ashley Judd; viewers also hear from famous and not-so-famous Kentuckians while taking in landscape, panoramic, and action shots of the wonderland that makes up the Bluegrass State.

"It doesn't seem to make a difference if you are in third grade or you are 93 years old, there is something in this for everyone," said Tim King, director of marketing and sales for *The Kentucky Show!* "As soon as the show starts, you do not hear a peep from the crowd for the next 32 minutes."

Since its debut on September 12, 2008, more than 25,000 people have enjoyed the show from the specially designed 100-seat theater.

The show was created by Donna Lawrence, of Donna Lawrence Productions of Louisville. No stranger to the field of multimedia, Lawrence has also created awe-inspiring videos for the Kentucky Derby Museum, the College Football Hall of Fame, and the US Capitol Visitors Center.

Every Kentuckian, as well as every visitor to the state, should see this magnificent show. For visitors it could reshape their trip and lead them to some of the greatest places in the state. For residents, well, seeing the Bluegrass State looking her finest on that big screen will inspire pride and possibly a lump in your throat.

Check the web site for show times. Closed Monday. Admission $7; seniors and students $6.

GALLERIES Mellwood Arts and Entertainment Center (502-895-3650; www.mellwoodartcenter.com), 1860 Mellwood Ave., Louisville. This huge old warehouse—a former meat-packing plant—is now home to more than 100 artists and entrepreneurs who use the space for studio and storefront. Watch the artists at work and browse their wares as you wander through the amazing collection of talent all under one roof.

Zephyr Gallery (502-585-5646; www.zephyrgallery.org), 610 E. Market St., Louisville. As the oldest cooperative, contemporary, fine-arts gallery in the region, Zephyr's 20-plus years of experience shows. It is owned and operated by the members, which allows visitors direct contact with the artists.

The Higgins Maxwell Gallery (502-584-7001; www.higginsmaxwell.com), 1200 Payne St., Louisville. Featuring fine examples of vintage American and European art. Knowledgeable staff are on hand to help you with anything you need.

ANTIQUES Joe Ley Antiques (502-583-4014; www.joeley.com), 615 E. Market St., Louisville. Located in an 1890s schoolhouse downtown, this well-known antiques store has been a Louisville attraction for more than 35 years. Not just knickknacks and dainty items, at Joe's you'll find architectural pieces like old gas pumps, hundreds of mantels, and an impressive assortment of carousel horses. They have china, books, toys from your (and your grandmother's) childhood, and more than 5,000 doors for that house you are restoring on the weekends. You just never know.

✳ Special Events

Spring: **Humana Festival of New American Plays** (www.actorstheatre.org). Rub shoulders with actors, producers, playwrights, directors, journalists, critics, and theater lovers from around the world who gather each year for a sampling of the newest American plays. For more than 30 years, the Actors Theater of Louisville has hosted this festival, which presents more than 500 performances of both classical and contemporary plays. It also encompasses meet-the-cast parties, discussion panels, and social events.

July: **Lebowski Fest** (www.lebowskifest.com). A celebration of all things Lebowski, a tribute to the Coen brothers' 1998 film and cult classic, *The Big Lebowski*. It's kind of like a *Star Trek* convention for bowlers, True fans gath-

photo by Deborah Kohl Kremer

JOE LEY ANTIQUES

er for unlimited bowling, trivia contests, and the overuse of movie quotes like "Not on the rug, man," and "The Dude is not in." Some of the actors from the movie have shown up from time to time. Lots of music, too.

♿ *October:* **St. James Court Art Show** (www.stjamescourtartshow.com). One of the largest juried art shows in the country, the St. James draws 700 artists and a quarter of a million people to the open-air show held in historic Old Louisville. Surrounded by 100-year-old trees and Victorian homes, art lovers can stroll the historic neighborhood and browse paintings, drawings, prints, watercolors, ceramics, pottery, and hand-decorated porcelain. There is also jewelry, floral arrangements, metalwork, wood work, furniture, toys, crafts, stained glass and art glass, windows, clothing, needlework, quilts, leather goods, and enamel work, just to name a few.

MAY: THE DERBY AND ITS FESTIVAL

Okay, so the race lasts two minutes. Still, preparations for the Kentucky Derby are years in the making. After all, these young thoroughbreds have been groomed and trained for this event since their birth, three years prior. Just a few minutes in town will clue you in to the fact that the city of Louisville does not take this event lightly. And for this reason, you will find over-the-top galas, star-studded formal balls, an open-to-the-public Governor's Breakfast (please see *Special Events* in the Frankfort chapter), and Derby Festival events that usually start to kick in two weeks prior to these sacred two minutes.

Produced annually since 1956, the **Derby Festival** entertains 1.5 million people during the 70 special events held each year in the lead-up to the most prestigious horse race in America and the first jewel of the Triple Crown. The events, which are scattered around town, are fun to enjoy on their own, but add to the excitement of the two weeks before the derby. Don't forget to pick up a Pegasus Pin, a cute little lapel pin that serves your ticket into most of the big events. It is available all over town, costs $3, and instantly becomes a collector's item. A few of the notable events are:

The **Pegasus Parade** is held the Thursday before Derby day. This parade has been a tradition since 1956. One of the largest parades in the United States, it's full of floats, inflatables, marching bands, equestrian acts, and celebrities. The route is downtown on Broadway. Bleacher seats require tickets, but free viewing is available along the route, too.

Thunder Over Louisville is a huge fireworks display, one of the largest in the county. The fireworks are launched from barges right on the Ohio River. Phenomenal viewing sites are all around the Louisville area.

Watch as more than 35 hot air balloons chase the lead, or hare, balloon at the **Great Balloon Glow and Race**.

The annual **Great Steamboat Race** on the Ohio River takes place between the *Belle of Louisville* and the *Belle of Cincinnati.* Stand along the shore and listen to the calliope play as the two paddle-wheelers race— well, they don't really go very fast—to the finish line.

Kicking off two weeks prior to the Derby and running right up through the big day, the **Fest-a-Ville on the Waterfront** features music, socializing, and gobs of food. It is also known as the Chow Wagon, and you'll know why when you see all the food vendors.

Be sure to check the Kentucky Derby Festival web site (www.kdf.org) for dates, times, and further information.

SHELBYVILLE, LAGRANGE, AND THE SURROUNDING AREA

J ust north, and slightly east, of Louisville city limits is a lesser-known area of Kentucky. Shelbyville, LaGrange, Eminence, and Crestwood are examples of small towns that are misleadingly known as bedroom communities. Although quite a bit of their residents do commute into the big city each day, the fact is they return each night to darling hometowns that offer cute shops, restaurants, and attractions that make this the kind of place where you want to live. So veer off the main expressway routes and take the back roads for a change. You will find scenic byways, farming communities, and out-of-the-ordinary eateries that will make you want to stay awhile.

GUIDANCE These towns are fairly small, so tourism isn't their main focus. For helpful advice you can always turn to www.kytourism.com, which offers regional information and a searchable database broken down by city. The city of LaGrange does have a web site (502-269-0126; www.discoverlagrange.org) that will help you plan your day in the downtown area. In surrounding Oldham County, contact Kim Buckler at the Oldham County Tourism Commission (800-813-9953; www.tour oldhamcounty.com). She can direct you to all the hot spots, and if your group is larger than four people, she'll even create a whole itinerary for you. In the tiny berg of New Castle, during warm-weather months, you'll find three men who sit on a bench in front of the Henry County Court House all day long. You can set your watch by these guys. They chat with passersby and solve all the world's problems. So if you need information, there's a good chance one of these three will have the answer.

GETTING THERE The area is served by the **Louisville International Airport** (502-367-4636; www.flylouisville.com). Car rentals are available at the airport. **Greyhound Bus** (502-561-2805; www.greyhound.com) is located at 720 W. Muhammad Ali Blvd., Louisville. The **Amtrak** station (800-872-7245; www.amtrak .com) is also located at 720 W. Muhammad Ali Blvd.

GETTING AROUND Bounded by I-64, which runs east–west, and I-75, which runs north–south, these expressways have exits for LaGrange, Shelbyville, and Crestwood—but take the back roads to see them in style. While the downtowns are tiny, you'll still need a car, because the only public transportation is a few commuter bus routes into Louisville.

MEDICAL EMERGENCY **Baptist Hospital Northeast** (502-222-5388; www .baptistnortheast.com), 1025 New Moody Ln., LaGrange. This full-service hospital serves patients primarily from Oldham, East Jefferson, Henry, Trimble, and Carroll Counties.

ALCOHOL If you are looking for alcohol in this region, you might need to plan ahead. The communities in this section spread across several counties, each with its own version of the law. Jefferson County is a wet county, so alcohol sales are permitted everywhere. In Henry County, which is moist, you will find alcohol within the city of Eminence and the Smith-Berry Winery. Oldham and Shelby Counties are considered limited, which means that certain restaurants can sell alcohol by the drink. So if you want a glass of wine with dinner, call the restaurant first to see which county they are in and what the law is in their neck of the woods.

✳ To See

✿ **Yew Dell Gardens** (502-241-4788; www.yewdellgardens.org), 6220 Old LaGrange Rd., Crestwood. Call for directions or check their web site for a map, as some Internet mapping systems are incorrect. Summer hours (Apr.–Nov.) Mon.–Sat. 10–4, Sun. noon–4. Winter hours (Dec.–Mar.) Mon.–Fri. 10–4. This spectacular 33-acre garden is certainly not your run-of-the-mill collection of geraniums and marigolds. This is the former home of Theodore and Martha Klein, horticulturalists who ran a successful nursery on the property for more than 40 years. Now run by a nonprofit organization, their collection of more than 1,100 species of trees, shrubs, and flowers is breathtaking. Wander through the themed gardens, which include roses, dwarf conifers, hollies and evergreens. Also on site are a relocated log cabin, a stone castle, and a tobacco barn. They have classes and demonstrations throughout the year, but you can also just take a self-guided walking tour. Bring your iPod and download the guided tour so you can follow it without the guide. $7 adults, $5 seniors; under 12 free.

Smith-Berry Vineyard and Winery (502-845-7091; www.smithberrywinery.net) New Castle. Walk the grounds of the vineyard and then stop by the tasting room (Tue.–Sat. 10–6) to taste the benefits of harvesting grapes by hand and fermenting them in small distinct lots. Smith-Berry hosts concerts during the summer, where you can kick back and relax with some great music and home-grown wine.

Rob Morris Home (www.discoverdowntownlagrange.org), 110 Washington St., LaGrange. Open by appointment only. Tour this beautiful home, which was once owned by Rob Morris, the poet laureate of Freemasonry and founder of the Order of the Eastern Star. The two-story white-clapboard house, which was built in 1840, was home to the Morris family from 1862 through the 1890s. Furnished with several pieces of the Morris family furniture, the home also features artifacts of Morris's life and pieces of history from the Order of the Eastern Star.

Oldham County Historical Society (502-222-0826; www.oldhamcountyhistorical society.org), 106 N. 2nd Ave., LaGrange. Open Tue., Wed., Thu., and Sat. 10–4, Fri. 10–8. Housed in three pre–Civil War buildings, this museum does a good job re-creating Oldham County's past.

photo by Deborah Kohl Kremer

OLDHAM COUNTY HISTORICAL SOCIETY

GOLF **Henry County Country Club** (502-845-2375; www.hccc.com), 2200 Campbellsburg Rd., New Castle. Quite the gathering place for Henry County residents, this semi-private club features an 18-hole, par-71 course. An excellent value: You pay one greens fee and golf from dawn to dusk. So load up your cooler and try to beat one local's personal record of 54 holes in one day.

Clear Creek Golf Course (502-633-0375), 717 Burks Branch Rd. Shelbyville. This 9-hole par-4 executive course is perfect for beginners but gets high recommendations from serious duffers, too. Carts are available, but it's a nice course to walk. Call for a tee time on holidays and weekends.

Weissinger Hills Golf Course (502-633-7332; www.weissingerhills.com), 2240 Mount Eden Rd., Shelbyville. With a clubhouse as nice as the 18-hole, par-72 course, you might want to stay awhile. This scenic course also offers friendly staff and a well-stocked pro shop.

SCUBA **Falling Rock Park Scuba Diving Park** (502-939-5049), Fendley Mill Rd., Oldham County. Open Sat.–Sun. May–Oct. This former rock quarry is now a 50-foot diving lake. Pay one fee and dive all day. Loaded with fish, sunken boats, and even an old school bus, all for your diving pleasure.

TOURS **Spirits of LaGrange Ghost Tours** (502-356-3293; discoverlagrange .org/ghosts), Thu.–Sat. evenings in Sept. and Oct. Reservations necessary. Get to know some former residents of LaGrange on this 1½-hour lantern-lit walking tour. The expedition covers about 12 city blocks and is led by an entertaining and knowledgeable tour guide. $15 per person.

✳ Green Space

Guist Creek Lake (502-647-5359), 11990 Boat Dock Rd., Shelbyville. Primarily known for its stock of largemouth bass, hybrid stripers, catfish, crappie, bluegill, and rockfish, it is a fisherman's dream. During the summer months, the lake also has an area set aside for water-skiers. A fully stocked marina on site offers gas, bait, snacks, and fishing licenses. They also have a boat ramp and some small motorboats available for rent. A campground is available March 1–Nov. with primitive sites as well as pull-through RV camping with electric and water hookup.

Lake Jericho Recreational Area (502-743-5205) This 137-acre lake located in Henry County offers bank fishing for largemouth bass, bluegill, crappie, and catfish. They also have a 62 RV camping sites with electric and water hookup. Throughout the property there are tent sites available, too. The fishing lake is open year-round, but camping is only available Apr.–Oct.

✳ Lodging

❝❶❞ The Bluegrass Country Estate B&B (502-222-2009, 877-229-2009; www.bluegrasscountryestate.com), 1226 Bluegrass Pkwy., LaGrange. For those traveling with a horse, this B&B will pamper you as well as your equine traveling companion. Although innkeeper Cheryl Sabin refers to her inn as a bed & breakfast, it is more like a luxury retreat that you won't want to leave. Inside the gorgeous home are five well-appointed guest rooms loaded with horse decor and antiques, which make them warm and inviting. But wait until you try the beds. Each room features a top-of-the-line Swedish sleep system that practically cuddles you into dreamland. It might be the best night of sleep you have ever had. Even though you won't want to get out of bed, wait 'til you see what else Cheryl has available. There is a fabulous home gym, a heated pool and hot tub, and a theater room with a giant screen, hundreds of movies, and a popcorn machine. More draws to this room are the comfy reclining theater chairs and the personalized Hollywood photographs featuring movie legends like Don Ameche and Ava Gardner. These original photos belonged to Cheryl's mother, who worked in the commissary at Paramount Pictures in the 1950s and '60s. Listen to her fascinating stories over gourmet omelets and scones or pecan waffles, just two of her oft-requested breakfast specialties. $$$

Colonial Hill Inn (502-558-4504), 316 E. Cross Main St., New Castle. Innkeeper Tina Stambaugh considers her B&B to be a retreat destination, where people come to unwind and unplug. So for that reason, you won't find a television in every room. This 1830s Greek Revival home offers two antiques-laden guest rooms that feature a welcome basket and homemade cookies upon your arrival. Tina is happy to accommodate special requests, like a favorite dessert in the evening or acknowledgment of a special occasion. Wander along the walking path that winds through the home's 22 acres. For breakfast, enjoy the deluxe continental array that always features Tina's signature scones. $–$$

✳ Where to Eat

♿ **DINING OUT Claudia Sanders Dinner House** (502-633-5600; www.claudiasanders.com), 3202 Shelbyville Rd., Shelbyville. Tue.–Sun. 11–9. When the wife of Colonel Sanders decided to open a restaurant, she put her own chicken on the menu. The chicken dishes are "finger-lickin'" . . . but Mrs. Sanders knew how to make southern favorites like hot brown, country ham and biscuits, and Kentucky pie with pecans and chocolate chips, too. $–$$

♈ **Westport General Store** (502-222-4626; www.westportgeneralstore.com), 7008 KY 524, Westport. Serving dinner Tue.–Thu. 5–9, Fri.–Sat. 5–10; lunch Sat. 11–4. Head west of LaGrange a few miles and you'll come to the tiny burg of Westport, where this store has been in business almost continuously since Westport formed in 1780. You can still pick up the sorts of things you would need from a general store, but their restaurant is the real reason to come. The wood plank floors, wood-burning stove, and old black-and-white photographs really add to the ambience. Yet their southern-style (with a hint of upscale) menu options are what brings people back time and again. You can't find dishes like black-eyed peas, collard greens, and fried bologna sandwiches alongside filet mignon and bison rib eyes just anywhere. Inexpensive kids' menu and nice dessert selection too. $$–$$$

The Science Hill Inn (502-633-2825; www.wakefieldscearce.com), 525 Washington St., Shelbyville. Tue.–Sun. 11:30–2:30, Sat 5:30–7:30. More than 100 years ago, young ladies of a certain pedigree attended the Science Hill Inn to learn social graces. Today the upscale dining room has an air about it that makes you try harder to use your manners. So put the cloth napkin on your lap and get your elbows off the table and carefully browse the southern-inspired menu. With choices like shrimp and grits, Kentucky hot brown, and country ham and pimiento cheese sandwiches, the decisions are tough, but your final decision will be a good one. The entrées are first-rate, and the dedicated servers will keep your table supplied with hot corn bread pone during your visit. $$

♈ **Arbor Ridge Vine and Grill** (502-241-5544; www.arborridgevineand grill.com), 6402 Westwind Way, #1, Crestwood. Tue.–Fri. 11–9, Sat. 5–9, Sun 10–2. A mix of Mediterranean and Californian specialties, the menu focuses on fresh and flavorful. They have a full line of sandwiches and soups, but entrées like pan-seared mahimahi, salmon in orange rum sauce, and slow-simmered chicken and sausage stew all make Arbor Ridge unforgettable. Speaking of unforgettable, their stuffed fried olives appetizer and amazing grilled cheese with raspberry sauce are out of this world. Owner Neal Gilder carefully chose the 33 wines on the wine list to complement his menu offerings. Casual but classy decor makes everyone feel at home. If the weather is nice, order their signature Maryland crabcakes and eat on the patio. $$–$$$

♈ **Old Stone Inn** (502-722-8200; www.old-stone-inn.com), 6905 Shelbyville Rd., Simpsonville. Serving lunch Thu. and Fri. 11–2, dinner Mon.–Sat. 4–10. Completed in 1818 and built from local limestone, the Old Stone Inn is a historic gem located in Shelby County. Touring the building and admiring the construction is worth a stop alone, but while you are there you have to experience their wonderful southern-inspired menu. Dive into Grandma Mary's chicken livers, southern-fried chicken, or their bourbon barrel pork chops for a real treat. Side dish options include southern greens, okra, and grits, reminding you that you are south of the Mason-Dixon line. They also serve more standard fare like burgers, sandwiches, and salads, which are all good, too. If the weather is nice, eat out on the patio and soak in that country air. $$–$$$

EATING OUT Our Best (502-845-7682; www.ourbestrestaurant.com), 5728 Smithfield Rd., Smithfield. Open for lunch and dinner Tue., Wed., Thu., and Sun. 11–8. They stay open until 9 PM on Fri. and Sat. Breakfast is served on weekends only, Sat. and Sun. 8–10:30. Slightly off the beaten path, about 8 miles east of LaGrange, you'll find this cozy hometown eatery. Housed in the former Smithfield Milling Company, Our Best serves up old-fashioned favorites like fried chicken, bean soup, and fried corn bread. One of their signature dishes is the fried green tomatoes, which you can have as a side dish or on a BLT, which they call BLGT. The creaky wood floor and enormous collection of business cards tacked to the walls add to the ambience. $–$$

Red Pepper Deli (502-225-0770), 103 E. Main St., LaGrange. Mon.–Fri. 10:30–6, Sat. 10:30–4. Known for their huge portions; you won't go away hungry. Their impressive lineup of homemade soups and salads, as well as sandwiches all served on fresh bread, make it hard to choose. $–$$

DELIZIE ITALIANE ITALIAN GOURMET MARKET

photo by Deborah Kohl Kremer

Delizie Italiane Italian Gourmet Market (502-565-4481; www.delizie italianemarket.com), 208 E. Main St., LaGrange. Open Mon.–Thu. 11–7, Fri. 11–8, and Sat. 10–8. Tucked into an adorable little pink house on Main Street, you will find this delightful little Italian eatery. The name means "Italian delights" and owners Sandra Gugliotta and Caroline Davis aren't handing you a line; this place is delightful. They specialize in traditional dishes like lasagna Bolognese, spinach fettuccine and cream sauce, and hand-rolled meatballs with pasta. All the pastas are fresh and homemade, and you will certainly be able to tell. They also serve up European rustic sandwiches made with imported luncheon meats and cheeses. The tiny restaurant also serves as an Italian market, stocked with hard-to-find Polly-O ricotta, Pomi tomatoes, Cerignola olives, and European packaged cookies. Speaking of cookies, they have several that are to die for, so order some with your meal or to go. You won't be sorry. $–$$

Big R's BBQ Shack (502-222-0058), 209 E. Main St., LaGrange. Mon.–Thu. 11–2, Fri and Sat. 11–8. Wander about a block farther down Main Street, and you'll find a barbecue lover's dream. When you smell the slow-roasted barbecue, you will know you are at the right place. Featuring baby back ribs, pulled pork sandwiches, and pulled chicken and brisket sandwiches, all swimming in sauce and lip-smacking good. Their potato salad is so good, some people are tempted to order it as an entrée. $–$$

Serendipity (502-222-4216), 116 E. Main St., LaGrange. Mon.–Sat. 10–5. Serendipity is a darling mix of café, gift shop, and tearoom. Stop in to browse their unique collection of home decor items and country-inspired art, then have a seat and enjoy a warm bowl of soup, a grilled sandwich, or a cup of tea. Everyone gets treated to a piece of scone to whet their appetite. $–$$

Ÿ **Irish Rover Too** (502-222-2286; www.theirishroverky.com), 117 E. Main St., LaGrange. Open Tue.–Thu. 11–9, Fri. and Sat. 11–10. With a perfect combination of Irish favorites transformed into American bar food, this pub is a perfect choice for a group trying to please several appetites. Nowhere else in LaGrange will you find a Welsh rabbit sandwich, a salmon burger, shanagarry fish cakes, or an order of bangers and mash. For those not feeling so Irish, they have a big hearty cheeseburger, stuffed pork loin, and a flavorful chicken salad sandwich. Nice assortment on their kids' menu, too. Save room for an Irish-cream-liqueur-laced cheesecake or bread-and-butter pudding that is soaked in whiskey-caramel sauce. Yes, you do have room for it. $–$$

Ÿ **Cutters Wharf** (502-228-3100; www.cutterswharf.org), 1902 Victory Ln., Prospect. Open Mon.–Thu. 11–10, Fri. and Sat. 11–11, Sun. 10–10. Cutoffs and flip-flops are welcome at Cutters. Eat outside on the floating wharf and enjoy watching the boats go by as you feast on casual selections like chicken fingers, wraps, and sandwiches and burgers. Cutters also offers a few unexpected entrées like salt and pepper seared tuna, filet and shrimp, and BBQ chicken pizza. The food is good, the prices are right, and dining on the river makes you feel like you're on vacation. $–$$

✎ ✿ S N A C K S **Morgan Drug Store** (502-255-3540), 325 US 42, Bedford. Open Mon.–Fri. 8–6:30, Sat. 8–2. Closed Sun. About 9 miles east of Campbellsburg, you will find the tiny community of Bedford. Although it is off the beaten path somewhat, it's worth your while to slip back in time to this old-time soda fountain that has been serving up treats to Trimble County natives for more than 50 years. The malts, shakes, and ice cream cones are still hand dipped the way they always have been, but the real draw is that this is probably the only place in Kentucky where you will find a nickel Coke. Yes, they really are a nickel.

Sweet on La Grange (502-222-5959), 114 E. Main St., LaGrange. Take a break from all the browsing along Main Street and treat yourself to some hand-dipped Blue Bell Ice Cream or a few decadent pieces of Kentucky's own Ruth Hunt candy.

✳ Selective Shopping

Cherry House (502-425-7107; www.cherryhouse.com), 2419 S. KY 53, La Grange. This furniture business started out selling cut glass and handmade solid cherry furniture in a small showroom in 1969. Today you can browse through several homes and buildings, where you'll find furniture displayed as it would be in your house. The Cherry House is widely regarded as the premier resource for upscale, yet affordable, fine home furnishings.

Wakefield Scearce Galleries (502-633-4382; www.wakefieldscearce.com), 525 Washington St., Shelbyville. Closed Sun. Housed in a former all-girl academy known as Science Hill, these galleries concentrate on British antiques, mint julep cups, and fine silver. The historic building also features smaller shops offering fine clothing, linens, and silk flowers.

The 1887 Corner Store (502-222-4454), 101 E. Main St., LaGrange. This building, which has been lovingly restored to its 1880s grandeur, is one of the first things visitors see when

THE GATHERING ROOM QUILT SHOPPE

owned toy store has shelves and shelves of wonderful toys for the kid in everybody. The story is so inviting, you really will want to play for a while.

The Gathering Room Quilt Shoppe (502-222-1044; www.gatheringroom quiltshop.com), 109 E. Washington St., LaGrange. Closed Sun. and Mon. Just browsing through this 1880s-era home and looking at all the quilts, patterns, and fabric makes you want to start stitching. One whole room is dedicated to Civil War reproduction fabrics and patterns, inspiring to both quilters and nonquilters.

✱ Special Events

⌀ ♿ ✿ *Weekends, May–July:* **Highland Renaissance Festival**, Eminence. Spend a day steeped in the Renaissance period of the Dark Ages around the 15th and 16th centuries. See jousting demonstrations, knights in shining armor, and period-appropriate musical acts. Wear a costume from that era in history and you'll make friends quickly. They have food like turkey legs but also festival-type fare to appeal to the whole family.

⌀ ♿ ✿ *July:* **Annual Harvest Showcase and Farmer's Market**, Henry County Fairgrounds. Although it feels a lot like a county fair, this huge farmer's market is really a way to bring goods from the garden to the table. Agriculture is the main attraction, with chefs cooking up the homegrown products like meat, honey, and produce. There are also kids' games like Thimble in the Haystack, a husband-calling contest, and a tractor pull. Spend the day and feel like a local.

arriving in historic downtown LaGrange. The warm and inviting shop is full of gift items you'll want to keep for yourself. They have pottery, linens, home decor items, and an assortment of upscale pieces for your home.

☕ **Karen's Book Barn and Java Stop** (502-222-0918; karensbook-barn.com), 127 E. Main St., LaGrange. Order up a coffee, cappuccino, or fresh fruit smoothie and wander through this cozy shop bursting with both new and used books.

Gardner House Antiques (502-633-1971; www.gardnerhouseantiques.com), 525 Main St., Shelbyville. Specializing in china, furniture, and antique rugs, this shop has sort of an upscale air about it. Stop by and see what's new.

⌀ **The Treasured Child** (502-225-9646; www.thetreasuredchild.com), 115 E. Main St., LaGrange. The sign out front says COME IN AND PLAY, and they mean it. This independently

Western Kentucky 6

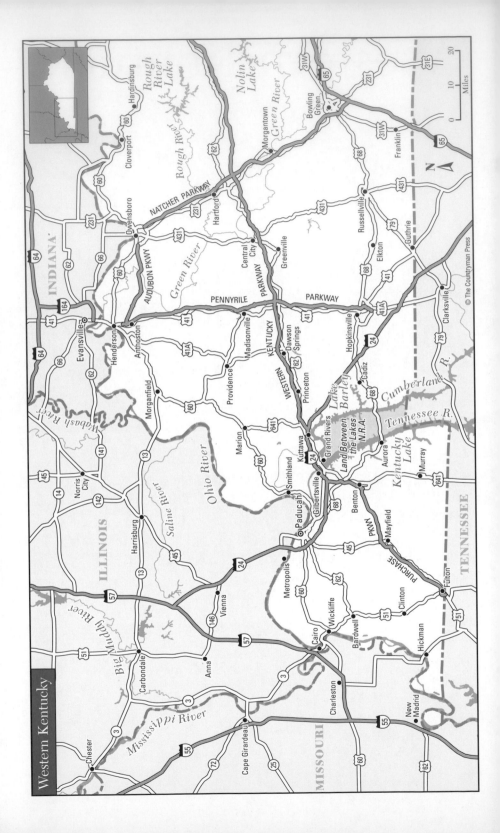

INTRODUCTION:
WESTERN KENTUCKY

Western Kentucky differs from the rest of the state geographically, because it's primarily flat. Vast open plains, giant farms, and dense wooded areas blanket Kentucky's lower left quadrant. Its beauty differs from the rugged mountains in the east and rolling bluegrass plains of central Kentucky, but it is beautiful all on its own.

The Ohio, Cumberland, Rough, Green, and Tennessee Rivers make up the myriad waterways that allowed this area to grow and prosper as Kentucky's settlers moved west. Now, 200 years later, it is these same rivers, along with the human-made Kentucky Lake and Lake Barkley, that bring people to the area. Although the flatboat has been replaced by luxury houseboats and the dugout canoe has evolved into a speedboat with a water-skier hanging on the back, it is the same water and shoreline that help the area flourish.

Western Kentucky is twangy bluegrass music, succulent barbecue restaurants, intricately stitched quilts, and the aforementioned water-related recreation. Yet although these are major factors in the area's character and charm, they merely scratch the surface. You have to go there, meet the people, and participate in these activities before you really understand what makes Western Kentucky special.

L ocated just about 30 minutes apart via US 60, you'll find the two river cities of Owensboro and Henderson. Although both are delightful on their own, they each deserve a place in Kentucky's history, as well as your vacation travels.

The third largest city in Kentucky, **Owensboro** is located on the banks of the Ohio River. The area is known for its famous barbecue and bluegrass music, but that's certainly not all this river city has to offer. They have a fine collection of museums, parks, and golf courses, as well as a lively downtown. But somehow everything seems connected to the bluegrass or the barbecue.

Let's start with the bluegrass connection. As the birthplace of Bill Monroe, known as the Father of Bluegrass, Owensboro residents know and understand this music. Locals claim that if it weren't for Monroe, there would be no genre of music called bluegrass. So it seems natural that the International Bluegrass Music Museum is in Owensboro. This is where you can learn all about Monroe and other pioneers in the industry. It is also home to the Bluegrass Music Hall of Fame.

Now on to the barbecue connection. Folks in this town know how they like their barbecue. It's not something that comes out of a can, and it's not something that people would refer to as "Sloppy Joes." It is a meal of various kinds of meat, preferably mutton, served with, depending on the restaurant, trademark sauce. Locals grow up going to one of these barbecue joints, and that is where they go for barbecue their whole life. They are a loyal bunch. So whether you are going to Moonlite Bar-B-Q, George's Bar-B-Q, Ole South Barbeque, or Old Hickory Bar-B-Q, you'll be getting a real authentic Owensboro barbecue. You might need to try them all so you can be a fair judge.

The river city of **Henderson** is a favorite stop for the paddle-wheel riverboats like the Mississippi Queen and the American Queen because Henderson is a perfect example of a darling, small Kentucky town. The city, home to about 27,000 people, has a nice park area along the river, which gently rolls into the downtown area.

Henderson's most famous former resident, John James Audubon, who spent most of his life painting birds, is honored in the downtown area with bird sculptures scattered about. He is also remembered at Audubon State Park, where you'll find camping, trails, a nature center, and a collection of his original artwork.

Another famous resident was W. C. Handy, aka the Father of the Blues. To preserve his memory and honor his lifelong achievements, Henderson stages its free W. C. Handy Blues & Barbecue Festival on the riverfront each June.

GUIDANCE **Owensboro-Daviess County Tourist Commission** (270-926-1100, 800-489-1131; www.visitowensboro.com), 215 E. 2nd St., Owensboro. Open 8–4:30 weekdays. Located in a refurbished historic building right in the heart of downtown. Lots of information, maps, and advice here, and it also houses the Hometown Hero Hall of Fame (see below). **Henderson County Tourist Commission** (270-826-3128; 800-648-3128; www.hendersonky.org), 101 N. Water St., Suite B, Henderson. Open weekdays 9–5. The Henderson Welcome Center is located in a replica of a historic riverfront railroad depot and has all the brochures and advice you could ever need. It is also the site of the Henderson Historical Society, so it is like a mini museum covering Henderson's past. Stop in and look around.

GETTING THERE The area is served by the **Evansville Regional Airport** (www.evvairport.com) just 12 miles away from Henderson. This airport offers commuter flights to connecting airports. **Greyhound Bus** (270-821-3086; www.grey hound.com) serves the Madisonville and Western Kentucky region. The station is located at the Red Cardinal Inn, 4765 Hanson Rd., US 41N, Madisonville.

GETTING AROUND **Owensboro Transit System** (270-687-8570; www.owens boro.org). Runs several route around the city, Mon.–Fri. 6–7, Sat. 8–4. Check the web site for route maps. The **River City Trolley** loops around to all the Owensboro attractions, restaurants, and shops. Tue.–Sat. 9–5, Sun. 1–5. The trolley does not operate during the months of Jan., Feb., and Mar. Running several routes through Henderson is the HART Bus System. They do not have a web site, but you can call 270-831-1249 for a schedule or pick one up at the Henderson County Tourist Commission.

OWENSBORO VISITORS CENTER
photo by Deborah Kohl Kremer

MEDICAL EMERGENCY **Owensboro Mercy Health System** (877-888-OMHS; www.omhs.org), 1006 Ford Ave., Owensboro. Serving 11 counties in Western Kentucky and Southern Indiana, this hospital provides medical services to the regional community. **Methodist Hospital** (270-827-7700; www.methodisthospital .net), 1305 N. Elm St., Henderson. Originally known as Henderson Hospital, it was built in 1946 and has 160 beds.

ALCOHOL Both Daviess County, home to Owensboro, and Henderson County, home to Henderson, are wet counties, which means alcohol is available at bars, restaurants. and liquor stores.

photo by Deborah Kohl Kremer

HOMETOWN HERO HALL OF FAME

✳ To See

♿ 🐾 **Hometown Hero Hall of Fame** (270-926-1100; www.visitowensboro .com), 215 E. 2nd St., Owensboro. Open weekdays 9–4. Attached to the visitors center, you'll find information about local residents who have made it to the big time via sports, movies, television, and politics. The Owensboro area is the former home of the Everly Brothers, Johnny Depp, and America's mom, Florence Henderson. Free.

✎ 🐾 **Sassafras Tree**, 2100 block of Frederica St. (US 431), Owensboro. See this 100-foot-tall tree, which is thought to be the world's largest.

♿ **International Bluegrass Music Museum** (270-926-7891; www.bluegrass-museum.org), 117 Daviess St., Owensboro. Tue.–Sat. 10–5, Sun. 1–4. This museum is dedicated to preserving the history of bluegrass music and the artists who created the whole genre. As a native from the Owensboro area, legendary Bill Monroe, along with his Blue Grass Boys Band, are celebrated in an impressive exhibit. Hands-on displays, photos, and memorabilia from the early days of bluegrass through today are all featured as well. $5 adults, $2 students; under 6 free.

✎ ♿ **Owensboro Area Museum of Science & History** (270-687-2732; www .owensboromuseum.com), 122 E. 2nd St., Owensboro. Mon. 10–8, Tue.–Sat. 10–5, Sun. 1–5. Kids can have fun while learning at the PlayZeum, an indoor playground for children under 10. They get to crawl through tubes and bridges and play on a riverboat and in tree houses. You'll also find science-based exhibits and a gallery depicting local racing history, and motorsports. $3 adults; under 2 free.

OWENSBORO AREA MUSEUM OF SCIENCE & HISTORY

photo by Deborah Kohl Kremer

♿ **Owensboro Museum of Fine Art** (270-685-3181; www.omfa.museum), 901 Frederica St., Owensboro. Tue.–Fri. 10–4, weekends 1–4. Lovers of fine art will appreciate a tour of Kentucky's second largest art museum, just behind Louisville's Speed Art Museum, in Owensboro. With pieces dating back to the 15th century through an impressive permanent collection of folk art and stained glass, the museum covers everything in between. Also on site is a 1909 Carnegie Library and the John Hampden Smith House, a pre–Civil War mansion. Voluntary admission fee.

Bill Monroe Birthplace (270-274-9181; www.visitohiocountyky.org), 6210 Blue Moon of Kentucky Hwy. (US 62E), Rosine. Open Mon.–Sat. 9–5, Sun. 1–4. About 40 miles south of Owensboro you can pay homage to one of the area's favorite sons. Take a guided tour of the birthplace of Bill Monroe, the Father of Bluegrass Music. The home, where Bill was born in 1911, is full of Monroe family memorabilia. Included with the furnishings are photographs of Uncle Pen, who was the subject of one of Bill's most beloved songs. Monroe, who is the only musician to be inducted into the Rock 'n' Roll, Country, and Bluegrass Music Halls of Fame, created the unique genre of music that today is known as bluegrass. Just down the road a bit is the cemetery where Bill and Uncle Pen are buried, if you'd like to pay your respects. Free, but donations are appreciated.

Ruby Moon Vineyard & Winery (270-830-7660; www.rubymoonwinery.com), 9566 US 41A, Henderson. Open Tue.–Sat. 11–6. Owners Jamie Like and Anita Frazer are proud of their award-winning wine and invite visitors to tour the vineyard and then stop for a sample.

✳ To Do

GOLF Ben Hawes State Park Golf Course & Driving Range (270-685-2011), 400 Boothfield Rd., 4 miles west of Owensboro. This course has 27 holes, an 18-hole course and a par 3 9-hole course. The front 9 was built on flat terrain and the back 9, on hilly. The Pro Shop offers pull carts, golf cars, and rental clubs.

Golfland U.S.A. (270-683-4963; www.golflandusa.net), 1864 Old Calhoun Rd., Owensboro. They have a pro shop, an 18-hole miniature golf course, batting cages, and a go-cart track. Bring the whole family for a day of fun.

Panther Creek Golf Course (270-785-4565), 4641 Hwy. 1514, Utica. This 18-hole, par-70, regulation-length public course offers 5,990 yards of golf from the longest tee.

Players Club of Henderson (270)-827-9999; www.playersclubofhenderson.com), 800 Wolf Hills Blvd., Henderson. With 13 lakes and more than 90 bunkers, this public 18-hole par-72 course can challenge even the best golfers. They also have a pro shop and Players Pub, a sports bar and grill right off the 18th green.

RACEWAY Windy Hollow Raceway Park (270-785-4300; www.windy hollowspeedway.com), 5141 Windy Hollow Rd., Owensboro. The park includes a 0.25-mile drag strip and D-shaped dirt stock-car track. Check the web site to see the racing schedule.

THOROUGHBRED RACING Ellis Park Race Course (800-333-8110; www.ellisparkracing.com), 3300 US 41N. Live racing July–Labor Day; simulcast races from other tracks year-round. Check the web site for schedules and post times. Come out and

OWENSBORO MUSEUM OF FINE ART
photo of www.kentuckytourism.com

enjoy Kentucky's only thoroughbred track that doesn't feel like it's in Kentucky. Originally built in 1922, Ellis Park is located on the shores of the Ohio River. Strangely enough, it's on the north side of the river, so it appears to be part of Indiana. But based on some long-drawn-out story about an earthquake and Kentucky's borders and the edges of the river, you just have to know that you are still in Kentucky. Don't let the fact that they use Indiana's 812 area code throw you off, either. A day of studying the race card can make you hungry, so while you're there, make reservations to eat at the **Sky Theater Restaurant**. They have a fantastic view of the track and finish line. It is an all-smoking restaurant, though, so keep that in mind if you don't care for smoke.

WALKING TOURS Audubon Sculpture Tour and Historic Walking Tour. Scattered about Henderson's downtown area are life-sized bird sculptures. These fabulous pieces of art were created by Kentucky sculptor Raymond Graf from John James Audubon's portfolio. Your tour includes Central Park, which is thought to be the oldest city park west of the Allegheny Mountains. Explore the downtown and see prime examples of 19th-century architecture in the homes, buildings, and churches. Get a map at the tourism office, or download from the web site, so you don't miss anything.

✳ Green Space

Pinecliffe Gardens (270-281-9791), 6745 Foster Rd., Philpot. You've never seen a garden like this. This daylily and hosta farm has more than 1,500 varieties on display. Although peak bloom season is the second and third weeks of June, the gardens are a nice place to visit all through the summer.

Western Kentucky Botanical Gardens (270-852-8925, 270-993-1234), 25 Carter Rd., Owensboro. Open to the public Mon.–Fri. 9–3. With six established gardens—Butterfly, Rose, Daylily, Iris, Herb, and Fruit & Berry—this small piece of Eden is chock-full of blooms you can enjoy and display ideas you can use in your own garden. Wander through and take in the glorious sights and smells.

Adkisson Greenbelt Park (270-687-8707). The 15-mile-long Greenbelt Park was designed to encircle the city of Owensboro. The 10-foot-wide paved surface is perfect for walking, running, skating, or bicycling.

Yellow Creek Park (270-281-0436) 5710 KY 144, Owensboro. Nestled along the wooded banks of Yellow Creek, the park offers 119 acres of recreation including plenty of softball fields, picnic shelters, nature trails, basketball courts, tennis courts, fishing, and a playground. They also have a disk golf course that is recognized by the Professional Disc Golf Association.

Audubon Mill Park, N. Water St., Henderson. Right alongside the Ohio River is this charming park. It features park benches where you can enjoy a take-out lunch, statues of James Audubon and some of the birds that he

AUDUBON SCULPTURE
photo by Deborah Kohl Kremer

photo by Deborah Kohl Kremer

AUDUBON MILL PARK

studied, and fabulous views of the river. The park sits on the land where Audubon ran a gristmill, one of several business ventures he participated in while living in Henderson. Some of the foundation stones are still on site, as is a huge gristmill stone from the mill.

🛶 ♿ 🌸 **STATE PARKS Ben Hawes State Park** (270-684-9808; www.parks .ky.gov), 400 Boothfield Rd., off US 60, 4 miles west of Owensboro. Situated on a former mining village. There are still nine buildings that were part of the Rudy Mines, which operated from 1820 to 1950. Enjoy 300 acres, a 2-mile nature trail, mountain bike trails, an archery range, a playground, and a picnic shelter.

🛶 ♿ **John J. Audubon State Park and Museum** (270-826-5939; www.parks .ky.gov), 3100 US 41N, Henderson. John James Audubon, renowned naturalist and artist, lived in the area 1810–1819, and it was here that he spent time searching for wild birds and sketching them. The park offers 6.5 miles of trails through the nature preserve and even backcountry hiking. For recreation they offer fishing, a 9-hole golf course, tennis, and paddle boats. The on-site museum includes memorabilia from Audubon's life and a nature center with hands-on exhibits. Museum hours: Mar.–Nov., daily 10–5; Dec.–Feb., Wed.–Sun. 8–4:30. Although there is no lodge, this park offers six rental cottages plus 69 campsites with utilities. Campgrounds are open year-round, although the water at sites is turned off during winter months. No reservations accepted.

✳ Lodging

River House Bed and Breakfast (270-295-4199; www.lastsummer .com/rhbb), 1510 Riverview Dr., Lewisport. Just 15 miles east of Owensboro, you'll find this modern inn that overlooks the Ohio River. Whether you stay in one of the inn's two nice guest rooms, or in the Executive Cottage out back, you will be able to make yourself at home. Immerse yourself in the lush, manicured grounds or enjoy the sunset views from one of the home's four balconies. The River House has a private dock and beach. Enjoy the exercise room and in-ground pool, too. $–$$

AUDUBON STATE PARK AND MUSEUM

photo of www.kentuckytourism.com

⁂ Helton House Bed & Breakfast (270-926-7117; www.bbonline.com/ky/helton), 103 E. 23rd St., Owensboro. Lovers of Arts & Crafts architecture will get their fill at this home, which dates back to 1910. They offer four guest rooms, plus a two-room anniversary suite, all decorated in warm and inviting period furnishings. Bring a good book or borrow one from innkeeper Grace Helton Conley and head for the comfy sunroom. You might never leave. Breakfast is memorable, too, featuring savory home-baked breads and muffins topped with Grace's delicious apple butter. $–$$

⁂ L&N Bed & Breakfast (270-831-1100; www.lnbbky.com), 327 N. Main St., Henderson. This 100-year-old Victorian home features soaring ceilings, a hand-carved staircase, stained-glass windows, and welcoming fireplaces. Close to the railroad bridge, the occasional train can lull you to sleep in one of the four gracious guest rooms. Innkeepers Norris and Mary Elizabeth Priest make sure you enjoy your stay. Norris loves magic and might do a trick if you ask. $

Victorian Quarters (270-831-2778; www.victorianquartersbb.com), 109 Clay St., Henderson. Overlooking the Ohio River, this Italianate home was built in 1865. The house is fully restored to its original days, with authentic antique furniture in each of the three cozy guest rooms and common areas. $

CAMPING Diamond Lake Resort and Campground (270-229-4900), 7301 Hobbs Rd., located 11 miles west of Owensboro on KY 56. It is worth the drive to this wooded park with 270 campsites on 157 acres. This resort is full of family fun: fishing, swimming, a go-cart track with carts for all ages, and even a paint ball field.

Windy Hollow Campground Recreation (270-785-4150; www.windyhollowcampground.com), 5141 Windy Hollow Rd., Owensboro. Not just a 110-site campground, they have all kinds of fun things to do. They have a swim lake with waterslide and a sandy beach. They also have a fishing lake stocked weekly with farm-raised catfish. Grill up your catch on their 40-foot barbecue pit.

✳ Where to Eat

Ⓨ Wolf's Tavern & Restaurant (270-826-5221), 31 N. Green St., Henderson. Open daily for lunch and dinner. This family-style restaurant has really friendly service. Try their famous Kentucky hot brown or their bean soup. They are true blue, which means they offer drink specials when the Kentucky Wildcats play. $

Famous Bistro (270-686-8202), 102 W. 2nd St., Owensboro. Open for lunch and dinner every day. In this land of barbecue, this is the place to go for a slightly upscale Mediterranean or Greek meal. Try the gyros and spanakopita for an authentic treat. $

Ⓨ Briarpatch Restaurant (270-685-3329; www.brpatch.com), 2760 Veach Rd., Owensboro. Open Sun.–Mon. for lunch 11–2. Open every day for dinner 5–9:30. This locally owned steak house has been around since 1971. In addition to steaks, they have a large assortment of soup and salad bar items, as well as a full bar service and fine wines. Save room for dessert: They offer the Official Kern's Kitchen Derby Pie direct from Louisville. $

Hunan (270-827-2229), 1765 S. Green St., Henderson. Open daily for lunch and dinner. Whether you are in the mood for Chinese, Mandarin, or Szechuan, you'll enjoy your meal at Hunan. They have reasonably priced lunch specials and a buffet on Sundays.

Try the Hunan chicken, hot-and-sour Soup, or garlic chicken; all are local favorites. $

Thomason's Barbecue (270-826-0654), 701 Atkinson St., Henderson. Call ahead for hours. This small stand-alone restaurant has just a few tables and a counter because most people order their barbecue to go. Thomason's barbecues everything: pork, mutton, beef, spare ribs, baby back ribs, chicken, ham, and turkey. Grab a few bottles of their barbecue sauce—or, as they call it, "Dip"—before you go. You'll want more of that flavor once you get home. $

❝❞ ♉ **Rookies Sports Bar** (270-826-1106; www.rookiesrestaurant.com), 117 2nd St., Henderson. Open Mon.–Thu. 4–11, Fri.–Sat. 4–2. The kitchen closes at 10 PM. With 27 TVs scattered around, you're not going to miss one play of the big game. While you're here, you might as well eat. They have everything from Buffalo wings and potato skins to filet mignon and pork chops. $

Downtown Diner (270-827-9671), 122 1st St., Henderson. Call for hours. Located in an old dairy building right in the heart of town, this is the place to go for burgers, fried green tomatoes, and typical diner fare. Not fancy but very friendly. $

SNACKS Diamond Delights Bakery & Café (270-831-2050), 115 N. Main St., Henderson. Open weekdays 6:30–3, Sat. 6:30–noon. If you need a quick lunch or a bakery-style snack, this is the place to go. They have hot and cold sandwiches, salads, soups, coffee, and bakery items, plus they are wide awake at 6:30 AM, even if you're not. $

❝❞ **Planters Coffeehouse** (270-830-0927), 130 N. Main St., Henderson. Open for lunch weekdays. Housed in an old bank building, this is a cute

place to stop for a coffee or light lunch. Even though the vault is gone, you'll still find the original woodwork, bank railings, framed savings account statements, canceled checks, and financial-looking stuff all around. Order the chicken salad sandwich if you can't decide. $

❝❞ **Crème Coffee House** (270-683-7787), 109 E. 2nd St., Owensboro. Open Mon.–Thu. 7 AM–9 PM, Fri.–Sat. 7 AM–10:30 PM. Stop into this coffee shop for a strong café mocha and enjoy the charm of this historic building with high tin ceilings, exposed brick walls, and a comfy conversation pit in the back room. Wake yourself up with a gourmet coffee, specialty drinks, desserts, soups, and panini sandwiches. $

CRÈME COFFEE HOUSE

photo by Deborah Kohl Kremer

OWENSBORO BARBECUE

Owensboro proudly proclaims to be the Bar-B-Q Capital of the World. Although they can't agree on how to spell it—you'll see *BBQ*, *Barbeque*, *Barbecue*, and *Bar-B-Q*—you will find hickory-smoked meats slow-roasted for hours and accompanied by a secret sauce at the acclaimed restaurants in town. The meats, be they mutton, pork, chicken, or beef, are served up on a plate of hamburger pickles, fresh onions, and a few slices of white bread. This is how barbecue is served in this part of the country, so roll up your sleeves and dig in.

Mutton, which is lamb, is also a staple on the menu of these barbecue restaurants. Although you can order it sliced or chopped and soaked in sauce, it is the primary ingredient to burgoo, another dish that claims Owensboro as its home. Burgoo is a thick stew full of meat (usually mutton, but other meats can be substituted), vegetables, and spices; it resembles a similar porridge made by sailors in the 1700s. The name either came from a sailor with slurred speech who was trying to say "Bird Stew" or was derived from the word *bulghur*, which is wheat that was added to the pot. It's also sometimes called poorman's stew or roadkill soup. The jury is out as to why burgoo is primarily found in this part of Kentucky and nowhere else in the country, but while you are here, you need to try some.

There seems to be no official recipe for burgoo, just an inclination to add all the meat and veggies you have on hand to a large pot and cook for about 12 hours. The seasonings and spices vary from restaurant to restaurant, so try it wherever you are, because you are in for an unexpected treat.

MOONLITE BAR-B-Q   photo by Deborah Kohl Kremer

&. **Moonlite Bar-B-Q Inn** (270-684-8143; www.moonlite.com), 2840 W. Parrish Ave., Owensboro. Open Mon.–Sat. 9–9, Sun. 10–3. Moonlite is largest and perhaps best-known barbecue restaurant in Owensboro, and maybe Kentucky. In business since 1963, the huge dining room and a parking lot full of tour buses are your first tip-offs that this is a popular tourist attraction. The Bosley family have been running Moonlite for three generation now, and they say the secret to their fine barbecue is simply the hard work and 12 hours of slow-roasting that goes into the process. They must be doing something right, because they serve up 10,000 pounds of barbecue a week. They offer an enormous buffet during lunch and dinner hours, and it is the perfect way to get a sampling of the fine mutton, pork, chicken, and beef barbecue they are known for. The meat, cooked over hickory wood and dunked in a vinegar-based dip as it cooks, is served without sauce. Their famous tomato-based sweet barbecue sauce is available on the tables, so you can add a lot or a little, based on your tastes.

photo by Deborah Kohl Kremer

OLD HICKORY BAR-B-Q

Luckily for you, the sauce is also available in the gift shop area near the checkout and online for real emergencies. This sauce is addicting; you might want to stock up before you leave. $–$$

 ♿ **George's Bar-B-Q** (270-926-9276), 1362 E. 4th St., Owensboro. Open Mon.–Sat. 7–8. Closed Sun. This is the place to go for stick-to-your-ribs burgoo and barbecued mutton slow-roasted over hickory and sassafras wood. In business since 1955, the folks at George's seal their meats in a vinegar-based dip that is mopped onto the barbecue as it smokes. Order your mutton "off the pit"—which means sauceless or slathered in its natural gravy. Either way you're in for a treat. Stop by for breakfast, too. Their country ham is smoked out on the pit for an entire day before it ends up on your plate, alongside your fried eggs, pancakes, or omelet. $

♿ **Ole South Barbeque** (270-926-6464), 3523 KY 54E, Owensboro. Open Tue.–Sat. 6 AM–8 PM, Sun. and Mon. 6 AM–2 PM. This homey restaurant is known around town for their mutton, pork, and beef brisket, which are all cooked slow in a pit and then covered in their homemade sauce. And even though it's a barbecue restaurant, they have usually have quite a breakfast crowd that come in for Ole South's huge portions. $

♿ **Old Hickory Bar-B-Q** (270-926-9000), 333 Washington Ave., Owensboro. Open 9–9 every day. Before you even enter Old Hickory, you see the massive pile of chopped hickorywood stacked up against the building. Looks like they are preparing for a long winter, but actually they're just keeping the home fires burning so they can barbecue their meat over the open flame as they have since 1918. Back then, Pappy Foreman, an Owensboro blacksmith, hung up his horseshoeing tools and started roasting mutton over an open pit, selling it to locals. It became all the rage, and now this family-run business is into their fifth generation. Their dedication to cooking exclusively on hickory-wood is evident when you breathe in that strong hickory-smoked scent wafting through the dining room. They are primarily known for their Western Kentucky barbecue chopped mutton and melt-in-your-mouth pork, but they also have awesome potato salad and blackberry cobbler. This casual restaurant is always packed with locals, which oughta tell you something. If you don't have time to dine in, they offer a to-go counter with barbecue by the pound and even bread, buns, pickles, and, of course, jars of their Old Hickory sauce. $–$$

Miss Daisy's Tea Room & Gift Shop (270-684-5001; www.missdaisystea .com), 404 E. 24th St., Owensboro. Open 10–5 Tue.–Sat. You'll feel relaxed just walking through the door to this charming spot. Try some finger sandwiches or a light dessert with a cup of warm or iced tea. They don't welcome smoking or children under 10 years of age. Reservations suggested. $

Andria's Candy (270-684-3733), 217 Allen St., Owensboro. Mon.–Fri. 10–5, Sat. 11–5. Making candy since 1959, they have melt-in-your-mouth choco-lates and bourbon balls. Stop in for a treat.

✳ Entertainment

Goldie's Best Little Opryhouse in Kentucky (270-926-0254; www.goldies opryhouse.com), 418 Frederica St., Owensboro. Why go all the way to Branson, Missouri, when you can find a full schedule of music and variety shows right in Owensboro? Check the web site to see the lineup of acts.

Henderson Fine Arts Center (270-850-5324; www.haaa.org), 2660 S. Green St., offers a wide range of pro-fessional performances in its 1,000-seat auditorium with an enormous stage.

The gallery hosts changing art exhibits year-round.

RiverPark Center (270-687-2770; www.riverparkcenter.org), 101 Daviess St., Owensboro. Hosting more than 1,000 events each year, the RiverPark Center is home to the Owensboro Symphony Orchestra, as well as musi-cal concerts and Broadway touring productions.

✳ Selective Shopping

Baker's Rack (270-684-6130), 2690 Frederica St., Owensboro. Owned by the Baker family, this darling gift shop is known for their distinctive brown-and-white-spotted wrapping paper. When you see a gift wrapped like this, you know you're in for a real treat. They specialize in Waterford crystal, Vera Bradley bags, and unique jewelry.

Kentucky's Best (270-683-2733), 5000 Frederica St., Towne Square, Mall, Owensboro. Featuring products made in Kentucky such as Louisville's Hadley Pottery, Frankfort's Candleberry Can-dles, and Kim Cabbage hand-painted gourds from Sacramento, Kentucky. They also have some items from Owensboro artisans as well as Ken-tucky-made candy, sauces, and honey.

Memories Past and Present Antique and Gift Shop (270-844-0014; www.hendersonmemories.com), 425 N. Main St., Henderson. Wed.–Sat. 10–5. Located in a historic home, they have 12 rooms filled with gifts, home decor, vintage jewelry, hats, gloves, glassware, china, and decorative items and furniture from the past.

Gabbi's Boutique (270-827-1567; www.gabbisboutique.com), 137 2nd St., Henderson. Offers one-of-a-kind, uniquely designed, and hand-sewn fashions for dogs. Bring your dog while you shop for food, treats, collars, leashes, toys, and gifts. Closed Sun.

Homefolks Hardware & Gifts (270-827-5745), 120 N. Elm St., Henderson. Shop for a hard-to-find tool or even a hard-to-find gift in this old storefront, complete with creaky wood floors and authentic tin ceiling.

Owensboro Antique Mall (270-684-3003), 500 W. 3rd St., Owensboro. With about 50 booths, you are sure to find a little bit of everything. They have furniture, glassware, toys, and collectibles. Open seven days a week.

✳ Special Events

✐ ♿ ♒ *May:* **International Bar-B-Q Festival** (www.bbqfest.com). Recognized as one of the top 100 events held in the United States each year. Owensboro has become known as "the Bar-B-Q Capital of the World." Each year for about 30 years, Owensboro has welcomed about 80,000 people to the downtown riverfront to enjoy "two days of barbecue heaven." Experience live bands, carnival rides, pageants, a car show, and backyard barbecue competitions while enjoying the hickory-smoked chicken, pork, beef, and mutton.

✐ ♿ ♒ *June:* **International Blues Music Museum** presents River of Music Party, better known as "ROMP" Bluegrass Festival (www.bluegrass-museum.org/riverofmusic). Performances held at the International Bluegrass Music Museum, Yellow Creek Park, and the River Park Center, Owensboro. Four days of blues performances, musical workshops, and even a bluegrass film festival. This is a huge gathering of blues musical performers and fans.

✐ ♿ ♒ **W. C. Handy Blues & Barbecue Festival** (www.handyblues.org). This weeklong festival celebrates the life and legacy of Henderson resident and "Father of the Blues" William Christopher Handy. Held on the riverfront each year, this free festival is one of the largest blues festivals in the nation. The opening day of the festival is highlighted by the "Taste of Henderson Barbecue," where you can enjoy barbecue of all varieties and listen to some of the hottest names in blues.

BAR-B-Q FESTIVAL

photo of www.kentuckytourism.com

THE HOPKINSVILLE AREA

T ucked in to the rolling farmland of Southwestern Kentucky is the small town of Hopkinsville. Although it appears small in size, the 30,000 residents of this city and nearly 80,000 residents of surrounding Christian County know the huge benefits of the area.

Several places in this region are named for an indigenous plant, the pennyroyal or pennyrile, depending who you ask. Both names are accepted, and the plant itself is a member of the mint family. It has been used for everything from an upset stomach remedy to an insect repellent, but the jury is still out on whether it is a medicine or a toxin. So if you see any, don't eat it. Whether the plant is good or bad, the Pennyrile Forest State Resort Park is a wonderful place to kick back and unwind. Situated on a secluded lake, the park offers lodging, camping, and various outdoorsy recreations.

In the 1830s, Hopkinsville was a campground for the Cherokee along the Trail of Tears, a route of forced western migration for Native Americans. This brutal trail took the lives of many Natives, and today you will find a park that includes the grave sites of two chiefs, White Path and Fly Smith. In September, Hopkinsville hosts the annual Intertribal PowWow in the park. This event includes storytelling, music, and Native Americans in full regalia. To the north of Hopkinsville, you'll find Madisonville, a quaint town full of antiques shops. To the south is Oak Grove, which is known as the "Hometown of Fort Campbell." The US Army's 101st Airborne Division, better known as the Screaming Eagles, calls Fort Campbell home.

Come to Hoptown, as it's known to locals, for its small-town charms and get a sprinkling of history and nature while you're there.

GUIDANCE Hopkinsville/Christian County Convention & Visitors Bureau (800-842-9959; www.visithopkinsville.com), 2800 Fort Campbell Blvd., Hopkinsville. Just 16 miles to the south is the city of Oak Grove. Contact the **Oak Grove Tourist Commission** (270-439-5675; www.oakgroveky-tourism.com) for information on the goings-on there. They are located in a log cabin replica right off Exit 89, I-24, leading into town.

GETTING THERE The closest airport is just over the border in Tennessee. The **Nashville International Airport** (615-275-1675; www.nashintl.com) is 70 miles from Hopkinsville. **Greyhound Bus** (270-821-3086; www.greyhound.com) serves the Western Kentucky region. The station is 35 miles away, located at the Red Cardinal Inn, 4765 Hanson Rd., US 41N, Madisonville.

GETTING AROUND Hopkinsville is a small town and doesn't have public transportation, but if you need a ride, you can call **Haddock Blue Line Cab** (270-886-3262).

MEDICAL EMERGENCY Jennie Stuart Medical Center (800-887-JSMC; www.jsmc.org), 320 W. 18th St., Hopkinsville. Founded by Dr. Edward Stuart in 1913 and named for his deceased wife, whose savings were used to build the hospital. This is a respected medical center serving Western Kentucky and Northern Tennessee. It began with just 12 beds; today JSMC is a thriving 194-bed state-of-the-art hospital.

ALCOHOL Hopkinsville is the seat of Christian County, a wet county that allows alcohol sales everywhere.

✳ To See

✍ ⅙ ❀ **The Trail of Tears Commemorative Park** (800-842-9959; www.trailof tears.org), US 41 (Pembroke Rd.), Hopkinsville. This historic park is one of the few documented sites of the actual trail and campsites used during the 1830s forced removal of the Cherokee people from their southeastern homelands across the Mississippi River to Oklahoma. More than 13,000 Cherokee camped here and received provisions for their forced migration. This park is the burial site for two Cherokee chiefs who died during the removal, Fly Smith and White Path. There is also a heritage center on site, housed inside a log cabin that dates back to this time period. Here you will find more information about the trail as well as the Cherokee people. Stop by the park anytime; the center is open Thu.–Sat. 10–2.

✍ ⅙ ❀ **Pennyroyal Area Museum** (270-887-4270), 217 E. 9th St., Hopkinsville. Weekdays 8:30–4:30, Sat. 10–3. Housed in the town's historic post office, which dates back to 1914, this museum portrays the history of Southwestern Kentucky through exhibits of antique clothing, toys, and local memorabilia. They also feature rotating exhibits by local artists. Admission $5.

✍ ⅙ ❀ **The Woody Winfree Fire-Transportation Museum** (270-887-4270), 217 E. 9th St., Hopkinsville. Open most days 10–4, but call first to make sure. Just across the street from the Pennyroyal Area Museum, housed in the original city fire station, is a unique museum. It features historic fire trucks, automobiles, carriages, wagons, and various firefighting memorabilia. The building's original 22-foot brass pole has been returned to its home, along with the city's first fire truck. The museum features several historically significant fire trucks, automobiles, wagons, and buggies. Admission $5.

✍ ⅙ ❀ **Jefferson Davis State Historic Site** (270-889-6100; parks.ky.gov), US 68E, Fairview. Open May 1–Oct. 1. Visit this towering 351-foot concrete obelisk honoring Jefferson Davis, the president of the Confederacy during the Civil War, who was born on this site in 1808. Visitors can take an elevator to the observation deck for a panoramic view of the countryside. While there, you can learn more about Davis in the visitors center museum. They also have picnic shelters, a playground, and a gift shop. The admission fee includes an elevator ride to the top of the obelisk and access to the small museum.

photo by Deborah Kohl Kremer

VIEW FROM THE JEFFERSON DAVIS
OBELISK

🖉 ♿ 🎖 **The Don F. Pratt Museum**
(931-431-2003; www.fortcampbell
.com), 5702 Tennessee Ave., Fort
Campbell. Open Mon.–Sat. 9:30–4:30.
This museum offers artifacts and memorabilia related to Fort Campbell and
the 101st Airborne Division, better
known as the Screaming Eagles. The
exhibits really tell the stories well. A
new facility, Wings of Liberty Military
Museum, is scheduled to open in 2010.
It will feature an 80,000-square-foot
museum as well as an IMAX theater.
Free.

🖉 ♿ **Christian Way Farm** (270-269-
2434; www.christianwayfarm.com),
19590 Linville Rd., Hopkinsville. Open
for tours on Sat., or call for an appointment during the week. Tour this working farm and learn what it takes to
keep a 350-acre spread going. The
Corley family welcomes guests to help
with chores or to take part in one of
their educational programs, like "growing hamburgers and french fries." $4
per person, children under 2 free.

✳ To Do

GOLF **Cherry Grove Golf Course** (270-466-3610), 1006 Dixie Bee Line Hwy.,
Trenton. This 18-hole, par-71 public golf course has a natural creek running
through it, so watch for ducks and beavers. There is also a driving range and putting green.

The Links at Novadell Golf Course (270-886-1101; www.novadell.com), 500
Nova Dell Way, Hopkinsville. This links-style 18-hole championship course sits on
the rolling terrain of former Kentucky farmland. Practice your game on the 10-
acre driving range, 8,000-square-foot putting green, and practice bunker.

SCUBA **Pennyroyal Scuba Blue Springs** (270-885-2585; www.pennyroyal
scuba.com), 602 Christian Quarry Rd., Hopkinsville. Open Wed.–Thu. 10–4, Fri.
10–6, Sat. 8–6, Sun. 8–5. With the nearest ocean about 700 miles away, if you're in
the mood to scuba dive, you'll need to stop here. This former quarry has been
turned into a diving destination with more than 40 sunken attractions in its crystal-
clear water. Diving ranges from 5- to 130-foot depths. They also have a full line of
rental gear. Rates vary.

WALKING TOUR **Historic Downtown Walking Tour** (270-498-5180). Grab a
map at the Hopkinsville/Christian County Convention & Visitors Bureau and get
started. You can enjoy the intricately detailed historic architecture and see land-

marks such as the Old Fire Station and Clock Tower, Carnegie Library, and Christian County Courthouse as you stroll along the shops and eateries that give Hopkinsville its small-town charm.

✳ Green Space

Tie Breaker Park and Aquatic Center (270-890-0730; www.tiebreakerpark .com), 9503 Eagle Way Bypass, Hopkinsville. This park features a softball complex, sand volleyball courts, a paved walking trail, and a playground and picnic area. The new water park has twisting tubes, a lazy river, and a splash zone interactive playground, along with a poolside café. Don't forget the sunscreen.

Jeffers' Bend Environmental & Botanical Gardens (270-886-6719), Metcalfe Lane and US 41, Hopkinsville. Formerly a water treatment facility, this park is perfect for bird-watching and nature trail hiking.

✐ ઙ "ï" **STATE PARK Pennyrile Forest State Resort Park** (800-325-1711), 20781 Pennyrile Lodge Rd., Dawson Springs. Located within the 14,648-acre Pennyrile State Forest, this park has all the amenities you need for a relaxing vacation. They have 14 miles of nature trails, tennis and golf courses, and swimming, boating, and fishing in Pennyrile Lake. It was named for the tiny pennyroyal plant found in the woodlands surrounding the park; this plant gives off a minty smell and is used in medications and herbal remedies. Stay at the **Pennyrile Forest State Park Lodge**, the rustic stone lodge high atop a cliff overlooking the shores of Pennyrile Lake. The lodge features 24 comfortable rooms, all with a view of the lake. For even more serenity, 12 private one- and two-bedroom cottages are tucked away in the surrounding woods. Watch for wildlife, which is abundant. There is also a 68-site wooded campground offering utility hookups, a dump station, showers, restrooms, and laundry. Open Mar. 1–Oct. 31.

✳ Where to Eat

BARBECUE Woodshed Pit Bar-B-Que & Restaurant (270-885-8144), 1821 W. 7th St., Hopkinsville. Open Mon.–Sat. 10:30–8. Even though it's a little bit off the beaten path, it's worth your effort to find this spot. The ribs are awesome, but they also have specials on catfish and prime rib. Start your meal with some of their flavorful Kentucky burgoo and end it with one of their signature fried pies. They have all kinds of flavors—Oreo, chocolate, coconut, peach—so you might want to order more than one. $

DINING OUT Timmon's (270-886-1800), 914 S. Main St., Hopkinsville. Open seasonally; call for hours. This elegant, upscale restaurant reeks with

class in its historic 1894 building right downtown. The menu features salads, soups, sandwiches, entrées, and signature single-serving desserts. $

Υ **Difabio's Casapela** (270-825-1900; www.difabios.com), 17 W. Center St., Madisonville. Open for dinner Wed.–Sat. Visit this authentic Italian restaurant, with seafood, steak, and chicken entrées in addition to Italian favorites. This family-run restaurant makes you feel like a relative from the moment you arrive until you polish off your three-layer cappuccino cheesecake. $

EATING OUT Ferrell's Snappy Service (270-886-1445), 1001 S. Main St., Hopkinsville. Open 24/7. This is a true burger joint. No fries, no shakes, just a counter, seven stools, and the best burgers around. In business since 1936, this is a true Hoptown landmark. If you want a side dish, grab a bag of chips, or just order more burgers. $

Charlie's Steakhouse (270-439-4592), 14850 US 41A S., Oak Grove. Open Mon.–Sat. 4–9:30. Look for the giant cow on the roof, and you'll know you've arrived at this 1950s-era upscale restaurant. The interior hasn't been updated much since that time, but it is a favorite of servicemen and -women of nearby Fort Campbell. Locals consider it an institution in the area. They are known for their giant porterhouse steaks but they also have juicy burgers and fresh salads. $

Las Fuentes Mexican Restaurant (866-421-1417; www.lasfuentesmexican restaurant.com), 3119 Canton Pike, Hopkinsville. Mon.–Thu. 11–10, Fri. and Sat. 11–10:30, Sun. 11–9:30. Serving the area for more than 10 years, the menu offers both Mexican American fare as well as true south-of-the-border dishes. $

✳ Entertainment

The Alhambra Theatre (270-887-4023; www.pennyroyalarts.org), 507 S. Main St., Hopkinsville. The majestic Alhambra opened in 1928, for both live stage shows and silent movies. Renovated in 2008, the restored 780-seat proscenium facility now offers live theater and musical performances. Check the web site to see what's showing.

✳ Selective Shopping

Gracious Me (270-886-8090; www .graciousme.com), 4537 Fort Campbell Blvd., Hopkinsville. Closed Sun. Stop in and see owner Sherry Calhoun and

find out what's new. Her shop offers china and crystal, picture frames and gift ideas from well-known names like Lenox and Noritake, as well as Olivia Mullin and Gorham.

Legacies Military Keepsakes (931-431-2003; www.fortcampbell.com), 5702 Tennessee Ave., Fort Campbell. Located inside the museum dedicated to Fort Campbell, this shop has all kinds of military gifts and souvenirs like shirts, hats, decals, and even Christmas ornaments.

ART GALLERIES Pennyroyal Arts Council (270-887-4295; www.penny royalarts.org), 425 E. 9th St., Hopkinsville. Housed in the late-1800s L&N Depot downtown, they feature monthly exhibits by a variety of local artists.

Brushy Fork Creek Studio and Gallery (270-424-5988; www.brushy forkcreek.com), 1550 Pleasant Green Hill Rd., Crofton. Featuring the award-winning art of Paul and Patricia Ferrell. They both produce bowls, lamps, and vases, but Paul specializes in woodturnings and Patricia in pottery. They also raise organic blueberries and herbs on their farm. Please call for hours.

✳ Special Events

✐ ♿ ✦ *September:* **Intertribal PowWow at the Park**. This annual gathering of Native Americans commemorates the beauty and integrity of their people. This public festival features Native American crafts, storytelling, demonstrations, and a competitive Indian dance competition.

THE LAND BETWEEN THE LAKES REGION

This region is truly one of a kind. This is the only place in the United States designated as a National Recreation Area, which is just a smidge below national park status. The area encompasses more than 170,000 acres and 300 miles of undeveloped shoreline. The largest island peninsula in the nation, it was created with the impounding of the Tennessee River on the west and the Cumberland River on the east. The creation of the dams brings flood control, hydroelectric power, and about two million visitors to the region each year. Kentucky Lake, which was created in 1944, is one of the largest human-made lakes in the world and contains about 160,000 acres of water. It is home to Kentucky Dam Village State Park, Kenlake State Park, and numerous marinas and docks.

When the Cumberland River was dammed in the early 1960s, it formed the 118-mile-long Lake Barkley, which was named for local resident and 35th vice president of the United States Alben Barkley. Lake Barkley State Park sits on one of the fingers of this huge 60,000-acre lake.

The actual land between the lakes is a huge recreational forest, where visitors can commune with nature. With the creation of the lakes, families and entire communities were removed from the land by eminent domain. The lakeside towns of Eddyville and Kuttawa were moved to higher ground; the original villages are now under 50 feet of water. The only thing that remained was the family cemeteries; some 250 of them are still undisturbed on the Land.

The Land itself has no commercial development, billboards, or fast-food restaurants, so plan ahead. The only major road, called The Trace, runs the entire 69 miles of the land from north to south. You'll find three helpful visitors centers along the way, as well as a few attractions that you won't want to miss. To the north is the Nature Station, an educational place to learn about the real natives to the area. In the middle you will find the Elk and Bison Prairie, the Golden Pond Observatory, and the Planetarium. On the south end is Homeplace 1850, where you can get a taste of how life was back then. Besides this, the rest of the Land is pure wilderness and recreation. There are five campgrounds with about 1,000 sites, 100 miles of horse trails, 200 miles of hiking trails, five beaches, and loads of access ramps and docks for boating and fishing.

There's no place like the Land Between the Lakes anywhere else in the United States. Come see for yourself what it is like and take time to enjoy nature at its finest.

GUIDANCE Kentucky's Western Waterlands Visitors Center (800-448-1069; www.kentuckylakebarkley.travel), 721 Complex Dr., Grand Rivers. This visitors center is located right off I-24 at Exit 31. They have all the information, maps, and brochures you will need for your stay in this area.

For information specific to the Land Between the Lakes, stop in the **visitors center** (800-LBL-7077; www.lbl.org) located just off US 68 in the middle of LBL. This center has exhibits explaining the origins of LBL and also has a gift shop.

GETTING THERE Greyhound Bus (270-442-2706; www.greyhound.com) serves Paducah, which is about 40 miles from Eddyville. The station is located at 301 N. 4th St., Paducah. The closest commercial airport is the **Nashville International Airport** (615-275-1675; www.nashintl.com). It is about 100 miles from the northern areas of the Land Between the Lakes Region. There is also the **Barkley Regional Airport** (www.barkleyregional.com), which serves private and charter planes.

GETTING AROUND The area has quite a few unmarked roads leading to marinas and lodging near the lakes. Several restaurants and attractions in the area recommend calling for directions, as some Internet map sites won't get you there. So get a good local map at the visitors center and call ahead if you're not sure.

Classic Carriage Service (270-825-1657), Grand Rivers. Take a romantic horse-drawn carriage right all around the cute city of Grand Rivers. Service runs Fri. and Sat. nights, 4–10 (weather permitting). Board your carriage in front of **Patti's 1880s Settlement** (270-362-8844, 888-736-2525; www.pattis-settlement.com), 1759 J. H. O'Bryan Ave., Grand Rivers.

MEDICAL EMERGENCY There are several hospitals in the area of the Land Between the Lakes. The visitors center recommends the Paducah hospitals: **Western Baptist Hospital** (270-575-2100; www.westernbaptist.com), 2501 Kentucky Ave., and **Lourdes Hospital** (270-444-2444; www.lourdes.com), 1530 Lone Oak Rd. Both hospitals can be reached in less than an hour from the Land Between the Lakes area.

ALCOHOL This region sprawls across five different counties, with five different laws regarding alcohol sales, so check maps to see which county you are in before ordering a drink. Marshall County is dry, but allows alcohol by the drink in restaurants. Trigg County, whose largest city is Cadiz, is a dry county that does not allow alcohol sales anywhere. Lyon County is a dry county, but you can purchase alcohol by the drink at certain restaurants in Kuttawa. In Livingston County, alcohol sales are prohibited everywhere within the borders. In Calloway County, alcohol sales are prohibited except at certain restaurants in Murray, where you can order a drink by the glass.

✳ To See

✐ ♿ ♞ The acres and acres of actual land situated between the lakes is mostly forest. There are a few attractions on this land, and you get to each of them by following The Trace, which is the main road running north–south through it. **The Homeplace 1850** (800-525-7077; www.lbl.org). Open daily Mar.–Nov., call for hours. Spend the day at this working farm that has been restored to represent the 1850s. Although it is located just over the border in Pryor Hollow in Tennessee, it

photo by Ellie Kremer

BISON RELAXING ON THE PRAIRIE

is part of the Land Between the Lakes recreational area. The tour includes 16 cabins with interpreters in period clothing demonstrating chores and activities from that era. Small fee. **The Nature Station** (800-525-7077; www.lbl.org). Open daily Mar.–Nov.; call for hours. Stop in to learn about the wildlife in the area. The station has an indoor discovery center with both live and stuffed animals and a staff to tell you all about them. Outside, the backyard is home to rescued animals that can't make it on their own. Stop by and see the bobcat, vultures, coyotes, and even a majestic bald eagle. Small fee. **Elk and Bison Prairie** (800-525-7077; www.lbl.org). Open year-round from dawn to dusk. Enjoy the 700 acres of rolling meadows from the comfort of your car. It's the perfect place to watch the buffalo roam, or in this case elk and bison. Just follow the winding road and see these huge animals in their native environment. Small fee per car. **The Golden Pond Planetarium and Observatory** (800-455-5897; www.lbl.org). Open daily Mar.–Dec.; call for hours and show times. Take a trip to outer space without leaving your chair. Learn about stars, planets, and even space exploration during the daily planetarium shows on the 40-foot screen.

The Adsmore House Museum (270-365-3114; www.adsmore.org), 304 N. Jefferson St., Princeton. Tue.–Sat. 11–4, Sun. 1:30–4. Located about 30 miles east of Grand Rivers. You'll be tempted to don your hoop skirt or top hat to tour this stately antebellum home. Built around the mid-1850s, the home is full of period furniture and memorabilia that belonged to the original owners. Located on the property is a restored log building, used as a gun shop, that dates back to 1844. $7 adults, $6 seniors, $2 ages 6–12; under 6 free.

ADSMORE HOUSE

photo of www.kentuckytourism.com

🚭 ♿ 🍴 **Lake Barkley Classic Car Museum** (270-388-1962; lakebarkleyclassic-carmuseum.com), 796 KY 293, Eddyville. Open seven days a week. Stop by the Classic Car Museum and enjoy the collection of about 40 mint-condition gems of the road. The collection is growing, so you never know what you'll see.

🍴 **Wrather Museum** on the campus of Murray State University (270-809-4771; www.murraystate.edu), N. 16th St. and University Dr., Murray. The museum is open weekdays 8:30–4 and Sat. 10–1. Highlighting the development of Western Kentucky and the Jackson Purchase with art, mementos, and artifacts of days gone by, exhibits cover everything from Daniel Boone to World War II. Housed in the first permanent structure on Murray's Campus, the building, which dates to 1924, is on the National Register of Historic Places. Enjoy the campus while you're here. Murray is home to about 10,000 students. Free.

✳ To Do

GOLF Marvel Golf Club (270-354-9050; www.marvelgolf.com), 466 Bay Hill Dr., Benton. This Palmer-designed 18-hole, par-71 championship golf course lies on the western shores of Kentucky Lake. After you shoot 18, stop in the southern-plantation-style clubhouse to relax. They also have a pro shop and full-sized driving range.

Arrowhead Golf Course (270-522-8001; www.arrowheadgolf.com), 183 Arrow-head Club Dr., Cadiz. With four sets of tees and a wide variety of teeing areas, you can make this 18-hole course as difficult or easy as you want. Designed by Gary Roger Baird, it is sculpted from forested hills and dramatic rock formations along the winding Little River.

HORSEBACK RIDING Wrangler's Camp (877-444-6777), located in central LBL along Lake Barkley and Ford's Bay. Offering 100 miles of trails in the seclud-ed area, which is laced with creeks and streams. Bring your own horse or rent one of theirs.

OFF-ROADING Turkey Bay OHV (800-LBL-7077) Get directions at the LBL Visitors Center. A true off-highway vehicle area, not just for ATVs and motorcycles; full-sized 4x4s and even dune buggies are welcome. They have approximately 100 miles of OHV trails that cover a variety of terrain and offer something for every skill level.

🚭 ♿ 🍴 **STATE PARKS Lake Barkley State Resort Park** (270-924-1131; 800-325-1708; www.parks.ky.gov), 3500 State Park Rd., Cadiz. With 120 rooms, most with private balcony and lake view, you'll love the surroundings. They also have cottages, cabins, and a 78-site campground available. Enjoy the fitness center, indoor and outdoor pools, sand beach, tennis courts, hiking trails, and even a trap-shooting range. Rent a boat or park your own at the nearby marina. Eat at the **Windows on the Water Restaurant** with floor-to-ceiling windows offering a panoramic view of the lake while you dine on good old country cooking like fried chicken, catfish, and meat loaf. $–$$

🚭 ♿ 🍴 **Kentucky Dam Village State Resort Park** (270-362-4271; 800-325-0146; www.parks.ky.gov), 113 Administration Dr., Gilbertsville. Located adjacent to the giant dam that created these massive lakes, you'll find the aptly named Kentucky Dam Village. **The Village Inn Lodge** offers a private patio or balcony in all of their 72 rooms. They also have 68 very nice cottages, some with up to four bedrooms. For more lodging options, try one of their 219 paved campsites. Rent just about any kind of boat at the marina, swim at the lodge pool, hike on the nearby trails or test your skills on the 18-hole championship golf course. Try the **Harbor Lights Restaurant**, serving all three meals every day, with fantastic views of the dam and marina. $–$$

✍ ♿ "👆" **Kenlake State Resort Park** (270-474-2211, 800-325-0143; www.parks.ky .gov), 542 Kenlake Rd., Hardin. Surrounded by serene gardens and the magnificent lake, this 48 room lodge is really inviting. They also have one- to three-bedroom cottages that offer lake, wooded, or golf course views and include decks and screened-in porches. If you want to camp, they have a 90-site campground, too. **The Aurora Landing Restaurant** overlooks both the gardens and the lake. They feature well-known Kentucky dishes like hot brown, as well as some Italian-inspired entrées. Open for all three meals, seven days a week. They have walking trails, tennis courts, and a full-service marina where you can rent boats and Jet Skis. $–$$

✍ **WATER PARK Venture River Water Park** (270-388-7999; www.ventureriver .com), 280 Park Place, Eddyville. This water park has all the makings of a fun day in the sun. Whether you want to float along Old Man River or take in the excitement of speed slides and giant water flumes, you're sure to have a good time. They have an area just for the little ones as well as a large area to just lie out and catch rays.

✳ Lodging

✍ ♿ "👆" BED & BREAKFASTS
The Rose of the Lake Bed and Breakfast (270-362-3233; www.bb online.com/ky/roseofthelake), 293 Lawson St., Grand Rivers. Innkeepers Steve and Gloria Estes take care of the little details to make sure your stay is relaxing. They have a pool and hot tub as well as four comfy guest rooms and a two-bedroom cottage. The Esteses are artists, and their works are displayed throughout the home. Speaking of art, the presentation of breakfast could win awards. The delicate china and wonderful meal is enjoyed with soft classical music in the background. Help yourself to the huge DVD collection or just relax with their big friendly dog, JoJo. $–$$

The Davis House Bed And Breakfast (270-388-5585; www.thedavis house.com), 528 Willow Way, Kuttawa. This historic home has a huge porch and an upstairs widow's walk, both decked out with comfy wicker furniture where you can take in the views. Inside, look for the original fireplaces and hardwood floors that are present throughout the house. The four guest rooms are filled with antiques and offer spectacular views of Lake Barkley. Innkeeper Betty Dixon has been making guests feel at home since 1989. $

✍ **Journey's End Bed and Breakfast** (270-388-5117; www.journeysendbb .com), 121 Spring Hill Dr., Eddyville. Right on the water, they offer a dock, a screened-in porch, a butterfly garden, and private boat parking. This nice B&B features the Anchor Room, a standard guest room. They also have the Morning Glory Family Suite, with two bedrooms and a kitchen, and the Eagles Nest, which is a lake-view studio apartment that sleeps four. $

RESORT MARINAS **Green Turtle Bay Marina** (800-498-0428; www .greenturtlebay.com), Grand Rivers. Located on Barkley Lake and at the canal that connects to Kentucky Lake, they offer luxury one- to four-bedroom condos. The marina offers boat rentals including Jet Ski rentals, fishing boats, pontoons, and houseboat rentals. Stop by the marina store, the Ship's Chandlery, a 3,000-square-foot nautical store with the latest fashions, home decor items, books, and marine parts and supplies. $$$

Buzzard Rock Resort and Marina (800-826-6238; www.buzzardrock .com), 985 Buzzard Rock Rd., Kuttawa. Try a two-bedroom cottage or a one-bedroom resort unit; either way you'll have comfy digs and a deck with a lake view. At the marina you can rent a fishing or pontoon boat, fill up on fuel, and stock up on food and fishing supplies at the marina store. $–$$

Lighthouse Landing Marina and Resort (270-362-8201, 800-491-7245), 320 W. Commerce Ave., Grand Rivers. Situated right on Kentucky Lake, they offer 200 open slips for boats up to 42 feet in a well-protected harbor. They rent everything from sailboats to kayaks. Cute cottages, from one to three bedrooms, sit lakeside. They are fully equipped for your getaway. They have lake views, air-conditioning, and gas grills; some even have Wi-Fi. $

Eddy Creek Marina Resort (270-388-2271; 800-626-2300; www.eddy creek.com), 7621 KY 93S, Eddyville. Situated on 102 acres of lakeside property, this resort offers motel-style rooms and log cabins for your lodging. They also have an outdoor pool and a sand beach. The marina opens at 6 AM, so you can get an early start on the lake. They rent fishing and pontoon boats and have all the things you need to head out. $–$$$

GREEN TURTLE BAY MARINA

✐ 🏕 **CAMPING Prizer Point Marina and Resort** (800-548-2048; www
.prizerpoint.com), 1777 Prizer Point
Rd., Mile Marker 55 on Lake Barkley,
Cadiz. Whether you want to sleep in a
tent condo, cabin, bungalow, or tree
house, this is the place to come. They
offer lakeside camping as well as boat
rentals (try the pontoon with a slide off
the back, known as the Slidezilla).
Their restaurant, **The Landing,** serves
breakfast, lunch, and dinner right on
the water. Family-friendly activities
include soccer fields, volleyball, a game
room, hiking and biking trails, mini
golf, and a swimming and splash pool.
There is even a huge "iceberg" floating
in the lake, perfect for climbing up and
jumping off. Cottage $

photo of www.kentuckytourism.com

LIGHTHOUSE LANDING MARINA

✳ Where to Eat

**DINING OUT The Brass Lantern
Restaurant** (270 -474-2773; www
.brasslanternrestaurant.com), 16593
US 68E, Aurora. Open mid-Feb.–Dec.
for dinner only, starting at 5 PM.
Closed Mon. and Tue. Western Kentucky's first three-star restaurant. Fine
dining with options like lobster tail,
grilled pork tenderloin, and salmon.
Try the homemade soups, which
change with the seasons. They also
have fried oysters and signature
grasshopper pie.

Patti's 1880s Settlement (270-362-
8844, 888-736-2525; www.pattis-settle
ment.com), 1759 J. H. O'Bryan Ave.,
Grand Rivers. Patti's is open every day
10:30–8 (Jan.–Mar.) and 10:30–9
(Apr.–Dec.). The restaurant is famous
for its cozy and casual ambience, but it
can seat hundreds of diners in intimate
dining rooms. Servers are dressed like
they just came off the prairie, and they
do a great job of making you feel welcome. If you go to Patti's, you have to
try the flower pot bread, which comes
with strawberry butter, and the 2-inch-

thick pork chops. Don't leave without
ordering a slice of mile-high meringue
pie. You'll be glad you did. The Settlement includes gift shops, a playground,
and even an animal park with sheep,
peacocks, llamas, and pigs. You can
also play a round of miniature golf or
get married in their wedding chapel.

🍸 **EATING OUT The Buzzard Rock
Café** at the Buzzard Rock Resort and
Marina (800-826-6238; www.buzzard
rock.com), 985 Buzzard Rock Rd.,
Kuttawa. Serving all three meals, they
open at 7 AM every day. This bar and
restaurant is a favorite of locals, as it is
the only wet spot on the lake in this
otherwise dry part of Kentucky. The
restaurant serves home-cooked meals
as well as their own big ½-pound Buzzard Burger. It is huge, so come hungry. $

Broadbent's (270-388-0609; www
.broadbenthams.com), 257 Mary Blue
Dr., Kuttawa. Open every day. Known
as the Pride of Trigg County, they have
been following a family tradition of
curing country ham, bacon, and
sausage for over 80 years. They serve
sandwiches, ice cream, and pies, but
try some of the hand-rubbed, hickory-

smoked meats like pepper bacon, sun-dried tomato bacon, and maplewood-smoked cinnamon bacon. $

⚓ Willow Pond Catfish Restaurant

(270-388-4354; www.willowpondcatfish restaurant.com), 124 US 62W, Eddy-ville. Open seven days a week, but call for seasonal hours. All guests get a free bowl of their signature hush puppies, and that's just the start. They are known for their pond-raised catfish fillets, shrimp, frog legs, and tilapia, but they also have grilled steaks, chicken and pork chops, burgers, and a kids' menu. Dessert choices are unbeatable: homemade cobblers, cheesecakes, and their signature items, double chocolate brownies bites and French coconut pie. This is a nice, homey, casual place to eat. $

Echo Charlies (270-388-2271; www .eddycreek.com), 7612 KY 93S, Eddyville. Enjoy the fabulous lake view 6 AM–9 PM seven days a week during peak season. Stop in for a breakfast omelets, if you're there before 11 AM, or grab a salad or a burger and fries. They also have a huge selection of entrées like grilled yellowfin tuna, strip steak, and hickory-smoked molasses pork tenderloin. Very casual and relaxing. $

⛾ The Oasis Southwest Grill (270-

388-0777; www.theoasissouthwestgrill .com), 42 Days Inn Dr., Kuttawa. Mon.–Thu. 11–11, Fri. and Sat. 11–midnight, Sun. 11–9, Sun. brunch 11–2. Whether you want a rib eye, sirloin, or filet, all their aged steaks are charbroiled over a mesquite flame. Slow-roasted prime rib, served au jus, is available on Fri. and Sat. after 4 PM; get it while you can. Eat outside on the patio or inside in the fun dining room. Enjoy free peanuts, too. $$

Lite Side Bakery and Garden Cafe (270-362-4586; www.litesidebakery .com), 2115 Dover Rd. (KY 453),

Grand Rivers. Open 7–2 all year round. Owners Bob and Irene have been serving up healthy breakfasts, lunches, baked goods, and picnics since 1994. Try an enormous Belgian waffle or fresh cinnamon rolls for breakfast or a veggie burger or que-sadilla for lunch. Well known for their muffins; try one of their 37 flavors (18 are available each day). $

Parcell's Deli and Grille (270-527-9300; www.parcellsdeli.com), 165 US 68E, Benton. Open 10:30–7. Closed Sun. Run in for sandwiches, box lunches, desserts, and even hand-dipped ice cream, milk shakes, and floats. They have good deli sandwiches and salads, and interesting burgers, like the Reuben burger and the pizza burger. Try one of their daily specials like the chicken cordon bleu sand-wich. $

Nelson Pharmacy (270-527-3616; www.nelsonpharmacy.net), 1112 Main St., Benton. Open weekdays for lunch only. Just a few minutes from the Ken-tucky Lake area, you'll find this local drugstore complete with a soda foun-tain. Everyone in town stops by for a hand-dipped ice cream cone, an old-fashioned float, or a creamy milk shake, but the lunches deserve a nod, too. Order up some homemade soup, burgers, or chili dogs; they're all quite tasty. But if you want to eat like a local, it's Nelson's taco salad that fills up that lunch counter every day.

HRH Dumplins (270-753-0000), 305 S. 12th St., Murray. Open Mon.–Sat. 10–4. Homemade bread really makes the sandwich; that's why they make it fresh daily. In fact, everything is home-made and delicious. They are known for their desserts, so think ahead while ordering. Big apple dumplings and yeast rolls served with honey butter are just two of the favorites. $

✳ Entertainment

Badgett Playhouse (888-362-4223; www.grandrivers.com/links/variety.htm), 1838 J. H. O'Bryan, Grand Rivers. The Badgett Playhouse is home to Branson-style musical performances with a professional cast of singers, dancers, and a live band. Check the web site to see what's showing.

✳ Selective Shopping

Newsom's Old Mill Store (270-365-2482; www.newsomscountryham.com), 208 E. Main St., Princeton. Closed Sun. A part of downtown Princeton since 1914, this old country store is home of the nationally renowned Col. Newsom's Aged Kentucky Country Hams. You'll find some modern-day products, but they still have the same counter used by the Newsom's almost 100 years ago. Stop in for seeds, plants, produce, preserves, relishes, sorghum, salad dressings, and, of course, a ham or two.

ANTIQUES Red Door Antique Mall (270-388-1957; www.thereddoorantiques.com), 35 US 641N, Eddyville. Specializing in a unique blend of country farm antiques and country primitives, all in a 7,000-square-foot showroom. Open seven days a week.

Days Past Antiques (270-362-4683), KY 952, Grand Rivers. Specializing in quilts, antique furniture, and pottery. Stop in to see what's new. Open seven days a week.

Lazy Ridge County Store (270-527-0427), 17 Cascade Hills Lane and US 68, Benton. Closed Sun. and Mon. They have antiques, folk art, and custom-made furniture. They also have handmade braided rugs, punched tin lamp shades, and quaint home decor items. Stop by this inviting barn with a front porch and visit.

OUTLET MALLS West Kentucky Outlet Center (305-893-5018; www.wkyfactoryoutlet.com), 385 Outlet Ave., Eddyville. With 11 stores and one restaurant, it's the kind of place you can slip in and browse around for a bargain. Stores for women's clothes, home décor, and even socks for the whole family.

✳ Special Events

🐾 ⚂ 🌸 *August:* **Hot August Blues Festival**. This two-day festival features blues performers from around the world. Performances take place at the amphitheater at Kenlake State Resort Park in Aurora, but you can listen from your boat, too.

🐾 ⚂ 🌸 *October:* **Hunters Moon Fall Festival** and **Grand Rivers Storytelling Festival**. These two festivals could be enjoyed on their own, but they run simultaneously, so why not catch both of them? The Hunters Moon Fall Festival features beauty pageants, street dances, craft shows, Taste of the Lakes, and a parade filled with floats and bands. The Grand Rivers Storytelling Festival features entertaining stories from professional, nationally acclaimed storytellers. Enjoy a variety of lively tales of Grand Rivers folk life. Both festivals are held in the downtown area of Grand Rivers.

THE PADUCAH AREA

A delightful mix of old and new, **Paducah** is the perfect example of a small Kentucky town that has successfully spruced itself up and put itself back on the map. Besides its flourishing, historic downtown, city leaders have created a growing arts community, centered in Paducah's Lowertown, that blends itself right in. You can feel the artsy vibe as soon as you arrive.

Since the creation of the Paducah Artists Relocation Program in 2000, the city has brought in more than 70 artists who are now full-time residents. The program includes both cultural and financial incentives for the artists to set up homes and studios in a 26-block section of Lowertown, once the city's most run-down neighborhood, now its prime attraction. All the artists who now call Paducah home say that this energizing community, so rich in residents who produce textile, fiber, paint, and glass art forms, makes this the place they want to live.

This river city is protected by floodwalls that not only keep rising waters out when necessary, but also show off a bit of the artistic bent of the city with the fabulous hand-painted murals by Robert Dafford. After perusing the giant murals, each a life-sized chapter into Paducah's past, head down to the river shore to take in the confluence of the Tennessee and Ohio Rivers. The rivers flow together,

PADUCAH TOWN CENTER

photo by Deborah Kohl Kremer

making a wide, calm portion of the Ohio as it flows westward and merges with the mighty Mississippi about 50 miles downstream.

Undoubtedly the biggest draw to Paducah is the National Quilt Museum of the United States. This one-of-a-kind museum displays more than 150 quilted works of art in an ever-changing gallery. Whether you are an avid quilter or know nothing about the art form, it should be a mandatory stop while in town. This ages-old craft, which started as a way to make warm blankets and grew into an intricate form of stitching and storytelling, can simply take your breath away. As home to this national museum, Paducah rolls out the red carpet each April to quilters and admirers alike for the American Quilter's Society Quilt Show and Convention, which draws upward of 30,000 people each year.

As you poke through the antiques shops, tiny diners, and artists' workshops of Paducah, don't forget to give a nod of appreciation to the legendary Chief Paduke. According to legend, Paduke was the hospitable chief of the Chickasaw Indians, a tribe that called the area, then known as Pekin, home in the early 1800s. He was well known for welcoming settlers to the area as they arrived on flatboats on the Ohio River and encouraging good relations between the Native Americans and these early pioneers. The community grew and prospered until around 1827, when William Clark, part of the famed Lewis and Clark adventure team, arrived with plans to lay out a city. Chief Paduke and his tribe graciously left the area, and Clark got to work creating the city grid that is still evident today. In a move of appreciation to the chief and his tribe, Clark renamed the city Paducah. A statue of the chief stands proudly at 1818 North 19th Street at Jefferson Street, Paducah.

GUIDANCE **The Paducah-McCracken County Convention & Visitors Bureau** (270-443-8784, 800-723-8224; www.paducah-tourism.org), 128 Broadway. Open weekdays 9–4. On your way through Paducah's historic downtown district, swing in for maps and brochures. **Whitehaven Mansion/Welcome Center** (270-554-2077), US 45, just off I-24 Exit 7.

Open 24 hours for travelers; tours of the home offered daily between 1 and 4. Come in for brochures and maps and get a free tour of the 1860s antebellum home that houses the welcome center. The Corinthian-columned white Classic Revival house is stunning. Whitehaven, Kentucky's only welcome center located in a formerly private home, showcases memorabilia of Paducah's native son Vice President Alben Barkley, who served under President Harry Truman. **Lower Town Arts District** (270-444-9191; www.paducaharts.com), 416 N. 7th St., Paducah. Open Wed.–Sun. noon–5. Pick up more information about the nearly 20 galleries, eateries, and studios in Lowertown at the historic Texaco service station on the corner.

PADUCAH VISITORS CENTER

GETTING THERE Paducah is located right off I-24, 137 miles from Nashville, Tennessee, and 176 miles from St. Louis, Missouri. To arrive by commercial air, your best bet is **Nashville International Airport** (615 275-1600; www.nashintl .com). It's about 130 miles from downtown Paducah. **Barkley Regional Airport** (www.barkleyregional.com), which is in Paducah, serves private and charter planes and makes connections to larger commercial airports. You can also get there by bus. **Greyhound Bus** (270-442-2706; www.greyhound.com) serves the Paducah and Western Kentucky region. The station is located at 301 N. 4th St., Paducah.

GETTING AROUND Paducah is easy to get around by car or by foot if you're in the downtown area. Look for a downtown trolley in the summertime that loops through the charming downtown area, stopping at all the popular attractions.

MEDICAL EMERGENCY Western Baptist Hospital (270-575-2100; www .westernbaptist.com), 2501 Kentucky Ave., Paducah, and **Lourdes Hospital** (270-444-2444; www.ehealthconnection.com/regions/lourdes), 1530 Lone Oak Rd., Paducah. Both offer an array of services to fill any medical need.

ALCOHOL McCracken County is one of those counties that is moist, not quite wet but not quite dry, either. Primarily, the county is dry, serving no alcohol, but within the county are five wet precincts. One of those precincts is the city of Paducah, where you can buy alcohol within the city limits.

✳ To See

&. **The National Quilt Museum of the United States** (270-442-8856; www .quiltmuseum.org), 215 Jefferson St., Paducah. Open Mon.–Sat. 10–5; Apr.–Oct., the museum is open on Sun. 1–5. Prepare to be amazed at the 150 modern-day quilts on display. Each a work of art, they look like they were created with paintbrush on canvas rather than needle and thread. The lighting and display techniques allow you to get up close to see the intricate stitches and tiny pieces of fabric used to create these masterpieces. There are also reader boards alongside each quilt so you can learn about the artist and how the work came to be. The display quilts are housed in three galleries, and the exhibits change throughout the year. No cameras allowed, and don't think about touching them, even though you'll want to run your fingers over this beautiful fabric. The museum also offers workshops throughout the year and has a gift shop full of quilt-related books and non-quilt-related pieces of art. $8 adults, $6 seniors and children.

NATIONAL QUILT MUSEUM
photo by Deborah Kohl Kremer

&. **Paducah Wall to Wall Murals** (270-554-3589; www.paducahtourism .org). These gorgeous life-sized floodwall murals depict Paducah's past.

photo by Deborah Kohl Kremer

WALL TO WALL MURALS

Hand painted by legendary artist Bob Dafford, the 48 panels are so life-like, you feel like you can walk right into them. Stroll along Water Street and take in their beauty while learning about Paducah at the same time.

& **William Clark Market House Museum** (270-443-7759), 121 S. 2nd St., Paducah. This darling museum tells the story of Paducah inside a historic building that used to be an open-air market. Evidence of the market stalls is still apparent, complete with old photos so you can envision what the place looked like when horses and buggies were parked out front. The museum has 4,000 square feet of rotating exhibits that do a good job of painting the picture of Paducah's growth and challenges.

Lloyd Tilghman House and Civil War Museum (270-575-5477), 631 Kentucky Ave., Paducah. Open Wed.–Sat. noon–4, Apr.–Nov. and by appointment. Tour the home of Confederate general Lloyd Tilghman, which dates back to 1852. Exhibits focus on the role of Western Kentucky during the Civil War and General Tilghman's efforts to keep the state neutral. Small fee.

The Paducah Railroad Museum (270-519-7377; www.paducahrr.org), 200 Washington St., Paducah. Open Fri. 1–4 and Sat. 10–4 or by appointment. Enjoy an interesting display of authentic railroad memorabilia, maps, and photos. Free, but donations appreciated.

MARKET HOUSE MUSEUM

photo by Deborah Kohl Kremer

✳ To Do

CARRIAGE RIDES Annie's Horsedrawn Carriage Rides (270-210-6095)
Weekends. Meet at the gazebo across from the Convention and Visitors Bureau,
take in a 20-minute tour of the river and floodwall murals, and get a feel for the
town.

GOLF Paxton Park Golf Course (270-444-9514; www.paxtonpark.com), 841
Berger Rd., Paducah. This 18-hole, par-71 course is a favorite of local residents.
They have a pro shop, driving range, and snack bar. If you forget your clubs, they
have rentals available, too.

PAINTBALL Paducah Shooters Paintball Field (270-443-3758; www.pssguns
.com), 3919 Cairo Rd., Paducah. Open weekends 10–5. Located next to their
Shooters Supply store, you can pick up all your paint gun necessities and head out
for a round of paintball wars.

RACEWAYS Paducah International Raceway (270-898-7469; www.paducah
internationalraceway.com), 4445 Shemwell Ln., Paducah. Enjoy high-profile
NASCAR events, like late-model stock-car and sprint-car racing, on the 3/8-mile
clay track.

Bluegrass Downs (270-444-7117), 32nd and Park Ave., Paducah. Live racing
from the end of Apr. to early June. Simulcasting Wed.–Sun. 11:30–8:30. This track
is home to live thoroughbred racing and harness racing, so come out and pick a
winner. Throughout the year, intertrack wagering is available from Kentucky's
other tracks.

WALKS Pick up a map at the Convention and Visitors Bureau, 128 Broadway, and
walk along the historic downtown. You'll enjoy the ages-old architecture, the revitalized historic buildings, and vibrant floodwall murals. The map will even take you
to Lowertown so you can find all the artists and their studios.

✳ Lodging

& ♂ "♪" **Executive Inn Paducah
Riverfront** (270-443-8000), 1 Executive Blvd., Paducah. This locally owned
hotel is simply massive, with 434
rooms. If you can't find a room else-
where in town, check the Executive.
This huge gray monolith that sits
alongside the banks of the Ohio is
nothing special to look at, but the
rooms have wonderful views of the
river and all the comforts you would
expect in a chain hotel. Their on-site
restaurant, fitness room, and indoor
pool round out the conveniences.
Great location, too; you'll be able to
walk to Paducah's biggest attractions. $

& "♪" **INNS Fox Briar Inn at River-
Place** (270-443-7004), 100-C Broadway, Paducah. You won't believe you're
still in Kentucky. This refurbished historic building houses loft-style apartments, making you feel like you are in
New York City. Located atop the storefront restaurants and shops of Broadway, you'll find these open, airy
apartments complete with exposed
brick, 12-foot ceilings, and creaky
hardwood floors. Each apartment,
which can be rented for the night or
long term, is decorated with cool contemporary furniture, whirlpool tubs,
and utensil-stocked gourmet kitchens.

photo by Deborah Kohl Kremer

FOX BRIAR INN SITS ATOP THE
STOREFRONTS

They even have washers and dryers.
$$–$$$

The Egg and I Guest Suites (270-
443-6323; www.eggandiarts.com), 335
N. 6th, Paducah. Located in a
pre–Civil War home in the Lowertown
district, the two guest rooms are above
The Egg & I Fine Art & Crafts
Gallery. Each room offers a queen-
sized bed and a sitting room with a
pullout sleeper sofa. Both rooms feature giant showers, measuring about 4
by 6 feet, so you can spread out and
enjoy yourself.

❝❡❞ **Fisher Mansion Apartments**
(270-443-0716; www.fishermansion
.com), 905 Jefferson St., Paducah. You
can walk to everything from this convenient location in Lowertown. Fisher
Mansion offers one- and two-bedroom
furnished apartments for the same
price as a motel room; the rooms are
perfect for both long- and short-term
stays. The 1,000-square-foot apartments are completely furnished and
offer linens, tableware, and all the
comforts of home. $$

Rosewood Inn Bed and Breakfast
(270-554-6632, 800-548-3840; www
.bbonline.com/ky/rosewood), 2740 S.

Friendship Rd., Paducah. Located just
15 minutes away from the downtown
area, this serene B&B offers one guest
room and two guest suites in a country
setting. Romance abounds with the
canopy-draped beds and the large
whirlpool tubs. Innkeepers Bob and
Nancy Platt focus on pampering while
you focus on relaxing. Sit on the porch
and watch their horses run in the
field. $$

❝❡❞ **1857's Bed and Breakfast** (270-
444- 3960; www.tribecarestaurant.net),
127 Market House Square, Paducah.
This building, which is listed on the
National Historic Register, was built
in, you guessed it, 1857. Located above
Tribeca Restaurant, they offer two
guest rooms on the second floor and a
giant guest room that covers the entire
third floor of this old building. The 12-
foot ceilings and old hardwood floors
blend beautifully with modern necessities and antique furnishings. They
offer a private deck, complete with
outdoor Jacuzzi and continental breakfast each morning. $–$$

✳ **Where to Eat**

❞ **DINING OUT C. C. Cohen
Restaurant and Bar** (270-442-6391;
www.cccohen.com), 103 Broadway,
Paducah. Open for lunch and dinner
Mon.–Sat. Located in a historic building near the center of town. The
Cohen building has a storied past,
which may include a ghost or two.
Patrons of this upscale restaurant
have reported chairs moving and salt-
shakers dumped mysteriously, but
whether you believe or not, it's worth
going for a nice meal. King cut prime
rib, lobster tail, and blackened swordfish are notable menu options, but if
you are in the mood for a basic burger, salad, or sandwich, Cohen's has
quite an assortment to choose from.
$–$$$

C. C. COHEN RESTAURANT
photo by Deborah Kohl Kremer

Ÿ **Ristorante di Fratelli** (270-442-7054; www.difratelli.net), 211 Broadway, Paducah. Open for dinner Tue.–Sat. Fine dining, Italian style. Enjoy the charm of the renovated historic downtown building while indulging in the elegant surroundings and upscale menu choices, featuring fresh fish and fine cuts of steak in addition to the authentic Italian options. Everything is made from scratch, and it shows. $$–$$$

Ÿ **Martin Fierro Argentinean Grill and Rodizio** (270-408-1300; www.martinfierrogrill.com), 314 Broadway, Paducah. Open for lunch Tue.–Fri. 11–2; dinner Tue.–Thu. 4:30–9, Fri.–Sat. 4–10. They also have a massive Sunday brunch 11–2. Carnivores take note: This is a meat restaurant. Although they do have an impressive salad bar, don't waste too much time there, because the focal point is the

Latin American meat. Served by authentic gauchos, skewered sausage, chicken, pork, and steaks that have been marinated and grilled to perfection start appearing at your table and keep on appearing until you've had your fill, which might be a while. Try everything. $$–$$$

Ÿ **Whaler's Catch** (270-444-7701; www.whalerscatch.net), 123 N. 2nd St. Paducah. Whaler's, as it is known to the locals, has been serving up market-fresh seafood since 1977. The building itself was built in 1878 and has housed everything from a distillery to a furniture warehouse to a union hall. The weathered brick facade and ornamental accoutrements add to the turn-of-the-century charm. This three-story building offers two levels of dining with seating for about 400. The first floor is a bit more casual and rustic, while the second floor has larger tables, six of them with large window views. Don't miss the 24-foot hand-carved mahogany bar that is a prominent feature in the dining room. This bar, which was built around 1863, is said to have been brought up from New Orleans by barge and called a roadside tavern in Cairo, Illinois, home. The legend goes that Ulysses S.

THE CROWS NEST AT WHALER'S CATCH
photo by Deborah Kohl Kremer

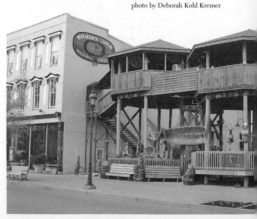

Grant was actually served at this bar during the Civil War. The building is on 2nd Street in historic downtown Paducah. Whaler's has added an open-air double gazebo-like dining area and bar called the Crow's Nest. Named for the lookout location on sailing ships, it's built on stilts that rise two stories above the street level, offering patrons a great view of the Ohio River. This area, which is naturally just open during the summer months, features live bands on weekends and can seat 150 people.

Whaler's Catch is known for their great seafood. One of the most popular entrées is the Boiling Bag, which is basically a bag made of cheesecloth, stuffed full of shrimp, crawfish, crab legs, and oysters. Diners can't wait to see what's inside. The menu really sticks to its promise of "A Taste of New Orleans." Appetizers like fried alligator, deep-fried okra, and oysters on the half shell are all very popular. Soup choices carry out the hint of New Orleans with offerings such as red beans and rice, jambalaya, and étouffée—fresh shrimp or crawfish and vegetables cooked in a roux to make a thick stew. That hint of New Orleans shows itself again on the dessert menu, with beignets and Bourbon Street bread pudding options. $$

♥ **d. Starnes at RiverPlace** (270-442-2122), 108 Broadway, Paducah. Open Mon.–Sat. for lunch and dinner. Known for hickory-smoked barbecue shoulders, this is where locals go for authentic Western Kentucky meals. They've been a Paducah staple for more than 50 years, so obviously they are doing something right. Try the homemade corn bread muffins with a piping-hot bowl of soup. Or skip the meal and go straight for the coconut cream pie, which you know was made fresh that morning. $–$$

♥ **EATING OUT Max's Brick Oven Café** (270-575-3473), 112 Market House Square, Paducah. Open Mon.–Thu. 5–10, Fri.–Sat. 5–11. Reservations are a good idea. Located in a converted warehouse, this hip restaurant uses architectural salvage items, like shutters, windows, and woodwork, to add to the ambience. The menu features delicious selections of gourmet pizza and sandwiches from their massive brick oven. Eat outside in the courtyard if the weather is warm. Live music sometimes on the weekends. $–$$

♥ **Toucan's** (270-450-0388), 119 Market House Square, Paducah. Open for lunch and dinner every day. This restaurant has a tropical theme but basic menu choices like soups, salads, and BLT sandwiches. The homemade potato chips and deep-fried onion rings served with the sandwiches are excellent. The most popular items are the chicken Marsala and warm chicken salad casserole. If the weather is nice,

TOUCAN'S

photo by Deborah Kohl Kremer

eat outside under one of the umbrella tables in their courtyard. Saturday nights they have a live band outside, too. $–$$

Tribeca Mexican Cuisine (270-444-3960; www.tribecarestaurant.net), 127 Market House Square, Paducah Open Tue.–Fri. for lunch 11–3, dinner 5–9; Sat. noon–9. This is the place to go for authentic fresh Mexican entrées served up in a fun, casual atmosphere. Order up a margarita and spicy enchilada, and save room for their famous cheesecake burrito. $–$$

Bob's Drive In (270-443-6493), 2429 Bridge St., Paducah. Known as the oldest drive-in restaurant in Kentucky, Bob's has thick creamy milk shakes and a nice selection of burgers. $

Serenitea (270-450-0749; www.sereniteateacompany.com), 121 N. 5th St., Paducah. This charming tea shop is located between downtown and Lowertown in a historic building. They sell all kinds of tea-related accoutrements so you can make your best cup at home. It's also a rejuvenating place to stop for a light lunch (serving weekdays 11–2). The menu offers an assortment of salads, soups, and even a quiche of the day. They also have fabulous scones and homemade desserts. $–$$

SNACKS Kirchhoffs Bakery and Deli (270-442-7117; www.kirchhoffs bakery.net), 114–116 Market House Square, Paducah. The bakery opens at the crack of dawn; the deli is open for lunch Mon.–Sat. Established in 1873, Kirchhoff's has been serving Old World and artisan breads, pastries, and cookies to the people of Paducah for generations. In addition to their fine bakery items, they offer a deli, with loaded sandwiches served on fresh-baked breads. Although they have fresh salads and homemade soups, you would be missing out if you didn't have a grilled sandwich on their focaccia or sourdough bread.

The Chocolate Factory (270-442-5222; www.chocolatefactoryky.com), 109 Market House Square, Paducah. Open weekdays, 9–4, Sat. 10–4. If the name alone doesn't make your mouth water, the smell of all the delicious chocolate will. This old-time candy shop, featuring jars of homemade chocolates and a fudge counter full of assorted must-try flavors, is pure heaven. It's owned by two sisters who have been making chocolates all their lives—and these ladies know what they are doing. Try the chocolate caramel fudge, the English toffee bark, or a tiger butter cup: white chocolate mixed with peanut butter, with dark chocolate swirled in.

TRIBECA MEXICAN CUISINE
photo by Deborah Kohl Kremer

photo by Deborah Kohl Kremer

KIRCHOFF'S BAKERY

✳ Entertainment

The Maiden Alley Cinema (270-441-7007, 800-442-7002; www.maiden alleycinema.com), 112 Maiden Alley, Paducah. Open Thu.–Sun. Located at the end of a brightly lit alley, this is where to go to see recently released international and domestic art films that are never on the bill at the big-screen megaplex.

The Market House Theatre (270-444-6828, 888-648-7529; www.mhtplay .com), 132 Market House Square, Paducah. Enjoy fine community theater in this historic 240-seat theater. Check the web site to see what this talented bunch is working on.

& **Luther F. Carson Four Rivers Center** (270-450-4444), 100 Kentucky Ave., Paducah. Enjoy live Broadway shows, the Paducah Symphony Orchestra, and even rock concerts at this 1,800-seat theater. Check the web site to see who's showing.

✳ Selective Shopping

ANTIQUES Antiques, Cards & Collectibles (270-443-9797), 203 Broadway St., Paducah. This shop is loaded, really loaded, with cards, books, furniture, and all kinds of old stuff.

Jeremiah's Antique Mall (270-443-3991), 225 Broadway St., Paducah. Closed Sun. Right in the heart of downtown, you'll find this shop full of both American and European antiques.

Just English Antiques (444-8454), 212 Broadway St., Paducah. Closed Sun. A not-so-ordinary collection of antiques from across the pond.

ART GALLERIES AND STUDIOS
Yeiser Art Center (270-442-2453; www.theyeiser.org), 200 Broadway St., Paducah. Open Tue.–Sat. 10–4. What began in the 1950s as an attempt to create Paducah's first art museum has emerged into a contemporary gallery that exhibits work by American, European, African, and Asian artists. Included in the permanent collection are works by Henri Matisse, Mary Cas-

ANTIQUES, CARDS & COLLECTIBLES
photo by Deborah Kohl Kremer

satt, Salvador Dalí, and Francisco Goya as well as regional artists. Free.

Wildhair Studios (270-444-6115; www.wildhairstudios.com), 201 Broadway St., Paducah. Open every day. The word *whimsy* comes to mind as soon as you enter this fun shop. Owner Sue Edwards keeps her studio well stocked with Paducah souvenirs, quilting-related T-shirts, humorous gift cards, and really fun jewelry.

In Lowertown

Bryerpatch Studio (270-444-8040; www.bryerpatch.com), 502 N. 5th St., Paducah. You have to see this studio of Caryl Bryer Fallert, three-time winner of the Best of Show award at the American Quilter's Society Annual Convention. Caryl's work can be found in museums and private collections around the world. Take in her exquisite collection of quilts on display, or peruse the collection of fabrics that she

CARYL BRYER FALLERT OF BRYERPATCH STUDIO

photo by Deborah Kohl Kremer

hand dyes and paints for use on her own quilts. She has bolts and bolts of brightly colored fabric and it is all for sale, in case her work has inspired you. If you have time, you might be able to fit one of her quilting workshops into your visit.

The Egg and I Fine Arts and Crafts (270-443-6323; www.eggandiarts.com), 335 N. 6th, Paducah. Visit with artists Steve and Carol Gabany and see their inspiring art created by carving ostrich, emu, and duck eggs. They painstakingly carve through the shell to expose the various layers underneath, resulting in treasured pieces of art. They also offer fine beaded jewelry.

Gallery 5 (270-444-2020; www.renzulliart.com), 803 Madison St., Paducah (entrance is on 8th Street). Open Wed.–Sun. Dr. William Renzulli, a physician and artist, showcases his artwork, which he creates from pastels, watercolors, and acrylics. The results are bold, colorful, and imaginative paintings.

Mentor House Gallery (270-442-1635; www.mentorhousegallery.com), 332 N. 6th St., Paducah. Open Wed.–Sun. noon–5. Okay, so you'd be hard-pressed to miss this 18-foot-tall giraffe sculpture right smack-dab in the middle of their front yard, so watch for it as you come down the street. Artist Paulette Mentor, herself a relocated artist, has brought her dramatic acrylic paintings to town. Her gallery features her own work as well as dramatic art glass, sculptures, and unique pieces from artists around the country.

Aphrodite Gallery (270-444-6871; www.julieshawdesigns.com), 503 N. 7th St., Paducah. Open Wed.–Sun. noon–5. See owner Julie Shaw's amazing designs of intricate, gem-laden jewelry pieces.

Dixie Leather Works (270-442-1058; www.dlwleathers.com), 306 N. 7th St., Paducah. Open Mon.–Fri. 10–5. With 38 years devoted to the art of leatherworks, owner Phillip Phillips can make anything from a guitar strap to a reproduction of a regulation field medical case from the Civil War.

Dixie Leather Works created countless pieces for museum displays and battlefield reenactors. They've had had cameo appearances in blockbuster movies like *The Alamo* and *Gettysburg*, and TV shows like *Dr. Quinn Medicine Woman*. They also produce and sell handmade leather purses, briefcases, and trunks. This interesting shop has all kinds of fascinating leatherworks that you didn't know existed. It also smells fantastic in there.

The Kentucky Oaks Mall (270-444-0440; www.kentuckyoaksmall.net), 5101 Hinkleville Rd., Paducah. With 12 anchor stores and 96 specialty shops, they probably have anything you need. The mall also has eight restaurants and a movie theater.

✳ Special Events

✦ *April:* **American Quilter's Society Annual Quilt Show and Contest**. Since 1984, quilters have been gathering for this annual quilt show where they can view a juried exhibit of some of the finest quilts from around the world, as well as see the latest in wares from quilt supply dealers. More than 30,000 quilters arrive each spring, and Paducah rolls out the red carpet for them. Events are held all over the city to coincide with the quilt show.

♪ ✦ ❀ *May:* **Lowertown Art and Music Festival**. Held every Memorial Day weekend right in the streets of Lowertown. Live music on stages throughout the district provides the backdrop for the artists who are demonstrating and displaying their art forms. Painters, sculptors, and even yoga instructors fill the booths along the streets, inviting you in to see what they do and how they do it.

♪ ✦ ❀ *Summer months:* **Downtown After Dinner** (800-723-8224). For some hometown fun, head for the middle of town on Saturday nights all summer long. The streets are full of live music, car shows, cloggers, and street artists who all come out 7–10 PM each week. Perfect for travelers and people who call Paducah home. You'll feel like a local before the night is through.

INDEX